MODERN DANCE
IN FRANCE

Lar

Choreography and Dance Studies

A series of books edited by Robert P. Cohan, C.B.E.

Volume 1
The Life and Times of Ellen von Frankenberg
Karen Bell-Kanner

Volume 2
Dooplé
The Eternal Law of African Dance
Alphonse Tiérou

Volume 3
Elements of Performance
A Guide for Performers in Dance, Theatre and Opera
Pauline Koner

Volume 4
Upward Panic
The Autobiography of Eva Palmer-Sikelianos
Edited by John P. Anton

Volume 5
Modern Dance in Germany and the United States
Crosscurrents and Influences
Isa Partsch-Bergsohn

Volume 6
Antonio de Triana and the Spanish Dance
A Personal Recollection
Rita Vega de Triana

Volume 7
The Dance of Death
Kurt Jooss and the Weimar Years
Suzanne K. Walther

Volume 8
Dance Words
Compiled by Valerie Preston-Dunlop

Volume 9
East Meets West in Dance: Voices in the Cross-Cultural Dialogue
Edited by Ruth Solomon and John Solomon

Please see the back of this book for other titles in the Choreography and Dance Studies series

MODERN DANCE IN FRANCE

AN ADVENTURE 1920–1970

Jacqueline Robinson

Translated by
Catherine Dale
University of Hull, England

harwood academic publishers
Australia • Canada • China • France • Germany • India
Japan • Luxembourg • Malaysia • The Netherlands • Russia
Singapore • Switzerland • Thailand • United Kingdom

Amsteldijk 166
1st Floor
1079 LH Amsterdam
The Netherlands

British Library Cataloguing in Publication Data

Robinson, Jacqueline
    Modern dance in France: an adventure 1920–1970. –
    (Choreography and dance studies; v. 12)
    1. Modern dance – France
    I. Title
    792.8′0944

    ISBN 90-5702-016-5

£25.00

Cover illustration: *Dancers* by Maurice Lang.

In memory of Laurent

CONTENTS

Introduction to the Series   xv

Acknowledgements   xvii

List of plates   xviii

Exergue   xxi

Foreword *by Valerie Preston-Dunlop*   xxiii

Prelude: Indelible Ephemera *by Dominique Dupuy*   xxv

INTRODUCTION
  An Epic   1
  The Sense of the Phylum   1
  Modern Dance in the Birth-Place of Classical Dance   2
  Virginity and Creation   3
  Terminology   4
  From Yesterday to Today   5
  Contemporary Opinions   7
  Fertility, Frivolity and Digressions   10
  Dance to Serve Man? Man to Serve Dance?   12
  Keys to Reading   13

PART I   1920–1930: THE GROUND-BREAKING YEARS
  Chronology   19
  Dance in the Roaring Twenties   23
  The Influence of the Ballets Russes (and Waslaw Nijinsky)   24
  Modern Dance is First and Foremost 'Individual'   25
  Isadora, the Symbol   26
  In the Wake of Isadora   27
  The Body Rehabilitated   29

Harmonic Gymnastics 30
Émile Jaques-Dalcroze 32
Rudolf von Laban 35
Other Influences 36
The Plastic Arts 40
Exoticism 42
Venues for the New Dance 44
A Similar Volapük of Movements? 44

THE ACTORS 46

INSTITUTIONS 47
The Ballets Suédois 1920–1924 47

THE DUNCAN LINE 49
Raymond Duncan 50
Elisabeth Duncan 53
Irma Duncan 54
Lisa Duncan *by Odile Pyros* 55
Ellen Tels-Rabanek 60
Postscript on the Legacy of Isadora *by Madeleine Lytton* 61

THE LABAN AND DALCROZE LINES 61
Dussia Bereska 61
Marie-Louise van Veen 63
Jacqueline Chaumont 64
Marie Kummer 66

THE INDEPENDENT ONES 67
Georges Pomiès 67
Alexander and Clotilde Sakharoff *by Denise Blanc-Raillard* 69
Hélène Vanel and Loïs Hutton 76
Yvonne Redgis 77
Paul Swan 77
Charlotte Bara 78
Yvonne Sérac 78
Isabel de Etchessary 78

THE EDUCATORS 79
François Malkowski 79
Renée Odic Kintzel 81
Irène Popard 84

THE ORIENTALS   87
Jeanne Ronsay   87
Nyota Inyoka   90
Djemil Anik   93
Uday Shankar   94
Raden Mas Jodjana   95

CONCLUSION   97

PART II   1930–1939: THE TILLING YEARS
Chronology   101
Dance: from the Ground-Breaking to the
    Ploughing of the Land   105
Mary Wigman   106
Mary Wigman in Paris in 1931   109
The Wave from Central Europe   111
Tours and Venues   114
A Diversity of Tendencies   115

THE ACTORS   117

INSTITUTIONS   118
The Archives Internationales de la Danse   118

THE LABAN AND WIGMAN LINES   126
Jean Weidt *by Dominique Dupuy*   127
Heinz Finkel   133
Ludolf Schild *by Lise Brunel*   135
Mila Cirul   140
Julia Marcus   143
Doryta Brown   144

THE DALCROZE AND HELLERAU-LAXENBURG LINE   145
Anita Wiskeman *by Florence Poudru*   146
Hélène Carlut *by Florence Poudru*   148
Doris Halphen, Maïan Pontan and the
    Hellerau-Laxenburg School   151

DEFECTORS FROM CLASSICAL DANCE   151
Jean Serry   152
Janine Solane   155

THE INDEPENDENT ONES   160
Marguerite Bougai   160
Tony Gregory   164
Freddy Wittop   165
Josette and Renée Foatelli   165

THE EDUCATORS   165
Fée Hellès *by Denise Coutier*   166
Liliane Arlen and Viennese Dance   167

CONCLUSION   169

PART III   1945–1960: THE SOWING YEARS
Chronology   173
The Return to Peace   179
New Landscapes   182
Our Own 'Modern' Dancers   183
Grafts   183
Turning Towards the Roots   183
Trends of 'Culture for the Masses'   184
Jacques Copeau and his Heritage   185
Travail et Culture (T.E.C.)   187
Éducation par le jeu dramatique (E.P.J.D.)   189
Spiritual Awakening   190
Scouts   191
Expression through the Body   191
Institutions that Foster Dance   193
The Birth of the Body   195

THE ACTORS   198

INSTITUTIONS   199
Jean Dorcy and Danse et Culture   199
Dinah Maggie and Association Française de
    Recherches Chorégraphiques (A.F.R.E.C.) and
    the Théâtre d'Essai de la Danse   203

FRENCH DANCERS OF EUROPEAN DESCENT   208
Anne Gardon   208
Geneviève Mallarmé   211

Raymonde Lombardin   212
Charles Antonetti   217
Jacqueline Levant   218
Suzanne Rémon   219
Claude Stéphane   219
Françoise and Dominique Dupuy and
    The Ballets Modernes de Paris   220

THE GRAFTS   233
Jerome Andrews *by Delphine Rybinski*   233
Jacqueline Robinson *by Geneviève Piguet*   240
Laura Sheleen   250
Karin Waehner   257
Muriel Topaz   266
Paul d'Arnot   267
Edith Allard   269
Katherine Henry d'Epinoy   270
Gilberto Motta   273
Régine Drengwicz   274

IN THE LINE OF JANINE SOLANE   275
Rose-Marie Paillet   275
Denise Blanc-Raillard   277
Marie-France Babillot   278
Titane Saint-Hubert   280

THE INDEPENDENT ONES   280
Olga Stens   280
Geneviève Piguet   284
Frédérique Franchini   286
Antoinette Guédy   287
Roger Ribes   287

THE EDUCATORS   288
Hilde Peerbohm *by Marie-Madeleine Cosnard,*
    Paul and Annelise Galland, Monique Golhen
    and Régine Le Bourva   288
Yvonne Berge   291
Phyllis Drayson   293
Mireille Fromantel   294
Anne-Marie Debatte   295

FROM DRAMA AND MIME   298
Bella Reine   298
Etienne Decroux   300
Jacques Lecoq   304
Marcel Marceau   305

IN THE DUNCAN LINE   305
Madeleine Lytton   305
Odile Hamelin-Pyros   306

CONCLUSION   306

PART IV   1960–1970: THE FLOWERING YEARS
Chronology   311
Social Changes   315
The Rights of the Body   316
The Institutionalization of Dance   317
Festivals   319
Companies and Schools   320
A Digression on Folklore   323
Competitions   324
The 'Militants'   324
Everything Changes   325
American Influences   326
The Wave from Latin America   327
Multiplication   328
Youth and Vulnerability   329

THE ACTORS   330

INSTITUTIONS   331
The Introduction of Dance into Parisian
    Universities *by Mireille Arguel*   331
The Growing Presence of Modern Dance in
    Physical Training Centres *by Mireille Arguel*   335
The Ballet Théâtre Contemporain   341
The Théâtre Français de la Danse   343
The Théâtre des Nations   343
The Châteauvallon Festival   344
Art, Recherche, Confrontation at the Museum of Modern Art   345

The Bagnolet Competition: Ballet pour Demain
  by Nathalie Collantes   346

FRENCH DANCERS, NOMADIC AND SEDENTARY   346
Françoise Saint-Thibault   346
Noëlle Janoli   348
Françoise Julliot de la Morandière   348
Claudine Allegra   349
Isabelle Mirova   350
Claude Decaillot   352
Dora Feïlane   354
Aline Roux   354
Annick Maucouvert   355
Suzon Holzer   358
Renate Pook   359
Poumi Lescaut   360
Anne-Marie Reynaud   361

THE SCHOLARS   361
Michèle Nadal   361
Francine Lancelot   363
Muriel Jaër   366
Claude Pujade-Renaud   367
Jacqueline Challet-Haas   369
Mireille Arguel   371
Alberte Raynaud   373
Pinok and Matho   375

THE EDUCATORS   378
Denise Coutier and 'Danse Ma Joie' (D.M.J.)   379
Jean Bouffort   380
Françoise Chantraine   381
Sylvie Deluz   382
The 'Science of the Body'   383

THE GRAFT FROM LATIN AMERICA   384
Arlet Bon   385
Sara Pardo   387
Graziella Martinez   388
Juan Carlos Bellini   391
Mara Dajanova   391
Noémie Lapzeson   391

Paulina Ossona   392
Paulina Oca   392
Diana Obedman   393
Gladys Aleman   393
Sonia Sanoja   394
Guillermo Palomares   394

JAZZ AND AFRICAN DANCE: ANOTHER
   TURNING TOWARDS ROOTS   395
Ingeborg Liptay   395
Christiane de Rougemont   396

EPILOGUE   401

Appendices   409
   The Specialized Press and Writers about Dance   409
   A Few Authors who Wrote about Dance   414
   Period Pieces: A Few Howlers   419

Bibliography   427
   Other books by Jacqueline Robinson   432

Index   433

INTRODUCTION TO THE SERIES

Choreography and Dance Studies is a book series of special interest to dancers, dance teachers and choreographers. Focusing on dance composition, its techniques and training, the series will also cover the relationship of choreography to other components of dance performance such as music, lighting and the training of dancers.

In addition, *Choreography and Dance Studies* will seek to publish new works and provide translations of works not previously published in English, as well as to publish reprints of currently unavailable books of outstanding value to the dance community.

Robert P. Cohan

ACKNOWLEDGEMENTS

I want to express my gratitude to all those who assisted me in completing this work:

to those who encouraged me in the validity of this project which had been taking shape in my mind for a number of years;

to those who were willing to talk to me about themselves, their teachers, comrades or pupils;

to those from whom I sought advice concerning the source or confirmation of information;

to those whose diverse knowledge helped to orientate my own thoughts and research: Dr Lia Andler, Jerome Andrews, Monique Babsky, Marie Bacharach, Alexandre Berlant, Arlet Bon, Lise Brunel, Alice Kohn Cahen, Janine Charrat, Jacqueline Chaumont, Selma-Jeanne Cohen, Gilberte Cournand, Ivó Cramer, Guy Darmet, Amala Devi, Françoise and Dominique Dupuy, Mireille Fromantel, Anne Gardon, Joëlle de Gravelaine, Antoinette Guédy, Georgette Guignard, Bengt Haeger, Philippe Henry, André Philippe Hersin, Muriel Jaer, Jean Jarrell, Poumi Lescaut, Edmond Linval, Léone Mail, Malavika, Le Mémorial Juif, Eric Näslund, André Perinetti, Michel Petit, Madame Pourtalé, Valerie Preston-Dunlop, Odile Pyros, Jérôme Rachell, Fernand Rouffi, Madame Jacinto Salvado, Monique Semprun, Paulette Serry, Claire Sombert, Corinne Soum, Alexandre Tansman, Jean-Pierre Viloin, Mara Vinadia … (and may those whom I have forgotten to mention forgive me!);

to those who so willingly contributed to the making of this book: Denise Blanc-Raillard, Lise Brunel, Françoise Chantraine, Nathalie Collantes, Denise Coutier, Roger Dabert, Dominique Dupuy, Philippe Henry, Thierry Lhote, Annelise Galland Peerbohm and friends, Geneviève Piguet, Florence Poudru, Odile Pyros, Delphine Rybinski; and to Jean-Marc Adolphe who judiciously edited my text.

In particular, my thanks must be extended to my daughters, Sophie and Dinah Gélinier, who followed the different stages of the project step by step and without whose confidence, patience and insight it would never have been realized.

LIST OF PLATES

1. Isadora Duncan and her pupils in 1909
2. Loie Fuller
3. Raymond Duncan at his Akademia with two disciples
4. Lisa Duncan and her dancers in November 1933
5. Dussia Bereska, *The Green Clowns*, 1927
6. Jacqueline Chaumont, *The Roman Chariot*, 1925
7. Alexandre Sakharoff
8. Clotilde Sakharoff in *Jeune fille au jardin*
9. Irène Popard and her Pupils in 1925
10. Jeanne Ronsay in *Funeral March*
11. Nyota Inyoka
12. Raden Mas Jodjana
13. Mary Wigman, *Russian Dance*
14. Gret Palucca
15. Jean Weidt
16. Heinz Finkel in Paris in 1939
17. Ludolf Schild in 1945
18. Mila Cirul in *Russisches Fragment* in 1929
19. *Symphonie du nouveau monde*, choreography by Hélène Carlut
20. Jean Serry in *La Danse des morts* in Lyons in 1945
21. Janine Solane, *Saint-Sébastien sous les flèches*, in 1943
22. Anne Gardon, *L'Appel*
23. Raymonde Lombardin, *Révolte*, 1949
24. Françoise Dupuy, *La Femme et son ombre*, 1968
25. Dominique Dupuy, 1965
26. Jerome Andrews, *Oedipus*, in 1951
27. Jacqueline Robinson in one of Mary Wigman's classes, 1953
28. *Cantique pour la terre*, 1959, choreography by Jacqueline Robinson
29. Laura Sheleen, 1956
30. Karin Waehner, *Extase*, in 1962
31. Karin Waehner and Jacqueline Robinson in their choreography *Le Seuil* in 1954

32. Paul d'Arnot and Françoise Dupuy, *Visages de terre*, 1957
33. Katherine Henry d'Epinoy and Laura Sheleen
34. Olga Stens and Jerome Andrews, *Rencontre* (*Encounter*), 1955
35. Etienne Decroux in *Le Menuisier*, 1940
36. *Quel temps*, choreography by Suzon Holzer
37. Pinok and Matho, *Présence d'Hiroshima*, 1969
38. Graziella Martinez in *Giselle after Tomorrow*
39. Hideyuki Yano, *Le Fleuve*, 1975, with Christiane de Rougemont and Elsa Wolliaston
40. Christine Gérard and Alejandro Witzman-Anaya in *Algorythme*, choreography by Jacqueline Robinson, 1970

Georges Pomiès, 1932. Photo: Maurice Tabard.

EXERGUE

In 1930 Georges Pomiès (yes, there already existed a great 'modern' French dancer as early as 1930) demanded the 'rehabilitation of dance' in a text that summarized both the struggle against indifference or disapproval that motivated these adventurers of yesteryear, and the high ideal of dance that urged them on:

'The rehabilitation of dance. A strange idea indeed.

'Has dance been so degraded, and what form did this degradation take? I believe rather that nobody even gives dance a second thought, especially in France. It appears as the most frivolous activity in the world, since its immateriality and intransience have prevented the handing down of important documents and episodes in its glorious history from age to age. It appears to have neither a past nor a future, and successive generations have constantly expressed surprise at finding themselves so strongly attracted to such a "passing fancy".

'And yet dance is without doubt the earliest artistic manifestation, and we will see that it is the most effective means of achieving the "wisdom" that leads to happiness.

'For some people, dance represents the very essence of what they call spectacle. It is an art that relies upon fine physical constitution and beauty, a discreet but frank allusion to pleasure, and a minimum of cerebral effort. It is a decorative element of the first order that sets great store by costumes, colours and general effects, and facilitates a means of listening to music that would be a little too indigestible without this sauce.

'The majority of people never progress beyond this conception.

'Then there are those who are seduced by technique and find it unbelievable that the body can achieve so many physical feats. Many of these people will never progress beyond this stage either and will remain admirers of spurious acrobats all their life.

'One begins to embark upon the right track as soon as one realizes that the dancer requires no instrument, or rather that his whole body with all its faculties is his instrument, the most primitive, complex and transient one, which alone has the power to create movement, for dancing amounts precisely to the creation of movement. Movement is the stuff of dance just as sound is that of music. It is the most tangible means by which the corporeal may create the incorporeal.

'Dancing represents a dilution of the body in movement, and is the surest way of achieving its disincarnation.

'This brief overview reveals that dance may help the individual to rise along the scale of human possibilities from the vainest of glorifications of the flesh to the painful striving towards spirituality. It is an endeavour that brings no external satisfaction for it creates nothing tangible, nothing that may even attest to its presence, or to which a hope or a happy memory may be attached. Dance creates nothing but the individual; it is the most effective method of human evolution.'

Georges Pomiès, 'Propos sur la danse' (1930),
Danser c'est vivre, p. 92, Tisné, Paris, 1939.

FOREWORD

Jacqueline Robinson's overview of modern dance in France, from 1920 to 1970, is a welcome addition to the growing literature on the beginnings of the European dimension to the twentieth-century innovations in dance.

The present translation will give the English reader access to this key part of dance history through the eyes and sensitivity of Robinson who was, and is, herself part of this evolution and influential in it.

Her knowledge of the diversity of the early seeds in France, their sources and their impact, gives an informed chronicle made enjoyable by her personal style.

Valerie Preston-Dunlop

PRELUDE

INDELIBLE EPHEMERA

by Dominique Dupuy

Without oblivion, neither individual nor society could escape the rule of insomnia. And yet, our struggle against the policies of oblivion is not over.
Nicole Loreaux

Repertory – Inventory – Census – Chronicle – Manifesto

Repertory: A corpus of material in which the contents are arranged in such an order that they are easy to find. All right.

A person who remembers many things and is always ready to impart these to others: ' . . . a living repertory'. Jacqueline Robinson is certainly one of these.

Inventory: A written statement of the property, furniture, deeds, documents of a person. 'To draw up an inventory of an estate.' We are getting on.

Taking stock of the goods in store and their various prices in order to ascertain the profits and losses and establish the balance sheet. This is certainly a kind of balance sheet.

An heir's right to settle the debts of an estate in proportion to the value of the goods he is to receive; 'without liability for debts exceeding the assets, according to the expected amount'. Our expectations will certainly be met.

Census: A population count. In this case a rather odd population, made up of nutty people suffering from a kind of St Vitus's dance, going before and following a wild and martial saraband.

Chronicle: This book claims to be a chronicle: a historical account of events in the order of time. It is not concerned with scandal, simply with truth. (The scandal lies elsewhere.)

Manifesto: A comprehensive and detailed list of merchandise. Dancers, forming the cargo of ship – this particular chapter in the story of modern dance, a cargo that must be declared at the

	port – contemporary public opinion. We are gradually getting there …
Census:	Let us return to the second meaning of the term: an examination of precious metals, gold and silver. Which means here that we are dealing with jewels. Good!
Chronicle:	If we pursue our investigations as glossarists and turn to the term 'chronic' in its adjectival form, we see that it can designate 'a prolonged illness that slowly pursues its course'.
	Modern dance a chronic illness, indeed! And which might last, one dreams! A worm, so to speak, in the fruit!
Manifesto:	Quoted once more: a written statement in which the leader of a party gives a public account of the previous conduct of the party in question and its aims for the future. I note with immediate pleasure that here we are concerned with a process of active memory that connects past and future and includes the present.
Chronicle:	Ultimately, finally and especially pleasingly, this means the earliest written traditions of a people, which brings us to the very heart of the matter. This is indeed what it is all about. And, as I go by, I salute the people concerned.

Had I written this book, I would have put more violence and anger into it.

By a reversal of the filiation through which according to Hesiod, theologian of the Greeks, Oblivion was the offspring of Quarrel, for me it would have been Oblivion that gave birth to Anger. Anger close to that of Achilles whom Homer praises in the opening line of the *Iliad*: 'Sing, O Goddess, of the anger of Achilles', placing the entire poem from the start under the sign of anger, 'the terrible memory of the only thing that cannot be forgotton: loss' (Nicole Loreaux).

We indeed suffered a great loss when Jean Weidt left Paris for Berlin in 1949, making us orphans of his dance.

Oblivion. As if remembrance were dangerous, memory has been excised for all actors of this period, a sort of amnesty which obliterates everything.

But were those people guilty? And of what? Of disturbing the peace?

This is to be an act of rehabilitation, and posthumously so in certain cases, in order to establish them, if not in the Pantheon (for which they care little) then at least in the collective memory, with the 'esteem' to which Saint-John Perse refers.

A little more anger, yes, the anger of raw memory confronting oblivion; as Nicole Loreaux claims, '*menis*, more formidable than *mneme*'; anger that endures, the anger of Achilles, yes, or that of Electra too. And yet that frequently carries within itself an ultimate renunciation.

I would have included more than memory alone: non-oblivion, something more active. For one must be constantly on guard against oblivion and, being thus vigilant, keep the echo ringing.

I feel this anger would suit those fiery individuals with whom we are concerned here – individuals who, far from making fashionable entertainment of their dance or cult objects of their bodies, have used the latter as a weapon to further their cause.

We don't just nibble at modern dance, it hits us right in the face.

We might, however, throw some of this anger back at these dauntless pioneers and bequeath them the guilty conscience, for they may indeed be reproached with having failed to hit out, so intent were they on contemplating their own navels.

And the difference between their struggle and that of their contemporaries in the theatre is striking; for the battles and victories of Copeau, Dullin, Baty, Jouvet, Pitoëff, and later Vilar and others, showed that they knew how to break through.

To the credit of these dancers, however, and in mitigation, it must be acknowledged that they were thrashing the water and thus the guilty conscience can be offered elsewhere.

Which institutions opened their doors to them; which venues, private or public, decided to welcome them?

Furthermore, who bothered to speak of them, or even recognize their existence? And when this did occur, it was clearly with no references, with above all a total lack of discernment and with so little intuition!

'Madame Sakharoff could have been a dancer', wrote someone, and we may read there his regret at not having seen her in *Giselle*, a role about which dear Clotilde could not have cared less. Was she to dance no other role?

Today our memory is like a sieve as far as this period is concerned. Contemporary/modern dance was born in the 1970s, they say, if not the 1980s and, at that rate, 2000. Which means only a century's delay.

I am reminded of the German texts we had at school during the war. Restrictions compelled us to use pre-war books; but the pages that referred to works by condemned Jewish authors had been carefully stuck together. Our first task was to unstick them.

Don't these blind people realize that, by scorning the dance of yesterday, they are amputating that of today?

For the latter is born of the former. 'One cannot be without having been' (Fernand Braudel). The dance of our children is that of our parents. There is no spontaneous generation.

I would like for a moment to imagine a play of correspondences between dancers of today and dancers of yesterday (other associations are possible): Catherine Diverres – Clotilde Sakharoff; Hervé Diasnas – Georges Pomiès; Daniel Larrieu – Ludolf Schild; Jean-François Duroure – Alexander Sakharoff; Isabelle Dubouloz – Françoise Dupuy; Régis Obadia – Jean Weidt ...

Suddenly one begins to imagine a future chronicle of 'young French dance', from the late twentieth century to around the mid-twenty-first. What an incredible patchwork of images ... A futuristic vision ...

This account (authentic statement of facts) is more than healthy; it is salutary.

We tend to stagnate beneath the memory of a kind of dance composed of tittle-tattle, knick-knacks or boudoir deco, Dresden china and other mantelpiece ornaments, a bust of Vestris or Noverre here and there to create an appearance of culture. (In the future we will no doubt collapse beneath the weight of the shelves of electronic gadgets that will furnish the libraries of dance and choreography and other arsenals of technological memorabilia!)

We live in a cocoon of dance that has come straight down from the nineteenth century, with a body-machine that needs to be warmed up (ah! the warm-up), trained, placed (ah! first of all we must place this object that we intend to displace!), tortured, a body condemned to perspiration, pain and mishap, that we nevertheless try to coddle, diet, bandage, nurse and repair ...

May this book enable us finally to enter, if not the twenty-first century, then at least a twentieth where dance would be given the place it deserves as one of the most subtle and profound creative activities – and most in tune with our time.

May this book make us take a step towards the acceptance of our history, past, present and future combined; in the affirmation of our identity.

Duck's feet exist only in the mind. They must make way for other mythologies.

Is it not strange to observe that a number of those who distinguished themselves, and continue to do so, came to dance relatively late in life by roundabout ways, and that they grew up outside the family: yesterday Pomiès, Weidt, Sakharoff ...; today Gallotta, Rochon, Appaix, Cré-Ange ... ?

Between the tradition that weighs so heavily on our shoulders and the excessive creativity required by competing productions, does there not exist a critical space in which the issues of the present and future may draw sustenance from those of the past?

Is it conceivable that contemporary dance should spring from the clear conscience of dance of good pedigree and no longer be the province of those noisy brats of the family against whom we should not bear too strong a grudge, since they might one day mend their ways?

But they will not mend their ways. Rather, they will continue to disturb. And this is how it should be.

Contemporary dance is revolutionary or it is not.

Dare I say that what surprises and perhaps delights me most about this adventure is that such a large-scale movement has practically created no school – unlike what has happened elsewhere.

There is no well-kept garden with calibrated produce but a field in which everyone sows his own seed. The field is not fallow but rich in the finest compost.

In it one finds many individuals uprooted from their native soil, some of whom chose to settle in Paris because of its image as an artistic capital, but the majority of whom came for more fundamental reasons, finding here a sheet-anchor, a haven of political, religious and philosophical freedom, and these included Weidt, Schild, Stens, Andrews, etc.

Now that circumstances are more peaceable, the grafts remain numerous: Carlson, Buirge, Nadj, Decina, Yano, Wolliaston, de Groat, etc.

Like all omissions, however, the lack of a school may be seen as a beneficial defect, since styles have a tendency to dictate.

Did not these sparse seeds produce the generous harvest we see ripening today?

We are not concerned here with the usual problems of dance, fruitless quarrels between different schools, styles or manners; we have reached the heart of modern/contemporary dance as these visionaries imagined it; we are in the domain of the spirit.

This book answers a need, fills a gap, rights a wrong; indeed a work of public salvation.

In rescuing modern French dance from Lethe, Jacqueline Robinson becomes twice over daughter of Mnemosyne through double filiation.

Though her work may be in large part heuristic, we can discern her wholehearted commitment.

She has acted with what Lorrina Niclas would describe as 'that vigilant care brought by one who reveals a poetic insight pertinent to the very core of the spirit'.

This book renders oblivion out of date, for 'it is always possible to appeal to the memory and awaken it against the oblivion of what happened' (Alain Fienkielkraut). It shows that we might hope in vain, like the chorus of Thebans at the beginning of Sophocles' *Antigone*, 'to forge the oblivion of today's battles', for there is always an Antigone keeping watch, a vestal of recollection.

It shows that however much one may seek to eradicate, scratch out, silence or conceal, 'complete obliteration does not exist' (Freud); and that those figures, considered for a time 'unmentionable', as were dissident Soviet writers, will one day return to haunt us.

It lends credence to Maurice Blanchot's pronouncement that dance, like literature, is 'condemned to be ineffaceable'.

It is not a question of merely turning the page but of opening a book.

Open this book.

It is the story of a gap in memory.

A fantastic tale of a brood of ducklings amidst a bevy of swans.

Memory is a form of courage.
Jean Vilar

How marvellous it is that the process of evolution is necessarily
composed of recurrences, as marvellous as the return of the recurrent.
At each moment, everything is both old and new.
Within a moment, or almost, a prime number may become a multiple.
At each moment, the new becomes old.
Paul Valéry

He who carries the obvious on his shoulders
remembers the waves in the salt warehouses.
René Char

INTRODUCTION

An Epic

For many years now, as I follow my path on the great journey of
contemporary dance, along with an ever growing crowd I have experienced a desire to pause for a moment, just to tell a story. As though I
were to stand on a slope on the side of the road, and looking backwards
and forwards, towards the past and the future, towards those who have
left the road and those who embark upon it, and I would call out to those
who pass by in front of me and I would say to them 'You (so-called
modern/contemporary dancers), you who give your life to dance, do you
know where you come from? Why this particular road? You who are
dancers, choreographers or teachers of a form of dance that you have
chosen as if it were a matter of course, do you realize that it has not
always been so? Do you realize that you are the heirs to a rich history of
events, struggles, discoveries, confrontations, hopes and humiliations,
tenacity and faith, wrong turnings, laughter and tears, and a great deal
of perspiration? An epic, in a way, upon your own ground'.

I would like to tell the story of the adventure of modern dance in
France from my point of view as one of the actors in this epic who
actually experienced certain episodes, fully conscious of the fact that
something of great importance was taking place.

This story will therefore assume the form of a chronicle, that is, a
personal reading of the course of events. The chronicler can only write
from his position within the field (be it the battlefield or the field of
observation). He sees only what he *is able* to see, and above all what he
knows how to see. His vision is partial (or partisan?), his interpretation of
events inevitably subjective.

The Sense of the Phylum

No member of my own generation launched himself into uncharted
territory, for the path was already marked out. It simply remained for us
to make it more accessible, to clear it more widely. Will the young
dancers of today take the time to glance back to the past; will they accept
this awareness of the artistic and human inheritance of modern dance?

Farewell to all references; long live the ephemeral! Our age is
characterized by a loss of historical or collective memory. As Michel

Foucault observes:

> *'This generation seeks to tear to pieces everything that made possible the comforting effect of recognition'.*[1]

This expresses the paradox of the individual who believes himself all the more free for having cut himself off from his own history!

It is with the aim of preventing this history of modern dance in France from sinking definitively into oblivion that I have the desire to establish this chronicle, in the hope of restoring to young dancers the 'sense of the phylum' that was so dear to Teilhard de Chardin.

Modern Dance in the Birth-Place of Classical Dance

The sources of modern dance are not exclusively American (a frequent statement), and the myth that Martha Graham (in spite of all my respect and admiration for her) is the mother of modern dance must be dispensed with once and for all! This new form of dance created by Western society arose simultaneously on both sides of the Atlantic where it experienced a similar gestation and first steps.

Since the days of Louis XIV and his Académie Royale de Danse, France has figured prominently as the cradle of classical dance. Gradually denying its roots in popular dance, classical dance became an entertainment of the aristocracy and gradually confined itself to restrictions of technique, styles and conventions, becoming ever more distant from personal and social life. Carving out its own perfection across two centuries, classical dance imposed a unique image of dance on Western society.

As a result, the earliest advocates of modern dance in France were forced to adopt a confrontational attitude towards classical dance. For it was not with impunity that France had conceived and nurtured classical dance, and this fact helps to explain the virulence of the reactions that the first promulgators of modern dance in France had to face. The conception of a new type of dance has been underway for almost a century now. But how many bold or tentative rebellions, how many thrusts, cracks, splits and surges had to take place in order that dance might rise once again, naked and vulnerable like a new-born child, and discover, define and develop its very self, in order that it may forge ahead in its essential universality and formidable diversity!

---

[1] Michel Foucault, *Nietzsche.*

Virginity and Creation

My chronicle charts the evolution of modern dance during the half century from 1920 to 1970, that is, from the point at which modern dance began to display identifiable characteristics to that at which the contemporary choreographic scene has become so complex as to make any attempt at analysis a matter for speculation.

It is impossible to apply the interpretative elements of classical dance to modern dance, and the specific nature of the latter in terms of its function, resources and semantic must be recognized. From this point of view, it is worth stating that the various impulses towards freedom apparent in the art of classical dance, such as the spurious adventures into 'naturalism', the neogothic reveries, and pastorals that replaced the old allegories, toe-dancing, daring exploits and new positions hardly changed the fundamental concepts of its language, vocabulary and internal procedures at all. Even the additional aesthetic 'novelties' introduced by the Ballets Russes at the beginning of the century had relatively little effect, with the exception of those of that great reforming genius, Nijinsky.

Modern dance demands both a specificity of material (movement before anything else), and a conception of creation as the expression/symbolic construction of the individual creator. Ex nihilo? Not at all. The creator is conditioned by thousands of unavoidable prejudices, but he must somehow try to preserve his *virginity*. How long it has taken for the public to understand this approach and accept this basic procedure!

As though it were indeed *unthinkable* that one might *invent* a movement oneself, or pursue an inner vision or feeling that were, by their very nature, unique, or that one may conceive and construct new forms and structures. But even the purest and most exacting of soul-searchers is, of course, unable to avoid, either as a consequence of the conditioning of his training, or more undefinably, of the weight of the 'collective unconscious', the subconscious assimilation of stereotyped movements and clichés that correspond to current gestural models of social behaviour.

Never before in the history of the world until the twentieth century had an individual been bold enough to stand before his fellows and speak to them with his body as the deliverer, subject and object of his own discourse. Never before had he tried to utter his singularity without reference to any known word, or a previously agreed language or discourse. In every remote civilization and society, dance has been shaped by the customs and codes in use. The desire for, conception and birth of a new dance form in the twentieth century was, therefore, a complete revolution and a revelation, so gigantic that its dimension may be occasionally betrayed, even by those who preach it. This new dance form, freed from all codes, indeed conformed to the vision of these early *revolutionaries*, who dreamed of such a return to sources. Such was the fundamental dogma of contemporary dance, whatever its diverse developments were to be. And yet, is it not a dangerous type of freedom that gives rise to a form of dance without any guiding principles, therefore elusive? But that is another story!

I am astonished by the number of theorists who have discussed dance in the period in question (and it is not over yet ...), with such concern for splitting hairs that they do not seem to have been able to see the forest for the trees. Perhaps this is because they have not experienced the research through their own bodies and have been content to observe and reflect, and, as a result, to classify and catalogue. One of the only thinkers to have understood the specific nature and implications of the procedures of modern dance in this key period seems to me to have been the American, John Martin, whose reference texts remain indisputable even today.

It may be argued that it was incumbent upon the performers themselves to better define their philosophy and methods. But during the early decades in particular, they were, on the whole, doubtless too absorbed in the actual process of their research, of which they were both the subject and the agent, too intoxicated by this exaltation of the 'self', this discovery of their soul as much as of their body, which they sought to fit in with 'The Great Whole'. The result of this was, from the very beginning, a type of discourse frequently imbued with mysticism on which it was difficult to establish any structure of a speculative nature.

Terminology

A significant symptom of the ambiguity of the very nature of (modern) dance has been and continues to be the problem of terminology. This operates on two levels, the first of which is the designation and nomenclature of a vocabulary. Certain theorists have attempted to produce a codification of contemporary dance that would provide a convenient counterpart to that of classical dance at any price. But according to what criteria and interpretative structures should the various steps, positions and movements be designated? It seems to me that there would be a fundamental antinomy in seeking to fix, and thus to render static and sterile, the organic material from which dance is constructed, without mentioning the crystallization of a style or vocabulary, whatever these might be. Indeed, this material is infinitely analyzable according to objective criteria involving precise and quantifiable elements such as time, space, energy, etc., and it is perhaps only this type of approach (namely, that of Laban), that would provide a valid means of categorizing movement and describing it in semiological terms.

Throughout these decades in which dance sought to define itself, many colourful terms and jargonistic expressions could be heard, ranging from the 'wild' and 'semi-wild' steps of Irène Popard, to the 'flexed feet' and 'triplets' of the Grahamians! The very identity of the type of dance known today as 'contemporary' has witnessed numerous problems of terminology: in the 1920s and 30s, 'free dance' (as it was called in Anglo-Saxon countries) was the most widespread terminology, followed by 'expressionist dance' (reflecting the artistic movement in German art and cinema), or even 'expression dance', a literal translation of the German *Ausdruckanz*. The term 'modern dance' appeared from the 1930s on and originated in America where it was first used in 1929 by the critic John Martin. In England in the 1930–50s, it was customary to refer to modern dance as 'Central European dance', emphasizing the importance of the phenomenon of the migration of artists from countries affected by the rise of Nazism.

In 1935, Pierre Conté wrote the following lines, which bring a smile to the lips today:

'One must include in free dance all those systems that are incorrectly termed:
– rhythmic dance
– plastic dance
– acrobatic dance
– danced music, etc.

I declare these terms incorrect, because one may indeed wonder how a dance that is not rhythmic, or that avoids all manner of acrobatics, or that is not danced to music, could be performed. The inventors and upholders of such terms will soon inform us, no doubt, that they have seen "quadrupeds with four legs", "birds with two wings", and that they have created "rhythmic" music.

Such terminology must be rejected, therefore, if one has any taste or common-sense, and the following terms should be used instead:
– rhythmic education
– rhythmic gymnastics
– musico-plastic rhythmic exercises'.[2]

From Yesterday to Today

The mode of dress in fashion in the studio as well as on the stage in a particular period speaks volumes about the evolution of concepts in modern dance:

---

[2] Pierre Conté, *La Danse et ses lois* (Arts et mouvement, Paris, 1952), p. 160.

– the Greek tunic of the Isadorians and Dalcrozians: yearning for
  a rediscovery of a golden age;
– the bathing costume of the early Germans: naturism and democracy;
– the long skirt of Wigman and her colleagues: feminization; the
  ability to express powerful human emotions through dance;
– tights, post-1950: autonomy of movement, abstraction;
– everyday dress at the end of the 1960s: social implications;
– rags in the 1980s: deconstruction and derision.

Over and above these few references to dress, I can detect obvious
important differences between the climate of modern dance at the time of
my Paris début in 1947, and that of today. We were at that time effectively
living an epic in full swing, doubtless too busy fighting for the existence
of the type of dance in which we believed to engage in much theorizing.
In seeking to immerse myself in the culture of the generation that
preceded my own, however, I have become aware of still more differences, in view of which the ideologies and practices of these brave pioneers
may indeed seem anachronistic to contemporary eyes.

It seems to me that one phenomenon has remained virtually
constant since the very beginnings of 'expression' dance and persisted
until the 1960s, constituting an essential difference with the new dance of
today. This phenomenon is in part philosophical with far-reaching consequences and represents a social value. I am referring to what Saint-
Exupéry calls *'the divine knot that ties things together'*: a concern for the
integration of mind and body, for the construction of an order and
meaning amongst things, an aspiration towards harmony, for want of
using that indefinable term beauty, and by way of a consequence, a
rejection of the 'ugly'. From this point of view, even if dancers or
choreographers wanted to express sad themes, or portray the tragic or the
horrible, they would not distort or depersonalize either the human being
or the discourse. There remains a core of dignity perhaps, an integrity in
the clinical sense, certainly a degree of logic that preserves a readableness
and understanding of the choreographic text.

Clearly, at worst, this falls into pleonasm, naïvety, a cult of the
angelic, and silliness. It is true that on re-reading the statements, mani-
festos and criticisms, in short, everything concerning expression dance in
the inter-war years, one may smile at the number of capital letters
attached to key words: Joy, Grace, Harmony, Freedom, Beauty, Youth,
e tutti quanti, and the spirit of optimism that refused to recognize the
darker side of human nature. The theories of Freud had not yet become
commonplace! This orthodoxy and prudishness of thought, this cult of

good taste and moral health must indeed have curbed the creative impetus of many individuals.

It was generally accepted that the function of dance (I refer to the infancy of modern dance) was the expression of man. But at that time it seemed that the concept of man was admissible only if he was presented in a certain way, disguised and idealized. This paradigm from the golden age in which the human being is perceived as ideally beautiful and harmonious, as in Greek statuary, was a necessary and detailed model. (The same idealization occurred in classical dance also, but the model was different.) Man may be tender or passionate or overwhelmed, but he was made for joy and splendour. This model was the most widespread one in France, but around the same time in Germany a style emerged that was not unrelated to the gothic 'grotesque' in which the human being was distorted by despair and anguish.

Modern dance in France did not escape a rather ingenuous but necessary transition through the 'grandiose' and a certain 'exoticism', as if an unadorned image of man were still impossible. In the 1950s, moreover, a similar phenomenon infiltrated neo-classical dance, then at its height in the work of Lifar, Charrat and Petit, out of a need for disguise, anachronism and metamorphosis, resulting in the abuse of literary artifices and mythological legends.

At what point did dance begin to cast off these images? Wigman and Graham settled their account with the angelic at least, letting loose the demons, exploring darkness and allowing cruelty to emerge. The extent of this change in direction is not fully realized today, accustomed as we are to the spectacles of Pina Bausch, amongst others.

Let us not forget, however, that as early as 1931 in France, the dancer and choreographer Georges Pomiès had the courage to affirm, with a new spirit of simplicity, the direct and frank expression of the human condition within an extremely sober theatrical setting.

From the 1950s there was a general change in attitude: naïvety gradually gave way to a distancing effect that went hand in hand with a certain maturity. The creator disengaged himself from his work, became increasingly concerned with abstraction, and established far more subtle relationships both with his own body and the space around him. The destruction brought about by the war, accompanied by new knowledge and awareness, all contributed to this change.

Contemporary Opinions

The ideological evolution of young choreographers is reflected clearly in observations such as those of Christine Gérard in *Ballet/*

L'Avant-Scène (1980):

> ' ... *dance is ever fragile. There are a number of reasons for this, but it is inherently fragile ... Dance and movement are graceful acts. It is true that there is an obsessive fear amongst dancers, particularly contemporary ones, of giving in to the ease of movement, the initial joy of gesture, and they play on this, degrading and deforming it, for they are afraid of falling into the trap of prettiness. Indeed, dance creates difficulties precisely because it may be pretty, and such prettiness has never led to anything worthwhile.*
>
> *Prettiness is one thing ... but it is not a sufficient basis for creation; it cannot support substance. It is a mere ephemeron, a passing moment that does not last; it is not a source of work: one cannot study prettiness or explore it in any depth. I believe there is a fear of falling into this trap'.*[3]

In the same text/interview Christine Gérard makes a further observation that seems to me to illustrate a more recent subtlety of contemporary work:

> *'some years ago now the expression "one must be" was frequently heard. One had to be what one claimed to be.*
>
> *My impression is that today this boils down to a question of existence, that the space in which one exists is reduced considerably, but that does not mean to say that it is any less rich; on the contrary it is perhaps much more diverse. But awareness is becoming more and more acute, more and more penetrating of the inner body, and within this new-found depth there is, indeed, an unsuspected richness ... visually, conceptually, there is very little space; it is so small that it may be held between two fingers, but within these two fingers there are billions of cells, billions of actions which are in fact the source of work and knowledge.*
>
> *It is not a question of minimalism in form but of minimalism in consciousness. Rather than being conscious of oneself in space, for example, one is conscious of oneself within the context of one's own choice. That is to say, external space is not defined by my relationship to a wall or an object, but rather by the relationship between space and body; it is the body itself that will travel through space, that will travel within itself'.*

Subtle feelings ... not that the work of earlier practitioners ever lacked subtlety. This was certainly true in the case of the 'greats' whose subtlety was innate, but it seems that the accent, in terms of the gestural schemata of creators as much as of the instructions of pedagogues, was placed rather on a *breadth* and fullness, a totality of feeling and action that existed primarily on a large scale, occupying its place to the full, stretching body and gesture to their limits, and seeking to rediscover schemata of simple, direct and organic actions. And once these well-oiled wheels were set in motion, the process of refinement could go on and on.

---

[3] Christine Gérard, in *Ballet/L'Avant-Scène* (Paris, April 1980), p. 109.

A key word of the 1950s was 'authenticity'. Dance, bodily expression and dramatic action all had to be authentic and 'valid'. This did not prove contradictory to the notion of subtlety, but placed the interest elsewhere. These differing procedures were not incompatible, moreover. It was simply a question of the range of the palette.

A second phenomenon that characterized the free dance of the 1920s and 30s was the strict dependence of the dancer on the music.

Émile Jaques-Dalcroze qualifies the relationship that existed between music and dance in previous centuries as *'combined-automatisms'*.

With the birth of new dance came the discovery of the possibility of listening to music *through the body*. Emancipated (more or less) from a codified vocabulary, the dancer was able to glide freely amongst the accents, dynamics and phrasing, and espouse the intimacy of the music. This indispensable stage in the development of the relationship between dance and music was both fundamental and enriching for the one as much as for the other (and for the choreographer as much as for the composer at a time when there was a true sense of collaboration between the two), but it led to a certain impasse also.

Another salient point to note, and a feature that was common to a number of dancers in the 1920s and 30s, is what we would describe today as amateurism, on a technical level at least. But this amateurism was particularly coloured by the extent of the personal culture of these practitioners, who frequently came from privileged backgrounds, and could exploit this fact to disguise the deficiencies of their feeble physical technique. There was no shortage of rich (and no doubt beautiful) women whose means enabled them to appear on the stage with all the required ostentation, but whose abilities were in reality rather poor. We may wonder whether one or another of them danced well, but according to which parameters should we judge?

The critics criticized (again, according to which parameters?) and the public either agreed or disagreed, sometimes moved, sometimes entertained and sometimes shocked by the new ideas they saw taking shape. It was precisely the novelty of these ideas in terms of gesture, costume, music (or the absence thereof) and scenography, their unprecedented emotional level and the hitherto unexpressed areas of the human soul they sought to reveal that established their market or moral value. The conviction of the artist, the extent of his audacity and richness of cultural reference, ultimately amounted to more than physical ability or even richness of vocabulary. Our attention today is focussed in an entirely different direction: we are blasé with regard to audacity and emotion, but ruthless in terms of bodily ability.

Fertility, Frivolity and Digressions

The adventure of modern dance in France has indeed been an adventure, and an epic one at times. Why, then, is it so relatively little known? It must be admitted that, unlike Germany or America during these ground-breaking years between the two world wars, France did not produce any personalities, works or trends of international stature. The French cannot pride themselves on having produced a Laban, a Wigman, a Jooss or a Kreutzberg, to mention only European examples. However, France, and Paris and Lyons in particular, was hardly a desert in relation to new dance.

She was certainly a welcoming nation; many artists, dancers, choreographers and pedagogues who had left their countries of origin for various reasons, settled in France where they became assimilated into the indigenous culture. During the first thirty years or so of the present century, there existed, amongst these immigrant artists and their fol-lowers, together with native French researchers, no small number of practitioners of merit who slowly established a following amongst the most enlightened strata of society.

It is interesting to consider the case of two countries, France and Germany, that were affected in very different ways by the phenomenon of the 1914–18 war, and to examine the reasons for this difference in terms of both the quantity and quality of their conception and practice of dance. The whole political, sociological, economic and cultural context must be taken into account in order to explain the imbalance in the fertility of these lands with regard to the appearance of new dance.

I venture to propose a hypothesis, which is a product of my thoughts during the many years in which I have lived and worked in France.

I have often thought that the French had a *frivolous* attitude towards the body and dance. (I was profoundly struck to read a similar opinion expressed by Georges Pomiès).

It is true that I am in part a foreigner (half English, half French), and that I have indeed been conditioned by my Protestant, musical and 'Wigmanian' upbringing, which has shaped my point of view. Neverthe-less, I was again and again annoyed by the attitude of those who appeared not to take dance – of whatever school, in France – seriously. I would be antagonized by writings, opinions and certain practices, as I would come across a valorization of prettiness, *'chic'*, elegance (in the fashionable sense of the term), prowess and a certain *'je-ne-sais-quoi'* that seemed to me to be light, affected and superficial in comparison with the values that were familiar to me. So be it!

As I wrote these lines a vision of Fragonard's painting *The Swing* came spontaneously and unexpectedly to my mind. The association of ideas is obvious! That charming and exquisite scene ... but is that not the very point?

Is frivolity not an elegant form of contempt? In a further association of ideas, I think of Dalcroze who claimed:

> '*I know many reasonable, intelligent and sensitive people who nevertheless only appreciate works of art as beautiful toys*'.[4]

It is generally agreed that contempt for the body constitutes a deviation from Judeo-Christian thought and, more recently, from Catholic as opposed to Protestant thought.

The body is both the location and the object of sin ... the sin of the 'work of the flesh' (and yet, there is no more beautiful expression than this, which seems to me to be strangely close to dance!) This attitude towards the shameful body, brought to heel, its sexuality denied, has, of course, figured prominently in Western civilization. As Desmond Morris maintained: '*we are our body*', and this body cries out its appetites and its wants. Accordingly, in order to make this constant cry bearable, we respond, but without appearing to attach too much importance to it.

If we examine the writings on dance, of previous centuries with the possible exception of those of Noverre, it seems to me that it is presented as something extraordinary, a manifestation that exists on the periphery of 'real life', something strangely unreal. Was it these attributes to which Dalcroze was also referring in 1912 when he wrote:

> '*Dancing has always, from the time of Lucian to that of Goethe and Theophile Gautier, been described in dithyrambic and aerial terms, calling up vague dreams of a supernatural order, in which bodily form, emancipated from the laws of gravity, floated high above the realities of human existence*'.[5]

Similarly, Philippe Muray stated in 1987:

> '*If there is an activity that sends one into raptures from the very start, it is indeed dance. It appears to be untouched, even untouchable, except through a kind of hazy, dazed enthusiasm that may be moving but does not lead to a lucid evaluation of the subject*'.[6]

---

[4] Émile Jaques-Dalcroze, *Le musique et nous* (Slatkine, Geneva, 1981), p. 107.

[5] Émile Jaques-Dalcroze, *Le Rythme, la musique et l'éducation* (Foetisch, Lausanne, 1965), p. 120. Translated in Émile Jaques-Dalcroze, *Rhythm, Music and Education*, trans. Harold F. Rubinstein (Chatto and Windus, London, 1921), p. 175.

[6] Philippe Muray, in *Art Press* (special article, no. 8, September 1987), p. 13.

In the first teetering steps taken by modern dance in the early years of
the present century, there was much concern with the expression of the
soul through the body, a body to which basic dignity had nevertheless
been restored. Before this dignity could in some way be rediscovered,
however, it was oddly necessary, as I suggested above, for some reference
to be made to a long-lost golden age. This was no doubt an inevitable
procedure, a necessary detour in order to escape the suffocation to which
the past, and above all the nineteenth century, had constrained the body.

Within this context, we must not forget that Germany and the
United States, which saw the most rapid development of modern dance
and gave birth to some of its most outstanding figures, belonged predominantly to the Protestant culture. Protestants? Puritans? The very
opposite of frivolity!

Spain would constitute something of an exception; a Catholic
country *par excellence* (and not exactly a frivolous one either), she
nevertheless had dance in her veins, but a strongly stylized, almost
ritualistic form of dance. This fact may account, therefore, for the time it
took for the very concept of 'free dance' to develop in that country in the
twentieth century. It is certainly no coincidence that Spain was slow to
admit and practise contemporary dance.

Dance to Serve Man? Man to Serve Dance?

In considering the recollections, testimonies, statements and experiences
of all the persons referred to, two phenomena stand out:

- the idealistic discourse of the majority of practitioners as well as
  the distinction between performers and 'educators';
- similarly, the distinction between professionals and amateurs,
  insofar as the parameters of this categorization may be defined.

What is the place of dance in society, in the lives of man and city alike?
These crucial questions remain a constant feature of society, even today.
There is an essential ambivalence and ambiguity: dance is an individual
manifestation, accessible and desirable to every human being. The right
to dance, dance for all. We are in agreement on the tenor of this discourse;
the evidence is undeniable. But, one might say, dance is also an art, and
where does the dividing line lie? This debate is not new. It may be found
again and again with regard to every artistic discipline: singing, drawing,
sculpture, dance, obvious activities that ought to be encouraged and
developed from childhood. And afterwards, who, then, would become a
musician, an artist or a dancer?

This debate is all the more ardent since dance (which type of dance?) effectively constitutes a unique and irreplaceable 'presence' in the world of each individual, and from this stems the passion of those who practise it.

This fundamental problem lies at the origin of the distinction between performers and 'educators'. The former tend to claim sole rights to competence, the latter to deplore the narcissim of the former; the ones displaying a corporate spirit, the others a sometimes invasive proselytism.

In the first half of our chronicle, there appear a majority of practitioners of the pedagogical type. At least, this is the aspect of their work that has been handed down to posterity most readily. The writings of some of these practitioners reflect didactic or ideological concerns; or could it have been that this aspect was the most marketable one, and so enabled them to survive? There were also prophet-like figures, even thaumaturges, but these featured much less prominently since the war. I would class Malkowski, Odic Kintzel, Berge, Peerbohm and Sheleen amongst these, without any pejorative implications.

There were the great performers, the stars of the stage, too. Isadora was one such, and Mary Wigman, Harald Kreutzberg and, closer to our own time, the Sakharoffs, Jean Weidt, Janine Solane, Jerome Andrews and the Dupuys could all be described in this way.

Then there were the rarer 'constructors' who served to advance systematic thought, and of whom Rudolf von Laban was the first example. Excellence in all of these categories is precisely what made the 'greats' truly great.

Keys to Reading

My aim in writing this chronicle was to reveal something of the history of these figures, to consider how and when they arrived on the French scene, what influenced them, and how they in turn influenced the subsequent course of events.

The accessibility of information proved particularly uneven in the case of those who had either passed away or of whom all trace had been lost; nor was the amount of information available necessarily proportional to a character's professional importance. I thus found myself confronted by a number of unforeseen imbalances.

One of the problems I encountered was the near impossibility of finding adequate terminology with which to describe movement, dance and dancers. Would I have to resort to poetic circumlocution?

I could only depict in the most crudely approximative way the individuality of the various characters discussed in this work in terms of style, mannerism and dynamic.

It must be taken as read, moreover, that all references in the text are to native French people, or to foreigners who made their career or established a following in France, and that they feature in this chronicle only *from the moment at which they began to acquire a certain notoriety in that country*. Thus, the foreigners may have already established a career elsewhere, whilst, on the other hand, the native French people who emigrated and created a career or following for themselves abroad are omitted from this study.

For a number of reasons, I did not want to write this book alone. It seemed to me more interesting for the reader to become acquainted with the various stages in this journey through the extraordinary story of dance, through the observations of its principal characters themselves, these travelling companions and occasional brothers-in-arms.

If this chronicle of the adventure of modern dance in France, which serves also as my personal testimony, has succeeded in redeeming certain great figures or noble enterprises from oblivion, and in thus paying them the homage they deserve, my aim will have been achieved.

It seemed to me useful to precede each part of this work, which corresponds to a decade, by a chronological survey* of events in order to establish certain landmarks. In view of the relative ebb and flow of things, it is sometimes surprising to note their contemporaneity, and, as a result, certain influences and convergences between them are illuminated all the more clearly.

It is evident, moreover, that dance did not develop in a vacuum. It submits to, benefits from and is transformed by the uncertainties of social, political, economic and cultural life. A chronological list of some of these events, on a world as well as a national scale, may help to situate this evolving dance form within its precise context.

---

* These chronological surveys have been drawn up with the help of **THIERRY LHOTE**.

PART I

1920–1930

The Ground-Breaking Years

CHRONOLOGY

1919–1925: FAILED REVOLUTIONS AND PAINFUL RECONSTRUCTION

Dates	Events in France	Events abroad	Contemporary culture in France
1919	Treaty of Versailles.	Establishment of the Comintern. Elimination of the German Spartacists.	*La Valse* by Ravel.
1920	Formation of French Communist Party.		Discovery of jazz and tango in Paris. Creation of the cabaret *Le Boeuf sur le toit*. Formation of "Les Six" group of composers.
1921		America fails to recognize the League of Nations.	Charles Dullin founds the Théâtre de l'Atelier. *The kid* by Charlie Chaplin. In Vienna, Schoenberg composes his first serial music.
1922		Stalin becomes General Secretary of the Communist Party of the Soviet Union. Mussolini becomes leader of the Italian government.	Diaghilev's Ballets Russes in Paris. James Joyce publishes *Ulysses*. Louis Armstrong makes his début.
1923	Franco-Belgian occupation of the Ruhr.	Economic crisis in Germany: 1919: 1$=8DM 1923: 1$=40,000 million DM. Primo de Rivera assumes Spanish dictatorship.	Louis Jouvet scores a success with *Dr. Knock*. In Paris the Ballets Suédois stage *La Création du monde* by Darius Milhaud.

Dates	Events in France	Events abroad	Contemporary culture
1923		Failed Putsch by Hitler.	
1924	Cartel des Gauches wins victory.	Death of Lenin. Assassination of the Socialist deputy Matteotti.	Surrealist manifesto by André Breton. Dance in Paris: Loïe Fuller, the Ballets Russes and Suédois, the Sakharoffs.

1925–1929: FRAGILE PROSPERITY RESTORED

Dates	Events in France	Events abroad	Contemporary culture
1925	Germany recognizes the inviolability of its frontiers to the west: Locarno Pact.		Success of Dufy and Poiret. Exhibition of Art Déco. Josephine Baker scores a hit in *La Revue nègre*.
1926	Poincaré recalled to power to rescue the franc. The Holy See condemns Action Française.	Pilsudski in power in Poland.	
1927	Creation of the Croix-de-Feu.		Advent of talking pictures. Disney creates Mickey Mouse. Isadora Duncan's final performance at the Mogador theatre.
1928	Loucheur's Law on cheap council housing.	Kellogg-Briand Pact of non-aggression.	Louis Jouvet stages *Siegfried* by Giraudoux and *Topaze* by Pagnol. Ravel composes *Boléro*.

Dates	Events in France	Events abroad	Contemporary culture
1929		Publication of Young Plan for re-scheduling German reparation payments. Black Thursday: 24 October, Wall Street Crash. Lateran Treaties: the Holy See negotiates the question of the Roman Catholic Church with Mussolini.	

1920–1930, designated by history and the sidelights on history as the Roaring Twenties, these years are doubtless thus called as a reaction to the long years of the Great War and the train of suffering borne by so many people, the destruction and countless deaths it brought with it. As though, like a strange echo of that horror and absurdity, there took place a sometimes nonsensical permanent fête: certain ties broke adrift, whilst other values found themselves overturned, as is always the case after a catastrophe of this nature. But the effect of this phenomenon is far from negative, for it serves to encourage creativity, audacity and a spirit of enterprise. After a period of convalescence, the early years of this decade saw, in France at least, an economic and cultural leap forward, together with an enormous change in moral habits. French industry experienced considerable growth, particularly in the fields of electricity and car manufacture (this was the age of the supremacy of Citroën). France profited from foreign investments, and her celebrated reputation as a country of the arts and high living attracted many foreigners, especially artists and intellectuals, to settle there. It was in this international melting-pot that the Paris School developed, including such artists as Picasso, Modigliani, Braque, Léger, Chagall, Delaunay, Cendrars and Carco, already resident and active during the war.

In *Le Roman vrai de la IIIème République* André Fraigneau writes of the Roaring Twenties:

> 'These were the years of the negro, the age of jazz, the shift dress, the cropped nape, a tractable form of cubism, sexual daring, gratuitous actions and senseless suicides. The golden calf was still alive, but nobody spoke of it. It was an ox that towered over the roofs of Paris now'.[1]

Memories of Fitzgerald. Extravagance was indeed in fashion, the modish sumptuousness of Paul Poiret, kitsch-culture, and the pursuit of ever more iconoclastic activities, such as surrealism and dada; there was, moreover, a ferment, an extraordinary stirring of ideas, within a sometimes unnatural sense of euphoria that did not continue long after the crisis of 1929. The turn of the next decade constituted a turn for the worse, for it must not be forgotten that the rise of fascism was already under way and that economic problems and political insecurity flowered over all the European chess-board.

---

[1] André Fraigneau, *Le Roman vrai da la IIIème République* (Livre de Poche, Gilbert Guilleminault collection) ("Le Boeuf sur le toit" – a famous cabaret.)

Dance in the Roaring Twenties

In the 1920s, when this chronicle begins, what was the state of dance in France, and in Paris in particular?

I propose to make only fleeting reference to the Paris Opéra and the 'great' dancers and 'classical' teachers, but the presence and/or work of some of these were so important that they featured prominently in the scenario and must, therefore, be emphasized:

- The mythical Anna Pavlova, of whom Jean Louis Vaudoyer claimed: *'Pavlova is to dance what Racine is to poetry, Poussin to painting, and Gluck to music'*,[2] remained omnipresent, and for a long time after her death in 1931 continued to represent, for many people the world over, the very essence and incorporeality of dance.
- Within the Paris Opéra, where in spite of a repertoire of an obvious academicism and poverty, the excellence of the technical teaching had been maintained. Such eminent figures as Carlotta Zambelli, then at the height of her career, Albert Aveline, ballet-master and teacher Léo Staats, Gustave Ricaux, Ivan Clustine and others, could be found under the direction of Jacques Rouché. It was, moreover, in 1929 that Rouché called upon the young Serge Lifar to replace the ailing George Balanchine, who was to have provided the choreography for Beethoven's *Die Geschöpfe von Prometheus*. As a result, Lifar was engaged as choreographer, principal dancer and ballet-master on a permanent basis.
- After Monte Carlo, Paris had been the favourite home-base of Diaghilev's Ballets Russes. The years in which they made their greatest impact and experienced their greatest glory occurred before the period with which this chronicle is concerned, however. Their world-shattering début was in 1909 (the Fokine years); 1912 began the Nijinsky years; 1917, the Massine years. By the beginning of the 1920s, the Ballets Russes had lost a little of its novelty and appeared somewhat exhausted. Nevertheless, they went on to produce *Sleeping Beauty* (Tchaikovsky) in 1921, *Les Noces, Renard*, (Stravinsky) *Les Biches*, (Poulenc) and other ballets by Bronislava Nijinska, and, with the arrival of Balanchine, most notably *The Prodigal Son* (Prokofiev) and *Apollon Musagète* (Stravinsky), which established a link between Diaghilev and his heirs.

---

[2] Jean-Louis Vaudoyer, *Pavlova.*

It is well known that on the death of Diaghilev in 1929, the company broke up and was later reconstituted as the Ballets Russes de Monte Carlo, under the direction of Colonel Wassili de Basil and René Blum.

> – The great Russian dancers who came either directly from Russia, as in the case of Olga Preobrajenska, or by way of Diaghilev as Lubov Egorova and Mathilde Kchessinska, opened their respective schools in Paris, and dancers flocked from all over the world to work with them.
> – Ida Rubinstein, who had danced with the Ballets Russes since 1909 before settling in Paris, played a role similar to that of Diaghilev as patron, organizer and occasionally star of dance productions almost until the outbreak of the Second World War. She could call upon the collaboration of choreographers such as Fokine, Nijinska, Massine and Jooss, and of musicians such as Ravel, Honegger, Stravinsky and Sauguet ...

The Influence of the Ballets Russes (and Waslaw Nijinsky)

To what extent did the Ballets Russes, in its first or second incarnation, influence the development of the new dance that was beginning to emerge? To a certain extent, the opposite was true: both in his writings and in his works (*Daphnis and Chloé*, for example), Fokine explicitly acknowledged the influence of Isadora Duncan, who opened new horizons for him and enabled him to make a more relevant adaptation of classical vocabulary.

The Ballets Russes, like the Ballets Suédois ten years later, was a melting-pot and point of convergence from which a new musical, graphic, theatrical and choreographic aesthetic exploded in the face of the public.

But was the actual choreographic vocabulary of dance cast into doubt? It seems unlikely, except, of course, in the case of Waslaw Nijinsky who undoubtedly could be considered as the 'father' of modern dance. This genius, in his so few choreographies, broke completely new ground, *'working from the inside'*, as the moderns would have said, without reference to the prevalent classical tradition. At the time, in spite of the scandals raised by *Faun* and *Le Sacre du printemps*, this revolution and all its implications were not fully recognized as such, especially within the classical context to which Nijinsky perforce belonged.

With regard to the Ballets Russes, there occurred a particular and easily recognizable phenomenon: Diaghilev's nomadic troop formed an organized company, an institution, that was itself descended from another institution, that bastion of classical dance, the Imperial Ballet of

St Petersburg. It held high the torch of choreographic tradition, whilst flirting with the avant-garde (in music and the graphic arts). But the weight of tradition and of the institution seems to have curbed this process of questioning of the very language of dance. In spite of superficial distortions and a few new contributions, the vocabulary, technique and, to a certain extent, the choreographic and creative procedures remained firmly rooted in the impregnable foundations of academic dance.

This fact may explain why the Ballets Russes, whilst representing the most 'modern', even shocking, face of dance at the time, was not really so modern in relation to the material of dance itself.

Modern Dance is First and Foremost 'Individual'

In its first teetering steps, modern dance ('expressionist' dance) appears to have been strictly the concern of the individual. This seems logical to the extent that the search for (and discovery of) a new vision and language may only be a matter of the greatest *intimacy*, and therefore personal and individual.

Vision and language must first of all be tested, incarnated and confirmed by the creator, and only later will they be amplified to the scale and scope of a dialogue or group piece. The ability to rally the cohesion of the group and, from this, form a dance company, depends as much on economic factors as on the strength of the creator's conviction. This was so in the case of Ruth St-Denis and Ted Shawn who founded Denishawn, and of Mary Wigman and her company also, to mention only two examples. In both cases, these companies were a direct offshoot of their director–choreographer, and formed, in a way, their own personal tool. At that time rather more than today, this type of company remained a strictly private concern, and could afford to take risks in the most extreme cases since only the financial interests (and opinions) of the director, and not those of a body politic, were involved.

Did any antinomy exist, therefore, between institutions and individual innovators, who were, by nature, iconoclastic? The innovators and early pioneers of modern dance were fiercely individual and generally self-financed (as in the case of later ones also, for this situation persisted for some time), and they existed largely on the fringes of the dance world.

Cursed artists? Not so. Simply hard-working people, firm in their beliefs, concerned in maintaining their physical prowess and securing a space in which they could devote themselves to their research. This situation explains in part why there were practically no groups or companies in the sense in which we understand these terms today in

France, during those inter-war years in which modern dance was seeking to define itself.

One can hardly speak of *French modern dance* in this period, but of *modern dance in France*, for the most important and influential personalities were foreigners.

Isadora, the Symbol

In Paris as elsewhere, the pole-star and leading light of new dance was undoubtedly Isadora Duncan. This was especially true in Paris where she remained most willingly for the longest period in her itinerant life, and was both understood and acclaimed. The 1920s saw her in the twilight of her adventurous, painful and exalted life. She made numerous journeys between Paris and Moscow in order to fulfil her dancing and teaching commitments, and in 1922 she married the poet Sergei Essenin, who committed suicide in 1925. The almost mythical death of Isadora herself came unexpectedly in 1927, a few months after her performance at the Mogador theatre.

Isadora's name, like that of Pavlova, had already become synonymous with and a symbol of dance for a large part of the general public. It would be superfluous to recall here the extent to which she inspired poets and plastic artists, and shook the very foundations of the dance establishment. There was a 'before' and an 'after' Isadora.

One of her most ardent French admirers, the writer and critic Fernand Divoire, wrote in *Découvertes sur la danse*[3] in 1924:

> 'And so, she continues along the route, always at the forefront, each time starting anew, her whole being at stake. The dance of Isadora follows her life'.
>
> 'For almost twenty years we witnessed the phenomenon of this woman who, in the face of all custom and fallacy, danced alone, her only décor a blue drapery; a saint to art, devoted solely to ''making the music heard'', and before her the public clapped their hands, went into raptures, and, in tears (yes, indeed), cried out her name: Isadora'.
>
> '... We are in the years 1920, 1921 and 1922. With each month that passed, Isadora Duncan appeared, to those who returned each time to see her, more supple and diverse, richer in easy, flowing fluidity, more unexpected and new, renewed ...'
>
> 'Now we see her resuming this course on which fate has forbidden her ever from settling in one place. She will leave us with the imperishable memory of the greatest genius of our time, of an artist, she who claimed that evening at the Trocadéro: ''I am not a dancer and I do not know how to dance. Life itself must be a dance ... I know only one dance, and that is the movement of the hands to

---

[3] Fernand Divoire, *Découvertes sur la danse* (Grès, Paris, 1924), p. 80.

the solar plexus and the opening and lifting of the arms, as if propelled by some inner force"'.

It is well known that Isadora had many imitators; some pale, or pathetic copies of this ardent, inspired original: "Disciples" who adhered in large part to the outer formal or expressive aspect of Isadora's style: Greek tunics, bare feet, loose hair, 'natural' movements, classical music and expressive mimicry.

It remained to penetrate to the very foundations of her dance and, without codifying or mummifying it, to make its principles susceptible to analysis, adaptation and development, and thus to transmission. This was achieved later by other means; Isadora herself simply followed her instinct and would have neither wished nor have known how to apply to her own genius the necessary analytical procedure to go beyond her fundamental discovery: the emanation of dance from inner movement, the expression of the soul through the body. And yet, she expressed such beautiful sentiments in her writings:

> *'true dance must be the transmission of the earth's energy through the medium of the human body ... man cannot invent, he can only discover. The Spirit of Dance enters into the harmoniously developed body, carried to its highest degree of energy'.*[4]

In the Wake of Isadora

Isadora claimed of her pupils in the programme of a gala at the Trocadéro written in 1914: ' ... *I believe that, in time, some of these girls will succeed in creating their own dances'*. Did Isadora mean (as we may suppose), that she wished to see her heiresses achieve a certain degree of autonomy, having been trained according to certain principles, rather than simply imitating the dances of their teacher?

As early as 1924, the critic Fernand Divoire posed the following problem:

> *'Anna, Lisa, Margot ... these girls were faced with many dangers. Had they not brought any personality or individuality to the dances they were taught, they would have been accused of being pale imitations, souless copies of Isadora's gestures. But had they contributed new elements, this would have been a worse danger, for Isadorism is not only a form of dance, it is a higher aesthetic scheme that would be tainted by the slightest hint of any inferior ideas; it is a simple, human, grandiose means of expressing the sentiments of the soul with no place for trivial anecdotes, pantomime, or veils in the manner of Loie Fuller, props, acrobatics or human tableaux. The girls are pure Isadorians, but each one retains*

---

[4] Isadora Duncan, quoted from the programme of her performance at the Trocadéro (Paris, 26 June 1914).

Plate 1 Isadora Duncan and her pupils in 1909. © Viollet.

her own personality. (...) All the boundless energy of youth is unleashed through them, but are they yet mature enough to perform the profound and tragic, almost motionless dances with which Isadora overwhelmed us?'[5]

In this passage, Divoire encapsulates both the charms and the boundaries of Isadora's style. I will retain his nomenclature for what he considers dance not to be: anecdote, acrobatics, human tableau, etc. Nevertheless, there appear amongst this list certain elements that served to nourish both new dance and, later, the very foundations of contemporary dance too.

The Body Rehabilitated

The most important influence on 'free' dance, and one that was widespread throughout the entire Western world, was without doubt a certain rehabilitation of the human body: a more wholesome education brought about through the practice of sport and gymnastics, the observance of hygiene, and plenty of fresh air. At the end of the nineteenth century there appeared, somewhat timidly at first, a huge overturning of thought and moral habits (symbolized by the abandonment of the corset) that swept through society's sudden leaps and bounds at the end of the 1914–18 war.

This phenomenon is perhaps so obvious that one might easily pass over it without further comment; but it seems to me particularly useful to refer to it once more since these increasingly widespread bodily practices influenced and sustained the course of action of anyone wishing to dance (either at an amateur or professional level) and modified the judgement of the spectator.

Underlying almost all forms of new dance, however, were the cult of Nature, together with its corollary, the condemnation of mechanized, urban life, the pursuit of harmony and a kind of primitive simplicity that may be misunderstood as a return to Antiquity. All this was expressed with a greater or lesser degree of emphasis, sentimentality or mysticism according to the temperament of the dancer.

I propose a hypothesis that reconciles two phenomena:

- firstly, the appearance in Germany after the 1914–18 war of those 'ecological', gymnastic, naturistic movements;
- secondly, the creation in France and the impact for several years after the 1939–45 war, of various 'popular culture' initiatives and organizations that shared a similarly explicit or implicit therapeutic

---

[5] Fernand Divoire, *Découvertes sur la danse* (Grès, Paris, 1924), p. 80.

goal: the moral and physical health of a community ravaged by war and defeat.

It is certainly no coincidence that the ideologies and practices of these diverse movements arose at similar moments of world or national crisis, and that, through them, man was valorized and nature was seen as a fundamental resource: man owed it to himself to make amends for the havoc wrought by the barbarity of war. From the ossuary sprang life, and the presence of a newly animated body made itself felt.

Gymnastic schools that were related either to sport or a kind of therapy tending occasionally towards spiritualism thus flourished throughout Europe. It was in Germany and Central Europe in particular that the majority of these types of establishments and initiatives arose.

Amongst these schools: Rudolf Steiner and Eurhythmics (in Switzerland), Gurdjieff and his Institute for the Harmonic Development of Man (which was located in Barbizon for a time), and Doctors Mensendieck and Bode and their gymnastic systems (in Germany). It should be noted that the Mensendieck system was practised in a large number of countries, including the United States.

In France there existed a particularly widespread practice of Swedish gymnastics that was rather militaristic in style (the Joinville school), and, in opposition to this, Georges Hébert's method of 'natural' gymnastics, known as Hébertism.

In this context, it is necessary perhaps to mention the work of earlier practitioners that proves relevant to our purpose, such as that of Georges Démeny who, at the end of the last century, preached a form of physical education that took the whole individual into account, and in which *'thought and action may only be productive as a result of their intimate interpenetration'*. His system of gymnastics extolled *'flowing, complete, rounded'* movements.

Harmonic Gymnastics

It was in this context that an entirely autochtonous movement developed in France, known variously as 'harmonic gymnastics' or 'rhythmics' (in obvious debt to Dalcroze), the principal representative of which was Irène Popard.

Irène Popard established her method and her school as early as 1916. For two generations of women the Popard method was synonymous with health and grace, a physical education from which the brutality and competitiveness of sport were excluded, a proper, well mannered artistic activity that transcended the dubious moral connotations that the image of the dance world continued to convey. Irène Popard maintained: *'harmonic gymnastics is not a method of dance, its sole aim is the promotion of a healthy mind in a healthy body'*. And yet, this widely practised form of gymnastics (which was even taught in high schools until the war), indeed passed for dance in the eyes of the public at large.

In 1935 Fernand Divoire claimed with a certain degree of relevance concerning a performance by the 'aesthetic gymnast' Odette Courtiade, that:

> *'It is clear that her method is formed outside the domains of classical dance and eurhythmics, in a sort of territory that borders equally on classicism, eurhythmics, Isadorism, and even Raymonduncanism, and shares with these methods a sort of common or average technique. Similar gestures, steps and preoccupations may be recognized between the various schools of harmonic, eurhythmic and aesthetic gymnastics. Each one demonstrates different degrees of vigour and delicacy, but they nevertheless remain cousins. The cousins on Marie Kummer's side are more adept in their use of the spinal column and demonstrate a sense of forceful precision; those on Irène Popard's side are often distinguished by their tremendous natural strength; whilst the cousins of Madame Odette Courtiade reveal a particular suppleness of the hands and a pleasing elegance ... It must be stated that this teaching is in no way harmful to girls'.*[6]

The Popard school, in the widest sense of this term (doctrine and method), was more than an individual realization, however; it formed part, as one may surmise, of an entire socio-cultural current, conveying an image of the body and woman at a given time.

We must not encroach any further upon the practices and influences at work, but turn rather to the fathers of modern dance, of whom the most obvious were Dalcroze and Laban. And it is almost with a feeling of relief that we may finally refer to male dancers, choreographers and teachers ...

It is well known that, even today, vestiges of the prejudice that considers dance to be the sole province of women still prevail. The female presence underlies the entire period covered by this chronicle, particularly the 1920s and 30s. Certain schools, and not the least among them, began to seem like gynaeceums. Oh, how Isadora's overwhelming femininity influenced these new generations of dancers! Both written and spoken language assume the *female* dancer, and in French one refers to 'pupils' (élèves) in the feminine as a matter of course. In English, on the other hand, the neutral noun 'dancer' implies nothing regarding the sex of the individual in question.

---

[6] Fernand Divoire, *Pour la danse* (Saxe, Paris, 1935), p. 101.

Émile Jaques-Dalcroze

Émile Jaques-Dalcroze was, in a certain way, and in the eyes of the general public at least, part of this movement of harmonic gymnastics. It must be recalled, however, that he was neither a gymnast, a dancer nor a choreographer, but a musician and teacher. He preached a system of education through rhythm:

> 'Rhythm establishes the circulation between our inner forces and those that assail them from the outside. The experimental (that is physical) study of rhythm should form part of every well constituted artistic education ...'[7]

Indeed, his philosophy extends beyond this to encompass the *complete* education of *every* human being.

The following passage is especially applicable to the dancer:

> 'The auditory, rhythmic and emotive properties necessary to every musician are a good ear, nervous sensitivity, a feeling for rhythm (that is, a keen sense of the relationships that exist between movement in time and space), and finally the ability to spontaneously externalize motor sensations and transform these into feelings and emotions'.[8]

Dalcroze thus proposed a systematic and extremely far-reaching study of all the elements of musical language (rhythm, melody, harmonic structure) that must pass through the mediation of the body and be expressed in physical feelings and movements, until a kind of materialization of the musical object in all its complexity was embodied in a choric choreography, for example. That is, in the process of learning music, priority was given to the physical aspect. Some people objected without doubt to the excessive systematization of Dalcroze's method, but it was perhaps necessary to tolerate this: a codification aiming in the first instance to circumvent all problems.

Dalcroze's system was appropriated by numerous dancers of his time. Even though one may observe a recuperation of the codes, which may represent an easy solution, Dalcroze's system, or rather, his philosophy, brought to dance certain analytical elements that had never been applied to it before. These elements included everything that was appropriate to the domains time and energy, elements that were indeed peculiar to music but which existed equally as factors, phenomena and

---

[7] Émile Jaques-Dalcroze, *La musique et nous* (Slatkine, Geneva, 1981), p. 235.

[8] *Ibid.*, p. 227.

qualities in the language of dance: pulsations, impetuses, accents, tension and relaxation, dissociations, periodicity, structure … in short, rhythm!

Dalcroze's work has influenced the entire subsequent history of dance in the twentieth century either directly or indirectly. It was recognized from the start, and as early as 1910 he began to establish his Institutes, first in Dresden, then in Hellerau, London, Geneva and several other European countries, and finally, in the United States through the intervention of Wigman and Hanya Holm.

Today his work lives on in the hands of certain individuals and institutions, based on the original principles and absolute validity of the remarks and aphorisms that may be found expressed to best advantage in the writings of this great thinker. His dream of a universal education that rests on man's earliest global experiences and aims to develop his sensory and analytical abilities together with physical and intellectual mastery, and in which all skill is at the service of inner equilibrium, may still be shared today.

It would perhaps be timely to reconsider the ways in which the relationships between music and dance evolved during these first decades in the development of new dance.

Not satisfied with using music conceived specifically for dance, which often seemed, quite justifiably, to be rather frivolous or like a kind of *passe-partout* to our intrepid pioneers, they followed Isadora's example in looking to 'great music' which they appropriated for themselves with new fervour. They drew on this emotional stimulus as a source of inspiration, aligning the structures of their dances with the already approved, indisputable (and indeed complex) structures of the music. Consciously or otherwise, they were thus guaranteed a form of quality assurance, since the quality of the music was already widely recognized.

All this proceeded from excellent intentions and aimed to provide a fusion of musical forms and language with the forms and language of dance. This dependence had an unfortunate and sterilizing effect, however, when it completely prevented the specific and autonomous development of movement in its own right. How many famous dancers in these heroic yet timorous times maintained that dance was inconceivable without music as a means of evoking an image or emotion, or as a formal, structural and temporal framework! A choreographic *language* with its own semiology, syntax and thematics, its own rhythmicized gestures with their own *inner* phrasing and intrinsic, autonomous structure seemed to them neither possible nor even desirable.

Numerous opinions and writings on this subject may be quoted. I have chosen one that is particularly revealing: Jérôme Bouxvilliers' 1949 preface to Janine Solane's *Vers une danse plus humaine*.

> *'If there is no guiding music, the expressive attitude intended by the dancer in imagining his poem either becomes fixed like a statue or evolves in his imagination according to a rhythm that may be extremely variable: it will hardly ever be practicable, for the real rhythm may only be determined by the place of his attitude within the context of the complete work.*
>
> *Because there is no fixed organic link between a body movement and a duration, it is impossible to proceed in both performance time (the sum of the durations of the expressive postures that are indeterminable) and the evolution of a preconceived scenario. It is only by choosing a piece of music appropriate to the general aspect of the proposed drama or poem in terms of its structure, movement and development, that the dancer may find the necessary "directional plan".*
>
> *Even before the dance exists, the music necessarily intervenes from the very first stages of composition. If the dance consists of two or more performers, their synchronism depends on a common beat which is external to each one of them. Music is to dancers what the conductor is to an orchestra'.*[9]

At this same time, certain pioneers, beginning with Mary Wigman and her descendants, followed the path towards independence in a series of successive stages: after a period of experimentation, there came a complete rupture, dance in silence, which served to reveal its inner song, and its own rhythmic and dramatic architecture. Next came a stage in which dance was performed to a minimal accompaniment that was entirely functional in its use of discreet instruments, such as flutes and percussion, for example, that are most closely suited to independent choreographic writing.

The time has long since passed, however, when there was a real sense of collaboration on equal terms between composer and choreographer, and the musical score could claim as much right to its existence as the choreography; the pendulum has swung once again, and today dance has assumed such a degree of independence that many young choreographers have returned to using music simply as an accompaniment, proceeding simultaneously with dance as a sonorous background, or as a means of evoking a dramatic atmosphere, or even as a factor in an aleatoric process. In each case, the morphology and very identity of these musics are taken into account to a greater or lesser degree. There is, however, still another type of relationship at work.

Returning to the period of the 1920s in which new dance was beginning to develop, it is interesting to quote Dalcroze's view expressed in 1918 on the relationship between music and dance:

> *'It remains for us to indicate under what conditions there might be created – as a contrast to absolute music – a special music adapted to gesture, and which, while distinct from the music of pantomime, would, like it, be deprived of all technical development, constructed on simple and regular lines, and would*

---

[9] Janine Solane, *Pour une danse plus humaine* (Jacques Vautrain, Paris, 1950), p. 23.

leave – at considerable sacrifice – a large scope for the collaboration of human movements.

A difficult and complex task, no doubt, but one that will certainly be accomplished, once the dancer has become a musician, and deserves that the composer may give up effects of merely decorative music, and devote his gifts along the lines of a more human and vital art. A new style will have to be created, the product of the collaboration of two equally expressive arts, with the potential participation of a whole public trained to co-operate with the artist, and to assume a responsible part in his performances'.[10]

Rudolf von Laban

Another of these progenitors of modern dance whose influence was felt in Europe in the 1920s was Rudolf von Laban. The depth of his research, the manifestations of which perhaps appear less immediately attractive than those of Isadora or Dalcroze, makes his particular contribution more difficult to determine; nevertheless, it proved without doubt to be more fruitful and lasting, for, more than half a century later, it continues to form the basis of much contemporary research and practice.

Artist, researcher, theorist, philosopher and practitioner, Laban pursued a training in graphic and theatre arts before deciding to devote himself to dance. His conception of dance was as a transposition of human behaviour, as an art in itself to which he supplied the missing link in its possibilities for development in the form of a detailed and exhaustive analysis of all the materials peculiar to it. Before Laban, would it have been possible to speak of a semantic, semiotic or syntactical language peculiar to dance? Was he not one of the first to make use of the trinity of time, space and energy, that the dancers of today evoke as a matter of course, an irrevocable reference?

It followed that such a penetrating analysis of movement should lead to the possibility of notation. His system, known as *Kinetography Laban*, Labanotation, which he had used as early as 1926, is now in use the world over, and in a way, it brought dance out of its quasi-illiterate state. A parallel may be drawn with that point in the development of Western music when musical thought began to be notated. Of course, not all dancers are able to read a movement score; indeed, they are not all aware that notation exists at all, and that there are a number of different systems. In spite of this, the practice of dance in general has nevertheless undergone the influence of a clearer and more refined thought process.

---

[10] Émile Jaques-Dalcroze, *Le Rythme, la musique et l'éducation* (Foetisch, Lausanne, 1965), p. 161. Translated in Émile Jaques-Dalcroze, *Rhythm, Music and Education*, trans. Harold F. Rubinstein (Chatto and Windus, London, 1921), p. 234.

Let us recall some of the concepts elaborated by Laban:

— the *Kinesphere*, the space occupied by the body and movements of
   each individual;
— *Choreutics*, the organization of the space within the Kinesphere:
   positions, forms, directions, trajectories, levels, etc. It forms a
   logical relationship with the motor phenomena which give rise to
   those skilful shapes and flights that he calls *scales*, designated
   according to the particular volume of the kinesphere (cube,
   dodecahedron, icosahedron, etc.);
— *Eukinetics*, the actual quality of the movement (timbre, colour),
   with all that this may imply in terms of emotional references over
   and above the quantifiable intrinsic factors of time – energy –
   space;
— and above all, a personal philosophy that encompasses the social
   aspect as much as the metaphysical, and at the heart of which lies
   rhythm.

Laban's journey is well known. From his native Hungary he travelled to
Paris, from Ascona to Berlin, and from Essen to Manchester. His earliest
followers are equally well known: Mary Wigman, Kurt Jooss, Sigurd
Leeder, Dussia Bereska, Suzanne Perrottet, Lisa Ullmann and many others,
as is his later work in the analysis of movement in industrial situations (the
Laban/Lawrence Industrial Rhythm), and, more closely related to dance,
the analysis of effort and shape, the research and pedagogy of which forms
a part of the curriculum at the Laban Centre for Movement and Dance in
London and the core of the teaching at the Laban/Bartenieff Institute of
Movement Studies in New York, to name but two of these great institutions that are flourishing more strongly today than ever before.

      During the 1920s, the influence of his work spread to France, but
it was not until the following decade that this influence, together with
that of Wigman, was to have a direct and lasting effect through the work
of his pupils who settled in Paris.

Other Influences

The influence of Loie Fuller was by no means negligible. She regarded
scenography as an integral part of dance. Her discoveries rested on the
play of light on moving fabric, and she appropriately named her company 'Les Féeries Fantastiques de Loïe Fuller'.

      Her stage pieces epitomized the stylistic and aesthetic features of
Art Nouveau: fluidity, drapery, floral shapes and animation, that occur
similarly in the glassware of Gallé, for example. Admittedly a producer

more than a dancer, Loie nevertheless appeared on stage until 1927, and her work was to have an important influence both on the theatre in general and the theatre of movement in particular.

She claimed:

> *'What is the body of the dancer if it is not an instrument through which the vibrations and sound waves of music that permit the expressions of every human emotion are emitted into space?'*

In reality, these sound waves and vibrations were embodied in manipulated veils, transfigured and metamorphosed by light. By means of this extension of the body, she shaped and animated space, evoking a dream-like world; the most astonishing aspect of all this is that it occurred as early as 1891.

Loie Fuller had her disciples too. How many kilometres of fabric must have been waved in front of projectors by her imitators? She cannot be considered an innovator with regard to the substance of movement, the body, or the vocabulary of dance, for, in her case, these were partly functional and were conceived in relation to the manipulation of the fabric. Nevertheless, she may perhaps be regarded as having opened up another part of the imagination.

Loie Fuller was classed as a music-hall rather than a concert or recital artist. The boundary between mere entertainment and serious art leaves us wondering, for sure. To move, amuse or impress the spectator? A question of the soul on the one hand, and sensuality on the other? This boundary was as ill defined then as it is today, but in a different way.

And yet, the importance of the role of dance in the music hall within the cultural scene is surprising, perhaps more so in Germany than in France, not only in terms of its live scenery (girls surrounding a star), but also of its entirely professional and serious treatment as an independent genre by the public, press and practitioners alike.

Contemporary documentation (photographs, articles) reveals the extent of the audacity of these dancers in their routines; they would appear to us kitsch today, but radical in gesture, costume (although in 1925 many danced nude) and aesthetic. It was as if the music hall at this time provided a framework for the kind of experimentation that was far more difficult to achieve in the concert hall. Of course, many concert dancers worked in the music hall for economic reasons, just as the pioneers of other periods worked in cabaret. But what could be seen as lying within the framework of the music hall in some way fell into the public domain.

A style of dancing that frequently occurred within the context of the music hall, known as 'fancy dancing', that is, dances of fantasy, or a whimsical way of dancing, must be noted here in passing. This was a

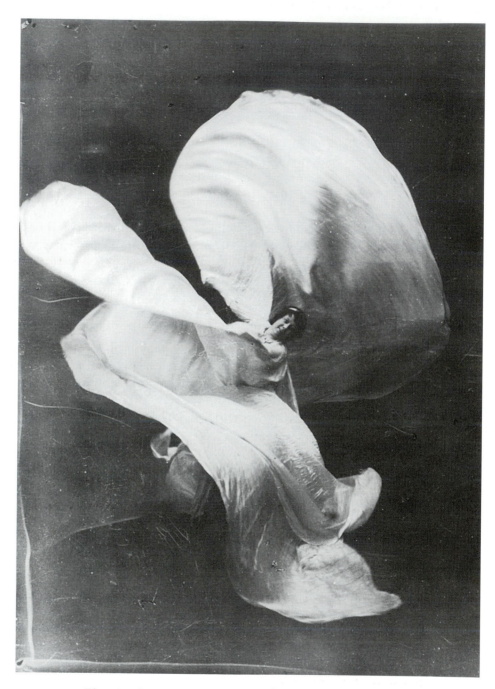

Plate 2   Loie Fuller. Photo: Jean Claude Marlaud. © Viollet.

graceful style, but one that could be humorous, employing props such as inflated balloons, acrobatic or erotic to; in other words, it was a hybrid mixture of everything. And it was taught in classes as a style in its own right.

The influence of the music hall could be seen, moreover, in the content and gestures of the concert dances performed by those occasionally naïve pioneers. How many puppets, golliwogs, 'minstrels', cakewalks, ragtimes and foxtrots appeared, either literally or transposed, in these programmes of old? They demonstrated clearly the influences of American folklore, jazz, Negro music and dances, and, quite simply, of fashionable ballroom dances.

Are we not witnessing the same phenomenon today in the appropriation of the popular music, gestures and dance practised in nightclubs, whether these be rock, funk, reggae, rap ... or styles such as punk, by young choreographers who certainly do not perceive themselves as lying within the framework of 'variety', but as belonging to the theatre proper, and who exploit a particular contemporary style derived from mass culture as the vocabulary and vehicle for a specific mode of discourse?

Thus occurred once more an interpenetration of genres, to be found at all periods, as when folk dance provided for the court dance in the sixteenth century, the ballroom waltz for the ballet one in the nineteenth ... This process took place again, logically, in the 1920s when dancers, in search of renewal and wishing to express their own age, sought nourishment from other sources.

In the words of Fernand Divoire quoted above, dance must not amount to *pantomime*, or what today might be known as 'mime'.

This pantomime that slipped into the repertoires of the early modern dancers descended from two traditions. The first was the *commedia dell'arte*, with its traditional stereotyped gestures and characters of Harlequin and Columbine, for example, and the second was the French tradition of Debureau, the creator of Pierrot.

However, it is equally probable that the commendable desire of these dancers to speak with their bodies, and to express genuine feelings and emotions, and touch by their very presence, led them to play in a somewhat raw manner. Expression was emphasized to such a degree of exaggeration that the danger of falling from the genre of dance into that of pantomime was obvious. This tendency was, however, received unfavourably by the critics of the time, who continued to uphold the incorporeality and refined character of classical dance.

This same type of exaggerated facial and bodily expression may be seen in the cinema of the period, where, as in mime, it proved necessary to mitigate the absence of the spoken word.

However, expressionist cinema succeeded in formulating a coherent style, an aesthetic in its own right, out of this exaggerated mode of expression, an achievement that did not occur in dance until a much later period, or in the hands of the very great, such as Wigman.

A further relationship between the emergent genres of cinema and modern dance that seems to me to be very important is the symbolic dimension of space. In classical dance, space was rarely considered as anything more than somewhere to move and best be seen. Its use may be decorative, as in the case of group dancing in which the displacement of the dancers may create geometrical patterns which have a pleasing visual effect; or it may be functional, as in the positioning of a series of turns on a diagonal or in a circle in order to create the longest trajectory. The concept of the dramatic or symbolic potentiality of space was rarely taken into account.

Isadora had without doubt already used space in a new way. She inhabited it, stretching herself out or curling herself up within it, and proved as sensitive to this dimension of movement as she was to all the others: rhythm, respiration, tension, etc. But these spatial (distance, orientation, direction) and spatio-temporal relationships, consciously organized according to their specific, intrinsic implications, and used for expressive and dramatic ends, were indeed found in both the style of dance that emerged in Germany with Laban, Wigman and others, and expressionist cinema of the same period. Such relationships included those between levels, shooting angles, and rhythms of sequences. *Space was capable of speaking out loud and clear.* All this was new.

The Plastic Arts

This brings us to a consideration of other influences at work on the evolution of new dance, and to those of the theoretical as much as the practical manifestations of the different movements in modern art (the plastic arts) in particular. Two opposing tendencies, expressionism and abstraction, coexisted and both, by means of a kind of osmosis, played a part in making dancers aware of the specificity of their art, a specificity that may be considered appropriately from two points of view:

- on the one hand, the objectivity of feeling and bodily expression, its absolute individuality, the *inner necessity* of a movement;
- and on the other, the careful and objective examination of the very material of movement as well as the formal and symbolic implications that proceed from it.

Many of the statements and assertions of the doctrines of painters in this period may be translated immediately in terms of movement and choreographic writing.

It is undeniable that the work and research carried out in the fields of architecture, the plastic arts and design at the Bauhaus, founded in Weimar in 1919 by the architect Walter Gropius and with which Paul Klee, Wassily Kandinsky and Oscar Schlemmer amongst others were associated, had a notorious influence on the theatrical arts and dance. In the words of its one-time director, Mies van der Rohe: *'The Bauhaus is an idea, and for this reason its influence has been so great'.*[11]

And with regard to Oscar Schlemmer's *Triadic Ballet*, produced at the Bauhaus in 1923, S. Gideon claimed:

> *'In order to be able to establish new creative principles, one had to set out from the beginning and try to extract the laws and secrets directly from the material itself. It is from and with these elements that artistic creation is born. Precision of line is sought even in dance. Of all the fields of activity practised at the Bauhaus, dance alone achieves perfect freedom'.*[12]

Kandinsky had already written so admirably in 1910:

> *'A simple movement, the simplest one imaginable, the goal of which is unknown, already acts alone, assuming a mysterious and solemn importance. It thus behaves like a pure sound. It is on this principle that the "new dance" that will develop the inner sense of movement integrally in Time and Space must and will be created. It will be the law of a necessary using of the inner sense of movement, the principal element of dance, that will decide upon its evolution and lead to the goal'.*[13]

Truly prophetic words that resulted from a mode of thought and an approach that were uncommon in the field of dance. A parallel might indeed be drawn with the work of Laban which facilitated such far-reaching development. It was a fundamental, essential approach that would lead, in the distant future, to abstraction and movement for movement's sake in post-modern dance, and even to minimalism.

At the other extreme (even if these two movements appear connected in some way), expressionism, which was promoted in Germany by the groups Die Brücke in Munich around 1916, Der Blaue Reiter in Dresden, and artists such as Emil Nolde, Edward Münch, Egon Schiele and Oscar Kokoschka, tended towards anguished subjectivity, eloquence and passion, expressed by means of schematic and systematic distortions

---

[11] S. Gideon, *Walter Gropius* (Neuenschwanden, Zurich, 1954), p. 17.

[12] *Ibid.*, p. 33.

[13] Wassily Kandinsky, *Du Spirituel dans l'art* (Denoël-Gauthier, Médiations, 1954, 1959).

of forms and colours, and a preoccupation with the social as much as the metaphysical aspect. Certain innovative dancers, notably Mary Wigman at the start of her career, were nurtured at this source, and exploited body language to the same end.

Dada and surrealism also influenced dance, albeit belatedly as will become apparent later.

Exoticism

Yet another influence on the European, French, and particularly the Parisian, dance scene that contributed either directly or indirectly to the development of modern dance was what might be termed exoticism, a phenomenon that was by no means peculiar to Europe. In America, too, many dancers inclined towards Eastern culture and dances, but with different motivations (Ruth St-Denis was one such dancer, to mention only the most obvious example).

The influence of foreign arts and cultures had long been felt, and was related, particularly at the turn of the century, to French presence in her colonies and protectorates in North Africa as well as in the Near and Far East.

Many dancers from foreign countries with deep-rooted cultures of their own, passed through Paris whilst on tour, occasionally leaving an ineffaceable mark. This was true in the case of the divine Argentina; 'la Argentinita', from Spain; Sakae Ashido from Japan; and the Javanese dancer Raden Mas Jodjana. Ethnic dance began to be known both through the experiences of certain dancers in the countries of origin of the various dances, and through visitors to French soil. The visit of the Cambodian Royal Ballet, first to the 1922 Colonial Exhibition in Marseilles, and then to the Paris Opéra, for whom the public developed real enthusiasm, may be noted in this context.

Midway between the music hall and exoticism lay yet another group of artists whose visits to France were so frequent, and who were so well loved by the Parisians, that they began to seem like permanent residents. 'La Chauve Souris' was a small and perfectly staged group of performers of Russian folk songs and dances, directed by Nikita Balieff, who offered a different type of folklore, performed with a concern for authenticity.

Some of these visitors to Paris simply passed through the city, whilst others settled there. But several European dancers adopted a foreign, and preferably distant culture. Thus, Spanish, Arabian and Japanese dances, evocations of bayadères and devadasis, subjective interpretations, studies in style of a more or less personal nature, seeking the authentic spirit and form in which these dances were conceived, frequently characterized the recital programmes and repertoires of 'free' dancers of the time.

In a sense, every available style was there for the taking in order to enlarge the palette or stock of the dancer/choreographer! And not only the imagination and creative powers but technique also could draw sustenance from these diverse styles. Thus prevailed a type of innocence with respect to the content and possible meanings of dance that contemporary sophistication would consider naïve, even kitsch, and this has without doubt survived until the 1960s. What would present-day ethnological purists think of these 'Eastern' dancers of yesteryear who performed in styles of both a real and imaginary exoticism (Berber, Egyptian, Hindu, Javanese, Chinese, Japanese) simultaneously and indifferently within the same programme? How could this possibly be authentic? And according to what criteria should such disparate dances be evaluated?

These dancers seemed to me to be aspiring towards an evocative rather than a documentary style, and worked not as ethnologists but as poets. This indeed left the way open for conjecture, and a confusion of styles and genres, but was it such a serious error at this point?

Many of these women sought to portray the sacred character of dance in these distant civilizations, and their fervour opened the minds of their audience, encouraging the public to see dance, and eventually to practise it, as something other than an entertainment or a form of gymnastics. It may be concluded that the development of new dance benefitted from the influence of these Eastern dances through the proposal of both a 'serious' approach and a wealth of material to be explored: unusual rhythms, hieratic balance and strength, fluidity, etc.

[Was it naïvety that led one to dream of foreign places and times gone by, and to identify oneself with characters, scenes and situations so alien to everyday life?

I wonder all the more about this choice of themes in dance since I belong to the generation that witnessed the last days of innocence. It seems to me that these choices resulted from the sheer joy of inner journeys and images of numerous past traditions that sustained, rather than stifled, the art, as certain commentators would have us believe.

At the beginning of my career, between 1945 and 1960, the majority of my companions and myself gave little thought to the political and psychoanalytical motivations and implications that our dance was able to convey. We existed, for the most part, above or alongside everyday life, however harsh the realities of this might be, pursuing our own idle fancies. I would indeed have been at a loss to respond to certain types of questions. I inhabited a universe of successive dreams, without hidden motives, conscience or ideological circumspection, concerned only to recreate with maximum clarity and accuracy a character, a scene, an atmosphere that had for a moment fascinated and attracted me.]

Venues for the New Dance

It is interesting to note the venues in Paris where new dance could be seen and free dancers could perform. There were few people besides Isadora Duncan, Jaques-Dalcroze, Loie Fuller, or others of the rich and famous who could afford to hire such large theatres as the Trocadéro, the Gaîté-Lyrique, the Théâtre des Champs-Elysées or the Mogador. On the commercial circuit, the following theatres provided venues for dance: the Comédie des Champs-Elysées (which was, for decades, one of the favourite theatres amongst soloists), the Ambassadeurs, the Michel, the Atelier, the Fémina, the Oeuvre and the Salle Gaveau. A further source was created by the 'clubs' (or associations), and these included the Club du Faubourg, the Interallié, the Université des Annales, the Théâtre Esotérique, the Cercle International des Arts, the Vieux-Colombier, directed by Jacques Copeau, in which the 'Samedis de la Danse' took place under the aegis of Suzanne Bing, the Salon d'Automne, an art gallery in which publicity for performances of dance was always on display, and the 'salons' of certain genuine private patrons, without mentioning the studios of particular individuals also.

An initiative created by Jacques Hébertot must be especially noted; in 1923 he established the 'Vendredis de la Danse' which took place at the Comédie des Champs-Elysées. It was there that the most outstanding, and particularly innovative dancers, from France and elsewhere, were received in the most favourable moral and material conditions of this well run theatre. They were provided with publicity and an audience, receiving no fee, but incurring no expense. (Jean Dorcy was to promote a similar venture after the war with Danse et Culture). The year 1923 alone saw performances by Jeanne Ronsay, Malkowski, Albertina Rasch, Djemil Anik and Jacqueline Chaumont, followed by la Argentina, the Sakharoffs, Harald Kreutzberg, Birgit Culberg, Ione and Brieux, Nyota Inyoka and Valeska Gert, for example. During the 1930s Jacques Hébertot transferred the 'Vendredis de la Danse' to the theatre on the boulevard des Batignolles which is named after him today.

A Similar Volapük of Movements?

Having provided a broad outline for the setting of this chronicle of free dance in France in the Roaring Twenties, it remains for us to consider the actors who took part in it. Although the text may have been clumsy, the actors were full of spirit and improvised as the need arose, exploiting every possibility to the full. We have seen that they came from numerous diverse backgrounds and were subjected to various different influences; animated by a tremendously proselyte passion, they aroused reactions of horrified rejection or sneering contempt as much as of ecstatic enthusiasm. There was nothing new in that. There were some great leading roles in this story, but a large supporting cast also, and, of course, mere walkers-on, some of whom have sunk into oblivion.

It seems to me very important, nevertheless, to place the key-point of this cultural revolution represented by new dance in context; for this reason, I propose to quote André Lévinson, the most formidable French detractor of new dance, who, in *La Danse aujourd'hui* (1929) devotes a whole chapter to 'Rhythmic Dance in the Concert Hall':

'The phenomenon of a single dancer occupying the stage alone for a whole performance is one of relatively recent origin. It was established by Isadora Duncan, creator of a new genre, and, indeed, of a new aesthetic. Her isolation was typical of all innovators. She danced alone because, at first, she was alone. Nevertheless, from the very beginning, she expressed a concern to establish a community, to educate the generation that surrounded her with her own enthusiasm, and to encapsulate this on stage. Whilst she was waiting for this to occur, the novelty of her conception which, fifteen or twenty years ago, coincided with the aspirations and illusions of a certain élite, combined with the strength and plasticity of her emotive personality, allowed her to hold the floor for one or more evenings. Until then, a protagonist of theatrical dance, a star of a school, would not have had the temerity to break away from her harmonic base, the ballet company, for an entire performance. The ballerina's solo, occurring at the climax of an act, was both prepared and led into, with the variation, usually in the form of a rondo, lasting some two minutes.

Duncan's example gave rise to a hybrid genre that fluctuated between spectacle and intimacy, between dance that was meant to be seen and arouse emotions in others, and dance that was a lyrical outpouring of the personality. Costumes and lighting added to the other elements of theatrical perspective in the way that intuition informs tradition.

Indeed, the irrational phenomenon of intuition evades any attempt at systematization and suppresses all criticism. It forces us into our unconscious, but how might we apply our scales of value to the incommensurable? A miracle cannot be reasoned, nor metaphysics disputed. Intuitive thrust shatters the logical relationships in dance, such as points of tension and relaxation, and stops and starts, and thus leaves the way open to chaos.

Duncan was a great force. She defied the spirit of the music, for some demon, some surfeit of exaltation, urged her on. Her lack of order appeared passionate and intense. Her vocabulary of movements may have been indigent, her syntax amorphous, but these were nevertheless vivified by a huge surge of emotion. The ambitions of countless dancers found confirmation in her example. The technical demands imposed on dancers in the past crumbled like a dam. This reassertion of freedom of expression meant that, whilst everyone could have their say, few *actually contributed anything new. Self-delusion raged. Vanity and feminine hysteria became incensed, and the public was overwhelmed by an alarming number of secrets revealed through dance. The most striking aspect of this outburst of individuality was, however, the extreme uniformity of production, the immediate and widespread adoption of the same choreographic stereotypes, the same gregarious spirit that governs every other manifestation of feminine intuition, and above all, fashion. The Greek philosopher, anxious to express the way in which phenomena are in a state of constant flux, claimed that man never enters the same river twice. But after attending fifty-five "Vendredis de la Danse" at the Comédie des Champs-Elysées, I am still left with the impression, a few exceptions apart, of always watching the same one; for nothing changes here; everything remains static.*

These intuitive dancers, imagining themselves to be drawing upon their own resources, relied in fact, with only minor variations in detail, upon the same volapük of movements, movements that derived from Duncan's basic Hellenism, as well as from certain sporting activities. All these dancers sought to establish more or less plausible relationships between the living complexity of music and the plastic corollary of it they claimed to offer. They attempted to do this most frequently by means of arm movements rather like those of an orchestra conductor. Some arrived from Bulgaria or Lithuania with the music of Chopin, Saint-Saëns and Schubert's Moments musicaux. Other, more enlightened ones regaled us with Debussy and Stravinsky. Tomorrow they will look to "Les Six", who will no longer be six; and then to the school of Arcueil, to Gounod and Chabrier. All of this was perfectly practicable, for they treated the spirit, the rhythm, the cadences and flow, the sentiment and style, of every musical work with the same degree of casualness, the same complete arbitrariness. They affirmed their "new spirit" with a philosophy of "anything goes", as long as it was based on modern music'.[14]

These remarkable paragraphs by Lévinson reveal clear evidence of rank prejudice and narrow-mindedness, but of soundly realistic insight also. By adapting and transposing the facts and context of Lévinson's claims to today's practices, we might indeed imagine that they would strike a few home truths.

These fiery dancers, these impassioned women, were ground breakers, working within the avant-garde of their own time, and we are greatly indebted to them. In their hands, not only did dance undergo a profound artistic transformation, but they also contributed in an entirely positive way to the development of new educational concepts and new ways of life, existence and thinking.

THE ACTORS

We turn now to the actors in our story, both leading and supporting roles, or, if we wish to pursue our initial metaphor, the first labourers in the fields. The selection was a difficult one to make, and access to information

---

[14] André Lévinson, *La danse aujourd'hui* (Duchartre et van Buggenhoudt, 1929), p. 463.

proved problematic in a number of cases. But the lines of descent are clear, and at this stage in our chronicle, classification is relatively easy. All of them taught, either out of economic necessity, or as a means of achieving recognition or spreading the word. Some prioritized their teaching; others saw it as merely secondary.

There were hardly any institutions that administered or even welcomed modern dance at this time, and there were practically no companies either.

The Ballets Suédois, although essentially classical, nevertheless demonstrated clearly that dance could proceed in other directions.

THE INSTITUTIONS

The Ballets Suédois 1920–1924

The Ballets Suédois have often been contrasted with the Ballets Russes, but in spite of their differences, it may be claimed that both companies, a decade apart, played a similar role in the panorama of twentieth century dance. Through the quality of their work, both contributed to the raising of ballet to the level of the other arts by instigating team work, a genuine collaboration with musicians and plastic artists of the first order.

The situation in 1920 was, nevertheless, entirely different to that in 1910, the year in which the sumptuous, exotic and occasionally disturbing marvels of the Ballets Russes hit Paris. The war had completely overturned the country, its inhabitants and their moral habits. Paris was a melting pot of new ideas and bold initiatives, and it was in Paris too that the Swedish patron and promoter, Rolf de Maré, chose to establish the home port of the classically trained company he created out of the Stockholm Opera. It was to another Swede, the young choreographer Jean Börlin, moreover, that he gave this company as an instrument with which to work. Maré and Börlin thus presided over the destinies of the Ballets Suédois during this brief four year period of intense activity, avant-garde experiments, triumphs, scandals and semi-failures.

These failures were indeed only partial, for the performances of the Ballets Suédois were, at one and the same time, both truly ahead of their time, beyond the comprehension of the majority of the public, including the critics. The company was incapable of dispensing completely with classical vocabulary and procedures because of their reliance on literary and visual, rather than strictly choreographic premises. The anomalies and gestural anachronisms that existed in Börlin's works only served to impair the coherence of the choreographic, musical and pictorial languages.

Influenced by Fokine, Jean Börlin certainly knew how to exploit the spirit of his age, and place his own aesthetic research in harmony with that of other adventurous creators. *'The Ballets Suédois represents intelligence and painting, rather than dance, music and sensitivity'*, remarked Fernand Divoire.[15]

A brief summary of their repertoire, choreographed entirely by Jean Börlin, indicates the exceptional character of these artistic events. It ranged from *Jeux*, music by Debussy, set by Pierre Bonnard (Nijinsky had choreographed this same score in 1913, with a set by Bakst), to *L'Homme et son désir*, libretto by Paul Claudel, music by Darius Milhaud, and the almost surreal *Les Mariés de la Tour Eiffel*, conceived by Jean Cocteau, in combination with the talents of composers of 'Les Six' and scene painters Jean Hugo and Irène Lagut. It included, moreover, *La Création du monde*, libretto by Blaise Cendrars, music again by Milhaud, set by Fernand Léger, Debussy's *La Boîte à joujoux*, and, as the parting shot in their brief existence, *Relâche*, which, not surprisingly, created a downright scandal in 1924. René Clair's film that served as the prologue and interlude to the ballet, together with experimental films by Fernand Léger, are available today and provide an impression of the extreme boldness of design and stage technique: visual flashes, disconnected scenes, Léger's constructivist sets, Satie's ironic music, and the whole conception orchestrated by Francis Picabia in order to strike a huge and unprecedented, grinding and absurd blow. After this adventure, the Ballets Suédois seem to have lost direction and, in fact, never resumed work. The company was disbanded and Börlin died prematurely in 1930.

It is interesting to quote Paul Demange's text of 1931 on the epopee of the Ballets Suédois:

> *'It would be no exaggeration to say that their four years of activity were four years of constant struggles. From the very first, the originality of their performances compelled attention. It was impossible not to express an interest in them. It was inevitable that everyone should come down on one side or the other, but they did so with bias, frenzy and passion. It hardly seems necessary to add that their detractors were more numerous by far and that the stubbornness of the latter testified eloquently to their complete failure to understand the scope and significance of this formidable movement created by Rolf de Maré and Jean Börlin.*
>
> *And yet, there had not been a more favourable time for the appearance of new aspirations. This was the post-war period in which everything that had existed in the past acknowledged its inability to survive. Creation was essential at all costs. But everywhere on this virgin soil that was thus laid bare to artists' aspirations, chaos reigned. There was no time for pruning or weeding; vigorous building had*

---

[15] Fernand Divoire, *Découvertes sur la danse* (Grès, Paris, 1924), p. 68.

to take place amidst the quagmires and the ruins. Such an enterprise attracted
pioneers of the most impetuous kind. Rolf de Maré and Jean Börlin were two of
these'.[16]

It is perhaps appropriate to add the remarks of Paul le Flem and
H. Malherbe to Demange's apposite comments which, although in reality
concern only the immediate post-war period, may be applied much more
widely than to the Ballets Suédois alone. Le Flem notes:

'Like the Ballets Russes, the Ballets Suédois stimulated the creative spirits of musi-
cians and elicited the composition of works that provoked bitter arguments and pas-
sionate diatribes. Like the Ballets Russes before them, they provided an opportunity
for a certain post-war musical tendency to develop and assert itself publicly',[17]

and in *Le Temps* of 10 June 1931, Malherbe commented:

'In the ardour of his youth, Jean Börlin appeared opposed to Serge de Diaghilev,
then at the height of his fame. The personal velleities of the Swedish dancer
revealed more flourish than real ability at work. Jean Börlin possessed qualities
of taste, curiosity and daring, but his artistic ambitions were vitiated by a rather
lax and indecisive attitude. In spite of his taking risks, he revived dramatic
spectacle in certain ways and brought it into line with changing morals'.

Let us return now to the beginnings of the Ballets Suédois in Paris: Rolf
de Maré sought a theatre that would welcome the company and provide
it with a base in which to work and perform. Without further ado, he
purchased the lease of the Théâtre des Champs-Elysées. Jacques Hébertot
was its first administrator. During the 1920s, following the dissolution of
the Ballets Suédois, Rolf de Maré founded the Opéra-music-hall there,
and brought to its stage a number of ballets and dancers as diverse as
Anna Pavlova, Vicente Escudero and Josephine Baker.

Then, having ceased to concern himself any longer with this
theatre, he elaborated the large-scale project that was to play a fundamental role in the development of dance, not only in France but throughout
Europe: the Archives Internationales de la Danse (A.I.D.).

THE DUNCAN LINE

The principal influence on the development of a new conception and
practice of dance in the first quarter of the twentieth century was undeni-
ably that of Isadora. Although exegeses and biographies of Isadora herself
exist in such abundance that it is superfluous to offer further discussion

---

[16] In *Revue des Archives Internationales da la Danse* (Du Trianon, Paris, 1932), p. 17.

[17] In *Comedia* (3 June 1961).

of her here, it nevertheless seems useful to outline the profile and itinerary of certain members of her (real and spiritual) family.

Her brother Raymond was a colourful character, who, over the years, initiated a large number of followers into the world of dance.

Her sister Elisabeth, who played an important role in transmitting the Duncanian spirit, was primarily a teacher.

Of her six adoptive daughters, Anna, Margot, Irma, Teresa, Erika (who died very young), and Lisa, I will consider Lisa mainly, for she made her career in Paris following the years she spent with Isadora, and it was through her in particular that the Duncanian tradition was perpetuated in France.

There was indeed a sort of spiritual family that gathered around the Duncans, and it is moving to assemble here the testimonies of figures such as Yvonne Berge, Odile Pyros and Madeleine Lytton.

Raymond Duncan

Born in San Francisco in 1874, died in Paris in 1966.

Although his role in the *fundamental development* of dance was not, in reality, a particularly important one (he even professed a certain lack of trust when confronted by professionals), he nevertheless converted thousands of dancers to the fertile stream he created both in relation to, and independent of, Isadora.

[I remember the first time I visited him in 1947 with June Fryer, my friend and partner at that time, who, like myself, was trained in the Wigman tradition. We were deeply moved: Isadora's brother!

He received us courteously, dressed in a long white tunic which, like his sandals, he had woven himself, his long white hair tied back with a ribbon. But throughout the conversation that ensued, it became apparent that he considered us not worthy to enter his holy chamber, at least as long as we had professional ambitions!]

The following extracts are taken from the autobiographical leaflets, printed on his own press, that he distributed to visitors – a promotional document of that time!

> *'Joseph Charles Duncan and Dora Gray were the parents of four remarkable children, Elisabeth, Augustin, Raymond and Isadora . . .*
>
> *The four children, inspired and guided by Dora Gray, established a school of arts in San Francisco in 1891. Here, Raymond Duncan, then a young man of seventeen, developed his theory of movement which remains the basis of his doctrine. During the following years he gradually evolved the system of movement now famous as the "Kinematics Raymond Duncan", a remarkable synthesis of the movements of labor and of daily life . . .*

Raymond Duncan had inherited the poetic fervor and the ardent physical energy which characterized his parents and has devoted it entirely to realize his first and unfading dream: the construction of a new world ... here began the first step in the direction towards an undiscovered world that the value of labor is the development of the workers and not production or earnings.

In 1898 Raymond Duncan with his sisters and his mother left America and worked years in London, Berlin, Athens and Paris where he devoted much of this time assisting Isadora to present and develop the art of the dance.

In Greece, Raymond Duncan built the house on the mountain outside Athens and there he and his wife Penelope tended their flocks of goats and sheep and led a pastoral life. During these years he developed a new approach to tragedy. In 1909 Raymond and Penelope went to America ... where they produced the Elektra of Sophocles. Though the tragedy was given in the original text, it was not an attempt to recall the Ancient Greek theatre but the presentation of an entirely new conception of stage craft wherein a style of orchestic action held equal importance with the text ...

In 1911 Raymond and Penelope Duncan returned to Paris and there founded the Akademia in which the arts and craftwork were taught free to all who wished to come and learn. Elektra was presented in Paris in the Châtelet and the Trocadéro where it met with a remarkable success ...

At the outbreak of the Balkan wars Raymond and Penelope went to Albania, founded hospitals and rebuilt the ancient city of the Onchismos in Epiros. The entire population of this city became self supporting on the product of the art and craft work. Because of civil strife, Raymond Duncan found it necessary to establish a republic in Albania; he organized his own army, printed his own money, and, during these wars, held his city against all Europe ...

In 1922 he built his theatre rue du Colisée ... Always with the ideal of a new world before him, Raymond Duncan then set himself to the creating of another city within the city of Paris. His school ... an open house for every new effort in theatre, literature, music and art ... a complete technique of living, being the synthesis of labor, art and the correct movement of the body ... During that period (of the Second World War), the house was a haven for part of the population ...'.

I cannot resist quoting several paragraphs from this document, which reveals something of the rather flamboyant character of this 'guru', 'prophet of the New Age', such as he would seem to us today, and his 'sophisticated simplicity' to which Adela Spindler Roatcap refers in her book *Raymond Duncan – Printer, Expatriate, Eccentric Artist* (The Book Club of California, 1991).

It must be noted that after Isadora's death, Raymond founded the 'Isadora Duncan Memorial School' on the rue de Grenelle, which in a way assumed the responsibility for the continuation of her work in France. This school was eventually included in the Akademia.

Raymond Duncan left a number of brochures: *La Musique et l'harmonie, La Danse et la gymnastique, Gestes*, etc. After his death at a ripe old age, the Akademia became an art gallery.

Plate 3 Raymond Duncan at his Akademia with two disciples. Photo: Harlingue, Paris. © Viollet.

Elisabeth Duncan

Elder sister of Isadora (born in 1873, died in Salzburg in 1948). She followed the same course as Isadora during those years in which the Duncan clan, after their initial Californian and national vicissitudes left America for Europe. Whilst Isadora shone in public in all her brilliance, Elisabeth pursued a more solid and sober path, oriented towards a philosophy of art and education. In spite of her stage appearances, she was infinitely more committed as a teacher than as a dancer. Her wide-ranging ability as a musician enabled her to capture perfectly the relationships between music and movement. Appearing somewhat severe and mystical in character, she did much to further Isadora's ideal of humanity dancing freely, joyously and in harmony.

From 1904 she directed Isadora's school in Berlin/Grünewald, where the 'Isadorables', Irma, Lisa, Teresa, Erica, Anna and Margot, took their first childhood steps. In 1909 Elisabeth opened her own school in Darmstadt, and this was followed by schools in Potsdam, and then Salzburg between 1925 and 1934. She married the musician Max Mertz, and Mary Howell was her principal collaborator. Unrivalled as a teacher, she remained in Prague until her death.

Yvonne Berge, one of her French pupils, described the course of a day's work at the school in Salzburg:

> 'At the age of fifteen, circumstances took me to Salzburg and to Elisabeth Duncan's school of dance. For several years I was thus able to absorb the unique artistic atmosphere of this rare school (boarder, 1924–1927) ... at the château in Klessheim ... we awaited the arrival of Isadora in the year of her sudden death.
>
> Every day we had the morning training session (held on the lawn in fine weather), which consisted of a form of gymnastic exercises in preparation for dance, to music improvised by Max Mertz, the school's director. He was a wonderful musician and teacher of music, sol-fa, singing and the history of the art. His improvisations provided extraordinary support for all the exercises.
>
> After lunch we had a compulsory quiet time in order to take a siesta. During this time we could either sleep or read our prescribed texts (in English, German and French), poems, Tagore, zen texts, etc.
>
> At three o'clock we had language or music lessons. We worked on our texts, and in music, we practised sol-fa, sight reading, dictation, and score-reading of works such as Haydn's 'Creation' that we were to hear subsequently in Salzburg.
>
> From five until seven o'clock in the evening we had dance lessons and improvisation. Then we could either go to the swimming pool or for a walk in the vast grounds.
>
> In autumn and winter we had rehearsals for the tours we were to undertake to Munich, Dresden, Berlin and Paris. During the "Isadora Duncan memorial week", organized by her brother Raymond, we danced most of Isadora's works at the Trocadéro with the Gabriel Pierné orchestra.

In the summer there was always a large number of famous visitors to Salzburg for the Mozart festivals. Amongst these was the renowned producer Max Reinhardt, who included us in the production of Shakespeare's 'A Midsummer Night's Dream', with music by Mendelssohn, that he staged in the grounds both of the château where we lived and those of the second château situated some five minutes away, which was normally reserved for receptions. The audience thus had to wander around the grounds, accompanied by an escort of young people brandishing torches; it was enchanting. And the lessons we learnt both from his way of adapting spontaneously to the location, and the production of the costumes, were of tremendous value to us. We worked with Elisabeth on the costumes, deciding on the most appropriate style of garments for the work, and also on the dyeing, draping, and even the weaving of the cloth.

Every morning we received drawing lessons from one of the best teachers from Csiseck in Vienna. In these classes we were introduced alternately to expressionism (on huge sheets of paper), kinetism, graphic musical and rhythmic expression, composition, lettering, placards and the nude. This graphic work, undertaken in conjunction with dance, was extremely enriching and stimulating. Music, painting, dance, theatre and literature all came together to form a perfect whole.

Was missing though the specific technical means to make the pupils' bodies well fitted for harmonious movement. Thus a whole underlying technical and psychological aspect could be guessed at that I have been able and have had to develop since' (extract from a letter from Yvonne Berge to Jacqueline Robinson dated 1986).

[We should perhaps recall that, as a child, Elisabeth, like Isadora, received her first lessons in dance and bodily expression from her mother, and that these amounted to little more than an application of François Delsarte's principles, as was the practice in America. These principles, neglected in France, had crossed the Atlantic with Steele MacKaye in the late nineteenth century, and it is interesting to observe the traces of Delsarte, or rather of his teaching, in the directions taken by certain actors and actresses who appear in this chronicle. He was their phantom grandfather.]

Irma Duncan

Of German origin, born Irma Ehrich Grimm (1897–1977).

One of Isadora's favourite pupils, to whom she entrusted the direction of the Moscow Duncan school in 1921.

Following their performances in Paris, the young dancers from this school, known as the 'little Russian Duncans', captured the imagination of the public, and, of course, of Fernand Divoire, who spoke of their ardour and lyricism and of 'Irma the perfect'. When the Moscow Isadorians went on tour to America in 1929, Irma remained in New York, where she opened the Isadora Duncan Dance Art School.

Her writings include *The Technique of Isadora Duncan* (1937) and *Duncan Dancers* (1965).

Anna and Teresa Duncan also settled in America where they created centres of Duncanism.

Lisa Duncan *by Odile Pyros*

Of German origin (1898–1976).
Isadora claimed:

> *'I conceive a dance school as a means of awakening in a child an awareness of the power of his soul so that ecstasy and beauty may direct his body according to the divine knowledge of the soul. This education is derived from music which speaks to the soul ... Although many "grown-ups" may have forgotten the language of the soul, this language is certainly understood by children, and they all understand me when I say to them in their first lesson: "Listen to the music with your "soul". Now, while listening, do you not feel it moving deep within you that it is by its strength that your head is lifted, that your arms are raised, that you are walking slowly toward the light?" This awakening is the first step in the dance, as I conceive it'.*[18]

It was to such a school, established by Isadora Duncan in 1904 in Grünewald, Germany, that the young Elisabeth Milker, Lisa, was admitted when she was barely six years old, and from that moment on, her whole life was devoted to dance. The school took charge of every aspect of the boarders' education. According to Fernand Divoire:

> *'it was essential that these children were able to spend ten years in this happy island atmosphere, free from all material cares'.*[19]

In order to provide for the needs of her school, Isadora frequently went on tour. During her numerous and sometimes lengthy absences, the children were entrusted to the care of Elisabeth, Isadora's elder sister. 'Aunt Miss', as the children called her, had a much stricter understanding of education than her sister, but by assuming control of the practical organization of the school, she was at least able to ensure continuity. Although a firm and intelligent teacher, Elisabeth lacked the inspired sparkle of her sister that made these young sensibilities quiver with excitement. As Irma wrote in her autobiography: *'one lesson with Isadora was worth Aunt Miss's entire routine'*; and Lisa often recalled the feelings of beauty and joy of existence with which Isadora imbued her childhood.

[18] Isadora Duncan, quoted from the programme of her performance in Paris on 26 June 1914. See also Isadora Duncan, *My Life* (Universal Publishing and Distributing, New York, 1968).

[19] Fernand Divoire, *Pour la danse* (Sate, Paris, 1935) p. 66 (whence are taken the other quotes).

The children's greatest joy was to be allowed to accompany Isadora on her tours, and it was in this way that, from 1908, Lisa and her companions were introduced to the different stages throughout Europe.

In 1914 Isadora installed her school in a pavilion in Bellevue, near Paris, and, on her request, her six eldest pupils left Darmstadt in order to be with her. Now that they were older, they were able to help Isadora and teach the beginners. The declaration of war created an abrupt interruption in the founding of this new school, and, after another year's separation, the six 'Isadorables' went to join Isadora in America, where she adopted them legally in order to avoid complications as a result of their German nationality.

The children, having developed into young ladies, well versed in their art, wanted to dance. With the support of Augustin Duncan, they asserted their independence and gave performances that were crowned with success. In 1920 Isadora, once again in Paris, was joined there by the girls, and when she took the decision to go to Russia in 1921, she was in the company of Irma, Lisa and Teresa. All four made a final farewell tour together, after which Isadora and Irma left for Russia in order to set up a school there. Lisa, for her part, returned to America with Anna and Margot for a tour that lasted several months; a number of engagements took her first of all to Algeria, then to Europe, and finally Paris, where she decided to stay and establish her own school. This was housed initially in rented studios at the Comédie des Champs-Elysées, and then at the 'Palais' on the avenue de Versailles, before being able to move into a large studio with living quarters on the rue des Sablons.

I began to attend her classes in 1932 at the studio on the avenue de Versailles where, as a member of the children's class first of all, then of the adults, and finally as an instructress, I grew deeply attached to her. I can vouch for the fact that, in spite of the problems involved in providing an education for a few hours a week to people immersed in everyday life, she succeeded in radiating and transmitting to us '*this joy of existence that still remains one of the principal characteristics of Isadorism*'.[20]

She knew also how to shape our bodies to make them capable of expressing our feelings, and it was not until some years later, when I became a teacher myself, that I realized that there was indeed such a thing as a Duncanian technique. What had always seemed so natural and simple to me in fact required a long apprenticeship.

At the same time as maintaining her classes, Lisa, soon surrounded by pupils, continued to perform both in France and abroad. She

---

[20] *Ibid.*, p. 75.

taught us the dances that Isadora had created for her own young pupils, and then those that, as adolescents, she had taught them later in her own characteristic way, dancing in front of them until they had grasped the spirit and form of the dance. These dances, conceived for her adoptive daughters, ranged from duets to sextets.

It would appear that Isadora rarely taught the dances that she performed herself, and it is likely that she varied her interpretation and steps, as many creators did, according to her particular mood. In order to become acquainted with some of these dances, the girls had to observe her from the audience, for when they appeared in a show with her, watching from the wings was strictly forbidden. Isadora used to say that seeing them there made her want to stick out her tongue at them, a sentiment that was hardly compatible with those she wished to convey!

There is nothing surprising in the fact that the same dance taught to several people should acquire slightly different nuances over the years dependent upon the character of each individual, but the fundamental essence of the choreography should nevertheless remain the same. Lisa was thus able to transmit the children's dances and ensembles, but few solos. Whilst preciously guarding this tradition, she created her own works which affirmed her personality. She has often been reproached with this 'modernism', but I agree with Divoire that:

> '...in her the sense of the modern is apparent at the same time as the unfailing dignity of her movements; everything that she learnt from Isadora became fused with that which she created for herself and resulted in an entirely new combination ... Lisa always retained her wonderful ease, her subtle delicacy and the extraordinarily expressive mobility of her hands and arms ... It would be no estimation of Isadora to praise Duncanian freedom whilst resisting all innovation in the name of this very tradition. In my view, the only intangible elements are the principles of the Isadorian aesthetic themselves: the suppression of anecdote and props, and the representation of human sentiments by means of postures and movements that are entirely natural to the human body'.

In 1930 Lisa made the acquaintance of Georges Pomiès and they created and performed together until 1932. Pomiès's strong personality certainly helped Lisa in asserting her own personality. A year and a half after Pomiès's premature death in 1933, Lisa staged her version of *Orpheus* to music by Gluck at the Théâtre de l'Opéra Comique. She introduced her new creation in the following way:

> 'Those who have seen Isadora will perhaps reproach me with failing to respect her interpretation entirely and daring to present these famous arias in a new light. I have retained Isadora's dances for the "Blessed Spirits", the serene and gentle charm of these being the only possible interpretation imaginable. For the suffering of Orpheus, however, I felt the imperious need to be alone and myself'.

Plate 4 Lisa Duncan and her dancers in November 1933. Photo: Lipnitzki, Paris. ©
Viollet.

She created the role of Orpheus and all the dances of the Furies that we performed too, and in recreating these enigmatic figures we were all made to look alike by wearing masks designed by André Barsacq. Once more according to Divoire, Lisa conceived

> *'a dance that was truly demoniac. They circled round and round, one after another, like a wheel that never stopped; they raised before Orpheus a lattice-work of legs, dancing like flames; they formed a ten-headed monster. The whole effect possessed a richness of invention and a dynamic violence that were acclaimed by the Opéra Comique audience'.*

This ballet indeed enjoyed great success; I remember that it was suggested to Lisa that she should produce it at the Théâtre d'Orange. As we were so few in number in relation to the size of this ancient theatre, it would have been necessary to supplement us with other dancers, but negotiations were never completed, for in this period (1935), roulades and tumbling were not part of the academic repertoire.

As in the case of her production of *Orpheus*, Lisa was always careful to indicate in her programmes the dances that were created by Isadora and those that were her own or her pupils' invention. I was able to appreciate her concern for precision when she taught me her *Valses d'amour*. Although Isadora had danced to several of Brahms's waltzes, Lisa knew only one of these for the reasons indicated above. Inspired by this same music, however, she created a suite comprising six waltzes, which she taught to me, showing me, in the case of the final one, both her own version and that of Isadora, and instructing me to retain the one that inspired me the most.

Lisa experienced many years of prosperity and success; she loved France and was adopted as a French citizen in 1937. Her whole life was a reflection and transmission of the beauty of dance 'awakened' in her by Isadora, who herself considered Lisa to be one of her most talented girls.

Then war broke out, and with it came the German occupation. Lisa, having been born in Germany and harbouring hostility towards the Nazi régime, did not wish to continue dancing in a Paris that was under German occupation, and sought refuge with friends in the provinces for the entire duration of the war. Her return to Paris was not an easy transition to make: she no longer had her apartment and had to content herself with staying in a hotel and renting a studio for her classes. Moreover, many of her former pupils had become scattered by the war. Courageously, she set to work again, and for several more years, was able to communicate her faith in dance to us, teach us her new creations and give performances. Her health had deteriorated during these difficult years, however, and she fell ill. With hardly any resources, and going from one hospital to another, she was unable to pursue her usual activities and was forced to end her existence in misery. As she could not be assured of an honourable end to her life in France, my mother, a friend of Lisa's for many years, contacted the latter's sister, who left Dresden for Paris and took Lisa to their native town where she was warmly welcomed and was able to live out her final years in safety, even resuming some of her artistic activities when her health permitted.

The memory of a life spent in the service of beauty remained with her until the very end, and a few years before her death she wrote to me:

> *'Dancing is a great happiness – like all manifestations of art – and communicating one's faith to others is the purest joy'.*

July 1983

Ellen Tels-Rabanek

Of Austrian origin. Married to a Russian. Born c. 1885, died in Paris in 1944.

Ellen Tels may be counted amongst those Eastern European 'ground breakers' who followed a different course, and were subjected to forces and influences different perhaps to those of the Western Europeans. Lying closer to their roots in popular folklore, they were distinguished by a different cultural context and character.

Ellen Tels was educated in classical dance, no doubt in Moscow and probably with Mikhail Mordkin. She was, however, chiefly a pupil of Irma Duncan, following the latter's appointment to the directorship of the school founded by Isadora. She was certainly acquainted with the theories of François Delsarte, who proved an inspiration to her subsequently. In Moscow she met Mila Cirul, and, sharing the same desire for freedom and experimentation, they left Russia. They performed together for several years in Germany and Austria where they experienced tremendous success.

Around 1920 Ellen Tels settled in Vienna where she established a reputable school and a group that was to spread a new image of dance. In 1927 she moved into a studio in Jasmin Square, Paris. Her teaching combined a classical basis (the bar), with Isadorian fluidity and Delsarte's principles of expressivity. She preached asymmetry of body position (as in antique statuary), and, in particular, the *'hanché'* (one hip higher than the other) position, which was in turn to form the basis of the technique of her attentive and devoted pupil, Janine Solane. Solane described her in the following way, which provides an accurate summary of her technical point of view:

> 'Her discovery lay in her understanding of the hips as the driving force behind all leg movements, in the way that the shoulders drive the movements of the arms. She made us try to achieve independence between our upper and lower limbs, and, in this way, restore the freedom of movement of Greek gestures ... the weight of the body must always rest on a single leg (whether in a static or dynamic position), the other leg being freed as a result and ready for departure (if one is in a period of rest) or arrival (if one is in a period of motion). Clearly, the 'hanché' position (the principle of relaxation) may be integrated with the initial motion and rest period of the rhythm and gesture ... An impression of clarity and power which is doubtless due to the 'hanché' position, emanates from all these studies, for it straightens the chest and forces the neck upwards like the stalk of a beautiful flower aspiring towards the light ...'.

Postscript on the Legacy of Isadora *by Madeleine Lytton*

Madeleine Lytton, who was trained in the Duncanian tradition by Lisa directly, and the followers of Elisabeth and Irma respectively, comments:

> 'I was too young to realize then that some of these teachers were not on the best of terms with one another. This was – and is – none of my concern; but realizing that rivalry still exists between the different schools which have inherited parts of the Duncan technique and repertory, my idea is to say "isn't it time to stop this antagonism?" Every one of us, whether from the schools in the Soviet Union, Czechoslovakia, France or the U.S. who continue the practice of exercises and dances created by Isadora Duncan, and who evolve new choreographies based on her style of moving, only know parts of the creative work of this genius! Few know the Wagnerian creations, the Marseillaise and the Ave Maria dances, and quite a few others are lost forever.
>
> It is important to keep the bulk of the tradition alive, but also to work on the theory, so that new exercises will help future pupils to understand better how to use the solar plexus in all motion. It is not betraying anyone to create new exercises absolutely based on the fundamental elements stated by Isadora the waving movement, the curve of the spine, the lightness and speed, and the technique which helps to portray emotion.
>
> ... The medium of Isadora is young and it is our task to keep it alive'.

THE LABAN AND DALCROZE LINES

Dussia Bereska

Of Polish origin, born c. 1900.

She was from early on the pupil, collaborator and companion of Rudolf von Laban in Zurich. During the 1920s she served as his assistant in Berlin, and was entrusted in particular with the direction of a small

Plate 5 Dussia Bereska, *The Green Clowns*, 1927. Photo: Werner Schuftan, Berlin.

group, creating works of intimate dimensions (as opposed to those of Laban, who specialized rather in choric works).

Dussia Bereska settled in Paris in 1930, officially charged with the direction of a branch of the Laban school, and thus establishing a Laban school in Paris on the boulevard Gouvion-St-Cyr. Gertrude Snell, also a pupil of Laban, joined her there as an assistant.

In 1935 she appeared at the Archives Internationales de la Danse, giving a lecture-demonstration, of outstanding quality. When Heinz Finkel arrived in turn from Germany, he stayed with Dussia Bereska and accompanied her classes in his capacity as a musician.

Until the war, she divided her activities between the different Laban centres, teaching, creating performances, and directing her Paris school. We lose all trace of her after the war. In his preface to Ann Hutchinson's *Labanotation*,[21] Rudolf von Laban referred to her with gratitude, as to an esteemed collaborator.

From the documents and photographs that survive, Dussia Bereska appears to have been an original choreographer, and her discoveries seem new and fresh in comparison with those of her peers.

Marie-Louise van Veen

Of Dutch origin, born c. 1900, died in Paris in 1985.

She was a pupil of Rudolf von Laban, probably in Germany. She appeared in Paris in 1929, as a member of Jacqueline Chaumont's group, and worked at the Odéon.

When Dussia Bereska opened the Laban school in Paris, Marie Louise van Veen was her assistant. In Paris, she performed either alone or with her pupils, and favoured dance set to poems. Fernand Divoire held her in high esteem on account of her sense of theatre. Considered as an actress perhaps more than as a dancer, she was a friend of Paul Claudel, whose texts she appears to have declaimed admirably. She continued to teach and perform until well into old age. Her work was strongly influenced by Laban's doctrines and emphasized the esoteric aspect of these. She succeeded in transmitting his teaching to a nucleus of people in France. Erudite and mystical, Marie-Louise van Veen also professed a predilection for Gregorian chant, and she drew inspiration from the spirit of this music as much as from its 'breathing' quality. At the end of her career, she composed a number of sacred dances.

---

[21] Ann Hutchinson, *Labanotation* (Phoenix House, London, 1954), p. 5.

Jacqueline Chaumont

Of Belgian origin, born in 1897, died in Paris in 1991.

Jacqueline Chaumont received her earliest training in theatre and dance in the Dalcroze method in Brussels, notably with the Genevese Jean Risler, and, as in the case of so many others, she experienced her first revelation of dance through Isadora Duncan. She came to Paris in 1920 with a Brussels theatre company, and was immediately noticed by Firmin Gémier, who engaged her as an actress, ballet teacher and choreographer at the Odéon, a position that she held until 1924.

Over and above her responsibilities at the Odéon (where she created *L'Homme et ses fantômes* by H.R. Lenormand amongst other works), she composed her own dances and gave numerous recitals. From her first appearances on stage, she was praised for the musical and theatrical qualities of her work, which, to music by Debussy, frequently sought to evoke the antique, as was the custom at this time.

Jacqueline Chaumont danced in all the favoured locations of the period, either alone or with her group, which comprised several dancers who pursued independent careers elsewhere: Anita Champagne, Marcelle Dazy, Lucienne Seatelli, Marie-Louise van Veen. Sonia Delaunay designed several of her costumes. Dubbed by the critics *'the dancer with a hundred faces'*, it has been said of her that *'what she achieves in the most masterly way is the ability to project beyond herself ..., always different, but always herself'*, whilst the redoutable André Lévinson, rarely indulgent as far as practitioners of non-academic dance were concerned, claimed:

> *'she is as refreshing as an oasis'.*[22]

In 1924 Jacqueline Chaumont married Pierre Guédy, a lecturer and man of letters, with whom she carried out research into various artistic and literary domains.

She taught under the aegis of the Conservatoire de l'Union des Femmes Artistes Musiciennes (U.F.A.M.) from 1923 until 1935. She then opened her own studio on the avenue de Wagram, where she worked with courage and enthusiasm until the end of her life. In 1928 Jacqueline Chaumont played the role of La Guimard in Sacha Guitry's *Mozart*. Until the war, she gave recitals with her pupils in Paris and the provinces, and abroad also. In 1933 Jacqueline Chaumont and Pierre Guédy founded the group Île-de-France within the Fédération des Groupes Folkloriques, and undertook work in the collection, repertoire and realization of the songs and dances of this hitherto unexplored region. This particular aspect of

---

[22] André Lévinson, *La Danse aujourd'hui* (Duchartre, Paris; 1929), p. 477.

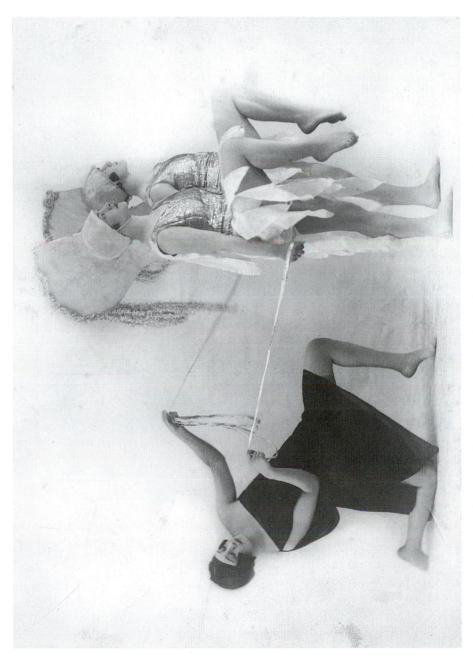

Plate 6 Jacqueline Chaumont, *The Roman Chariot*, 1925, with Lucienne Seatelli and Suzanne D.

Jacqueline Chaumont's work, which was especially dear to her, still exists under the name of the Ballet de l'Ile de France and is currently directed by her daughter, Antoinette Guédy. This interest in the cultural heritage of France led Jacqueline Chaumont to incline towards court as well as folk dances, and musicology; thus, it is not surprising that, during the war, she was entrusted with research at the Musée des Arts et Traditions Populaires.

In the late 1940s (Pierre Guédy died in 1942), Jacqueline Chaumont, as enterprising as ever, became associated with a new organization, La Scène Française, created by the barrister Pierre Masson in 1946. The aim of this organization was to promote the quality of French culture, an aim that was shared by a number of culturally oriented ventures at the end of the war, in the domains of music and dramatic art. Jacqueline Chaumont created a dance section there and established an annual competition from 1951. At this time, there were hardly any dance competitions in France, with the exception of those held by state institutions, such as the Opéra and the conservatoires. During the 1950s and 60s, this competition, organized by La Scène Française, provided a platform for a large number of young dancers and choreographers who have since made their own way in the field. The competition still exists and serves to unite hundreds of lay-practitioners from various disciplines. Jacqueline Chaumont was also one of the mainsprings of another organization that came into being after the war: the Fédération Française de Danse, which was itself a derivative of a syndicate of teachers of ballroom dance (known today as the Fédération Nationale Interprofessionnelle de Danse (F.N.I.D.)).

Jacqueline Chaumont's career spans precisely the period covered by the chronological framework of this book. In her youth she was enraptured by Isadora and in her maturity by José Limón. Eclectic in outlook, she was also influenced by memories of Ione and Brieux, Kurt Jooss, Janine Charrat and Roland Petit, Doris Humphrey, and the folk ballets of Eastern Europe.

Marie Kummer

Date of birth unknown. Genevese.

She studied initially with Jaques-Dalcroze, but finding his method too strict and not directed specifically towards dance, she went on to work with Malkowski in Paris. In her own sensitive way, she thus integrated Dalcroze's musical rigour with Malkowski's precepts of the analysis of natural, 'flowing' movement, economy and equilibrium of the body, and the fundamental role of the spinal column.

As a teacher in Paris in the 1920s and 30s, she demonstrated a particular talent as a choreographer of ensemble movements, and confronted the problems posed by the practice of Dalcrozian 'Eurhythmics' as a training for dance. In an interview with Fernand Divoire published in *Pour la danse* in 1935, she maintained:

> *'Rhythm must not create a mechanical body; it must let the body live. Can musical rhythm be adapted note for note to natural human rhythm? The subordination of the human body to any rhythm whatsoever leads inevitably to mechanization and a lack of sensitivity. On the other hand, through a logical education of the body (logical in relation to the body's own nature), one may succeed in realizing through it a synthesis of the proposed rhythm, its accents and essential lines (and not an arbitrary, mathematical, word for word translation). The study of rhythm is only possible when it is based on genuine physical technique'.*[23]

THE INDEPENDENT ONES

Georges Pomiès

French (1902–1933).

Georges Pomiès would perhaps have been the greatest French dancer of his generation and the one who brought French dance into an international sphere, had he not died at the age of thirty-one, after a career of barely more than six years.

Born in Paris in 1902 in the rue de la Gaîeté, where he lived all his life, his unusual career took him from dental school to the Théâtre des Champs-Elysées, via the music hall. As a student, he enjoyed singing as a hobby, and had some success in amateur circles, making a few tours, and eventually winning a variety act competition in which he imitated Maurice Chevalier. It was in this competition that he came to the notice of Paul Franck, director of the Olympia, not so much for his singing as for his innate talent as a dancer. Pomiès, who had never dreamed of making a career in dance, gradually began to drift away from the vocal circuit in favour of original choreographic research. He called himself an autodidact, was a perfectionist and tenacious worker, who devised a technique that served his purpose admirably.

His earliest dances remained close to the music hall: 'parodies' of fashionable artists, as he called them. Later he created dances such as *Clements Charleston* and *Georgian Blues* to the music of Jean Wiener, which, although derived from fashionable ballroom dances, were of a very personal expression and composition. He experimented with dance without music also. He gave his first recital in 1928 at the Comédie des

---

[23] Fernand Divoire, *Pour la danse* (Saxe, Paris, 1935), p. 88.

Champs-Elysées, and the novelty and quality of his work struck the audience from the very start.

In 1929 Charles Dullin welcomed him to the Atelier theatre where he taught and choreographed the dances for the English Restoration play, *The Beaux Stratagem*, by George Farquhar. Similarly, Gaston Baty invited him to the Gaîté Montparnasse, where he gave recitals, and created the interludes for Baty's original and memorable 1931 production of *Le Malade imaginaire*. He featured in several films, including *Tire-au-flanc*, *Ciboulette* (Autant-Lara) and *Chotard et Cie*. During 1931 and 1932 he became associated with Lisa Duncan and they performed together most notably at the Salle Pleyel and the Théâtre des Champs-Elysées. His final creations were *L'Homme sans bras* (Cliquet-Pleyel) and *Sonate au clair de lune* (Beethoven), tragic dances that prefigured the following six months in which he fought against the death that was finally to overcome him in 1933.

Numerous accounts and photographs evoke an image of Georges Pomiès: the clear, sharp lines and mass of his body, his sober and eloquent expression, the pullover or T-shirt and trousers he appears to have adopted as his costume which lent him a certain air of austerity and allowed his body and movements to speak clearly without constraint.

Pierre Abraham wrote of him:

> *'Naturalness, humanity and sincerity are the first words that spring to mind in association with the image of Pomiès. Rhythm, beauty and grandeur are those evoked by the memory of his dance. Sensibility, intelligence and profundity are those that come to mind on recalling his words on the art that was of all things most dear to him ... this tall, blond boy, with broad shoulders, slim waist, lozenge-shaped face, small bony forehead and wide brow ridge, beneath which lay two enormous, deep-set, clear eyes',*[24]

whilst the notoriously academic critic Maurice Brillant claimed:

> *'This intelligence, this gift of observation, this sensibility, this culture that is so indispensable to an art such as that of Pomiès that is so new and nurtured entirely on the substance of contemporary life, and which, whether through direct comedy or parody that strikes much deeper than apparent comedy, or through his own poetic inventions in the true sense of the word, or even a discreet sense of tragedy, aimed to express both the visible aspects and the secret soul through a powerful, delicate and ironic stylization that clearly revealed the essential characters. . . . Such was Pomiès's achievement, an achievement that he would have expanded in his own way and brought to a higher level had he lived longer. Certain critics have not been mistaken in calling him "the modern dancer" and in counting upon him to create and establish an entire art of "modern expression"'.*[25]

---

[24] *Danser c'est vivre. Georges Pomiès*, collected authorship (Tisné, 1939), p. 18.

[25] *Ibid.*, p. 53.

And in the words of his sister, Hélène Pomiès:

> *'Understanding, feeling more lucid every day, blossoming into a human being in which intelligence and intuition may act together in harmony were to him the greatest interests in life. His lesson to young people was that, although one may regret having been born, one cannot be excused from the obligation of cultivating the mind, for there is only one treasure and that is life itself, but one must know how to find it'.*[26]

Pomiès wrote about dance and contemporary dancers too. In an essay *La Bonne nouvelle*, he summarized his philosophical conceptions, and in *Propos sur la danse*, he maintained:

> *'Never has the unity of the individual been created more than in dance. All his zones, from the most physical to the most intellectual are united and condensed into a whole which, alone, may engender movement. No chinks, errors or carelessness are allowed.*
>
> *The two extreme attitudes in man are, firstly, action, during which consciousness is reduced to a minimum and physiological qualities are used to the maximum, and secondly, meditation in which physiological qualities are used to the minimum in favour of an intensification of the consciousness. Dance may be said to achieve the impossible in permitting a synthesis of these two extreme attitudes.*
>
> *It is well known that our feelings are intensified by the extension of their physical basis. The entire body, both external and internal parts, participates in dance.*
>
> *It is impossible to experience stronger feelings than through dance.*
>
> *Dance is not a means of glorifying the body or of submitting to it, but rather one of turning it into a hypersensitive instrument that makes no demands, a fluid entity that forms a geometrical basis for movement. ...*
>
> *A singer can hear his voice, an artist my see his paintings and a poet read his verses. The musician may listen, but the dancer creates nothing beyond himself. There is no end product with which he may satisfy or at least calm his senses.*
>
> *The dancer creates only himself. The wise man dances.*
>
> *But dance is the surest way of creating the wise man'.*[27]

Wonderful words! I think we would have loved Georges Pomiès.

Alexander and Clotilde Sakharoff *by Denise Blanc-Raillard*

Alexander Sakharoff, born in Russia in 1886, died in Sienna in 1963.
Clotilde von Derp, born in Berlin in 1895, died in Rome in 1974.
The name 'Sakharoff' permeated my entire childhood. It had a magical ring to members of my family ... My father, a theatre doctor,

---

[26] *Ibid.*, p. 78.

[27] *Ibid.*, p. 87.

used to go to the Opéra late in the evening to see them perform! I was not old enough to stay up; yet!

I cannot remember whether the first dance I saw was by Alexander or Clotilde: lines, colours, supple, moving bodies that travel led through space, advanced and turned with movements of the arms and hands that fascinated me. With each dance came a new surprise, a new marvel. I carried with me a signed photograph that I clasped tightly against my body so that nothing could escape me of this evening in my childhood when something beyond expression mysteriously occurred!

Before the war, I had the opportunity to see them again when Marseilles welcomed them as enthusiastically as it always had done. Then they departed for South America. Many years later, in Sienna, where they gave classes and performed their dances, I was able to appreciate their way of expressing only the essential elements, of playing on musicality, and their concern for precision and poetry of movement.

I saw Clotilde again in 1966, following Alexander's death. She had been engaged to direct a choreography course in Paris. But who knew her? Unfamiliar to the majority of students seeking technical perfection, Clotilde Sakharoff's course found itself deserted. Only two of us remained with her and we enjoyed some marvellous moments thanks to her extraordinary, exquisite, and richly experienced presence. She was always ready to offer advice and help in a kind and sensitive way; she demanded precision and rigour and encouraged a sense of personal creation.

From whence did these two prophets come? Alexander Sakharoff was born in 1886 into a middle-class family in Russia beside the Sea of Azov. He was a studious, docile, dreamy child whose ambition was to dedicate his life to painting, which had been revealed to him by an evocatively coloured theatre curtain representing the Bay of Naples. 'Paint or die', he used to say.

Thanks to his sister, who played the piano, he listened to the rhythms of classical musicians, and his body felt the need to move.

He also liked to drape himself in white cloths and improvise in the garden at nightfall. His mother had warned him not to go out of the garden, for 'bands of passing gipsies steal little children and take them to their caravans where they make them work in their circus'. From that moment on, the young Alexander dreamed of being carried off and of becoming an acrobat, a juggler or a trapeze artist, so he opened the garden gate and waited.

At seventeen, he was sent by his father to study law in Paris. On seeing Sarah Bernhardt in the role of 'The Eaglet', he was dazzled. This actress, although not a dancer herself, revealed to him what dance ought to be; through her, he discovered the inner self expressed through the body, this instrument capable of modulating tension, breathing, muscular

Plate 7 Alexandre Sakharoff. Photo: Lipnitzki. © Viollet.

action and the energy of movement. He watched Sarah Bernhardt come on stage, cross the floor, stand up, sit down, open her arms, bow her head, and thus discovered the language of plasticity, the magic of gesture; he decided to devote himself to dance there and then.

He was twenty years of age. He closed the lid of his piano, tore up his canvasses and began to work at training his body. He threw himself into acrobatics and soon attained a degree of physical virtuosity that enabled him to perform at the Odéon in 1910, where he gave his first recitals and danced before an audience that welcomed new choreography, such as that of Isadora Duncan, Ruth St-Denis, and Diaghilev's Ballets Russes. He then went to perform in Munich. There he became associated with the artists of Der Blaue Reiter, who fuelled his artistic conceptions. There too, in 1913, he met Clotilde.

Clotilde Edelfon der Planitz was born in 1895 into an aristocratic family in Germany. She lived alone with her mother, a remarkable pianist, who introduced her to the violin at an early age. Munich was an intellectual and artistic centre. Clotilde took lessons in rhythmic dance with two English women to whom she revealed her secret hopes. Later she pursued her initial training in dance with a star of the Munich Opera. At fifteen, she possessed a wide artistic culture, and felt sufficiently prepared to give a dance recital to music by Strauss, Schumann and Schubert, in which she scored a shining success. She was engaged to appear in the large Reinhardt productions, went on tour, assumed the name Clotilde von Derp, and went to dance in Munich ... where she met Alexander.

Both dancers felt admiration for one another, and they featured together in the programme of an artistic performance in which Alexander played the part of Bacchus, and Clotilde that of the Knight of the Rose. Amidst thunderous applause, Clotilde offered him a rose ... Their destinies were linked through their work initially, each one retaining his own personality, but their personal lives soon became entwined and in 1919 they married.

[Alexander and Clotilde travelled the world with their dance programmes, and were acclaimed as the poets of dance. They performed frequently in Paris, where they were held in high esteem. In 1940 they left for South America (Brazil, Chile Argentina, Peru), where they taught and performed, leaving a marked impression wherever they went. After the war they returned to Europe and settled in Italy. They continued to give recitals for a few more years, performing at the Théâtre des Champs-Elysées in Paris in 1949, for example. They taught in Sienna and Rome, then, having gradually retired from the dance scene, died in their final adopted country.]

Plate 8 Clotilde Sakharoff in *Jeune fille au jardin*. Photo: Stone, Brussels.

'*Dancing*', claimed Clotilde Sakharoff,

> '*may be described as particular states of existence that are transposed by the mind and expressed by the body – the mysterious depths of our being ... It has always seemed to us that the fundamental law of dance was to materialize the spirit, and spiritualize the materials*'.

Alexander maintained:

> '*First of all the dancer experiences a certain feeling out of which the desire to express oneself in a certain way is born; this is the moment in which the work is conceived .... the artist must experience this feeling, he must know how to become aware of it intellectually, and then embody it; these are the three stages of aesthetic creation. But*', he added, '*in modern art, artists frequently express what they think rather than what they feel. ... The artist is altruistic by nature he wishes to share with others the marvellous gift of being able to see that which is hidden to the eyes of the world and which fate has revealed to him*'.

They perceived the human body as a '*keyboard of flesh*' from which magnificent harmonies and resplendent runs may be drawn. '*Technique is created by the need to express something personal in a precise way*' (Clotilde). '*The dancer must attain this harmony, this state of joy in which everything seems easy, and technique no longer seems to pose any difficulties*' (Alexander).

They appeared stern to '*the artist who forgets that technique is only a means that he must choose carefully; if he forgets that, he runs the risk of deviating from the essential and falling into virtuosity, which strips the work of its grandeur and, if carried too far, often conceals a complete lack of artistic sense*'.

The Sakharoffs wrote extensively on the relationship between dance and music. Alexander revealed the complex nature of this in his book *Reflecciones sobre la Danza y la Música* (*Reflections on Dance and Music*), written in Spanish and published in Buenos Aires.

Both Clotilde and Alexander 'respected' music and saw it not merely as an accompaniment. They strove to fathom the deepest intentions of the composer, and rediscover the very emotion that lay at the source of his imagination. They did not wish to dance to music, or with music, but to '*dance music*', a view that reflected that of Isadora. However, they wanted to go further in their research into this harmony/conflict between dance and music, and Alexander stated that

> '*dance without music is the final stage towards which we are aiming. The music that is used to accompany our dances at present is for us only temporary. It existed before our choreography; it was written independently of the latter. We only used it because we believed that the time of dance without music had not yet arrived; but we fully realized that it restricted our creative freedom. For the principal fault of this music lies in the fact that, as a result of its own structure*

and possibilities, it influences our choreographic compositions and often imposes
upon them movements that are not in keeping with it'.

Alexander maintained of the other arts that

'All harmony between the elements is music; there is music in movement, just
as there is in colours, scents, lines and forms'.

Clotilde claimed:

'Dance is a whole in which each part plays a role similar to that in painting:
composition, colour, rhythms, values, light and shade are the elements that form
this whole. The dancer is, therefore, a multiple being, a synthesis of all the other
arts, and he may, indeed must, create correspondences between them. The more
complete the dancer, the more numerous the correspondences will be'.[28]

I believe sincerely that the Sakharoffs were all too quickly forgotten. But
why was this so?

The disturbing events of their respective fatherlands do not
appear to have affected the subjects they expressed in their dances. Two
world wars, the Russian Revolution, Nazism ... They somehow passed
over these catastrophes that, in contrast, other artists felt the need to
express. Could this be why these other artists made a deeper impression
on their time and left a more lasting memory? How can one fail to evoke
the dances of Wigman, animated with such force and passion.

The Sakharoffs were never 'committed' in that direction, nor did
they effect an aesthetic or technical revolution. As Jacques Baril claimed
in *La Danse moderne* (ed. Vigot, 1977):

'Their work, which is in no way revolutionary, is a unique example of artistic
conscience, of fidelity to a message that has no other ambition than to express
itself in a personal language that rejects every external influence other than their
love of dance'.

There is perhaps another reason for their sinking into oblivion: they did
not establish a school or form a company; neither did they seek to
cultivate a following. Perhaps they felt in a vague sort of way that their
extremely personal language was too difficult to communicate. And yet,
they sought to advise and demand attention of those who wished to enter
the *'religion of dance'*, insisting upon the *'neutral point'*, that moment of
concentration in which the body is prepared for the *'journey to the inner*
self'. In his lessons, Alexander insisted upon the value of silence (*'He who*

---

[28] Quotations from Clotilde and Alexander Sakharoff from *Esprit et art dans la danse*, Alexander
Sakharoff (Maurice Bridel, Lausanne, 1968); *Ce que la danse est pour nous*, Clotilde Sakharoff (in
Conferencia, August 1939); *Clotilde et Alexandre Sakharoff*, Émile Vuillermoz (Centrales, Lausanne,
1933).

is able to listen to silence can see sounds and hear movements'), and also upon the importance of the intimate desire, a force situated in the solar plexus, the secret of all equilibrium.

The Sakharoffs lay within the current trend of modern art that sought 'inner necessity'. Kandinsky, who was acquainted with and often referred to them, wrote prophetically in 1910:

> *'Inner beauty will replace outer beauty. A hitherto unsuspected power, a living force will emanate from the very movements themselves. Beauty will suddenly burst forth. From this moment, the dance of the future will soar into existence'.*

The development of contemporary dance demonstrates the accuracy of his vision, and the Sakharoffs indeed constituted a part of this evolution.

Hélène Vanel and Loïs Hutton

The encounter between Hélène Vanel and Loïs Hutton around 1925 gave rise to a type of artists' co-operative known as Rythme et Couleur, which was based in Saint-Paul-de-Vence.

Loïs Hutton was English by birth and originally of Dalcrozian training. She had taught in London where she already formed part of that group of British intelligentsia known as the Bloomsbury Set (comprising principally writers and graphic artists such as Duncan Grant, Clive Bell and Virginia Woolf) through contact with whom she had become appreciative of literature and the graphic arts. In this same period, Margaret Morris, a follower of 'free' dance and the inventor of an embryonic system of notation, was working in the picturesque artists' quarter of Chelsea. Margaret Morris organized summer courses in Antibes, home to an important Anglo-Saxon colony.

At one of these courses, Loïs Hutton met the Frenchwoman Hélène Vanel and, as a result of this meeting, these two young women settled in Saint-Paul-de-Vence. In the interests of both an early form of multi-disciplinary artistic decentralization, and ecology, their house in Saint-Paul became either a theatre or a gallery as the case required, and a centre where meetings and creation could take place. For a number of years they ran this home with scant resources, doing everything for themselves, and turned it into a true nucleus of artistic activity. They also gave dance recitals in Paris and elsewhere, and appear to have made considerable progress for their time in the search for a theatrical language that was perhaps closer to mime than dance. They were more interested in creating than in teaching, this was particularly so in the case of the more audacious Hélène Vanel. She was the only dancer to perform at the

Surrealist Exhibition of 1937, held in the rue du Faubourg-St-Honoré. After the war she worked at the Musée de l'Homme.

Yvonne Redgis

Franco-American, born c. 1895.

Trained in classical dance. Later she studied with Loie Fuller, and was probably a member of her company. During the 1920s she taught at Loie Fuller's school. She was an eclectic, like the majority of dancers of the time. Fernand Divoire referred to her sympathetically, praising the recitals she gave in her studio on the rue Victor-Massé, drawing attention to a 'well balanced' Spanish dance in particular.

[For my own part, I remember Yvonne Redgis in her studio on the avenue de Wagram, and the years of my childhood spent working with her, once a week … a bit of classical (oh, that beautiful sky blue satin tunic!), a bit of rhythmic dance, but a degree of freedom also, improvisation, and a lot of music.]

Yvonne Redgis gave a lecture-demonstration at the Archives Internationales de la Danse in 1935 in which she declared that

> '*dance, like all the arts, demands a solid technical basis, but perfection must not be achieved at the expense of the personality.* [Solid technique=classical technique.] *Study should sustain the individual's own character, and lend him support, so that he may develop his instinctive qualities with greater assurance … The role of the teacher should be to awaken this personality and to respect it if it is already formed in a child. The teacher must be aware of and recognize everything, and not deny what has been achieved already for the sake of novelty*'[29]

Yvonne Redgis disappeared during the war and all trace of her has since been lost.

Paul Swan

Of American origin.

Paul Swan was also a sculptor, and appears to have been known as such as much as for his work as a dancer. He gave a recital at the Théâtre des Champs-Elysées in 1925, which probably represented his first appearance in Paris. His dances were held in high esteem in both Paris and Germany, and he was regarded by the critics with definite respect.

---

[29] Yvonne Redgis, lecture quoted in the *Revue des Archives Internationales de la Danse* (Paris, November 1935), p. 10.

His studio was a place where other artists were always welcome and could exhibit their work. He featured prominently until the war, when he returned to the United States.

Charlotte Bara

Of Belgian origin.

Like Laban before her, she settled in Ascona, Switzerland. She studied with Alexander Sakharoff, Uday Shankar and Raden mas Jodjana. She appears to have been an unusual character. She directed her school and San Materno theatre in Ascona, and specialized in sacred dances in a Medieval or Renaissance style, inspired by the Christian faith. She was extremely cultured. She sometimes danced in silence. A soloist, choreographer and producer, she toured Europe and was highly acclaimed in Paris. Fernand Divoire said of her:

> 'She bore on her brow the mark of mystic genius ... she is one of the most moving and extraordinary dancers we have ever encountered'.[30]

Yvonne Sérac

French.

She aroused attention in 1917 as a member of Gaston Baty's circle. She surprised her audience and the critics by the fact that she danced in silence. Sérac gave her first public recital in 1921 at the Salon des Indépendants and reappeared at the Théâtre des Champs-Elysées during the early years of the decade. In 1924 Fernand Divoire reproached her with miming:

> ' I have come to consider mime as the worst enemy of dance. Mime reduces dance to anecdote in some individual cases. Yvonne Sérac's dances, fail to measure up to silence'.[31]

He compared her with:

Isabel de Etchessary

Argentinian.

She was principal dancer at the Colón Theatre in Buenos Aires, and was therefore of classical orientation. Like Sérac, she too made her début in Paris in 1921. She appears to have retained a basic vocabulary

---

[30] Fernand Divoire, *Pour la danse* (Saxe, Paris, 1935), p. 95.

[31] *Ibid.*, p. 96.

of classical steps (including toe-dancing), but she also dispensed with music, *'unable to perceive any relationship between muscular sensation and musical feeling'*. She preached 'polyrhythmic' dance and composed 'danced poems'. All this puzzled the good (?) Divoire:

> *'This young and beautiful woman is an intelligent dancer. She rushes headlong into intelligence with a terrible feminine logic. There is nothing quite as appalling as an intelligent female dancer. To all appearances, Mademoiselle de Etchessary's polyrhythm seems like a complete lack of rhythm'.*[32]

These two rather baffling dancers do not appear to have remained in the public eye for long. During the second half of the decade they were no longer to be found on the Paris stages. Nevertheless, their work must have gone some way towards establishing the autonomy of dance in relation to music. And in this respect the contribution they made was perhaps a useful one.

THE EDUCATORS

François Malkowski

Born in Czechoslovakia in 1889, died in France in 1982.
Malkowski's pupil, Françoise Chantraine, testifies:

> *'The greatest elegance results from the greatest simplicity. How many times have I heard François Malkowski (Malko to his friends and pupils) express this thought that he held so dear. It served as a warning against all lack of genuineness, whether of gesture or word, in dance and in life. François Malkowski gave me a feeling of "oneness" between what he preached and the way in which he danced and lived. "Show me how you walk and I will tell you who you are"; "one may see from a person's gait whether he has found his way in life": how he liked to quote these phrases from Nietzsche to us!*
>
> *After studying singing in Prague, Malko discovered Paris around 1912, and met Isadora Duncan also. This meeting appears to have had a crucial and enlightening effect on him. In 1914 Malko joined the Foreign Legion, and, after the war, he chose dance as his art. Like Isadora, he was inspired by the music of the great composers together with Greek aesthetics, and was opposed with similar strength to the structures of classical dance, and saught to establish a harmonious way of life. He followed a career as a solo dancer, giving recitals, accompanied in his programmes by one of his disciples and his pupils. His final recital took place in the Salle Gaveau on 18 June 1948, with the participation of his disciple Christiane Reynaert.*
>
> *Since his youth spent in the Carpathian mountains, he had been a lover of nature in all its manifestations, and excelled as an amateur dancer and*

---

[32] Fernand Divoire, *Découvertes sur la danse* (Grès, Paris, 1924), p. 106.

*sportsman; his instinctive knowledge and observation of movement thus gave
him great insight into the analysis of natural mechanisms.*

*From around the age of seventy until his death, François Malkowski became
increasingly interested, over and above his choreographic activities, in redis-
covering the exigencies of basic movements, the logic of which is governed by
universal principles. In this way, he facilitated the experience of movement
radiating outwards from the solar plexus. He demanded a free and erect body,
and aspired towards a degree of transparency that revealed itself in his own
movements through a state of suspension.*

*Due to this state of suspension and awareness of the solar plexus, the
displacement of the centre of gravity required by each step gradually became
natural, with a distribution of movement between the upper and lower parts of
the body. This shift of balance also enabled one to feel the shoulders pulling
in the opposite direction to the legs, like a wheel, and increased the awareness
of the centrifugal force created by the pendulum-like motion of the arms drawing
the body further and higher in an entirely natural way. He liked to use so many
tripartite maxims, such as "active, passive, neutral", "escapement, diffusion,
confirmation", or "obtaining, accumulating, releasing", in order to encourage
the different phases of the tripartite pendulum movement.*

*His quest for truth took the precision of a movement almost to a vibration. I
will never forget François Malkowski's expression or his tone of voice when he
used to solemnly recite to us Nietzsche's phrase: "It is only through dance that
I can express the symbols of the most sublime things"'.*

François Malkowski belonged to that breed of mystical dancers/teachers
(that is, those who were imbued with the need to listen to the great
natural/cosmic laws and to try to place mankind within the context of
these). He enjoyed such a long career that he taught several generations
of enthusiastic pupils, the most recent of whom still endeavour to preserve his teaching today.

As early as the 1920s he defined the fruits of his observations on
movement in number of principles based on the fundamental notion of
economy of effort: *'The stars, plants, oceans and air, birds, fish, earthworm,
dog and monkey, the elements and the animals are, like all things, a part of the
universe in which they fulfil a certain function. The fitter they become to fulfil
this function, the more they evolve towards the attainment of their respective
perfection. The more agile the greyhound, the more perfect a greyhound it is. The
more indefatigable a navigator the frigate, the more perfect a frigate. For a
greyhound to be a good greyhound, it must be able to run and run well. For it
to be able to run well, it must have spirit and special limbs that develop and
evolve by means of the very movements that are proper to it: the more economical
these are, the simpler and more graceful they will be; the more elegant, the greater
its ability as a greyhound and the better it will become. The same applies in the
case of the frigate. Each well executed movement possesses a precise inner and
outer rhythm (which has absolutely nothing in common with the pseudo-rhythm
of the regular steps through which rhythm is claimed to be learned). It recalls*

the rhythm of the pendulum which must clearly be understood if we wish to truly exploit the body's weight in order to conserve energy' (quoted by Fernand Divoire, who added to Malkowski's remarks, *'when a dancer has reached this depth in the analysis of movement, he must not encumber the purity of his movements with trivial stories').*[33]

' *... I advise my pupils to avoid every kind of poison: meanness, falsehood, ugliness, vulgarity, snobism, injustice, mechanical movements, and everything that drains the sap of their life, distancing them from themselves and the states of receptivity that are indispensable to the perception of the particles of universal rhythm, and the profound and mysterious life that speaks to them through everything around them that is worth hearing and to which they must learn to listen. In helping them with all my heart to blossom into their own true flowers, I seek to create a favourable atmosphere and a sense of communion in work, for if a long period of silence is required before a perfect harmony may be achieved, it takes a long and perserving initiation to penetrate the white magic of dance ... '*

'The basis of human movements is the gait: the continual falling motion, accelerating and decelerating with each step due to the alternate displacements of the centre of gravity (regulated by our solar plexus). The shoulders, imperceptibly describing a double wheel, draw our arms and legs in opposite directions, allowing the spinal column to curve freely, thus becoming the shock-absorber, or spring, that protects us against damaging the nervous system.

... Knowledge and ability are not one and the same thing; in indicating the true way towards the greatest of all the arts, the art of living, to those who have been entrusted to our care, we should not simply force them to learn by heart the ready-made thoughts of others, but teach them how to think, how to become their thoughts even, how to realize and merge with the harmony of the spheres, the Great Whole, the One. In our teaching, we must begin by awakening receptivity, and try never to forget that it is only in helping others that we may help ourselves, that in sowing the seeds of joy we may discover our own joy, and that in giving we may receive'.[34]

Renée Odic Kintzel

French (1890–1969).

She was an artist of remarkable all-round ability. She began her career by studying music to advanced level at the Schola Cantorum, where she was a pupil of Vincent d'Indy and Blanche Selva amongst

---

[33] Fernand Divoire, *Pour la danse* (Saxe, Paris, 1935), p. 82.

[34] François Malkowski, *Toute la danse* (February 1954).

others. Later she discovered dance, adopting an autodidactic approach at first, and devoting herself finally to this art in which she saw the source of and solution to many of her questions about music, art and human nature. Her aesthetic and pedagogical research was characterized by a genuine spirituality. Like the majority of free dancers of her time, she dedicated herself to the cult of nature, and preached harmony and grace in a way that transcended the sentimentality and affectation typical of that period. She was inspired also by antique statuary, not only on account of its poetic, expressive and evocative qualities, but as a means of conducting a systematic investigation of the support, weight and balance of forces.

Odic Kintzel (or simply Kintzel, as she signed herself), referred to her dance as 'redemptory dance'. André Gaudelette introduced her work in the following way:

> 'in her understanding, dance operates on three levels: the spiritual, the moral and the material, and is one of the most complete, reliable and effective means of achieving the purification, regeneration and betterment of humanity. This is the reason for her choice of this significant designation: redemptory dance. There is indeed a sovereign power of re-education, and therefore of correction, improvement and reparation – in short, of Redemption – of all physical and moral discord in the Art of Choreography'.

This avowed mysticism might be suspected of concealing a lack of solid technical ability, but this does not appear to have been the case. Her work was admired and supported by many of the foremost artists and intellectuals, and she benefitted from the collaboration of composers such as Florent Schmidt, Albert Roussel and Arthur Honegger. During the 1930s her recitals at the Salle Pleyel and the Vieux-Colombier theatre were notable events in Parisian cultural life. She was commissioned to write articles for various journals, and gave many lecture-demonstrations in a number of different locations on her doctrine of dance.

In 1925 she published *Le Corps harmonieux,* aimed at parents and teachers, as a guide to the teaching of movement to childern. *Cultive ta statue!* (1930) warned against the harmful effects of defective bodily postures, inviting a greater awareness of the self, whilst *Ce que peut la danse* (1935) presented a collection of poetic and philosophical writings.

In a communication to Fernand Divoire, she wrote:

> 'You, apostle of my faith, have known for a long time that I am the servant of harmony. I seek this harmony in the forms of the bodies that have been entrusted to me, in their balance, and in the living quality of their movements, composed of breadth, suppleness, sincerity, precision, subtlety, truth and accuracy in relation to the expressive or useful ends they aim to serve. I seek it in their souls ... and why not? It is almost inevitable. Thus, for the sake of my serious students, I have renounced these "educative games", these gilded pills destined for feeble bodies.

I aspire to create suppleness, energy and breath; it does not matter if the exercises that have proven their effectiveness are not very elegant; a path is only a path, it is the edifice to which it leads that counts. And whilst physical work follows its course without bluff, cheating, or false modesty, aesthetic formation may occur in parallel with the same strict rigour.

My dear friend, in the past you have reproached me in all fairness with dancing with my brain ... Do you not consider it necessary that I should have done so in order that my pupils may now realize with their bodies the joyful, moving or passionate poems suggested to them by music? Of course it was necessary, for if ordinary physical culture is more like market-garden culture, tending merely to produce well formed human fruits, then the pursuit of beauty belongs rather to the realm of spiritual culture.

What cannot be achieved through dance? Is there any more complete art? Is it not music and poetry combined when it expresses the human soul in time, plastic art and painting when it creates visual images, and architecture when it connects and arranges these images? What more perfect means of teaching the laws of art in all their diverse manifestations and essential unity could one ever hope to find? If, as my old teacher Vincent d'Indy, used to say, "art elevates man on the scale of existence", dance of all art forms may achieve this since it requires not only the soul, but also the body"'.[35]

The following extract from *Ce que peut la danse* reveals a subtlety of thought unusual for that time.

'*Such is the multiplicity of dance that it is too diverse to be systematically approved or condemned.*

Those who speak ill of it because it committed the error of expressing sentiments of which they disapproved, or of assuming forms that shocked them, ought rather to have regretted that they did not either wish or demand that it were better ... for it is a necessary means of expression.

There are different types of dance because there are different types of people and affinities and categories exist amongst current styles of dance just as they exist amongst people and there are such clear relationships between one and the other that it may be claimed, in the words of the proverb, "Tell me how you dance and I will tell you who you are".

All gesture is primarily a form of confession, not intentionally as much as through the sometimes minute but always eloquent nuances it conveys an imperceptible trembling, a flickering of the eyelids that betray a secret emotion, an all too delicate feeling a mark of conceit or vanity that nevertheless reveals so much an infinite scale of degrees that connects openness to dissimulation, sponta- neity to calculation, caution to enthusiasm, clarity of thought to indecision, indolence to ardour, and cowardice to courage by means of everything that rises irrepressibly from the very heart of man's existence to the surface where it may be read.

---

[35] Renée Odic Kintzel, *Ce que peut la danse* (published by the author, 1932).

> *Now if these almost unconscious gestures can disclose so much about the nature of a human being, what might the movements of dance, chosen freely according to the character and criteria of the individual reveal! ...*
> *Indeed, if this expressive dance, this creation in which the whole being participates with his corporeal and incorporeal self, had a place in our education and in our lives – for art should not only be reserved for show, music exists outside the concert hall, the plastic arts outside the museum, and lyricism and poetry outside the theatre – many things might be changed.*
> *But this must be demonstrated step by step'.*

Odic Kintzel appears to have been one of the first to speak of dance in such evidently modern terms that set out from an acute observation of movement and behaviour. She continued to teach in her studio after the war. Jerome Andrews made her acquaintance on his arrival in Paris in 1952, and was struck by her immense culture, her sense of observation of the body, and the harmony that emanated from her style. He worked for a while at her studio.

She died in 1969, leaving many notes on dance, art and teaching that are worthy of publication. She was also a visual artist and made many quick charcoal sketches encapsulating movement. In the opinion of her friends, *'a message such as hers should not be allowed to be forgotten'*.

Irène Popard

French (1894–1950).
After an initial career in high fashion, Irène Popard trained with George Demeny, a pioneer of a more natural form of gymnastics. During her apprenticeship in Boston, she discovered Isadora Duncan and dreamed of introducing this type of education through movement to young French girls. On her return to Paris, she embarked upon a study of pure gymnastics, became a teacher of physical education, and opened her school under the aegis of the Union Chrétienne de Jeunes Filles (the equivalent of the Y.W.C.A.), where one of her most loyal supporters, Elizabeth Fuchs, had just established the French girl guides.

An initial performance at the height of the war in 1916 launched 'Popard gymnastics' into orbit, but although she secured the support of a sector of the medical and sporting professions, she had to contend with the narrow-mindedness of the 'establishment'. After the war, however, the Popard school performed in all kinds of circumstances, in stadia and theatres alike; the Popard method continued to spread, instructresses swarmed all over France, and Popard courses became almost a national phenomenon.

With her strong personality and impulsive, intransigent nature, Irène Popard never stopped working throughout her life, even in the face of illness and the vicissitudes of the war, during which she worked at the École Normale Supérieure d'Éducation Physique (E.N.S.E.P.) (a teachers' training college for sports). In the year before her death in 1949, she took part in the *Chorégies d'Orange*, in which her group danced in *Sept contre Thèbes*. Then she collaborated with Serge Lifar on the production of Honegger's *La Naissance des couleurs* at the Opéra, in which her feeling for the deployment of large forces was most appropriate to the subject matter concerned.

As the leader of a movement, Popard left her mark on an entire age. This movement pertained more to physical education than to dance and existed, it must be admitted, on the fringe of the commonly held view of dance. Marie-Thérèse Eyquem, Inspector General at the Ministry of Youth and Sports in 1959, and an indefatigable promoter of modern dance, wrote at this time:

> *'Irène Popard's work does not provide a substitute for that of Jaques-Dalcroze, for whom physical exercises were initially only a means of increasing the awareness of music. Moreover, as Irène Popard's system of harmonic gymnastics developed, eurhythmics came to assume a growing place in her method. She did not pretend to be a dancer in the traditions of classical or expressive dance, but her musical adaptations nevertheless lay on the boundary between gymnastics and dance. Irène Popard's most original and lasting contribution was the coherent structuring of a system of gymnastics devised by a woman for women, and in this, she may be regarded as a pioneer. This idea, which was revolutionary in France at the time of her arrival on the scene, became, largely due to her, more and more customary'.*

Training at the Popard school today remains faithful to her original precepts; a more creative procedure and the study of certain contemporary techniques (Graham, for example) have been integrated into its curriculum, however, in a deliberate attempt to bring it closer to dance. The discipline and style of these techniques remain hybrid, nevertheless. Amongst the French pre-war schools of harmonic, aesthetic or artistic gymnastics, those of Simone Jacques-Mortane, Odette Courtiade, Andrée Joly and Simone Caquille must be mentioned in the wake of Irène Popard.

It is interesting to try to recapture contemporary thought and practice by quoting a few lines written by Fernand Divoire in 1935:

> *'The movements do indeed seem to be hanging from a circle rather than setting out from a central point. Moreover, they do not belong to any sensual or intellectual domain, but to the physical one. We have in Irène Popard's work an example of what is, perhaps, the art of the movement of the masses, such as is already making its cry heard in America and Russia.*
>
> *In summary, Mme Irène Popard makes a constant effort that must not be overestimated, as certain critics have done, by placing it on a level with real art,*

Plate 9 Irène Popard and her pupils in 1925. Photo: Harlingue. © Viollet, Paris.

but, within the limits she appears to have imposed on herself, she cannot be applauded or encouraged too greatly'.[36]

THE ORIENTALS

Jeanne Ronsay

(Text written in collaboration with *Roger Dabert**)

(1890–1953).

Jeanne Ronsay enjoyed a considerable reputation as a dancer, choreographer, teacher and theorist. Few details of the development of her career have survived, however. Born in La Rochelle towards the end of the last century, into a middle-class family with a long-standing military tradition, she was not destined in any way to follow a career in dance. Little is known of her early training, however, it was on seeing Isadora Duncan, of whom she will always consider herself a disciple, that she received a revelation of the art that was to occupy her whole life.

Her public life began in 1912. Like Isadora, she took her inspiration from musicians such as Mozart, Debussy, Ravel and Satie. She already had a group of pupils, and had posed for the sculptor Antoine Bourdelle, which enabled her to appear beside Isadora on the large frescoes of the Théâtre des Champs-Elysées, then under construction. *'Young and beautiful like an ancient Diana, she dances'*, wrote Pierre Thiriot. This description brings us very close to Isadora ... but its continuation tells a different story:

> *'Perhaps her expression was a little too heavy for the Dyonisiac dances she often performed, like an illustration by Pierre Louÿs. Her face was always burdened with thought: one could see that she "knew many things"'*[37]

At the same time as her summons to pure dance, she was in demand in the theatre too. She set the ballets for Maeterlinck's L'Oiseau bleu for Réjane, and worked for Firmin Gémier and Jacques Copeau also. Copeau had always associated dance with the theatre, and Lucienne Lamballe from the Opéra taught for him at the Vieux-Colombier, with the whole weight of the classical tradition behind her. The free dance of Jeanne Ronsay appeared closer to a theatrical procedure committed to the

---

[36] Fernand Divoire, *Pour la danse* (Saxe, Paris, 1935), p. 101.

* Roger Dabert: born in 1928; a dancer (studied classical dance with Olga Preobrajenska and modern with Raymonde Lombardin), mime artist and actor. Also an author and historian. Currently technical and pedagogical adviser at the Ministry of Youth and Sports (classical and contemporary dance).

[37] Pierre Thiriot, 'In mémoriam Jeanne Ronsay', *Toute la danse* (June 1953).

exploration of new paths, however, and Georges Pomiès was later to fulfil the same role, for the same reasons, in collaboration with Copeau's heirs, Gaston Baty in particular. Jeanne Ronsay studied with Raymond Duncan also, and she may have found through him an extension of her early emotions. Her future lay in an entirely different direction, however.

Like many others at this time, she was fascinated by the East. She was commissioned to create an Oriental ballet for the 1925 Exhibition of Decorative Arts, which was to be performed on the steps of the Grand Palais (a similar image of the East as that represented by Griffiths's films and Ruth St-Denis, to the strains of Delibes's music). It was at this exhibition that she met Uday Shankar, and through this young Indian, as handsome as a god, a different image of the East began to take shape in her mind. The relationship that ensued as a result of this meeting was both a social and a professional one, for, with Uday Shankar, Jeanne Ronsay and some of her pupils developed a deeper knowledge of Indian dance.

Jeanne Ronsay also inherited the memory of Cambodian and Ceylonese dances from the experience of Art Déco, and she studied and exploited these with her pupils. At the same time, in the Grenelle district of Paris, she observed the dances of North African immigrants, and drew from these the inspiration for her *Danses chleues*. The 1931 Colonial Exhibition opened up a wider audience to her for a time, but it was within a much more restricted circle that the majority of her essential creations were produced. Nevertheless, during this period she also set dances for the Palace company, nude dances for the stars of the music hall, and Eastern-inspired ballets for her pupils.

Some time later, a young student named Janine Charrat entered Jeanne Ronsay's class where, under her tutelage, she was to discover the East through dances and museums. She attended Djemil Anik's classes concurrently with those of Madame Egorova.

In 1940, with the outbreak of war, Jeanne Ronsay left Paris and retired from dance. She tried to build a new life in the still rural Seine-et-Oise, where she lived dedicated to nature, surrounded by pet animals. In her retreat, she wrote her memoirs and gave lessons to the local children, who appeared with some of her former pupils in a final performance. She died in 1953, after a long illness.

She described her method of working in a clear, but rather dogmatic way in a lecture given at the Archives Internationales de la Danse in 1953:

'1. *The source of the dance is the idea that appears to a person in a plastic or musical form. This is the subject that determines the purpose, and therefore the*

Plate 10 Jeanne Ronsay in *Funeral March* by Grieg: the mourner contemplates death.
Photo: Branger, Paris. © Viollet.

limits of the dance. 2. This idea must be associated as early as possible with the general line, the plan on stage ... thus creating a set of geometrical lines analogous to the stays used by a sculptor in constructing a rough outline. 3. The plastic style that is either imposed by the character of the music or chosen deliberately, and serves as a strict discipline in circumscribing the movements, should be determined straight away. 4. Up to this point, the process has been a rather cerebral, static one; the structure of the music must now be studied in order to gain an understanding of its architecture and balance, and inscribe it, without distortion, into the context of the general plan. 5. A study of the rhythmic detail, the accentuation and balance of the steps, must then be made. In order to achieve this, the dancer must somehow submit to the music, allowing it to guide him, without ever distorting it in order to repeat a lesson that has already been learned. 6. The dancer may then investigate the expression, that is, an element over and above movement, that communicates the emotion of the dancer to the mind of the spectator by means of the entire body, including the face. This may be effected only through a splitting of the personality; the dancer must be able to submit to the character he wishes to portray whilst remaining conscious of his own resources and effects. This brief study, which is inevitably rather arbitrary and incomplete, does not pretend to be a methodological type. Each dancer may, indeed must, create his own method of working according to his culture and sensibility, for art without method is nothing but a trivial amusement, and those who brave the stage have a duty to present to their audience an art that is nurtured on hard work, struggles and toil'.

Such a realistic, objective approach was uncommon in a period in which Grace and Harmony (with capital letters), and a rather vague technique were proclaimed more widely. With the benefit of hindsight, however, we may conclude that Jeanne Ronsay and her colleagues had not yet perceived that the *idea* could be associated still more closely with the body and movement, and did not require the mediation of the plastic arts or music. Unavoidable and indispensable music! What would they have done without it? Movement had not yet discovered its autonomy and specificity. But it would do so in the future!

Nyota Inyoka

(1896–1971).

Nyota did not form part of the so-called modern dance movement, but she was certainly a *creative* dancer in her own sphere. She was without doubt the most exemplary of these Oriental dancers in France, the one who left the most vivid memory, and from whom the entire dance world benefitted.

Reference has already been made to this Easternizing trend in dance in Europe and the United States in the 1920s and 30s. The East that was evoked was one that existed only in dreams, however, and was unknown to ethnologists and Orientalists. It was sometimes a shoddy

East, but sometimes a poetic East. It was indeed a dream of another world, the seduction of the exotic, but more than this, it was the dream of an indissoluble unity between body and soul, spirit and flesh, gods and men. And so it became, in the hands of certain dancers, sheer magic.

This was true in the case of Nyota Inyoka, whose exquisite beauty, purity of dance, generosity and luminosity of character aroused a sense of wonder and admiration throughout the whole of her career. She embodied this dream! *'A living jewel, an exquisite magician, a tiny golden statue, a little oasis of music'* (she was in fact very small!).

She was born of a Vendean mother, a schoolmistress by profession, and an Indian father who taught English. She was brought up in Paris in a cultured environment in which her taste and curiosity for things Oriental could flourish easily. As a young girl, she would work through her studies with passionate intensity, in order to decipher the dance she could read in Oriental statuary.

Loulou Roudanez claimed:

> *'Nyota Inyoka always wanted to dance. From an early age she was attracted by Eastern and Far Eastern culture and aesthetics. Unable to accept that her dance was only an imitation of traditional dances, however, she aimed to understand the idea of a symbol before accepting its form. In order to achieve this, she had to rediscover the creative essence of the tradition, not through its everyday routine, but in the mythological and religious legends, as well as in the sculpture, painting and architecture of India, Egypt and Assyria. Her fate was, therefore, to search, one might almost to say to fathom, the very depths of her dances. She thus stepped completely out of the conventional frame. Her dance conveys meaning; through it she attempts to express her inner life and emotions, whilst restoring life to the old ancestral traditions and seeking to reconcile them with the present time. With Nyota Inyoka we have the good fortune to rediscover dance in the form of regenerative magic'.*[38]

Nurtured on Indian (and Egyptian) literature and art, and having finally 'invented' an adequate physical technique, Nyota created her first evocations in dance, appearing in New York in 1920. In 1921 Paul Poiret launched her Paris career (and provided her costume) at the Oasis theatre and the Salon d'Automne. She achieved immediate success and was praised for her equilibrium, delicacy, strength, rhythmic complexity, and conviction. She married a Polish aristocrat around 1923 and they lived in Tahiti until the latter's premature death.

Nyota returned to Paris where she resumed her teaching and performing careers, both in France and throughout Europe. Her performances at the 1931 Colonial Exhibition scored a triumph. She appeared

---

[38] Loulou Roudanez, *Nyota Inyoka; les danseurs sortent de leurs cadres* (J. Susse, Paris, 1947).

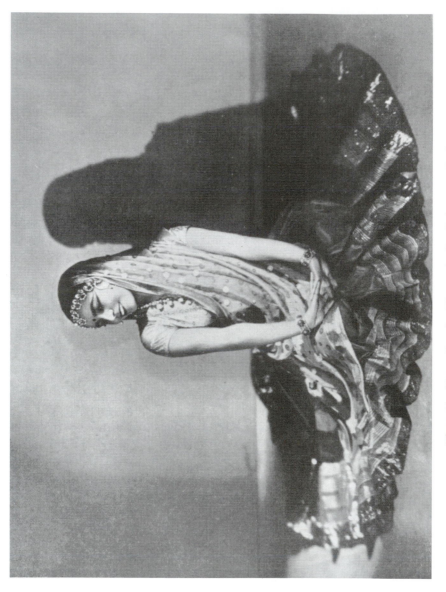

Plate 11 Nyota Inyoka. Photo: Atelier Robertson, Berlin.

in public for over twenty years, alone and with her company which consisted largely of European dancers, trained by Nyota herself, and steeped, as she was, in the philosophy and culture of India. In 1952 she took part in the Biennial Festival in Venice with a work that was commissioned as part of the 'Silk Route' exhibition. (The young Kumari Malavika was a member of her company at this time.)

Nyota Inyoka never ceased to seek to perfect herself and enter further into the worlds she had chosen to inhabit. The *Bhagavad Gita* was her bed side reading, and she was a friend of Uday and Ravi Shankar and other Indian artists and philosophers. She was a regular and valued visitor to the Musée Guimet, and throughout her life enjoyed excellent relations with learned Orientalists, musicians, plastic artists and philosophers. She also practised yoga which she taught until the end of her life. She died from a stomach cancer in 1971 at the age of seventy-five, radiant, serene and luminous to the last.

Djemil Anik

(1888–1980).

Born of a Javanese mother and a French father (a former colonial administrator), Djemil Anik was brought up in a convent in France and began her studies in classical dance with Léo Staats from the Opéra (as Janine Solane was later to do). Like the majority of dancers embarking on a career in dance at that time, she also worked briefly in the music hall before leaving for Java, where she absorbed the culture of the country in which her roots lay, and familiarized herself with the rather austere forms of Javanese and Indian dance. On her return to Europe, she gave recitals, and, like many of her fellow Oriental dancers, must have created a large number of these dances/exotic evocations, for, in 1924, she gave a programme at the Comédie des Champs-Elysées that consisted of dances from eight different countries! Until 1939 she appeared on the stages of all the popular venues of the time, such as 'Vendredis de la Danse', the Salon d'Automne and the Vieux-Colombier.

In 1935 Fernand Divoire commented on her in a passage that is quoted here not only for the light it sheds on Djemil Anik, but also for the insight it reveals into the author's own very subtle thought:

> 'In her reigns a type of discretion that is peculiar to great art. Is it a transposition? Certainly not. Rather, it is a sign of transposition. A stylization? A sign of stylization. A fluctuation of the rhythm? A pause that comes before the beat of the music? No. A sign that requires a great deal of attention if it is to be perceived. There are no "silences" in Djemil Anik's dances, but there is an imperceptible silent beat lasting only a fraction of a second which lends the

*dance an extraordinary nobility ... What a great dancer! How well she obeys
the rhythms and the inner rhythms, the movements and silences of dance'.*

Over the years her dance seems to have become purer, and doubtless
more fundamental (it should not be described as more authentic, however, since this would introduce the notion of an ethnological parameter,
which does not fit into the context of the particular poetic of these
dancers). She was indeed considered a force to be reckoned with in dance
circles, and one very interesting aspect of her work lay in her creative
initiatives, for although she will no doubt be remembered by posterity
primarily as an Oriental dancer, she also created her own personal dances
and was the first to use the new ondes Martenot.

She enjoyed a long career in teaching, concentrating mainly on
classical dance after the war, since few people at that time appeared to
have been interested in Oriental dance and the particular disciplines with
which she was involved.

It is tempting to reflect upon the similarities between these two
women, Nyota Inyoka and Djemil Anik, both half-French, half-Oriental
by birth, both held in high esteem by their public, and greatly loved and
appreciated by their pupils, both regarded as receptacles of wisdom, and
both surviving to a great age, lucid and dynamic to the last.

Uday Shankar

(Text written in collaboration with *Roger Dabert*.)
(Uday Shankar cannot be counted legitimately amongst the immigrant
dancers who settled in France, for, like the Sakharoffs, he neither
remained there for long nor showed any particular inclination to put
down roots. Nevertheless, he was a frequent and much appreciated
visitor to France, and left an undeniable mark on the country.)

Born in Bengal in 1902, Shankar studied painting initially, as
many pioneers of new dance had done, and forged a personal style
derived from his vision of Indian plastic arts, painting and sculpture, and
the folk dances of Bengal. Indeed, Uday Shankar's work has often been
compared by purists with that of other dancers who showed greater
concern than he to observe the purity of their source. He was, nevertheless, if not the only promoter, at least the reformer of the latent taste for
Indian dances, the deep-rooted tradition of which he was to study later.

He made his début in Anna Pavlova's company, for whom he set
Rhada and Krishna and *The Frescoes of Arjanta* in 1923, and in 1925 he took
part in the Exhibition of Decorative Arts in Paris. He founded a company
of Indian dancers and musicians who performed his choreography in

an exquisitely tasteful, if ethnologically impure manner. He later became a great friend of Jeanne Ronsay, the pupils of whom blended into the Indian company until they became completely absorbed. Two of these, Michelle Damour, and Simkie in particular, became Uday Shankar's regular partners and accompanied him on his tours until the end. It is piquant to note that in 1932 he participated in a week-long festival of dance held in New York, in which he was billed alongside Mary Wigman and Vicente Escudero! Around 1940 the Indian government invited him to open a school in Benares, where he remained for the rest of his life, teaching and carrying out research. Agnes de Mille remarked of him in *L'Âme de la danse:*

> *'He was without doubt the first Asiatic to attempt to express contemporary themes and movements in a traditional language, and thus arrive at modernism without ever becoming Westernized'.*[39]

Raden Mas Jodjana

Born c. 1870 in Java, Indonesia, died c. 1960 in France.

As a prince at the court of Jodjakarta in Java, he was brought up in the purest tradition of theatrical dance. He later studied in Holland, eventually becoming a very famous actor and dancer, and was one of the first to introduce the theatrical art of his country to the West. He began to attract attention in Paris in the 1920s, and performed there regularly, greatly acclaimed for the power and elegance of his sober, ritualistic dance, and his strong stage presence. He enjoyed a world wide reputation as a teacher, and had an important influence on many modern dancers in all countries.

He married a Dutch dancer whom he introduced to Javanese art and dance. Over and above this traditional art, they based their later work on an investigation of the fundamental laws of movement, which were applicable not only to dance but also to dramatic performance. Their work, which united both spiritual asceticism and a rigorous observation of neuro-motor mechanisms, may be seen as lying within the domain of therapy, and may be compared with contemporary research into those domains that prepare the body for the acquisition of 'techniques', such as relaxation, ideokinesis, and numerous other methods frequently inspired by Far Eastern philosophies.

After living in Holland, the Jodjanas settled in the French Pyrenees, and their home radiated with artistic as much as pedagogical activity.

---

[39] Agnes de Mille, *L'Âme de la Danse* (Golden Press, New York, 1963 – and Flammarion, 1964), p. 164.

Plate 12   Raden Mas Jodjana. Photo: Atelier Robertson, Berlin.

Raden Mas Jodjana appeared with his wife and son Roemalaseilan, until well into his old age. In 1957, at the age of ninety-two, he made one of his last public appearances at the Atelier de la Danse where, impressive to the last, he danced and taught 'Living Traditions' and 'Universal Principles of Movement'.

In this context it would be appropriate to mention a number of other dancers who, either by birth or adoption, may be classed as Oriental or exotic, and who performed widely in Paris in the pre-war period, settling there in some cases. These include the Kurd Leila Bederkhan, whose dances in Kurdish and Persian styles were much acclaimed; the Japanese dancers Toshi Komori, Ashida, Marsuyama, Rikuhei Umemoto, and the great Yeichi Nimura; Vanah Yami, who was of uncertain racial origin, but who nevertheless created some Oriental compositions; and gave frequent performances. She created Florent Schmitt's *La Tragédie de Salomé*. And finally, the Persian dancers Nahide and Medjid Rezvani, who were said to be of the highest calibre.

CONCLUSION

Thus it was, to pursue our initial metaphor, that French soil became prepared for new ploughing. Considering our chronicle thus far, we must indeed admit that our land did not experience the same spontaneous generation, the same degree of genius, as occurred elsewhere, in America, Switzerland and Germany, for example. In spite of this, French soil made itself so welcoming that the work of these foreign geniuses was eventually able to take root there, and, alongside these, new shoots began to spring up, inspired to work all the more ardently as the land became more fertile.

PART II

1930–1939

The Tilling Years

CHRONOLOGY

Dates	Events in France	Events abroad	Contemporary culture in France
1930	French troops evacuate the Rhineland.	Primo de Ribeira resigns. Collectivization and anti-Kulak drive in the U.S.S.R.	Costes and Bellmonte cross the North Atlantic from east to west.
1931	Paul Doumer elected president of the Republic.	Failure of the Kreditanstalt in Vienna. Devaluation of the pound.	Colonial exhibition in Paris.
1932	Assassination of Paul Doumer. Victory of the Left in the parliamentary elections.	12 million unemployed in the United States. Great Britain abandons free trade. Roosevelt elected president of the United States.	Louis-Ferdinand Céline publishes *Voyage au bout de la nuit*. Jules Romains, *Les Hommes de bonne volonté*. François Mauriac, *Le Noeud de vipères*. René Clair directs *A nous, la liberté*. Choreography competition: *The Green Table* by Kurt Jooss.
1933	Creation of the National Lottery.	Hitler appointed chancellor. Establishment of the New Deal.	André Malraux writes *La Condition humaine*. Louis Jouvet creates *Intermezzo* by Jean Giraudoux.

Dates	Events in France	Events abroad	Contemporary culture
			Jacques Becker directs *14 Juillet*. The Archives Internationales de la Danse regularly programme 'modern' dancers.
1934	Death of Stavisky. Anti-parliamentary demonstrations in Paris. Assassination of the Yugoslavian king in Marseilles.	'Night of the long knives' in Germany. Death of Hindenburg. Assassination of Dollfuss, chancellor of Austria. The U.S.S.R. adheres to The League of Nations. Numerous political assassinations in the U.S.S.R.	Alain, one of the three founders of the Anti-fascist League. Jean Cocteau stages *La Machine infernale*.
1935	Pierre Laval administers a policy of deflation.	The Saar votes for restoration of German control. Italian aggression in Ethiopia.	Jean Giraudoux writes *La Guerre de Troie n'aura pas lieu*.
1936	Victory of the Popular Front, granting paid holidays and a 40-hour week to all workers.	Olympic Games in Berlin. Outbreak of the Spanish civil war.	Georges Bernanos writes *Journal d'un curé de Campagne*.
1937	Downfall of minister Blum. Creation of the S.N.C.F. (French National Railways).	Purges in the Soviet army.	International exhibition in Paris. Marcel Carné directs *Drôle de drame*.

DATES	EVENTS IN FRANCE	EVENTS ABROAD	CONTEMPORARY CULTURE
			Pablo Picasso exhibits *Guernica*.
1938		Anschluss. Trials in the U.S.S.R. Racial laws in Italy. Munich conference.	Jean Cocteau stages *Les Parents terribles*. Marcel Carné directs *Hôtel du Nord*. Charles Trenet and Mistinguett score a hit in the music hall.
1939	War declared.	Czechoslovakia invaded by Germany. End of the Spanish civil war. Signing of the German-Soviet pact. Invasion and partition of Poland by the U.S.S.R. and Germany.	Saint-Exupéry writes *Terre des hommes*. Jean Giraudoux writes *Ondine*.

On re-reading the history and the sidelights on the history of this decade, what turmoil may be seen! With hindsight, its progress appears much clearer; at the time it was fraught with paradoxes and ambiguities. These were difficult and savage years for Europe, as for the entire world, along with grand and courageous projects and the perverse effects to which these have constantly given rise throughout history: power struggles, intrigues, scandals, mistakes, claims, hopes and disappointments.

This period was characterized by the rise of totalitarianisms: Stalin; Mussolini; Hitler; Franco; Chiang. These went hand in hand with poverty and unemployment.

In France the accession to power of the Popular Front (the Left Party) brought about deep-seated changes in society, both morally through a new awareness, and materially through the obvious improvement in working conditions: increased social security; paid holidays, a virtual revolution in mores; reduced working hours; pensions. Nevertheless, the economic and political crisis continued to weigh heavily on the people of France. State finances were frequently in jeopardy, devaluation gave way to strikes and bargaining to base actions, with consequences that are all too well known: moral and material weakness, and a country caught unaware in the face of the German invasion.

During this same decade, French culture flourished and was even resplendent. This was the age of great theatre in the hands of the celebrated cartel, Charles Dullin, Gaston Baty, Louis Jouvet and Georges Pitoëff. The young Jean-Louis Barrault was also beginning to make a name for himself with Cervantes's *Numance* and *Tandis que j'agonise*.

It was the golden age of French cinema too, with Duvivier and Carné amongst others. Both theatre and cinema were typically French in the way they united poetry, vigour and tenderness with a certain elegance of style. Gide, Malraux, Mauriac Montherlant, Saint-Exupéry and Claudel were the most appreciated writers, whilst composers such as Darius Milhaud, Olivier Messiaen and André Jolivet were held in no less esteem.

The spirit blew about with unquestionable force. This was a time of great artists and great works, whose renown and popularity show no signs of fading with the passage of time. Our view of this period might betray a certain nostalgia, as if, beneath the surface, there lay an awareness of the gradual disappearance of certain ideals, such as the valorization of quality and a life of the spirit.

Dance: from the Ground-Breaking to the Ploughing of the Land

The dividing line between the 1920s and 1930s is an arbitrary but convenient one. There was, of course, an important, but progressive line of evolution, and those influences and tendencies that were emphasized in the preceding chapter remain valid throughout the present one. Nevertheless, new dance began to stride out with increasing confidence and emerge from those veils that had complacently blurred its contours. Thanks to the experimenting of certain pioneers, it gradually became independent of music and literature, and revealed its own specific properties. It began to take root in France and developed through the work of native dancers and choreographers.

The influence of Isadorism was a little less pervasive; a more or less Dalcrozian form of eurhythmics had, on the other hand, acquired more and more status and was practised by a whole population of children and young women in private dance classes or school settings. I am still referring to what lay outside classical dance. Ballet was also widely practised, by an increasing number of children in private dance classes. Dance gradually permeated educational projects and moral habits, thanks to eurhythmics, to be sure, but the majority of parents and teachers continued to prefer classical dance, based as it was on secular tradition, to new dance forms which would nevertheless be more suited to amateur practice. In this context, we must refer once more to the Popard schools and other forms of harmonic gymnastics mentioned earlier.

The Dalcroze school, from which came a large number of practitioners teaching in France, changed somewhat in style and orientation during this decade. We must recall that Dalcroze's point of departure was *musical education through movement*. The Dalcroze institute in Hellerau was about to change its perspective, however, to one in which the training it offered became more closely adapted to dance; advanced gymnastics was practised there also. The great Austrian dancer, choreographer and teacher, Rosalia Chladek, became director of the institute in 1930, after having been a pupil there from 1921 to 1924, and then a teacher. Hellerau-Laxenburg rose to be one of the foremost centres of modern dance in this period, radiating an approach and skill of immense value, and many European dancers flocked to study there.

Returning to France, a number of important figures who had defected from classical dance were also to play a significant role in the second half of the decade, the most notable of whom were Janine Solane and Jean Serry. Although both of these continued to rely to a certain degree on the classical tradition, they had the tremendous merit of bringing dance to a wider audience and of raising an awareness in the cultural milieu during these and the succeeding years, that dance might be a true expression of man. The innovative pedagogical work of the independent dancer, Marguerite Bougai, is also worth mentioning.

A consequence of the Nazi persecutions was the arrival in France of foreign artists who, finding shelter, settled there. Some French dancers went to study in Germany and other Central European locations, thus establishing a new and extremely fruitful graft. The two principal German sources were, of course, Laban and Mary Wigman.

Mary Wigman

Laban was sufficiently referred to in the preceding chapter; Wigman's influence is perhaps a little more difficult to determine in that her teaching left a more subtle and universal mark. One cannot draw from her work easily recognisable stylistic mannerisms and *method*, but rather an authenticity of language, a fullness and intensity of body expression and form, and a specificity of material and language expressed most notably through the use of space.

Musically inclined, and discovering dance relatively late, she received her earliest training in movement with Dalcroze in Dresden at the age of twenty-five. This somewhat rigid method served only to exacerbate her desire to find her own personal language, however, and the second stage in her education came through her contact with the group of expressionist artists known as Die Brücke, especially the painter, Emil Nolde. She found in their violence and exalted, dynamic power, an approach that lay close to her own nascent aspirations. Nolde directed her towards Laban, with whom she worked for several years, sharing in his spiritual and formal discoveries.

She later turned to painters once again for her artistic nourishment, first to the Munich-based group Der Blaue Reiter, which included Kandinsky and Franz Marc, and then to the Zurich-based Dadaists, that group of revolutionary, iconoclastic artists from diverse disciplines, to which Arp, Janko and Tzara belonged. Through a process of skillful deconstruction, they sought to invest these fragments of language, reconstituted at random, with poetic meaning. Dance and gesture clearly could play a role in this procedure.

Mary Wigman was then ready to go out into the world alone, independent and autonomous. She created her first dances and productions, set up her first groups, made her first tours, and enjoyed huge success. She crystallized the obsession of the youth of this still shattered and feverish country in 1920, with 'Ausdruckstanz' (expressionist dance), and *Tanzgymnastik*, which was practised fervently by thousands of

Plate 13   Mary Wigman, *Russian Dance*. Photo: Charlotte Rudolf, Dresden.

followers. Wigman opened her first school in Dresden, and later established a network of schools in other towns.

Mary Wigman then became involved in both stage work and teaching. A prolific choreographer (she has more than thirty solo cycles and as many ensemble pieces to her name), she toured extensively throughout Europe, inspiring many imitators, and in 1931, 1932 and 1933 she toured the U.S.A., scoring great triumphs. Her pupil Hanya Holm remained there and succeeded in integrating 'Wigmanian' dance into the American artistic scene.

All this was achieved in the first half of the decade before she was black-listed by the Nazi government, her school put under surveillance, and her art decreed 'degenerate'. After several years of relative retirement, a more or less enforced stay in the Russian zone in Leipzig, and a number of sudden turns of fortune, the post-war period saw her settle in Berlin. As before, her school attracted dancers from all over the world and she created her last great works: *Alceste, Orphée, Carmina Burana* and *Le Sacre du printemps*. Her final years were extremely difficult ones as she was consumed with ill-health and blindness; nevertheless, she displayed exemplary courage until the very end.

What was Mary Wigman's unique contribution to dance and to French dance in particular? The French critics of the period held her in rather poor esteem, as we will see, and it was only through the intervention of intermediaries, first in the 1930s and then in the 1950s, that the 'Wigmanian spirit' began to spread. It remained somewhat underground at first, for, clearly, it was necessary for a second generation of French dancers, themselves nurtured on this spirit either at first or second hand, to integrate it into their own work before they could communicate it to others.

This spirit may perhaps be said to consist of a *fusion* of passion and reason, freedom and strictness, and a fullness of being and gesture with the most searching awareness. She also had effected a return to sources, paying careful heed to every inner impulse and movement, but she went further than Laban, for example, in the analysis and application of the numerous variations and developments to which the elements of choreographic language may be subjected, and which had previously been used in arbitrary or instinctive ways.

With her acute sense of theatre and exceptionally powerful presence, she freed dance from its dependence upon music, turned space into a symbolic and dramatic entity, and enabled *movement* to achieve its expressive and functional independence. Her teaching was a perfect illustration of the fusion referred to above.

Mary Wigman in Paris in 1931

Mary Wigman came to Paris in 1931, where she danced at the Théâtre des Champs-Elysées, and gave a lecture on the philosophy of dance at the Sorbonne. She met with a definitely restrained reception, however, and in 1970 she wrote to Walter Sorell (who had interviewed her with a view to writing a biography):

> 'I would gladly give you all the information about the Philosophy of Dance. But is there such a thing at all? Certainly not from the viewpoint of dancers, who, if at all, think in quite different terms. In May 1931 I danced in the Théâtre des Champs-Elysées for the first time and, shortly before my performance, I had to deliver a speech on La Philosophie de la danse – and to top everything – in French. What an excursion into anxiety!!! Unfortunately, the manuscript of this lecture has been lost, otherwise I would send it to you'.[1]

In 1935 Fernand Divoire claimed:

> 'Mary Wigman is a "great fellow"; a real "somebody". This must be acknowledged before anything. I have seen her close up: her eyes are clear, her hair a deep golden colour, her face as though burned up; she has the very look of intelligence; a simple yet profound nobility; a sweet yet melancholy tone of voice. To judge Mary Wigman on her method and theories, or the analysis of her movements alone, would be to fail to understand her. We find in her a certain quality that surpasses all theories, nationality, intelligence and forms of dance. What is this quality? We may call it soul, an invisible crowd that envelops her, giving her best dances a superhuman, but never divine, feeling, repercussions that fill the audience with respect ... Mary Wigman's contribution is difficult to evaluate from the reactions of several of her critics. Nothing could be more true than to say that she creates a strange atmosphere that can upset some people, and please others; but nothing could be further from the truth to say that she possesses that heavy, baroque, macabre, sadistic Germanism that is so displeasing to French sensibilities. Mary Wigman is a kind of magician who can impose on the public a certain rhythm, an obsession, the colour of a feeling ... Yes, Mary Wigman is someone very great and noble who may err, who may appear to build an extraordinary construction outside of our own values, but before whom we must nevertheless bow down.
> We may indeed feel fortunate to have experienced the greatness of her dances, which concede nothing to facile charm or brevity, but are, rather, vast compositions in which paroxysms alternate with choreographic silences. Can Mary Wigman be classed simply as a dancer? She creates the invisible'.[2]

Divoire's text, which must be carefully restored to its original context, seems to me to display an undoubted degree of intuition and accuracy of

---

[1] Mary Wigman, letter to Walter Sorrell, cited in Walter Sorrell, *The Mary Wigman Book* (Wesleyan University Press, USA, 1975), p. 141.

[2] Fernand Divoire, *Pour la danse* (Saxe, Paris, 1935), p. 197.

judgement in the face of the Wigman phenomenon. Representing the opposite camp, as it were, may be quoted the great critic and exegetist of dance, André Lévinson, who fiercely defended a kind of dance that conformed closely, from every point of view, to certain aesthetic canons of a more academic and classical nature. On this same occasion of Mary Wigman's 1931 performance at the Théâtre des Champs-Elysées, he wrote in the cultural events journal *Comedia*:

> *'Zealous, but imprudent propaganda, proclaiming Mlle Mary Wigman the greatest modern dancer in the world, has done this German artist a great disservice in the eyes of the Parisian public. If this is so, they might indeed wonder what the world was coming to. So great is the discrepancy between the image of her created by such a slogan and the reality, that many sceptics might have believed that there was some kind of hoax. They would have been wrong; Mlle Wigman's reputation in her own country had been immense; it was falling rapidly into decline when a fruitful tour of the United States came at just the right moment to restore her deflated prestige. Mary Wigman is (or was and still remains) truly famous: and this is what is most astonishing about this whole affair. For there is a risk that what might appear to the naturally smart French as an encroachment is the result of a kind of collective illusion, a phenomenon of nervous and moral ill-being characteristic of post-war Germany, that may spread like an infection to other countries, as we have seen, with the help of a demagogic attitude, for Mlle Wigman is very talkative.*
>
> *This oratorically exaggerated and psychologically inflated art deceiving us with regard to the poorness of content and form, by extreme gestures and affectation of violence, reflects the convulsed, delirious condition known as expressionism that lately spread throughout Germany. Mlle Wigman is a belated representative of this frenzied aesthetic and plastic vaticinations within the context of a now wiser, more realistic and authoritarian Reich ... Mlle Wigman's style thus conveys a crisis in German sensuality and thought, a state of mind that is no longer relevant today, but which nevertheless explains the influence on her compatriots of this dark woman, neither young nor beautiful, of Mongolian appearance, of mannish ways, half Pythia, half Fury, performing pantomines with sharp, clashing movements, thrown out, slung with an unjustified expenditure of energy, with the accents savagely stamped by her bare feet, and increasingly loud gong strokes. Her eclectic style, depending not only on Isadora's "reforms", but also on Dalcroze's research, Asiatic choreography, dancing dervishes and Javanese serimpis, is a rough and scant adaptation of these different kinds of saltation. Some three years ago I wrote in connection with her Le Sacre [Die Feier], a secular mystery play officiated by the Dresden mystagogue and her sect, of "the savage's tam-tam adopted by civilized barbarity". But the very exaltation of this art that sought to be incantatory fell into a less overheated atmosphere, and what seemed to me at the time to be intense was, in that performance at the Théâtre des Champs-Elysées, nothing more than affectation. The climate of the Ile-de-France is not favourably disposed towards such disturbing spells. We must nonetheless be grateful to the organizers of this performance for a lesson that, although without doubt long overdue (imagine, if Dr. Caligari were shown for the first time in 1931 ...), was*

both explicit and conclusive: they helped to destroy an aesthetic superstition and dissipate a cloud'.[3]

The quotation of this article *in extenso* seemed to me to be worthwhile since it provides a good illustration of the state of mind of a number of the French intelligentsia at this time, and it is obvious that such an attitude did not make for an understanding, and therefore growth, of this new conception of dance. For good measure, and in order to summarize those aspects of Wigman's dance that were truly novel and augured well for the future, I will quote another writer of this period, the American John Martin, one of the shrewdest commentators who ever lived, who wrote in 1939 in his admirable book *Introduction to the Dance:*

> 'With Wigman the dance stands for the first time fully revealed in its own stature; it is not storytelling or pantomine or moving sculpture or design in space or acrobatic virtuosity or musical illustration, but dance alone, an autonomous art exemplifying fully the ideals of modernism in its attainment of abstraction and in its utilization of the resources of its materials efficiently and with authority. This brings it, however, to no state of finality, no crystallization, but only to a complete statement of its selfhood, to a revelation of the principles upon which it may enlarge its borders and deepen its awareness of itself... Heretofore it had been at best simply an emanation from a person ... Now it assumed the dimensions of an objective work of art, for it had entered into the full-bodied world of relationships. Instead of being lyric – that is, consisting of a simple outpouring of feeling of whatever depth and intensity – it became dramatic, presenting the conflict between two forces ... With Wigman's sense of space as a tangible symbol of universal forces, the dancer is supplied with something outside himself, which he may shape to his purposes, and toward which he may direct his emotional reactions so that even his most subjective experiences become visibly externalized'.[4]

The Wave from Central Europe

Mary Wigman's first great pupils, Harald Kreutzberg, Hanya Holm, Yvonne Georgi, Max Terpis, Gret Palucca and Margaret Wallmann, must be recalled, for their shining example took the new kind of dance in its autonomy, humanity and rationality to all four corners of the earth. There was some contact between these dancers and France, but very little, since France did not have the reputation of being particularly welcoming with regard to German dance, as Wigman's own case proved. Nevertheless, her influence penetrated the French dance world through the intervention of others.

---

[3] André Lévinson, in *Comedia* (31 May 1931).

[4] John Martin, *Introduction to the Dance* (Dance Horizons, USA, 1965), pp. 235, 231–32.

Plate 14 Gret Palucca. Photo: Suse Byk, Berlin.

More effective than the actual but fleeting presence of Wigman herself in Paris at this time was the presence of dancers who had worked with her. These dancers were either foreigners who had settled and made their career in Paris, the most notable of whom were Doryta Brown, Julia Marcus and Mila Cirul, or native French dancers, such as Hélène Carlut. Amongst other dancers who acknowledged having been influenced by her were Marguerite Bougai, Hilde Peerbohm and, later, Anne Gardon.

A number of dancers encountered in the previous decade, in addition to some new arrivals, also made their careers in France, especially as teachers:

- in the Isadorian line, these were Odic Kintzel, Malkowski, Lisa Duncan and Ellen Tels;
- in the Dalcrozian line, Anita Wiskemann, Doris Halphen, Marianne Pontan, Marie Kummer, Jacqueline Chaumont and many others;
- in the line of descent from Elisabeth Duncan, Yvonne Berge;
- in the Laban line, Dussia Bereska and Marie-Louise van Veen.

Jean Weidt, Heinz Finkel and Ludolf Schild arrived later from Germany, and will be discussed in detail below, for their influence was enormous.

All these artists who implanted themselves in French soil served as rich fertilizers, or even grafts, and succeeded, each in his or her own way, in integrating themselves more or less into French cultural life. They took root there and affected a kind of interpenetration of different cultures and ways of thinking that opened up new horizons to practitioners and informed members of the public alike. These dancers were the earliest pioneers of what was beginning, and would continue even in the 1950s and 60s, to be known in France as 'expressive' dance, a translation of the German '*Ausdrückstanz*' ...

The younger generation of French dancers who, in the 1930s, were seeking new directions in the theatre of movement and dance could, from then on, find more substantial nourishment in their own country. A great deal of work had been achieved, often in the dark, in preparation for the future.

It must be recalled once again that at that time the conditions of work and opportunities for bringing dance to the public at large were in no way comparable with those of today. The activities of these dancers could only be practised and made known within a relatively limited sphere: that of their own studios; amongst their pupils; and in the few organizations that programmed dance. It would have needed enormous resources in order to bring dance to the wider public who were, in any case, no doubt not yet ready to appreciate or understand this new and bold theatrical language that threw into question the whole conception of human behaviour and the very function of dance itself.

It was inevitable that our brave pioneers should remain somewhat on the fringe of the 'establishment', and it could be that the influence they radiated upon a nucleus of disciples was all the more powerful because of the feeble impact they had upon the public at large. If we are to judge by various documents of the period, it would appear that some of these groups and schools took on an appearance of coteries, of cliques, even of sects.

And today? Perhaps we are more fickle! For reasons of economy and a growing market, the majority of dance studios are rented, anonymous, functional, a situation which is clearly far less favourable to a gathering of the faithful. In the past, every practitioner who could had a studio of his own: his shell or temple, and at times his theatre. Such a large number of strongly personalized places may have had the twofold consequence of affirming the individuality (real or imagined) of each one and of creating a withdrawal into the self.

Tours and Venues

Alongside the artistic and pedagogical work of certain individuals, dance in France in the 1930s was characterized by a few of large-scale collaborative ventures, most notably the Archives Internationales de la Danse, which contributed to its development. The initiative already undertaken in the previous decade by Jacques Hébertot, known as the 'Vendredis de la Danse' may be considered similarly as a collective venture.

Some of the venues frequented by the merely curious and experts alike, in addition to the studios of those who, either from choice or by force of circumstance, performed only in their own surroundings, included:

- the Archives Internationales de la Danse, whose mansion in Passy comprised a small but extremely adequate hall where performers could show their work without expenditure (as in the case of the 'Vendredis de la Danse'), and a whole range of new dance from all over the world could be seen paraded before one's very eyes;
- the Vieux-Colombier continued to programme dance on a regular basis.

Over and above the theatres, clubs and institutions mentioned above, the Mutualité, 'Journal' and Iéna halls together with the Pigalle theatre were all receptive to dance.

Some of the dancers who appeared regularly in Paris, willingly breaking their tours there and opening up new horizons, included:

- modern dancers (excluding native French dancers and those immigrants to France already mentioned) such as Harald Kreutzberg, the Sakharoffs, Rosalia Chladek and her group from Hellerau-Laxenburg, Birgit Akesson (a pupil of Wigman from Sweden), Agnes de Mille (from the U.S.A.), Trudi Schoop, and Charlotte Bara (from Switzerland);
- the Spanish dancers la Argentina, la Argentinita, Teresina and Vicente Escudero;
- classical companies such as the Ballets de Monte Carlo (1932), Colonel de Basil's Ballets Russes (1936) – following in the footsteps of Diaghilev, the Ballets 33 (directed by Kochno who went on to direct the Ballets des Champs-Elysées after the war, the Ballets de la Jeunesse (Egorova, 1937) and, of course, the Opéra, where Lifar reigned supreme, and the Opéra Comique;
- Asiatic dancers such as the Cambodian and Bali ballets, the great Javanese dancer Raden Mas Jodjana who settled in France after the war, the Persians Nahidé and Madjid Rezvani, Nyota Inyoka and Djemil Anik, Uday Shankar and the Japanese Toshi Komiri, Yeichi Nimura and Rikukei Umemoto;
- the stars of the music hall such as Josephine Baker and the Americans Albertina Rasch, the Charleston Babies and the Blackbirds.

Dance lovers certainly had plenty to get their teeth into, but most likely preferred styles that they could place in clearly defined categories such as classical, Spanish or Indian. The new, unclassifiable dance remained without exception a curiosity.

A Diversity of Tendencies

To conclude this cursory glance of the 1930s, it is interesting to quote the opinion of another contemporary writer, the anatomist and designer Paul Bellugue. We owe to him a fine work entitled *Introduction à l'étude de la forme humaine*, which is closely related to dance, from which Bellugue draws many of his examples. He enjoyed a close association with the team at the Archives Internationales de la Danse, and in the November 1935 issue of the review, devoted to the different techniques of dance taught in France, he expressed a number of relevant thoughts by way of a commentary on a series of lecture-demonstrations that had just been given at the A.I.D. Certain paragraphs of Bellugue's text clearly reveal the state of mind of a public aware of current practices:

> '*Now, in view of the diversity of modern tendencies, it is perfectly justifiable to wonder whether today there is such a thing as a style of dance.*
>
> *If it is acknowledged that there is no dance without style, that is, without definite, permanent and transmissible choreographic form, it could be said that, with the exception of ancient and exotic dances, "Dance" as such does not exist today, only a throng of dancers. Style and aesthetic must not be confused. Duncanian or expressionistic movements may correspond to an aesthetic, therefore, but they do not amount to a style. Their artistic principle is the complete opposite of this, for it aims to give each individual the means to express his own ephemeral personality. Style, like language, is a social phenomenon, and has its own grammar and syntax, that is, a system of conventions familiar to everyone. Style is a collective, and in a way, anonymous phenomenon. Heaven only knows that this is not the case in contemporary works!*
>
> *There is no small number of different trends – classical, Duncanian, Dalcrozian eurhythmic, culturist, expressionist – some of which have grown rapidly whilst others have become less prominent, and we find ourselves tossed about in their back-wash. Indeed, this chaos is not dissimilar to that which occurred in the Renaissance. Thus the application of the elemental movements of man, found today in gymnastics and on the sports ground, is to dance what the application of Greek roots were to literature; they enriched choreographic language immensely. Expressionism is a kind of Reformation, and, like the latter, is German in origin and spirit. As in the fifteenth and sixteenth centuries, a new world is created within and around Man. Our culture no longer seeks to raise us above ourselves, but to realize the potential within ourselves. The dancer aims to be a complete athlete, and likes to imagine movement emanating from the centre of his body.*
>
> *But we must not be deceived, for contemporary choreographic art only appears to be anarchic, and its disorder is simply the result of the search for a new order. Do we not already see the nymphs and bacchantes of our gymnasia and sports grounds mounting the stage with a more restrained step. Indeed, they are beginning to suspect that the stage is not a sports field, that a complete athlete does not necessarily make a good dancer, and even that a theatrical dancer is a highly specialized kind of athlete, and they are coming round to the belief that whilst Dance may be healthy, health does not necessarily result from dance. Meanwhile, principal ballerinas, having discarded the rigidity of their corsets, are beginning to question why they dance as if they are still wearing them. Certain expressionist dancers may be attracted to ballet, whilst other, classical ones, recognize the eloquence of expressionism; a eurhythmic dancer may practise toe-dancing. An Oriental feel at home in turn-out, and an acrobat take up the castanets.*
>
> *What confusion, one might say. Yes, but a fusion too! And this is perhaps the most significant point to emerge from the lecture-demonstrations given at the A.I.D. These divergencies, although still very pronounced, are without doubt beginning to disappear. A new choreographic language is in the process of being born, a language that is awaiting its Malherbe and its Boileau but has only got*

as far as Rabelais and Ronsard. These lecture-demonstrations will indeed have helped its development by pointing out the weakness of certain forms, the strength of certain traditions, and the promises of things to come. The more the contacts between technicians are increased, and in particular, the wider the field of inquiry becomes, the more chance there will be that a style of dance will take shape. Will originality have any less value when all the teachers have pilfered each others' steps?

It would, nevertheless, be unfortunate if dancers limited their curiosity and concern to technique alone. Dance can expect nothing from each of these special techniques individually, whether saltatory, musical, pictorial or whatever, but it has everything to gain from their co-ordination. Dance is greater than the dancer. Mother of all the arts, she cannot exist without her children. If one would only listen, after the dancers, to the architects of the hall and stage, the scene-painters, the lighting engineers, the costumiers, the librettists and musicians, and the great directors too, then the investigation would be complete and the laws of a required aesthetic might proceed from a better knowledge of realities.

Does this mean that we are approaching a classical era? I do not believe this to be the case and we must continue to enjoy the clouds of darkness and flashes of lightening of an uneasy romanticism for many years to come. It has a charm of its own nevertheless and corresponds so well to the troubles that we endure on every front! But to indulge in it would be disastrous and we must congratulate the Archives Internationales de la Danse on having sought to guide us away from to it ... by opening our eyes to it all the more clearly'.[5]

THE ACTORS

New actors were beginning to come on to the scene, or, pursuing the metaphor underlying this book, new 'farmers' entered the field and began to plough it, whilst some of the older ones had disappeared. The climate was unsettled; there were violent storms and a cyclone gathered overhead. The whole scene was beginning to change.

At this point in our chronicle we must recall that characters are discussed only from the moment at which they begin to make a name for themselves in France either as choreographers, performers or teachers, irrespective of their age or previous career. Thus appear in this landscape a large number of people whom we have encountered already, who continue to develop their old methods, or invent new ones, in addition to those at the start of their careers who were looking for new directions, certain institutions, and those refugees or immigrants who brought new influences to bear on the art.

---

[5] Paul Bellugue, 'La Technique de la danse' (special issue of the *Revue des Archives Internationales de la Danse* (du Trianon, Paris), (November 1935), p. 41.

INSTITUTIONS

The Archives Internationales de la Danse

In 1932 the Swedish patron Rolf de Maré, who had founded and financed
the Ballets Suédois which broke up in 1924, went on to establish and
provide funding for the Archives Internationales de la Danse (A.I.D.),
which was to become the home or melting-pot for all forms of dance.
Widely receptive to current trends, this institution enabled the new dance
to establish itself, and a number of initiatives: performances, lectures,
exhibitions, and writings, contributed to launching it into orbit. The
A.I.D. was to a certain extent exemplary, and played a leading role
during the years preceding and following the war.

I would like to quote here the prefatory remarks to the first issue
of the *Revue des Archives Internationales de la Danse*, which was published
in 1932 and continued to appear regularly until 1937, for better than any
summary or exegesis, it takes account of the context and most significant
aims of this enterprise.

'The Archives Internationales de la Danse ... founded in memory of the
Ballets Suédois and their choreographer Jean Börlin.

When the Ballets Suédois ceased to exist, their prestigious promoter
M. Rolf de Maré continued to take an interest in dance simply as an inquisitive
and enthusiastic observer. But he was not content to take a back seat for long,
and he began to dream of creating a vast organization devoted entirely to the art
of dance in all forms and from all times. Thus it was that the Archives
Internationales de la Danse came into being.

It never ceases to be a constant source of amazement that, unlike the arts
of painting, sculpture, literature and music that have formed part of the
imperishable heritage and means of expression of man throughout the centuries,
one of the most ancient art forms practised by humanity, the art of movement,
was not until this time endowed with any institution, either private or official,
in which a record of its various stages of evolution and development could be
found.

But whereas these other arts received extensive documentation through
museums, libraries and archives, dance had nothing to call its own. Everything
concerning it was scattered in all directions. It was not ignored, simply
neglected. It needed a cathedral and had only many tiny chapels into which one
could not venture without a guide.

The Archives Internationales de la Danse was to fill this gap. Deciding
upon its constitution, assembling the most suitable collaborators to carry out the
work that would be entrusted to it, drawing up the statutes, all this was mere
child's play to a man of action like Rolf de Maré.

The first point to be debated was the location of the head office of this new international institution. There were strong arguments in favour of Paris, and nobody doubted Rolf de Maré's own preference. A magnetic centre of artistic endeavours, retaining all the prestige of its legendary past, receptive to new ideas, vibrant and enthusiastic, the great city deserved this gift. For none better than those who came from the four corners of the earth to rekindle their creative flame, or to remind themselves of the fearless struggles carried out in the past in the name of some dearly held idea or fiercely defended work, were in a better position to appreciate its value.

Something new had to be done, everything created afresh. Only the boldest solutions would do in this case. New premises were obtained at 6, rue Vital in Passy. The organizers knew exactly what they wanted. Plans were laid down and every detail of installation foreseen. It simply remained to act.

This was no small task. The A.I.D., true to its programme of assembling and centralizing everything concerning dance, had to consider the creation of a museum of dance, a library, a documentation and information office, and archive service, a sociological and ethnological department, a lecture theatre and an exhibition hall.

This general statement of the aims and of the different sections set up in order to achieve these, will enable a greater understanding of the working of the A.I.D. as it has developed since.

It must be remembered first and foremost that the Archives Internationales de la Danse are open to everyone, irrespective of status, and that not only artists, professionals or specialists will be able to consult the studies and research that may be useful to them, but that anyone who, for whatever reason, is interested in dance, will have free access. It is with the aim of helping them in the task they have assigned themselves, and guiding them in the preferences they show, that the following different sections have been created.

Firstly, there will be a museum which already possesses a number of important exhibits, some of which are notoriously rare. In this museum, models of sets and costumes, paintings, drawings and photographs relating to dancers of former times or certain of their works will be on display. Various items of memorabilia and relics of the late great stars will also be on view. In summary, this museum will contain all the documentation relating to dance throughout the ages.

It will be judiciously completed by an exhibition hall in which all the artefacts relating to a specific period of choreographic history, or to the artistic activity of the great servants of dance, will be periodically on display. Thus we may now announce that an exhibition dedicated to the memory of the recently deceased great dancer, Anna Pavlova, will be held.

Moreover, anyone who has had to deal with choreographic creations will be aware of the constant difficulty of making an informed choice of the collaborators and materials (models, orchestral scores, etc.) they will need for their realization. The aim of the documentation and information office will be to help these people avoid such wearisome tasks, and it will serve as a point of connection between artists, endeavouring to give them all the useful information they require. The strict contact maintained between this office and all the other services provided by the Archives will, moreover, enable it to offer those wishing to use it, immediate guidance on the quickest and best way of carrying out their plans.

As for the library, this will assemble all the books, magazines and journals from every country and in every language, that are relevant to dance, and will centralize in a number of card-indexes a complete bibliography relating to the art of movement.

It goes without saying that this huge task cannot be accomplished in a day. It will take many years, and the international profile of the documentation will add to its size.

This library will in turn be completed by a cinematographic section that will house a collection of films relating to dance, and a music section consisting of ballet scores classified according to an extremely simple system.

A lecture theatre, put free of charge at the disposal of those invited to speak on dance, has been equipped in such a way as to lend itself either to a theatrical demonstration or the projection of instructional or documentary films. The task of the sociological and ethnological department will be not only to collect the huge body of material on dance belonging to primitive peoples, but also to carry out a comparative study from a sociological point of view, and encourage aesthetic, psychological and physiological studies on dance and movement.

The sociological and ethnological department will work in strict collaboration with the other sections of the Archives. Its books and card-indexes will be housed in the library, and it will put on exhibitions, show films and organize lectures. It will be a scientific section first and foremost, but its artistic work will be no less effective, for it will also serve to inspire choreographers, dancers and painters by bringing new art forms derived from exotic peoples to their attention.

The Archives Internationales de la Danse will organize annual competitions which will take an entirely unprecedented form, the repercussions of which promise to be of the utmost interest. Readers will find in the article devoted to them in this review, all the details concerning those competitions that will take place shortly at the Théâtre des Champs-Elysées. The enthusiasm that their announcement has aroused amongst dance professionals, artists and public alike, proves that the time is ripe for their introduction and that the need to galvanize the art of dance by allowing it the greatest and most effective freedom of expression has been recognized by everyone.

The Archives Internationales de la Danse thus exists and functions in the most minutely detailed and enlightened of ways, and all the cog-wheels in its mechanism have been described above.

One very important point that remains to be emphasized is that this institution does not seek to make any sort of profit. This must be repeated constantly: all the services listed above are available free of charge to everyone. And of all the realizations that have just been mentioned, this is the one that permits the greatest understanding of what the creation of the Archives Internationales de la Danse represents for choreographers the world over.'[6]

This text leaves the reader somewhat amazed for various reasons – if only because of the promotional aspect of this formidable project, in which all available resources would be set to work. In fact, the programme that was announced took shape effectively in stages: the premises, the library, the lectures and performances, and the exhibitions.

Rolf de Maré's dream (which was interrupted by the war and lasted only a few years) nevertheless still remains a dream today, in spite of the sundry local and isolated efforts of the last decades. It is undeniable that the structure of the enterprise provided by the A.I.D. was admirable, due largely to the willingness and enthusiasm of certain people, and exploited the full potential of the technical possibilities of the time. It is all the more unfortunate to note that this episode in the history of dance has faded into the past and remains in the memory or knowledge of very few people today.

Another striking point is that the services offered by the A.I.D. were free of charge. Where did the organization's undoubtedly colossal funding come from during the years of its existence? Quite simply from the personal fortune of Rolf de Maré, a very rich diamond dealer and true patron of the arts.

The Archives Internationales de la Danse was thus launched in 1932, with a flourish marked by this famous first choreography competition that took place in July, and in which the most notable participants were Pierre Conté and Janine Solane (France), Gertrud Bodenweiser and Rosalia Chladek (Austria), Lubov Egorova, Boris Kniaseff, Trudi Schoop, and, from Germany, Oskar Schlemmer with his *Triadic Ballet* and Kurt Jooss and the Folkwangsbühne of Essen. The reader may recall that Jooss took first prize with *The Green Table*, a true masterpiece, evidenced by its continued presence over fifty years later in the repertoire of several companies in the world today. Its subject, both contemporary and timeless, its bare yet human and theatrical language, all had a staggering impact. The second prize was awarded to Rosalia Chladek, and the third to Trudi Schoop from Switzerland.

It would be interesting to compare the works presented at this first competition in 1932 with those that appeared fifteen years later at

---

[6] *Revue des Archives Internationales de la Danse* (du Trianon, Paris), 1932, p. 2.

the third, held in Copenhagen in the summer of 1947. These works, by choreographers based in France, England, Central Europe and Scandinavia, were all marked to some extent by the events of the recent world war. Modern dance had taken its course, but we may wonder, with all due allowance, whether the works that appeared in 1947 were of an equally revolutionary nature as those of 1932. Jooss's *Green Table* and Schlemmer's *Triadic Ballet* were truly surprising for their time. In 1947, too, there was indeed a significant number of extremely forceful, original and climactic works that demonstrated total mastery of content, vocabulary and structure. The first prize was awarded to Jean Weidt and his Ballet des Arts de Paris for *La Cellule*, in which Françoise (then Michaud) and Dominique Dupuy danced. We will have occasion to return to this work and to Weidt himself later in this book. Weidt was one of those young Germans who settled in France in the 1930s. Also worthy of note were the contributions of the Swedes Birgit Culberg, *The Three Musketeers*, and Ivo Cramer, *The Message*, which related the life of Christ in scenes full of sobre grandeur and theatrical effect. The Parisian dancers taking part included Mila Cirul, Madika and Léone Mail.

There should be chronicled in detail the activities of the A.I.D. since its creation, documenting all the events that took place, the people who frequented it and the ideas that were in circulation; for such a chronicle would indeed represent the progress of dance during some twenty years. Beyond the fact that my purpose here is not to write a book exclusively about the Archives (although this would be an exciting project), it has often proved quite difficult to assemble the necessary data, for the holdings of the Archives were variously transferred, even dispersed, during the 1950s. By means of a chronology of the major events, however, it is possible to gain some idea of the breadth and eclecticism of the enterprise, and of the leading role it played at a time when modern dance was in its bubbling adolescence.

Let us return, therefore, to an account of some of the events that took place in Paris in the elegant, discreet and functional setting of that charming house on the rue Vital in Passy, which called for a certain *quality* of approach. We must mention first of all the Russian writer and historian, Pierre Tugal, educated in philosophy at the University of Heidelberg, to whom Rolf de Maré entrusted the management of the A.I.D., together with the direction of the museum, from the very start. Tugal thus took the helm of this delicate and complex ship, assumed responsibility for the editing of the review, and writing articles and other works on dance; he attended every choreographic event in Paris and elsewhere, and was acquainted with dancers from every walk of life.

Moreover, he had an eye for recognizing and encouraging young talents, many of whom remain indebted to him for having set them on the first rung of the ladder.

Here follows a catalogue, albeit brief and incomplete, of the events that took place under the aegis of the A.I.D., either in the premises on the rue Vital or in other locations:

1932 – Founding of the Archives Internationales de la Danse by Rolf de Maré, in memory of the Swedish choreographer Jean Börlin. Curator: Pierre Tugal.

– Publication of the quarterly *Revue des Archives Internationales de la Danse* (40 pages; 24 × 30 format; glazed paper, illustrated. Price: 10 francs; circulation unknown).

– First choreography competition held at the Théâtre des Champs-Elysées in Paris. First prize awarded to Kurt Jooss for *The Green Table*. Second prize to Rosalia Chladek.

1933–34 – Exhibition: 'About Anna Pavlova'.

– Lectures and performances by, amongst others: Marie-Louise van Veen (Laban method), Marie Kummer (Dalcroze), Dr. Mensendieck, Lisa Duncan and Georges Pomiès, and Clotilde and Alexander Sakharoff (with a commentary by Émile Vuillermoz).

1935 – Exhibition: 'Dance in Painting and Sculpture from Bosch to Degas' (this appears to have been a particularly sumptuous event).

– Exhibition: 'Festivals of Yesterday and Today'.

– Lecture series of thirty-four lecture-demonstrations on 'The Techniques of Dance', aiming to demonstrate the methods used in dance teaching. A special issue of the *Revue* was devoted to an account of these sessions, and it is not without interest to note the styles and genres of dance discussed: classical, eurhythmic, plastic, harmonic, acrobatic, expressionist, exotic and folk.

In the introductory text to this series, the author 'P.B.' (Paul Bellugue?) wrote:

> *'It is not a question of individual recitals or competitions between different schools, but simply of the demonstration of methods of dance teaching in use today, explained by the teachers themselves and illustrated by their collaborators or a group of pupils.*
>
> *For the purpose of these demonstrations was to reveal the variety of trends, to confront the theories and to see if, from this vast panorama, a single, more pronounced characteristic might stand out that would enable us to predict the future. To this end, representatives of the various schools of both French and*

foreign origin, currently teaching in Paris, were invited. Thirty-four different teachers presented the theory and practice of their pedagogical systems. These lecture-demonstrations were further commented on by a listener'.[7]

Amongst the teachers who took part were:

- Odic Kintzel, Ellen Tels (Delsarte method), Mila Cirul (Wigman method), Judith Marcus (Wigman method), Rudolf von Laban (Hellerau-Laxenburg group), Yvonne Redgis, Dussia Bereska (Laban), Doryta Brown (Wigman), Heinz Finkel and Jeanne Ronsay;
- Eurhythmic dance: Jacqueline Chaumont, Odette Courtiade, Irène Popard and Andrée Joly;
- Oriental dance: Djemil Anik, Madjid Rezvani and Rao.

1936 – Exhibition: 'Old French Dances'.

- Receptions involving various personalities.
- Lectures by the dance critic Pierre Michaut.
- Performances by Leila Bederkhan, Nyota Inyoka, etc.

1937 – The *Revue* ceased publication as a result of its excessively high costs.

- Various activities continued to take place during these years, about which little record is left.

1939 – Javanese dancers, Nana de Herrera and Hans Rijbeck. Films about dance.

- The Second World War. Pierre Tugal took refuge in the South, where he became involved in the activities of a mutual aid association for artists and intellectuals. Underground performances.
- Activities concerning dance came to a halt at the A.I.D., but Sunday concerts featuring contemporary music continued to take place. Certain measures allowed the protection of the collection and library during these difficult years.

1945 – End of the war. Rolf de Maré, now in Stockholm, organized a second international choreography competition. However, it was still too soon after the war for many countries to be able to take part. The main participants were choreographers from Scandinavian countries together with refugees from the Baltic countries and Poland. The first prize was awarded to the German dancer Julian Algo for *Visions*; Algo was a pupil of Volinine and Laban, who had

---

[7] *Ibid.* (November 1935), p. 2.

been greatly appreciated in Northern Europe before the war, and was ballet-master at the Stockholm Opera.

1946 – Pierre Tugal returned to Paris. Rolf de Maré, whose health was failing, relinquished the direction of the A.I.D. A new team comprising Pierre Tugal, Baird Hastings, Bethsabée de Rothschild, Alexandre Berlant, Edmond Linval, Thomas d'Erlanger de Rosen and Jeanne Ranay undertook the reorganization of activities.

1947 – 'Exhibition: Ballet in Great Britain' (photographs).

– Third international choreography competition held in Copenhagen and presided over by Rolf de Maré. This competition undoubtedly occurred at a key moment, enabling the changes in dance that took place after the war in various countries, notably France, England, Finland, Holland, Sweden, Czechoslovakia and Denmark, to be seen. This competition was without doubt the first large-scale *professional* meeting of the post-war period.

– The lecture-demonstrations were resumed as before, the list of participating artists demonstrating a high degree of eclecticism. These included:

– the junior classes of the Paris Opéra, presented by Paulette Dynalix;

– songs and dances of Spain, by Maria Kousnetzoff and a flamenco group;

– the Ballets de Monte Carlo, presented by George Reymon;

– Marie-Louise Didion from the Opéra;

– mystic dance by Josette and Renée Foatelli;

– 'Inspiration and Technique', a lecture by Janine Charrat, with the co-operation of Ethéry Pagava and Youly Algaroff;

– 'Ballet in the U.S.A.', presented by George Skibine, with Hightower, Tallchief and Eglevsky;

– June Fryer and Jacqueline Robinson (Wigman-trained).

1948 – Exhibition: 'The Salon of Dance and Movement'.

– 'Mardis de la Danse' performances: Jeanne Ranay, director of the Ethnology Department, presented amongst other dancers: Nyota Inyoka and her company, Filemon and Emilia Torrés (Spain), Pedro Ortus (Chile), Simkie (India), Mrinalini Sarabhai (India), Indra Kamadojo (Indonesia), José Torrés, José Greco, Susanna and José.

Other dancers from various disciplines, including Mila Cirul, Madika, Olga Stens, Jerome Andrews, Françoise Michaud (Dupuy), Nadia Sauvage,

Srimati Usha, Judite and Felix Fibisch (hassidic dances), Jacqueline Robin-son, continued to perform there until the dissolution of the Archives.

In effect, the A.I.D. became, in a series of successive steps, the Centre International de Documentation pour la Danse. Pierre Tugal and the critic Ferdinando Reyna were its first organizers and directors. The premises in the rue Vital were sold, the holdings of the archives and library passed into other hands, with one part, in particular, going to the library at the Opéra. On Tugal's death in 1964, the C.I.D.D.* was administered by a team consisting of Alexandre Berlant, Pierre Goron, Jeanne Ronsay, André Schaikewitch, Alexandre Tansman and others.

This chronicle, however sketchy and incomplete, clearly indicates the importance of this institution. It was indeed of international standing, but its location in Paris and the presence of French nationals meant that it was French dance that benefitted from it the most! Here was a particular time and place, the coming together of people and initiatives, the trace of this phenomenon living on in a few memories, but it must not be allowed to sink into greater oblivion.

THE LABAN AND WIGMAN LINES

We come now to three particularly important figures in the story of dance in France, for it was perhaps these three Laban pupils, Weidt, Finkel and Schild, who established their powerful vision of modern dance most firmly in France. Their pupils and descendants in turn became the key workers in the ensuing post-war phase of development of modern dance in France. Their work and memory live on in part due to their own intrinsic qualities, but also because their descendants are still working amongst us today. The same may be said of Mila Cirul, whose active presence in France was to continue for several decades. Historically, she might be seen as forming part of the Wigman line, but the eclecticism of her style and the individuality of her personality and teaching in fact place her amongst that heterogeneous group of 'unclassifiables'.

---

* The Centre International de Documentation pour la Danse must not be confused with the Conseil International de la Danse since their abbreviations are identical. The latter is dependent upon U.N.E.S.C.O., and its official organ of representation in France is the Comité Français de la Danse.

Jean Weidt *by Dominique Dupuy*

This chapter on Jean Weidt does not claim to be an exhaustive biography. More specifically it aims at providing an account of the periods he spent in France both before and after the war, through my own childhood and adolescent memories.

Setting out from Hamburg, where he was born in 1904, Jean Weidt arrived in Paris (via Berlin and Moscow) for the first time in 1934. A pupil of Sigurd Leeder (principal collaborator of Kurt Jooss for many years, since the start of their careers with Laban), Weidt had already established himself as a dancer and choreographer. Fleeing from a political régime to which he was fiercely opposed, he had, in his own words, *'ein emigrant geworden'* (become an emigrant).

As a communist, he became acquainted with the party leaders in Paris and took part in numerous popular festivals. He appeared in two films, *L'Apprenti sorcier* by Paul Dukas and Ravel's *Boléro*, and frequented contemporary activist theatrical circles, becoming friendly with Mouloudji, Jean-Louis Barrault and the Blin brothers, Roger and Noël. Noël Blin later became a member of the Ballets 37, the company that Weidt went on to establish through sheer tenacity, and which appeared at the Atelier theatre, amongst others, at Dullin's invitation.

My father, R. L. Dupuy, met Weidt at the home of the photographer Maywald, an exile like himself. Dreaming of dance, my father grew fascinated by the man and his work, who reminded him in so many respects of another dancer, Georges Pomiès, who had also filled him with enthusiasm. Passing through the Cour Carrée of the Louvre one day, my father noticed a masked man who was dancing and passing his hat round. Recognizing him as Jean Weidt, he tapped him on the shoulder, saying: *'There is no need for you to do that any longer. I want to help you ... '.* Weidt thus entered our house, where he taught my father, my two elder brothers and myself the basic principles of German dance. This initiation was threatened at one point by Weidt's departure to Moscow for several months. Upon my father's request, he found us a replacement in Doryta Brown, a student of Wigman and one of the great figures in German dance, who had settled in France. Somewhere within me a seed was sown ...

One of the last appearances of the Ballets 38 in Paris took place in March 1939, in the Salle Pleyel. The programme included a new version of *Parade* by Cocteau-Satie. In the programme, Jean Cocteau wrote:

> *'With Weidt a miracle takes place. This apostle of rhythm makes dancers. A couple of young manual workers, a man and a woman, who did not dance before, begin to dance and perform acrobatic exercises. No sooner work allows time for rest than Weidt's pupils eagerly seek it in dance. Dance frees them and ceases*

to be a toil. Overwhelmed with fatigue, they begin to relax, and willingly, lovingly grow exhausted. I know of nothing more noble or more youthful or extraordinary than this little company who leap and turn and stamp upon the dreams they should experience whilst sleeping'.

Amongst the cast lists may be found the names of Eydé Fortin, who reappeared after the war in the Ballets des Arts, Nguyen Van Tu, an elegant dancer of Indo-Chinese origin, who unfortunately was unable to resume his place after the war, and became a weaver, providing fabric for the company's costumes. We may also note the names of Noël Blin and Gaby Morey, my mother's sister, who established a link for me between Weidt's two French periods.

At the outbreak of the war, Jean Weidt was considered a stateless person, arrested and deported to a labour camp in North Africa where he was held in particularly harsh conditions. He escaped from this situation by enlisting in the English army with whom he fought, first in North Africa and then in Italy.

We heard from him regularly. His morale remained high, and he occupied his mind with thoughts of dance, of his return after the war and of the company he would establish. He continued to train so as not to lose his body strength and technique.

My aunt Gaby Morey, who, like my parents, had taken refuge in Bourgogne, pursued her musical studies and set up a choral society. We were able to profit from her experience of movement with Weidt and, for a time, I found with her the logical continuation of the work I had already begun. She put on performances in which I took part, and, on seeing my enthusiasm, she declared: *'Dominique will take up acting'*, to which my father replied: *'before anything he will work with Weidt'*. The die was cast.

After his demobilization in the spring of 1946, Weidt returned to Paris with the firm intention of settling there. With the money he had carefully saved from his pay, he was able to establish the Ballets des Arts. Charles Dullin put a studio in the Sarah-Bernhardt theatre at his disposal (the very studio that Diaghilev had arranged for Nijinsky in 1909). It was there that, the seed having germinated within me, I had sought Weidt again in order to join his company, and had met for the first time an exceptionally talented dancer called Françoise Michaud.

Jean-Louis Barrault, who had recently installed himself in the Marigny theatre, engaged Weidt for *Baptiste*, the pantomime taken from Carné's film *Les Enfants du Paradis*. Weidt played the part of the 'old clothes dealer', created by Etienne Decroux, appearing beside Marcel Marceau and Madeleine Renaud.

Weidt assembled a little company that included, besides Françoise and myself, Paul Dougnac (a pupil of Finkel), Mathilde Roelens (a pupil of Decroux), Suzy April and Nicole Chauchet (pupils of Hélène Carlut in Lyons), Pierre Sonnier, René Pélikan, Rudolphe Roelens and Eydé Fortin. The work of the company, which consisted of daily classes taught by Weidt himself, and rehearsals, took place during the late afternoon, thus enabling each member to work during the day or evening. The rest of the day was spent by Weidt and two or three others, of whom Françoise was one, giving classes, making costumes and taking steps to ensure the survival of the group.

By November, an initial programme was ready, and the Ballets des Arts appeared for the first time at the Marigny theatre at the invitation of Barrault. There were three works: a revival of *La Victime*, and two new creations, *Ode après l'orage* and *Abel et ses frères*, each treating the theme of war in a different way.

La Victime tells of the influence of war on the destiny of the individual, and the theme of conflict between the Montagues and Capulets is transposed to two enemy Indian tribes. *Ode* concerns the annihilation of the family by war, and the rebirth of the survivors through faith, whilst in *Abel et ses frères* it is the effect of war on the entire community, half black, half white, that is evoked. In the first part, blacks and whites fight side by side against an imaginary enemy; in the second, the prisoners return, and the work deals with the toil and struggle of those who are left and the joy that breaks out on the restoration of peace.

At the beginning of 1947, the company had just completed an extensive tour of occupied Germany. Pierre Tugal, director of the Archives Internationales de la Danse, encouraged Weidt to take part in the international choreography competition that was to take place in Copenhagen in June.

So, Jean Weidt began work on a new creation, *La Cellule*, that we rehearsed throughout the spring. Émile Damais, a pupil of Honegger, was commissioned to write the music, which was scored for piano and a new instrument that was beginning to attract attention, the ondes Martenot. We set off for Copenhagen as if on some great adventure. There was little money, and living conditions during the days we spent there were particularly difficult. But once again Weidt knew how to maintain the morale of his dancers, and our faith and ardour were rewarded when *La Cellule* took first prize ahead of a whole pleiad of choreographers from all over Europe, some of whom, such as Birgit Cullberg and Ivo Cramer amongst others, have since made a name for themselves.

Even today *La Cellule* is hailed as a 'masterpiece' by the great Swedish critic, Bengt Haeger, director of the museum of dance in Stockholm, who was present at the time. It is a premonitory work, just as that by Jooss was before the war. (The striking relationship between the

1932 and 1947 competitions is that both were won by Germans with equally premonitory works, although in different circumstances.)

La Cellule was in the line of action ballets that denounced modern life, as *The Green Table* had succeeded in doing; it is not the collective act of society that is stigmatized here, however, but man's position within that society – man seized by the throat by a life of drudgery from which there is no escape, even in dream. Going beyond actual form, which was indeed ahead of its time, with the introduction of flash-backs, of theatre within theatre, props etc., the hero, Andréas Kragler is a Kafkaesque hero. The work anticipates Ionesco, and even Beckett. (Andréas Kragler, personified by Weidt, is thrown into a prison cell. He falls asleep and in his dreams relives part of his life, in particular the events (a murder) that led to his imprisonment. Ghosts and masked, hallucinating characters return between each scene like a *leitmotiv* of anguish).

The return to Paris came as a bitter disappointment. Acclaimed in Copenhagen, where he was recognized as a creator of the first rank, able to take over from those whom the war had forced into inactivity, Weidt found no echo to his success. His triumph remained unacknowledged, his talent unrecognized, and apart from a short article by his fervent admirer O'Brady, this exceptional event was not reported in any newspaper.

At first, Weidt reacted positively and, following a tour to the Netherlands, decided to relaunch his company in a Paris season once more; for this event he chose the superb Pigalle theatre, which was later destroyed. The repertoire of the company was enriched by three new works, *Nuages, Les Villageois* and *La Ballade d'Ana et Olivier*, which, together with the existing repertoire of the company, enabled them to present a different programme every evening.

The title of Maurice Brillant's article in *L'Aurore*, 'Les danseurs existentialistes de Weidt crient, hurlent, trépignent, remuent, mais ne dansent pas' ('Weidt's existentialist dancers shout, scream, stamp and shake, but they do not dance') provides ample illustration of the tone of the critics' reaction. 'Existentialist dancers!' This is indeed an insult of rank prejudice, for Weidt's conceptions had nothing to do with the philosophy of Sartre that was just beginning to dawn.

Fortunately, this did not prevent a large public following. The theatrical and popular cultural associations, such as E.P.J.D., T.E.C., T.E.T., and the Maison de la Pensée Française, rose to collaborate. Neither did it prevent the company from being invited to make another lengthy tour of occupied Germany, and not only of the area under French tutelage, but also of the allies. Thus the company was able to perform its repertoire over several days in Berlin. It was there that Weidt had the

Plate 15 Jean Weidt. Photo: Picto.

opportunity to renew relations with his old friends and received an invitation to work at the Komische Oper in East Berlin.

On his return to Paris, Weidt bade us farewell, sick at heart, for France was his first love (it should be noted that throughout his life, Weidt referred to himself as *Jean* Weidt), and the Ballets des Arts, his child. He left Paris for Berlin in 1949, never to set foot there again.

In Jean Weidt, Paris lost an artist of the greatest calibre. First and foremost a dancer of exceptional talent, he was also a choreographer, and, above all, a master of theatre art. He conceived every aspect of his ballets himself: libretto, production and choreography. He was a builder and his choreographies were constructed with the utmost care.

Above all, he was a man of faith. He held fast to a strong and lofty ideal of modern dance, which was, to him, not entertainment, but a weapon of combat, artistic combat, primarily against the omnipresent and omnipotent academicism as well as against the ordinary incorrigible balletomania that reigned supreme.

This combat represented, moreover, an ideological and political struggle against a society whose vices he denounced, whilst magnifying the virtues of the individual. Dance for Weidt was an exacting art: at the most difficult times in his life (and he certainly knew a few!), he always kept his body in training, and for this show of respect, dance rewarded him well.

Dance, combat and life were one and the same thing to him.

With Weidt gone, the company broke up and its members dispersed. The fire was not extinguished, however. Weidt's departure was the logical consequence of the Parisian dance world's complete refusal to accept modern dance. It was not long after, we should recall, that the arrival of Martha Graham at the Théâtre des Champs-Elysées caused such an outcry that the slighted Graham vowed to strike Paris off her itinerary of European tours, a resolution to which she held firm for twenty years.

Paris was for the time being entirely under the reign of Serge Lifar at the Opéra and the 'Parisianism' of the Ballets des Champs-Elysées. Modern dance's day had not yet arrived (and was far from doing so); it survived only on the fringe, in schools, and hardly existed at all at the level of creation.

Weidt had a different perspective. He had no interest in creating a school as such, but sought to establish modern dance through a direct appeal to the public, in a form that spoke in a contemporary language. He realized that the ways of ordinary balletomania would not serve his purpose and that he had to look elsewhere. As a result of this came his search for a theatrical dance, and his fight to impose a company.

This was the path that Françoise Michaud and I followed in 1950, when, renouncing the experiences we had each undergone individually since the demise of the Ballets des Arts, we decided to combine forces for better or worse and take up the torch once more. This marked the start of a new battle.

We were unconcerned with quarrels between different schools and styles, over and above fashions. We worked towards the pure and simple theatrical qualities of dance; we sought a new public outside traditional circuits and balletomania. Remaining faithful to Weidt's spirit, we retained the sense of a dance dedicated to combat, testimony and passion, fully aware that we needed to dance the world of today for the public of tomorrow.

Heinz Finkel

German (probably born in Hamburg c. 1908 of a German father and Russian mother; died in 1946).

He was educated in dance at the Laban School in Hamburg, and also received a training in music and the graphic arts.

Around 1930 he was a member of the ballet companies of various theatres, becoming a member of the Vereinigten Bühne in Duisburg/ Bochum in 1931. He gave recitals of his own dances which brought him several very positive reactions, amongst which was the advice and encouragement of Kreutzberg. But what struck both critics and public alike, was the fact that he composed his own musical accompaniments to his dances (after their choreographic composition) and made his own costumes.

In 1932 he gave a recital in Berlin; the critic of the review *Der Tanz* of 17 April 1932 described him as a *'self-made dancer'*. But was he really an autodidact? He was certainly an eclectic, for his work revealed the multiple influences of classical, Bauhaus, exotic and expressionist dance, within a programme of highly contrasted dances. The clarity of construction and purpose of his works nevertheless received much praise.

He emigrated to Paris in 1933 around the same time as Jean Weidt. It is interesting to note that the specialist German press of the time continued to report news of these artists who left (indeed, were forced to leave) their country because they were either Jews or communists: of Jooss, in particular, who left Germany as a show of solidarity with his Jewish dancers and settled in England, as did Sigurd Leeder; Julian Algo for Stockholm, whilst Weidt, Finkel and Julia Marcus all settled in Paris. They were then reported in the foreign news as if they had always lived in these countries – a somewhat ambiguous attitude.

Plate 16 Heinz Finkel in Paris in 1939.

Heinz Finkel was welcomed to Paris initially by Dussia Bereska, who had directed the Laban School there for several years, and he worked within this organization as a dancer, accompanist and choreographer. In 1935 he appeared at the Archives Internationales de la Danse within the framework of a series of lecture-demonstrations on the techniques of dance. He advocated the independence of dance from music (but allowed for an accompaniment after the initial stage of choreographic composition was complete), distinguished between a freer method for the teaching of amateurs and a more rigorously exacting one for professionals, and impressed his audience with an 'abstract' dance, *Construction*, which had already brought him praise in Berlin.

In the same year he gave a successful solo recital in the hall of the École Normale de Musique (a favourite venue amongst dancers). Our old friend Divoire did not appear to appreciate it, however, describing Finkel as *'an unfortunate young man, reserved and sickly looking, with a grimacing intellectuality'*.

Heinz Finkel began to teach also, in the Laban tradition, naturally, and amongst his pupils was the young German dancer, Ludolf Schild, also a refugee.

Then war broke out and for four years Finkel was forced to live under cover, and thus in a state of choreographic inactivity. When the Liberation came, he reassembled his pupils with the aim of resuming creative activity. Amongst these was Raymonde Lombardin who became his partner. He later formed a group of dancers and instrumentalists (piano, flute, xylophone, percussion) and staged a performance which was given in the Sarah-Bernhardt theatre and other locations.

Death overcame him in 1946, shortly after having resumed his activities, and before he had time to train many pupils or create many works. He was in the process of preparing a tour to Germany with Raymonde Lombardin when he died. Raymonde directed his group for a time. She said of him: *'He expressed himself in dance with rigour and mastery of both a bodily and an emotional nature'*. She believed that, like Weidt, he had been influenced by French culture in the sense that he *'freed himself from an elementary sentimentalism and a leaning towards a priori ideas'*.

Ludolf Schild *by Lise Brunel**

Note: When Ludolf Schild settled in Paris, he gallicized his name to Loudolf Child in an attempt to integrate himself into his adopted country.

---

*See p. 418.

The original spelling has now been restored officially in accordance with the wishes of his family. In documents of the time, therefore, he would be found under the letter 'C'.
German (1913–1949)

An expressionist dancer of the 1930s and 40s, Ludolf Schild was, with Weidt and Finkel, one of the foremost representatives of German expressionism in France. Due to the brevity of his career, his name is all too frequently overlooked in writings on the history of dance, a lacuna that I am pleased to be able to fill, so deep was the impression he left on all of those dancers, pupils, spectators, artists and friends alike, who knew him. A human and artistic impression, a memory in which the corporal language of dance was united with the mind, and strove towards physical, emotive and intellectual globality, with an element of both sensitivity and the metaphysical that belongs only to the most exceptional beings. He was one of these.

Born in Hamburg on 12 April 1913 of a Jewish father, Ludolf Schild studied dance in a local school according to a method based on the principles of Wigman and Laban (theory, group work, technique, creativity, anatomy), and received his diploma in 1933. He danced for a time at the Hamburg Opera, before leaving Nazi Germany in order to take refuge in Paris and carry out his own research into what was known at the time as 'expressionist' dance.

He gave recitals in which he performed solo most of the time, or with his Bulgarian partner, Ludmilla Menslova, before joining the little company established by Finkel, also a German refugee. (Ludolf Schild also collaborated with Julia Marcus in 1935 on the choreography and production of a modern ballet.)

The innovatory ability and radiant presence of this *'tall, thin boy, clad in a black jersey, who beat on his drum'*, made a great impression on a young Russian therapeutist named Nadia Chipiloff, who became his wife, and assisted him throughout his career. The war took them to Algeria where, after serving in the army for a time, Schild began to reflect once more on dance, and, from 1941, he embarked upon a series of solo recitals without music, which ran parallel to his educational work with the Centre d'Éducation par Méthodes Actives courses and scout groups. Followed by his pupil Hélène Faure, costume designer Jean Aubert, and Alexandre Leupert who composed the musical scores for Schild's choreographies (*Don Quichotte* amongst others), he returned to Paris in 1945.

On Finkel's death in 1946, Schild established his own school in a little studio in the rue Lammenais, before installing himself in Studio 121 in the Salle Pleyel. He worked in conjunction with Travail et Culture and Éducation par le Jeu Dramatique (E.P.J.D.), a school of actors opened by Barrault, with Jean-Marie Conty, Mytho Bourgoin and Roger Blin amongst others, and formed a little group, of which I had the immense joy of being a member, that subsequently became his company.

His teaching, well balanced between technique, theory, the relationship with space (internal and external), rhythm (which was related to movement through the use of percussion instruments), and creativity (improvisation and composition), was complete, effective, dynamic and stimulating, and aimed to produce the unity of the individual. '*A future dancer*', he once said to me, concerning the expressivity of movement, '*does not only learn the correct functioning of his body, but strives to express his thoughts through the smallest movement*'. Exacting, precise, and humourously 'pulling our leg' in his charmingly gauche accent, he was a 'tutor', a spur to action, whose quick-wittedness enabled him to respect our own personalities and budding sense of creativity.

Studio 121 became a greenhouse for the discovery of dance, of oneself and others. It became the centre of a real passion for dance where Jacqueline Levant, one of Schild's principal collaborators, was to pursue the pedagogical activity begun by him by opening the doors of Studio 121, following his death in 1949, for courses taught by important guests such as Merce Cunningham and Helen MacGehee in 1950. Although few in number, the performances he gave between 1945 and 1948, solo in Algiers and Paris, and then with his company, the Ballets Modernes Français, seem to have aroused the interest of the small élite of contemporary critics who were sympathetic to modern dance. The importance that Schild accorded to thought and the continuity of thought (which was not unrelated to his encounter with the Javanese dancer Raden Mas Jodjana) often led him to be regarded as an intellectual – wrongly so, however, through the failure to understand its deeper motivation. He was more concerned with the type of dance he called 'absolute', which was freed from all conventions and drew on the various resources of the dancer's body in order to express itself. [Mary Wigman also spoke of 'absolute dance'(J.R.).]

In an interview of June 1946 he claimed:

> '*For my part, I am anxious above all to develop each individual in his own way to the realization of his full potential. Dance is a language that extends as much from intellectual and abstract creations as from purely expressive, human ones*'.

Already in 1945, in Algiers, the Journal *Rafales* had emphasized '*the expressive magic of the Sept figures de la vieille*', observing that '*in Schild we find a harmony and balance of gestures executed with precise and marvellous*

Plate 17   Ludolf Schild in 1945. Private collection: Lise Brunel.

musicality. This relationship creates the impression, even in extreme vivacity, of developing with the same logical rigour as a human being, starting in the spinal column, progressing to the fingertips and continuing into space'.

In *Arts* Maurice Pourchet recalled *'the picaresque and Picassoesque style of Don Quichotte, and the delicacy of its circular, clockwork movements'.* When this same work was performed in the Salle Pleyel in December 1946, the review *Paysages* described *Mouvements sphériques* as *'a circular dance that generates strange spirals, characterized by a sort of sidereal gravity'.* Two months later, in *La Vie intellectuale* of February 1947, Émile Damais described Schild's *'passionate, ardent nature, his exacting sincerity'*, and admired his *'concern for plastic expression allied to his sense of forms and colours'.*

Passion, ardour, sincerity. Schild possessed all these qualities and more besides, revealing the sensitivity of a poet shaping images with impressionist touches. F. Vezin wrote with regard to a performance organized by Travail et Culture at the Maison de la Chimie:

> *'Schild appeals as much to intuition, to the atmosphere of the work, to fantasy, silence and immobility, in his intense interpretation of Tableaux d'une exposition as in the plastic diversity of Don Quichotte. Through the infinite nobility of the postures, the style and technique, the dance of Loudolf Schild holds its place amongst the humanities' (L'Enseignement, February 1946).*

When Schild fell ill in 1947, we were preparing to tour North Africa with *Tableaux d'une exposition* in a revised version for the company. Did he know Kandinsky's work on this piece? Was he acquainted with the Bauhaus? There are so many questions that remain unanswered, for want of having asked them at the time. Struck down by cancer, he was to die on 3 June 1949, bringing to an abrupt end a career in which teaching, dance and choreography featured on an equal basis.

Glancing through the notes I took in the Studio 121 one day, Alwin Nikolaïs was struck by the intelligence of Schild's comments, his method and philosophy, a philosophy in which the dancer did not seek to show off as in classical ballet, but simply to exist.

Too young to have ever really known him, his daughter Louba follows her own path in India in a Kathakali school she created in Kerala.

(I would like to thank Nadia Schild-Chipiloff and Jacqueline Perrin-Levant for their valuable help).

[I cannot resist the desire to add a few lines to this evocation of Ludolf Schild who received me so generously at the time of my arrival in Paris in 1947. He welcomed me, penniless, into his classes, and showed such delicate concern over me . . . He was a truly exceptional person; as a teacher he knew how to inspire. Unfortunately, I was not acquainted with his work as a choreographer. (J.R.)]

Mila Cirul

Latvian (1901–1967)

Mila Cirul was born in Riga in 1901. As in the case of many other dancers, she received her first revelation of dance through Isadora. She trained initially in classical dance with Mordkin in Moscow, and then with Ellen Tels, whose teaching was imbued not only with the 'Isadorian' spirit, but also with the research of Delsarte and Meyerhold, with the latter of whom Mila also worked.

Numbering Lenin amongst her admirers following her first public appearances in Russia where she made her début, Mila pursued a career as a dancer and choreographer for several years in Austria and Germany with Ellen Tels and a little group. She met Mary Wigman in Frankfurt in 1916 and fell under her influence, along with that of Laban. She then embarked upon a period of personal research in which she attempted to free herself of everything she had learnt in order to find what she believed to be her own dance, expression and style.

After working in Berlin, where she was principal dancer at the Opera, Vienna and Hanover, she settled in Paris in 1932, where she opened a school and had an undoubted influence on a number of young dancers who were seeking a teacher in Paris who was not only an independent personality, but who also established a link with the German school. Several followers of classical dance, such as Edmond Linval, for example, experienced their first awakening to modern dance through her.

Mila Cirul was a colourful character. She never lost her Russian accent, and was distinguished by her fiery red hair, pale blue eyes set in a triangular face, milky complexion and extraordinarily supple body; she was voluble and exalted: in short, a tornado! Finally, she was very Russian: romantic and mystical.

She soon made a name for herself in Paris. The prolific critic and champion of free dance, often quoted in this book, Fernand Divoire, was one of her greatest admirers, and produced several texts and libretti for her. In 1934 she gave an enormously successful performance at the Théâtre des Champs-Elysées in which she danced her version of Richard Strauss's *Salomé*. In 1935 she showed her work at the Archives Internationales de la Danse with her sister and partner, Elia, and her pupils. She danced until the war, and even during the war, in various European cities.

Afterwards, Mila taught in Paris where she performed with her pupils.

[This was the period in which I knew her, and I have already referred to the ballet she presented in Copenhagen in 1947 at the

Plate 18   Mila Cirul, *Russisches Fragment* in 1929.

choreography competition organized by the A.I.D., in which I took part. *Le Chemin de la vie*, with a libretto by Fernand Divoire and music by Liszt (Marius Constant who had recently arrived in Paris was our pianist), related, in contrast to the implications of its title, the coming of death to various characters in a series of tableaux that included a ball, war, revolution, and lovers, culminating in an apotheosis with a procession of all these souls claimed by Death! Romanticism of the first degree, which may cause one to smile, but unquestionably theatrical and generous nevertheless! (J.R.)]

Amongst her pupils in this period were Olga Stens, who acknowledged her great debt to her, Sonia Millian and Geneviève Mallarmé. Later, Mila enjoyed fruitful relations with the new generation of dancers who came from abroad, most notably with Jerome Andrews whose deliberately romantic and baroque style resonated in a way rather like her own. She succeeded in awakening something of her own ardour and boldness in her pupils.

She left Paris in 1962, married, and settled in Nice, where she continued to work. In 1969, she returned for a while to Paris to teach the pupils of Olga Stens at the Salle Pleyel. She never ceased to keep abreast of everything that was happening in Paris. She died in Nice in 1977.

In an interview with Fernand Divoire in 1935, Mila claimed:

> *'dance is a confession of human beings facing life, revealing endless shimmerings of the soul. The body must be educated, and made to work as a tool until it attains perfection (in the same way as an instrument created by Stradivarius). When it has achieved its greatest efficiency, the soul begins to vibrate. Each dancer requires an appropriate technique, for there is no dance school capable of developing dance in all its manifestations: spiritual, emotional and intellectual. It is only on leaving school that one really begins to work effectively. Each dancer must find his own technique, the precise expression of himself, and if he is not afraid of making sacrifices, he will succeed'.*[8]

For his part, Fernand Divoire said:

> *'I have written that I love Mila Cirul because she is not perfect. Indeed, she is like a flame, a strange, supple and powerful flame, a flame that escapes all ordinary aesthetic types. Mila Cirul needs the space afforded by a vast stage so that she can develop the expansiveness of her magnificent leaps and bounds, the grandeur of her compositions, and the frantic, passionate barbarity of certain of her dances'.*[9]

---

[8] Fernand Divoire, *Pour la danse* (pp. 87, 88).

[9] *Ibid.*, p. 285.

Critics from different countries referred to her strange, feline beauty, her technique that was adapted perfectly to what she wanted to express, and the incandescent passion that emanated from her dances. Today we would call her a star.

Julia Marcus

Of German nationality, Julia Marcus was born in 1905 in Switzerland where she began her first studies in dance, initially with Madame Bienbaum, and subsequently with Suzanne Perrottet who was closely associated with the work of Rudolph von Laban. Julia Marcus also studied with Laban in Zurich and Elisabeth Duncan in Salzburg.

In 1927 she went to Dresden to work with Mary Wigman with whom she remained for several years (in the same 'group' as Margarete Wallmann). She was later employed by the Berlin Opera in the first generation of modern dancers to work within this framework and of which Mila Cirul also formed part. Julia Marcus appeared as both a choreographer and an independent soloist.

She was part Jewish and politically active, circumstances that forced her to leave Germany and settle in Paris in 1933. She was in sympathy with Marguerite Bougai, Odic Kintzel, Lisa Duncan, Bella Reine, and her compatriots, Heinz Finkel, Jean Weidt and Ludolf Schild. She *'was fortunate in being able to adapt herself'* and her original talent was quickly recognized. She specialized in a way in *'social and political parodies'* with much success. Pierre Michaut wrote in 1939 of *'the ever intelligent, captivating, spiritual and ironic Julia Marcus. Boldly pushing to the extreme without ever losing the line of a concise style, Julia Marcus's dance draws on everything: the hard worker; the young ballet girl; the pianist; the conductor; there is nothing that it does not reveal'*. In spite of these satirical themes, these sketches of real life, Julia Marcus has not been categorized as a mime artist. Her vocabulary was sufficiently transposed to remain *dance*.

In 1935 she appeared at the A.I.D., and other interesting places; she was a member of Nadia Wanger's circle, the critic and patron who did so much for dance. She met Jerome Andrews there who initiated her to the technique of Martha Graham, who was completely unknown in France at that time, and she shared a gala at the Gaîté Lyrique with him in 1936.

In 1937 Julia Marcus collaborated with Ludolf Schild in the creation of a ballet entitled *La Marche du temps* that was performed at the Pigalle Theatre. This ballet, inspired by cinema newsreels, was a humorous evocation of the events of contemporary life. The scenario was by Jean Yachec Vinot and the music by Fernando Lopes Graca. The dancers came from different backgrounds, and were brought together to form the

Compagnie des Ballets Internationaux specifically for the event. Although one of the scenes might be passed off as plagiarism of the first scene of *The Green Table*, this work nevertheless constituted an event: the collaboration of two modern choreographers on contemporary themes.

Julia Marcus worked in the theatre also, notably with Alice Cocéa. She performed at the Salon d'Automne, and gave recitals. Unlike the majority of dancers of her generation, whether immigrants or French nationals, she rarely taught, although occasionally she gave gymnastics classes, she was attracted principally to the stage. She took part in the 1933 International Dance Competition in Warsaw and was awarded a special prize for humour for her dance *Ghandi et le lion britannique* (Ruth Abramowitch, also a pupil of Wigman, won first prize and Rosalia Chladek the second). This dance seems to have been one of her most successful creations, along with *La Machine à coudre* and *Parodie de Hitler*.

In 1938 Julia Marcus married M. Tardy, a French engineer. During the early years of the war, she appeared in Paris again, both as a soloist and alongside other independent dancers of the period. A review of 1941 recalled:

> 'Julia Marcus, who is seen all too rarely, enlivened the show with short humorous comedies that are both ludicrous and shrewd, like wittily mocking sketches'.

After the war, Julia Marcus resumed contact with dance, notably at summer courses in Macolin, Montreux and Zurich in Switzerland, where Mary Wigman, Harald Kreutzberg and Rosalia Chladek all taught. These courses were historic moments, characterized by rediscoveries, confrontations, revelations and developments. Although retired from active participation in dance, Julia Marcus has never ceased to show an interest in the new directions taken by contemporary dance, applauding the work of Françoise and Dominique Dupuy in particular, and, in a different category, that of Dinah Maggie. Today, at eighty years of age, she continues to show evidence of a rare degree of tolerance and insight. She writes regularly in *Quinzaine littéraire*.

Doryta Brown

Born in the early years of the century, of half-German, half-English descent. She studied with Wigman in Dresden in the late 1920s in that first heroic cohort of pupils.

In 1931 she taught with Mary Wigman at the main school in Dresden, where she was responsible for the children's and amateurs' department, and appears to have been particularly gifted in the teaching of children. She settled in Paris around 1932, where she opened a studio, and in 1933 she took part in the performances 'les Samedis du Vieux-Colombier'. She received extremely favourable reviews in the press:

'a remarkable dancer ... a highly individual art ... a very secure and personal technique, and the most subtle feeling for rhythm' (*Liberté*, 2 February 1933).

It should be noted that she often danced in silence (perhaps inspired by Wigman's current practice).

In the famous series of illustrated lectures given at the A.I.D. in 1935, she presented one on the 'Wigman Method' with great clarity and rigour, illustrated by studies, solos and group dances with her pupils. Her dances appear to have been extremely finished on a technical as much as on an expressive and theatrical level. In 1938 she was recommended by Jean Weidt as a teacher and, as a result of this, the young Dominique Dupuy could be counted amongst her pupils. She probably collaborated with other French dancers or foreign immigrants like herself. After the war, all trace of her was lost.

Fernand Divoire described Doryta Brown as *'lively, laughing, intelligent, she retained from Mary Wigman only her technique and taste for art. The life in her breaks every mould. She reveals an impetuous sense of harmony'.*[10]

THE DALCROZE AND HELLERAU-LAXENBURG LINE

Most of those dancers who followed in the Dalcroze line of succession at the Hellerau-Laxenburg school, continued by Valeria Kratina, and later by Rosalia Chladek, possessed a solid foundation: a certain technical rigour, acquired usually through the practice of gymnastics, and a degree of musicality acquired by the study of eurhythmics.

They generally moved away from Dalcrozian techniques, as if their initial training did *not* enclose them in a system (or, indeed, on the contrary, as if they felt the need to turn their backs on it).

At this point, the beginnings of modern dance may be seen not only in Paris but also in Lyons.

---

[10] *Ibid.*, p. 116.

Anita Wiskeman *by Florence Poudru**

Of Swiss origin (1901–1953)

When Anita Wiskeman died of cancer at Easter 1953, the review *Toute la danse* was the only one to pay homage to her in a few lines. The Lyons press remained silent: Lyons had forgotten her. And yet, thirty years earlier, a young Swiss woman, her hair in a neat bun, born at the turn of the century, had settled there. Her arrival would indeed have been insignificant if she had not come from Hellerau, that temple of rhythmic dance, for, at a time when the choreographic spectacles at the Grand Théâtre were the eternal *Coppelia* and *Faust*, the importance of the event may be noted. A former pupil of Dalcroze, Anita Wiskeman had also studied at the Dorothée Günther school in Munich, one of the numerous gymnastics and 'expressionist' dance schools in Germany in that period.

She was not the first eurhythmic dancer to come to Lyons, but she was the first who was both a dancer and a teacher. The phrase 'eurhythmic movements' appeared in the daily press following her first performance in the Salle Molière on 2 December 1922. Like Duncan, she danced to music that was claimed to be impossible to dance to: Beethoven, Couperin, Bach and Wagner, and to contemporary music such as Debussy and Satie, whom she loved for their wit, De Falla, Rachmaninov, Ravel, Stravinsky, Lewis, Schmitt and Ferroud. Florent Schmitt, then director of the Conservatoire, accompanied her at the piano when she danced her version of *Salomé*, but it was more frequently Ennemond Trillat, another renowned musician, who appeared at the piano. An extremely capable musician herself, and an excellent pianist, the critics were unanimous in praising her immense musicality. One of them wrote: '*in her hands, Beethoven is neither diminished nor caricatured*'.

Wiskeman's costumes were very varied: she was particularly sensitive to colours and materials, wore white chlamys and heavy robes of coloured velvet, not forgetting the wide Arab trousers of fluid silk or the more whimsical outfits worthy of the music hall, top hat, striped waistcoat and trousers!

She was young and pretty and intelligent, and found her audience principally amongst artists and writers (one of these, Joseph Jolinon, spoke of 'Anita' with tenderness and respect), for few dancers came to see her, refusing to accept the style of dance that gave such importance to breathing. As early as 1926, one critic suggested, not without a certain daring, that she might '*teach Dalcrozian technique at the Grand-Théâtre*'.

---

*Florence Poudru, author, Professor of Dance History at the Conservatoire National Supérieur de Musique de Lyon, Doctor at University of Paris 1, Sorbonne.

As time progressed, not content with disseminating Dalcroze's ideas through her programmes, she turned towards a more personal style, notably by dancing to the poems of Verlaine recited by her actress friend. Between 1922 and 1929, she travelled throughout the Rhône-Alpes region. The press always reserved an excellent welcome for the Trillat-Wiskeman duo, and it was no coincidence that Line Trillat, the pianist's daughter, like many children of her generation, took her first steps with Anita. In the 1950s Line Trillat was to return from Hellerau-Laxenburg and establish her own school. For her own shows, Anita very quickly surrounded herself first by one, then three of her pupils, of whom Hélène Carlut was one. Sixty years later, when I was fortunate enough to meet Carlut, she spoke of this period with simplicity and passion.

At the end of the 1920s Anita Wiskeman met the Spanish painter Yacinto Salvado, who designed the masks she wore for her performance on 6 December 1929 at the Comédie des Champs-Elysées. This performance clearly fell within the category of expressionism; she danced all these ballets masked and gloved, and Fernand Divoire confessed to having waited impatiently for her to reveal her face, which was set off, in this period, by a boyish hair cut. He praised her *'solid technique – solid rather than rich'*. As for Hélion, he described her ballet *Ombre* in the following terms: *'A point on the back-cloth moves a little, very slightly: a fold in the curtain protrudes, then a few more, and a grey form appears amongst them, sliding itself forwards, freeing itself from behind the curtain, and advancing slowly and continuously, like a cloud in a grey sky'*. In Paris, Anita chose to demonstrate the tragic aspect of her talent and received a mitigated welcome from a press that was tired of the attempts of innumerable practitioners of eurhythmics.

After a short stay in the south of France, the couple left for Barcelona: this was a turning-point. Artist, wife and mother, Anita brought up her two young children whilst directing her dancing school. She danced in public, and the excellent reception she received from the Spanish press may be judged by the numerous biographical articles that appeared. The approach of the Spanish Civil War forced the entire family to return to France, however.

Between 1936 and 1939, she often left the south to teach in Lyons at the Bobenrieth Studio. From this time on, she danced chiefly for her friends; nevertheless, she reappeared in Lyons in March 1939, accompanied by Ennemond Trillat. In 1944 she became known as 'Atina' in her native town of Zurich as a result of the inspiration of a journalist who adopted the erroneous spelling of a Spanish colleague! This was her last recital.

She was indeed both a dancer and teacher, but also a tireless lecturer who passionately loved to explain her method. From early on she

understood the need to reconcile techniques, and liked to claim that
*'rhythm does not constitute dance in its entirety; the gymnastics of the
music-hall girls expresses only one sentiment, the joy of existence. Ballet often
expresses only visual joy. I dream of a universal dance'.*

Beyond her specific artistic lineage, she left above all a spiritual
influence: a large number of retired but radiant women owe their present
interest in dance to their association with the studios of Anita Wiskeman
and later Hélène Carlut. Of all the people I have ever met, the memory
of Anita Wiskeman eclipses that of all others. Everyone talks of the
dancer, her painter husband, and one of their sons, a poet, who died at
the age of twenty. She has become a myth, but her engaging personality
must not lead us to forget her pioneering role in the Lyons region.

[The Salvado family spent the war in Switzerland, returning to
Paris after the Liberation. Anita had developed cancer, however, and,
with admirable courage, continued to run her classes for as long as she
proved able before retiring to their property in the Var where she died.

Of all these dancers from a former age, spirits who haunt the
pages of this book, certain speak to me ... ones that I would like to have
known. Anita was one of these. (J.R.)]

Hélène Carlut *by Florence Poudru*

French (1908–1979)

Born in 1908, Hélène Carlut took her first steps in dance with
Anita Wiskeman, as did the majority of women of her generation in
Lyons. She did not begin to dance until she was seventeen years of age,
but from that moment on, this belated passion became an inseparable
part of her life.

As early as 1928 Hélène Carlut became one of Wiskeman's three
partners and stood in for her when Wiskeman was away from Lyons. She
soon felt the need to study with the masters, and in addition to her
summer courses with Jaques-Dalcroze, she studied with Rosalia Chladek.
According to Line Trillat, Hélène Carlut was the first French woman
to go to Hellerau-Laxenburg. She also studied with Harald Kreutzberg
in Salzburg and Mary Wigman in Berlin. This training would not have
been complete without a musical education, and her teacher was César
Geoffray, founder of the choir 'A Coeur Joie'. Freed from Dalcrozian
archaisms, she was to become the driving force behind post-war choreographic life in Lyons.

During the course of the 1936–37 season she opened her school
with the gymnast Lily Contamin and directed it single-handedly after the

war. In her view, *'there was no language without vocabulary'*, and so it was essential to provide a musical, rhythmic and physical education. If Anita Wiskeman's dance had strong contact with ground level, that of Hélène Carlut was more physical, positively bounding! In her classes, she accorded an important place to group work, believing that *'the individual, incorporated into the group, enjoys the satisfaction of being an integral part of a coherent whole, subjected to order and the rule of the majority. What was an effort becomes a joy, what was a constraint, a liberation'.*

In spite of her technical demands, the plastic interest of dance was always more important to her, and this was expressed in her numerous choreographies. *Rhapsody in Blue*, to music by Gershwin, created in 1938, and inspired by the music in its treatment of the theme of the ambivalent relationship between jazz and classical, may be mentioned as an example: costumes and masks with two faces were created by the painter Combet-Descombes. She collaborated with Lily Contamin on the music for *Percussion.*

From Couperin to Ray Ventura, whatever its style, music was indispensable to her. *Les Soutiers* by V. Kosma, *Vitrail*, based on Bach's chorale *Jesu bleibet meine Freude*, or *John tu es mort* by J. Silvant, are evidence of her success. Her frequent collaboration with the theatre should also be noted.

Unfortunately, Hélène Carlut, whose qualities as a teacher were recognized by numerous critics such as Jean Silvant and Jean-Jacques Lerrant, did not possess much business sense. She was entirely preoccupied with her art and preferred to encourage her pupils with modest resources to the detriment of all profitability. At a time when only a dancing school could finance a show, it was foolhardy to harbour ideas for such great projects. Nevertheless, she succeeded in realizing many of these. She divided her life between her studio and her performances until 1966, when a fracture of the hip-joint kept her away from her school. After this accident, one of her best pupils, Suzy Cothenet, succeeded her. Françoise Michaud, another of her pupils, had already left in order to create the Ballets Modernes de Paris with Dominique Dupuy, whom she married. Although Carlut's vocation was to provide a good quality education for amateurs, Françoise Dupuy's career testifies to the success of her teaching.

After a number of difficult years, Hélène Carlut died peacefully in the autumn of 1979, nine months before the opening of the Maison de la Danse in Lyons.

[According to Françoise Dupuy, who studied with Hélène Carlut for a long time before going to seek her fortune in Paris, the level of

Plate 19 *Symphonie du nouveau monde,* choreography by Hélène Carlut.

technical and artistic competence of her pupils was remarkable, and all the more so since they studied for only a few hours each week. The rigour and clarity of her approach to technique (the emphasis being placed on bodily posture, leaping techniques, musicality and rhythmic mastery, for example) and creativity – *'those who do not feel anything have nothing to say and ought not to dance'*, she maintained – seem to have stood out from the usual practice of her contemporaries in France. (J.R.)]

Doris Halphen, Maïan Pontan and the Hellerau-Laxenburg School

In order to obtain a better understanding of the development of French practices, we must recall the continuation of Jaques-Dalcroze's teaching in the principal schools in Germany, and subsequently in Austria. Jaques-Dalcroze founded his school in Hellerau, near Dresden, in 1919; it was transferred to Laxenburg, near Vienna, in 1925, and placed under the direction of Madame Baer Fussel, who was succeeded by Maïan Pontan, Valeria Kratina, and Rosalia Chladek, amongst others.

Dalcrozian principles underlay the teaching that was provided there, but this was oriented towards dance by means of a physical training that included gymnastics, technique, a rhythmic and musical education, improvisation and composition. Around 1935 the Corposano Studio in Paris, directed by Doris Halphen and Maïan Pontan, aimed to become the French centre of the Hellerau-Laxenburg school and method. At this time, the teaching attracted mainly amateurs – those thousands of women who sought fulfilment through a form of rational and musical gymnastics and dance. One could indeed mention many more of these schools that attempted, with varying degrees of success, to *'give each individual the freedom to be entirely himself ... '.*

DEFECTORS FROM CLASSICAL DANCE

Janine Solane and Jean Serry both had a wide public following and a large number of pupils. They marked out an important path, or, to pursue our initial metaphor, ploughed a deep furrow, in the field of French dance. They were mediators in the sense that they erected a bridge (at the expense of some compromise, purists might say) between the firmly rooted classical tradition and a new vision of dance. They also figured amongst the rare *native French dancers* to realize this quasi-revolution in ideas. This certainly contributed to their success, for they indeed formed part of the continuum of French culture.

Jean Serry

French (1910–1987)

Born in Chartres in 1910, he was steered towards the Opéra by his father, a gymnastic teacher, who was able to recognize his gifts. He gained entry to Gustave Ricaux's class in 1922, and progressed rapidly through the grades, making a name for himself in competitions as much as on the stage. He became *'premier sujet'* in 1935, working principally with Serge Lifar and studying dramatic art with René Simon.

Along with his colleagues at the Opéra, he organized performances that were decentralized to the provinces. Possessing a true artistic temperament that needed to be expressed, however, he soon began to suffer from the impersonal, restrictive manner in which dancers were employed by the Grande Maison, which showed more concern for their virtuosic qualities as good performers than for their sensitivity and ideals.

Thus, when, in 1935, he was judged the most capable of organizing the benefit gala given by dance artists at the Salle Pleyel in aid of the Opéra Friendly Society, he accepted on condition that each artist create his own choreography, outside the repertoire. This enabled him to reveal that certain ones were incapable of doing so, and as a result, a choreography class at the Opéra was opened.

That evening represented a decisive moment in his artistic career. He experienced the importance of personal creation, and discovered that the method of training dancers would have to be radically reformed if it were to fulfil the desires of artists, the aspirations of great philosophers and teachers, and the demands of modern ballet and theatre.

This gala affected his life in another way too: he threw himself into it with such intensity that he fell ill and, in 1936, after another year of excessive work on his research and other large projects, he was forced to leave the Opéra for the sanatorium. In this retreat he began to draft a new conception of dance, and, recognizing Serry's preoccupations, Jacques Rouché, the director of the Opéra, entrusted him in 1939 with studying the means of perfecting the method of training dancers at the Opéra. However, Jean Serry, seized with a sense of doubt, decided to abandon, for a time, classical dance which had disappointed him so in the form in which it was currently practised.

He left for Provence and worked on a farm near Manosque where he immersed himself in nature. He sought there a relationship between his dance and the impetus of the cosmos, and from the observation of his experiences, of movements associated with work, folk dances, and the spontaneous movements of children, animals and even plants, his method of 'living dance' gradually emerged. From that moment on, he devoted himself to the teaching and organization of a type of show in which dance, song, music, dramatic art and cinema were united.

After 1943, Jean Serry's career became part of the renaissance of popular culture and effusion of artistic and pedagogical initiatives that took place in France at the end of the war, and he became associated with the activities of the Compagnons de la Chanson and the organizations Travail et Culture and Danse et Culture. In the heroic and tragic years of the Occupation and the Liberation, he produced an evocation of *Jeanne d'Arc* in Chartres, *Le Miracle du pain béni* (with Jacques Copeau) in Beaune, and *Les Feux de la Saint-Jean* and *Le Chemin de croix du prisonnier* also in Chartres. He was particularly gifted in creating large expressive effects of mass movements, and spectacular unfoldings.

A pilgrim of dance, he scoured France (often on foot), giving lectures and performances, and sensitizing the general public to his notion of dance founded on spiritual grounds. He tirelessly gave classes in Chartres, Paris, Bourges, Dijon, Brest and Lorient, thus enlivening the seats of 'Danse et Vie' as he called his group and method/philosophy of working. It was around him that a large group of young modern dancers of the post-war generation, some of whom were French, others who came from elsewhere, gathered for varying lengths of time, eager to discover this uncharted territory. Between 1948 and 1956, he produced numerous shows, frequently in Chartres cathedral or other churches in the city, and dancers such as Françoise and Dominique Dupuy, Paul d'Arnot, Anne Gardon, Suzanne Rémon, Olga Stens, Jacqueline Levant, Geneviève Piguet and Karin Waehner collaborated with him.

Jean Serry owed little to foreign influences. Trained in academic dance, which he reconsidered according to his spiritual aspirations, he drew upon the secular treasure of architecture, poetry and French popular dance. The titles of his productions and dances: *Cantate à Jean de France* (1951), *La Geste médiévale* (1956), *Jabadao* (1954), *La Marche à l'étoile*, *Légende de la ville d'Ys* and *L'autre île* by La Varende, bear this out. Specializing in period dances, he also worked for the cinema on films such as Delannoy's *Marie-Antoinette*, Christian-Jacque's *Lucrèce Borgia*, and *Le Vicomte de Bragelonne*.

In 1956 Jean Serry was appointed professor (of classical dance) at the National Conservatoire of Dijon, where he finally settled. For thirty years he directed his association Danse et Enseignement there, devoting himself in particular to the pedagogical concerns of dance (in classes, courses, lectures and a magazine) with a radiant fervour that remained with him until the end. He died in 1987.

In accordance with his unfailing convictions, he never ceased to seek to expand the personality of the dancer, whether amateur or professional, and to '*develop his love of life by developing his creativity*'.

Plate 20 Jean Serry in *La Danse des morts* in Lyons in 1945.

Numerous individuals active within the various currents of modern dance or theatre in France worked with him and came under his influence to some extent, including Marie-France Babillot, Anne-Marie Debatte, Geneviève Piguet, Georgette Watteau (ex-principal dancer with Solane), Jean-Pierre Kalfon and Gabriel Cousin, for example. His own daughter, Viviane Serry, is currently pursuing a career as an independent dancer with Jean-Claude Gallotta's group, Émile Dubois.

If not a classic, Jean Serry was nevertheless a classicist at least. He was certainly a mystic, and would not have denied this himself. He succeeded in creating a curious combination: he invested the vocabulary and particular forms and gestures of classical dance with a breath of real life, and in reverse, appealed to the creativity of his pupils whilst directing them towards certain recognized and classified forms. In this way he attempted to justify, after a fashion, the absolute validity and universality of the forms selected by classical dance throughout the centuries, as if he were unable to break the umbilical cord completely.

In this sense, it could be claimed that he was a *reformer* rather than an *innovator*. His radiance as a teacher and the inspiration he gave to others have been an important force until the present day; in the past he played a decisive role as both choreographer and producer, illustrating in a way the polyvalence of dance. He knew how to exploit and valorize it in different contexts and for different audiences, informed or otherwise, and how to marry it with other performance arts, making it appear rooted in the life of man and of the city.

In 1973 Jean Serry published *Par le mouvement*, a moving book that received an Académie Française award. It was a work of both poetic and didactic significance, somewhat missionary in intent, one might venture to say, for there emanates such a degree of faith and ardour from those aesthetic, historical, philosophical and spiritual considerations, despite the often dogmatic and simplifying limitations the author took upon himself as far as dance is concerned. It is nevertheless a rich and thought-provoking book that clearly reflects the personality of its author.

Janine Solane

French, born in 1912.

Amongst the most notable personalities to contribute, albeit indirectly, to the progress of modern dance in France, Janine Solane must be mentioned.

She began to attract attention as early as 1932 when she presented a 'ballet' at the choreography competition organized by the A.I.D. in Paris. The introduction to this work in the review of the Archives in

April 1932 provides a good example of the contemporary style of discourse about dance:

> '*Mme Janine Solane, director of a school of dance in Paris, has been pronounced champion of eurhythmic dances at the second Dance Championship, organized in 1929 by La Semaine à Paris. In the ballet of her own composition, entitled L'Abandon céleste (to music by Richard Wagner), that she will present, Mme Solane will be surrounded by the company she created, of which she remains the vital force, and will demonstrate the principles that have always guided both her teaching and the beautiful performances she has already given. Dance must never cease to be an intellectual diversion, and its essential aim is to express in beauty, with the deepest sincerity, the infinite scale of human feelings. It is the spirit, the soul, that must direct the body which thus becomes a perfect instrument, the creator of harmony, through the magic of pure lines and the splendour of rhythm. The spontaneous movements of dance are a function of enthusiasm and spirit, and each movement must be a new hymn to immortal beauty*'.

Fernand Divoire described her in 1935 as a representative of the Paris School.

She was born into a family of artists in 1912; thus, at the time of the competition, she was twenty years of age. She studied dance in the purest classical tradition with Léo Staats at the Opéra, and later with Ellen Tels, a pupil of Irma Duncan, and Vaslav Veltcheck, a pupil of Wigman and Laban. It was the eclectic nature of her training that led her to elaborate, as early as 1929, her 'classical-natural method'. She herself laid claim to Duncanian descent, and wrote to me in 1979:

> '*I received from Isadora free, human expression, and its finality: dancing the Heart of Man*'.

In her book *Pour une danse plus humaine* (1950), Solane wrote:

> '*Having learnt from Léo Staats what is indispensable: the technique of a stylized vocabulary of dance, a surprising subterfuge to transform the man-who-dances-for-pleasure into a man-instrument, I had the good fortune to learn from Ellen Tels the means of returning to source in order to feed on what is natural. My third stroke of luck was to love music. It is music that compels me to seek perfection. I want to be worthy of it*'.[11]

On her own admission, Janine Solane attempted to bring about a fusion of '*the basis of classical academic vocabulary with the expression of the German method*', a fusion that one could be justified in considering impossible, for it seems to me that it embodies a fundamental contradiction. The German method, the philosophy of modern dance, implies perpetual seeking and denies the very concept of a codified or stylized vocabulary. There is,

---

[11] Janine Solane, *Pour une danse plus humaine* (Jacques Vautrain, 1950), p. 91.

here, therefore, an ambiguity, a compromise that gave rise to a hybrid style and mode of thought. It is certain that Janine Solane shook up classical vocabulary and style, and made it more flexible, notably by transforming its characteristic verticality and introducing asymmetrical lines and curves. Similarly, the unbalanced '*hanché*' position that she owed to Ellen Tels, and which was a constant feature of her style, contained much dynamic promise. Did she replace one form of codification with another? This was perhaps the impression created by her choreographic and pedagogical work.

In this same book she gave extensive treatment to the relationships between dance and music, which was a constant source of inspiration to her; nevertheless, she placed dance in a position of extreme submission to music, which is to serve as a formal frame and to set in motion. I referred to this problem in a preceding chapter of this book in which Jérôme Bouxviller's preface, *Vers une danse plus humaine*, was quoted. In this preface, he expressed very dogmatic and limited opinions concerning the relationships between music and dance.

And yet, Solane wrote in the same work:

'If I dance in silence, if I invent within myself some rhythm or melody, or even if I listen to my heart and breath, the impression that I make is sufficiently rhythmic in space to become immediately so in time. That is to say, the spectator unconsciously fills the silence with inaudible music, perceptible only by each individual, a sort of music of the soul'.

Janine Solane thus grasped the nature of this fundamental point, an intrinsic quality of dance. But she did not take the step to achieve it, running the risk of pleonasm, and depriving her dance of a more original dimension. She stated further:

'I have often been asked "is it the music that inspires you, or are you filled by a dance subject for which you seek music?" Seeking music for a pre-conceived theme would reduce the principle of musical transfiguration to nothing'.

Unquestionably musical, as sensitive to the emotion of a work as to its structure, yet, Janine Solane did not make use of the potential independence of dance in relation to music – which does not infer that dance might lose its musicality. Was it too soon for dance to be truly freed?

This breaking apart and the experience of dance in silence were going on elsewhere. Not out of a lack of respect for music and the added dimension it can bring to dance, to be sure, but out of absolute respect for the intrinsic power of dance. This added dimension was probably just what some of these choreographers of yesteryear sought to

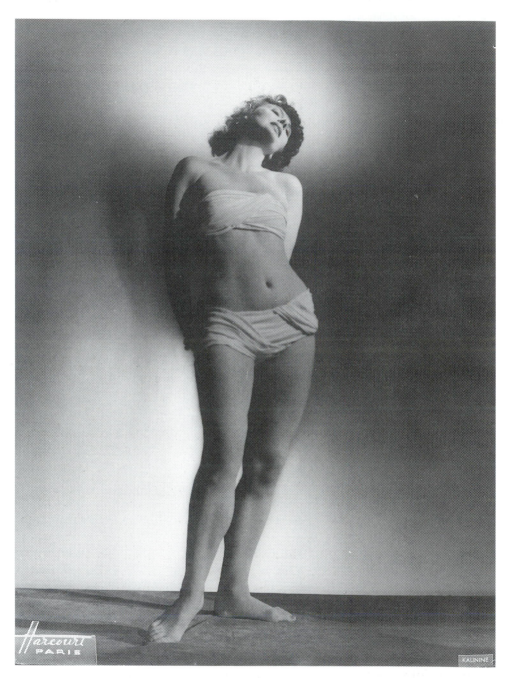

Plate 21 Janine Solane, *Saint Sébastien sous les flèches*, in 1943. Photo: Harcourt, Paris.

incorporate into their creation, not yet having confidence in the specificity of dance.

In 1932 Janine Solane established her school and company: the Janine Solane Dance Choir. As a result she undertook considerable pedagogical and artistic activity, both within her school, and within the framework of various official and private organizations of cultural or educational activity (particularly at the École Nationale Supérieure d'Education Physique). The Dance Choir performed regularly for forty years in Paris, the provinces and abroad.

Solane was a prolific choreographer and her most notable group works include *Fugue en sol mineur* (J. S. Bach), 1941, *La Symphonie Pastorale* (Beethoven), 1946, *La Grande Passacaille* (J. S. Bach), 1948, and *La Belle au bois dormant* (Vivaldi), 1957. All these works are large scale in terms of their subject matter as much as of their choric treatment, and all of them employ a large number of dancers. Respect for the music, together with a sense of theatre, lent them an unquestionable quality, whatever the restrictions on certain aspects of their style might be: mannerism, tinged with affectation at times, and recourse to travesty for male roles.

Janine Solane was equally sensitive to the problems of dance in education, presenting it not only as a physical activity, susceptible to harmonizing the personality, but also as a means of access to musical, literary and plastic art culture, thus classifying dance amongst the humanities. This represented an important issue at the time, and, also, rather like eurhythmic dance, her method offered an alternative to the extreme rigours of classical training.

She educated generations of young women (her school often seemed rather like a gynaeceum), some of whom went off to direct Solane schools throughout France. Others, especially those from her most recent classes, ventured to take steps towards a more personal language and procedure, and followed their own path. These included Anne-Marie Debatte, Sylvie Deluz, Suzon Holzer, Geneviève Piguet, Rose-Marie Paillet, Denise Blanc-Raillard, Marie-France Babillot, Titane Saint-Hubert and many others. Today, in 1994, the Solane school and company are directed by her daughter Dominique and, at a slight remove, by Janine herself.

Janine Solane presents something of a paradox: considered by modernists as a classicist, and by classicists as a modernist, she is, in fact, neither one nor the other. (Perhaps Béjart presents something of a similar case today, in a different context, of course.) She was a child of her time, and specifically of the French bourgeoisie of her time (this is not intended in any pejorative sense). She was brought up in the context of certain French cultural values: a taste for the harmonious, for grace and balance, a certain prettiness that does not exclude lofty aspirations, a tang of the soil, and genuine quality. She fought to impose her vision of dance, a vision that she unfortunately allowed to become set; throughout her career she worked with and trained thousands of young talents and gained recognition for her work from a large number of French artists and intellectuals. The form of dance she proposed was nourished by the values cited above from an artistic as much as from a pedagogical point of view, and drew from these both its qualities and its limitations.

THE INDEPENDENT ONES

These artists were mostly nurtured by diverse sources and generally remained apart from recognized or institutionalized groups or associations. They cannot be classified in terms of existing categorizations or lines of filiation. Nevertheless, their individuality is perhaps one of their greatest charms.

Marguerite Bougai

French (1910–1994)

She was interested in dance from childhood. The lack of choice in schools of dance at this time led her to take classes in the Cecchetti method at the Châtelet, where she became a soloist. However, her inquisitive and sensitive nature made her particularly attentive to new artistic trends, and in 1931 she left the Châtelet and obtained employment in various locations as principal dancer and choreographer. She took advantage of every opportunity, journey and tour to observe and learn.

Whilst still very young, she felt the need to research and concentrate on her own experience of dance in order to discover progressively the pedagogical considerations that emanated from it. As early as 1936 Marguerite Bougai was one of the pioneers to propose giving dance recitals in primary and other types of schools. This idea was accepted with interest and her recitals were received enthusiastically by children, young people, and the teaching body alike. This exciting but very poorly paid activity nevertheless enabled her to continue to develop her own work in form, expression and choreographic experiments with and without music. Out of all this grew an initial concert group, in collaboration with some of her pupils who were interested in and stimulated by this kind of work. This gave her the opportunity to continue her demonstrations in primary schools and gain access to high schools also. A real interest in her work was awakened which extended to reach a much wider audience.

Her first major recitals were held at the École Normale de Musique and the Maison de la Chimie, two of the most popular venues for the performance of dance of more intimate dimensions some thirty or forty years ago, and took place in 1948, at the end of the war years that were so difficult for everyone.

Marguerite Bougai was assisted in this task of awakening and sensitizing the public, particularly its younger members, by Mademoiselle Goupil, the open-minded headmistress of the Jules-Ferry high school, who introduced her to the university sector; as a result of this, she was entrusted with the direction of the refresher courses in 'Dance technique and notions of composition' intended for teachers from the City of Paris Teachers' Training College from 1946 to 1955. Within this framework she was able to train dance teachers and give numerous performances for children with her group, as well as performances by children. She was amongst the first to organize performances of choric dance which employed in stadia, amongst other places, a large number of participants, including children, who had been prepared locally for this event.

From 1947 to 1952 Marguerite Bougai was closely associated with the work of the Martenot School, on both a pedagogical and an artistic level, and she frequently used the ondes Martenot to accompany her choreographic realizations. Between 1949 and 1963, the charitable society La Chaussée du Maine provided her with a hall/theatre that became her home port, where she was able to pursue her teaching and give numerous recitals with her group. These performances were greatly appreciated by an educated public and the critics alike, as the following lines by Maurice Pourchet indicate:

> 'This performance illustrated to me that without any fuss or publicity, your courage and perseverance have succeeded in creating a choreographic language capable of translating, by means of its suppleness, variety and unity, the ever so delicate, discreet, and sometimes vigorously asserted nuances of your sensibility. Moreover, the faith and technique of your dancers testify to the radiant force that emanates from your sincerity and skill simply through their unadulterated interpretation of your choreography, which is most intimately adapted to the scores you have chosen to illustrate, and so richly endowed that it proved able to create its own music' (Letter from Maurice Pourchet to Marguerite Bougai, 1962).

Marguerite Bougai did use contemporary music by composers such as Stravinsky, Hindemith, Honegger and Bartók, for example, and occasionally early music also. Her interests led her more and more towards dance without music, however, and she experimented further with the use of a text as the sole accompaniment. During the 1950s and 60s she had the opportunity to work with Etienne Decroux, Roger Blin and

Jean-Louis Barrault, and whilst maintaining her independence, she collaborated on a number of joint ventures with other Parisian modern dancers, amongst others Françoise and Dominique Dupuy.

Marguerite Bougai continued her activities in her personal studio following the demolition of the Chaussée du Maine centre. Constantly driven by curiosity, she pursued her activities until the very end, and one could note her impassioned presence 'wherever anything was happening', be it individual teaching, work in schools, or group realizations.

Over the years, the principal concern of Marguerite Bougai had become the teaching of children, or, expressed another way, the evolution of dance through the evolution of young people. Her work in this field has been admirable, and moreover in conjunction with a deep awareness of music.

Marguerite Bougai was an important and engaging figure on the French dance scene. She herself claimed to have deliberately chosen an austere path, and she referred to her own work, with characteristic humour, as 'underground dance', no doubt indicating the years of uncompromising struggle and searching during which she initiated many new developments from which dance has benefitted. And maybe, because 'underground', her work is rich in inner feeling and lucid concentration.

A fluent writer, she published an eloquent collection of poems entitled *Le Mot et le geste*, in addition to texts of a didactic and philosophical nature.

> *'What concerns me and matters to me above anything else',* she recently wrote to me, *'is the future of dance. As far as I am concerned, anything relating to me personally is of little importance. What really matters is the "reason" for my struggle. I want the meaning of my work to be clear. My development was crucial; the strength of my instinct demanded such evolution, but I was only able to discover its meaning retrospectively by virtue of experience and after a long and patient study and a very strict and ruthless analysis. What we are ourselves, with all our weaknesses and qualities (as far as we may ever really know anything about ourselves), may be felt in the beating of our inner pulse. But what we truly believe in is so impalpable that it cannot be described.*
> *... Roger Blin used to say to me: "it is not the torments or the harshness of things that are harmful, but the INERTIA by which we are so often surrounded"'.*

A text by Marguerite Bougai

> *'Do you want to see a labour of art, work seized as the years go by?*
> *Perhaps it is a work of culture, or only of education. Perhaps it is neither of these. Would it then be only a labour of the mind?*

But then, we are asked, is it well organized?
Is there a signature to it?
Can you say: "Look, here is the masterpiece!"
Where is it to be found, where do you show it, have you programmed it clearly?
Well, no, comes the reply, with a hint of a smile.
It is true, the work has been going on for years, but it may not be seized in a concrete manner, no more than one can seize the morning dew.
Such an act is not an academic working out. It is ephemeral, but precious in an ephemeral way.
Why?
Yes, why?
In an activity in which knowledge is handed down from person to person, as it is in dance, for that is what we are concerned with, no dictates!
There is ebb and flow. To put it in a prosaic way, he who teaches also learns. No obligation, no contract.
We meet because it is necessary, an impulse of the inner life. It is not to be placed under a dome. It is not protected by institutional ramparts. It wakes and lives inside a human being. It is part of intrinsic life.
Vibrant life is not to be found in what is called today a market (although the market of dance has been heard of).
It is to be found inside the human being. This life speaks through the face, the eyes, the whole body of a person, through each and all of his cells. It brings about communication between human beings.
In the working out of such a project there is a kind of free will.
We are swept along by a kind of current.
And yet here we are, having to move our steel-like soles towards so many useful things.
Maybe we should say so many useless things.
And so, the building of the human being happens during lost time. We must be sparing therefore, and diligent.
To mould the living geometry of the body-spirit is a subtle undertaking. It reminds one of those beautiful grasses, plants of all kinds that spring up among stones, rockeries and ruined walls. But what vitality, what joy in life!
But, will you then say, how do you come to possess that? In what manner do you bring it about?
There appears another hint of a smile.
Form, organization, that certainly exists! It is alive and can be seen if we take the trouble. It can be planted anywhere, belong to every being who feels the need of it, and may even stimulate that need.
A feeling for creativity is not the exclusive property of that rare and precious race: geniuses. We need them imperatively to be sure, but in another manner.
Each one possesses this vibrant spark which makes him a human being.
Shall we then open those sordid doors that keep back those waves of life?
And bring it about that the impressive constructions made to house precious and sometimes sophisticated learning may let a few rays of sunlight filter through the cracks of the all too often hermetically closed shutters.
And go you now, here, there, everywhere it exists, go and see how is revealed the delicacy of the human being, and his strength and his affirmation.'

18 June 1986

Tony Gregory

Of Corsican origin; born c. 1907, died in 1947.

In the first issue of the *Revue des Archives Internationales de la Danse*, published in 1932, a short unsigned article introducing Tony Gregory, who was to participate in the choreography competition, appeared:

> *'In the current development of dance, especially in France, Tony Gregory appears as something of a precursor. To use a term that has frequently been abused, he belongs to the 'avant-garde' and is certainly one of the oddest performers of today. Like all the great pioneers, he is classically trained, as much from a literary as from a musical and choreographic point of view. M. Tony Gregory has therefore created his own technique on a very solid foundation. Attracted by the rhythmic beauty of the most humble and everyday forms of life, he strove to disregard the prejudices surrounding the beautiful and the ugly, the noble and the trivial, and having freed himself from such paralysing conventions, he conceived a mode of expression that is more direct in its objectivity and which retains a sharp and curious flavour'.*

This competition did not mark his début, however, for he had given recitals as a soloist or with different partners for several years, and had experimented with various styles that he appeared to have integrated. He created his own very beautiful costumes, danced to poems and used masks (some of which were specially made for him by Picasso). He was later to sing and write songs. The critics were unanimous in praising his personal style, *'his lively sense of humour and intense sensibility'*.

Equally remarkable was the pedagogical work he undertook from 1936, teaching adult amateurs and staging performances with them. He militated for access to artistic activities for the working classes, and created a choreographic production with Le Regard, a group of 'working-class artists'.

For over twenty years he organized weekly 'entertainments' in his studio, in which he danced, sang and recited, and which became the meeting place of a certain élite. This led Julia Marcus to declare recently that *'that delightful boy was really with it, and rather fashionable!'*. In 1939 Tony Gregory was appointed ballet master at Monte Carlo, where he danced and produced the choreography and scenery for the ballets also. After the war he resumed his Parisian activities. Maurice Pourchet wrote in *Arts* in 1947:

> *'Tony Gregory worked with the ardour of a neophyte. He had a taste for research and refinement, extending occasionally to affectation; but that in no way diminished his attraction for the masses and large popular shows'.*

He died during a Corsican gala in Neuilly, whilst performing one of his songs:

> *'life is a dance – you dance, then you die'.*

Freddy Wittop

Of Dutch origin; born c. 1912.

Classically trained. He appears to have made folk and classical Spanish dance his speciality. The critics claimed that *'he excelled at it so greatly that he had no need of Spanish blood in his veins'*. He also created his own dances that were frequently inspired by elegant, refined Spanish subjects, and for which he made the costumes himself. He enjoyed much success during the 1930s.

Josette and Renée Foatelli

Sisters; born in the first decade of the century. Possibly of Corsican origin.

Following their débuts and an eclectic training that incorporated classical, eurhythmic and 'Isadorian' influences, they specialized in 'religious dances'. They performed frequently in galas alongside early music groups, and taught until the 1950s. They published several works written in the late 1930s, including *Les Danses religieuses dans le christianisme* (Spes), *La Danse et nous, Pour le théâtre chrétien* (Enault), and *Méthode de danse religieuse chrétienne* (Desclée de Brouwer).

THE EDUCATORS

It is important to distinguish between two categories of dance artists. These should not be opposed; still less should they be compared. Certain artists devoted themselves principally to the stage, whilst others showed greater concern for education through dance. Different procedures and no doubt different temperaments. Certain dancers succeeded in following both paths. The work of the educators was perhaps less well known because less spectacular, and therefore less susceptible to be disseminated by the media, today.

It seems to me I could discern a certain degree of sadness amongst some of these great educators, as if they felt themselves insufficiently recognized, involved in dance but remaining on the periphery. We touch here on a problem that was outlined above: the opposition between dance for everyone and a practice reserved for the professionals.

A fundamental ideology is common to all these educators, however: that of the complete person in harmony with nature (the cosmos), and its rhythms, the union of mind and body, respect for the individual, the desire for personal expansion, and a certain sense of responsibility for the future. According to the individual, their practice may be more or less scientific or mystical. In this respect, these pioneers appeared rather like prophets.

Fée Hellès *by Denise Coutier*

(1886–1982)

Born in Poltava, Russia, of a French father and Norwegian mother, she travelled widely and, indeed, it is difficult to reconstruct the exact itinerary followed by this exceptional and all too little known character. From her very childhood, she made a close study of nature and life around her, and, in the evening, she would draw inspiration from the shadows:

> 'accustomed to looking and seeing, I learnt to perceive the synthesis of the truth by means of the shadows that dispense with useless details ... my beloved shadows taught me two things: to observe in a state of detachment and concentration and without worrying about time, those things that fade away, and to complete in my imagination, my creative thought, those that disappear all too quickly'.

She studied philosophy and plant biology in St Petersburg, but a serious attack of pleurisy forced her to interrupt her studies and spend three months in hospital. As a result of this experience, she discovered out of necessity exercises that later formed the basis of her method.

In her own words:

> 'An extraordinary event occurred in my life: I saw Isadora Duncan dance and I found in her what I had always been looking for: grandeur, purity, nobility and a certain spontaneity that allows everything to speak for itself; I understood the role of the creative element, the state of awakened consciousness, this receptivity to the spiritual that gives us a sense of worth, and the union of the human being with the universal. As a result of this emotional shock, Fée Hellès concerned herself with 'analysing the correct postures in order to understand the play of tensions, key to the harmony of movement, and primary condition of health; and with learning the use of the extremely delicate and unstable mechanisms of balance and good nervous control (a single emotion or simply an anxious thought may upset this ...) and I am forever struck and moved to observe the result of the fusion of the psychological and the physical, when the movement arises from the depths of a person'.

Married to the concert pianist, conductor, teacher and accompanist Arie Abilea, who accompanied Isadora Duncan amongst others, when she danced in Switzerland, Fée Hellès had three daughters: Debora, a medical researcher in London; Mira, resident in the United States, and Maïa, a dance teacher in New York.

At the age of fifty, Fée Hellès began her studies in medicine with Henri Wallon and became very well acquainted with Jean Rostand. She graduated from the Paris academy of medicine, and claimed that the guiding forces in her research were Descartes, François Delsarte, Claude Bernard, Henri Bergson and Alexis Carrel. After twenty years of teaching, she met Delsarte's grandson, Maximilien, and was astonished by the similarity of their ideas for helping man in his spiritual evolution. In 1938 Ria Delsarte herself lent Hellès a copy of the writings of Delsarte's pupils, and she made a study of the concepts of this great French thinker and forerunner. Throughout her life she collaborated, gave lectures and demonstrations in France and abroad, and never ceased to hold classes and pursue her own work.

In her teaching she aspired towards the development of the complete person and sought to appeal at one and the same time to the intellect, the psyche and the physical faculties. She aimed, moreover, towards the preservation of immunity and self-improvement, for Fée Hellès believed deeply in the perfectibility of man, such perfection being a natural and universal biological phenomenon. The education of the child was a major preoccupation in her life.

Some of the people who worked with Fée Hellès include Jacques d'Arès, Jean Babilée, Alain Cuny, Yvonne Berge, Janine Charrat, Marie-Christine Coutier, Lycette Darsonval, Dora Feïlane, Thérèse Hautval, Robert Hossein, Paul Lecour, Albert and Claude Lamorisse, Christiane Leckler, Nil Maillard, Maurice and Jean-François Martenot, Dr Minor, Dr Peillon, Raymond Rouleau and Nicole Verstenstein.

Fée Hellès wrote a thesis, under the aegis of the academy of medicine, and a number of articles, including 'Une âme saine' (*La Tribune de l'Enfance* review, no. 14, 1964), 'L'Éducation par le mouvement' (*ibid.*, no. 36, 1966), and 'Quelques réflexions sur la danse sacrée et ses rapports avec l'éducation générale' (*Atlantis*, no. 277, 1974).

Liliane Arlen and Viennese Dance

Of Austrian origin. Born in 1908.

For the first time in this chronicle we meet an Austrian dancer and this allows us to make a brief digression. The styles of new dance that arose in Germany and Austria in the twentieth century have perhaps been all too easily associated, for these two countries, although sharing a common language, have an entirely different culture.

Whatever, according to Liliane Arlen, who fully accepted her nationality and the culture of her origin, German expressionist dance, represented by Laban, Wigman and their followers, never really took hold in Austria, where it was considered too heavy from both a moral and a physical point of view. If dance may be regarded as the expression of the culture of a nation, new Austrian dance was more fluid, rounded, lively, and more feminine too (one cannot help thinking immediately of the waltz!).

Rudolph von Laban appears to have commented that German dancers were *deep* (*'tief'*) and Austrian dancers *light*. Fernand Divoire, for his part, maintained that:

> *'Our knowledge of Austrian schools and dances indicates certain tendencies that closely resemble German tendencies, but only in the most approximate way, for whilst Germany may imprison herself in theories, Austria frees herself from them'.*

Nevertheless, one can note, observing photographs and records of the period, that there seemed to radiate from these Austrian pioneers of the new dance during the early years of the century, a certain joy of life one cannot find in Germany, a feeling that owed little to Isadorism, in spite of the presence of Elisabeth Duncan and her school in Salzburg.

These pioneers included Grete and Else Wiesenthal (who inspired young Mary Wigman, forbidden by her family to pursue a career in dance), Anton Birkmeyer and Gertrud Bodenweiser, who, following her début in 1919, was appointed as a teacher at the Vienna Conservatoire (an interesting curriculum: classical technique, free dance, composition, music, history of arts, anatomy and pedagogy). And Ellen Tels, in charge for a time of an important school and group in Vienna may also be recalled in this context, together with the Dalcroze school, established near Vienna at Hellerau-Laxenburg, under the direction of Rosalia Chladek who later rose to great fame.

Liliane Arlen thus worked alongside these pioneers in Vienna during the 1920s and was particularly impressed by Ellen Tels. She studied classical dance with Victor Gsovsky, one of the great classical masters, and gymnastics and acrobatics in an English school. When she was still very young, she was appointed as a teacher at the Vienna Conservatoire of classical dance (the academy of music and art), and when she was only seventeen she met an Austrian prince who, at seventy-five, performed on stage like a young man. His secret? Hatha yoga. He initiated the young dancer to this, and it became one of the components of her teaching.

In 1936 she settled in Paris where she appeared as a soloist with much success, especially within the framework of the music hall, in character dances created for her chiefly by Gsovsky and Birkmeyer. She remained a soloist and did not seek to become involved with any Parisian group.

As time went on, however, Liliane Arlen devoted herself more and more exclusively to teaching. Today (1989), at seventy-nine years of age, she still works with a large number of pupils, including professional and amateur dancers, in her studio in the Salle Pleyel. Although she teaches 'officially' classical dance, it is not for that reason that I include her here. She teaches what she describes as 'bodily discipline', a study of basic technique that may be applied in numerous different situations. This encompasses an awakening of the body, breathing, placement, suppleness bordering on acrobatics, control and endurance, or, in her own terms, '*Body sculpture – Artistry and beauty of movement – Correction of bodily defects – Strengthening of the muscular system – Balance of the nervous system – Straightening of the spinal column*' (through 'hanging' from rib stalls, in particular).

Over and above her gymnastic, acrobatic and classical training, combined with her knowledge of yoga, Liliane Arlen is reputed to possess remarkable flair and intuition for making a diagnosis, encouraging correct movements and sensations, and evaluating the full potential of each individual, guiding him towards the realization of his utmost physical capacities.

Amongst the many dance pupils whose bodies she has helped to sculpt in this way are Jean Guizerix, Dominique Kalfouni, Noëlle Pontois from the Opéra, Francine Lancelot and Christiane de Rougemont, without mentioning the numerous foreign dancers.

Liliane Arlen told me with characteristic modesty that: '*You cannot make an artist; I am content simply to prepare the instrument*'. She also maintained that:

> '*The Viennese woman is a born dancer, with an uncontrollable enthusiasm for the joy of life, a joy that is fused with a feeling of tender, romantic nostalgia and unleashed passion. Her instinct and sharp mind constantly make her feel that she must jealously guard her nature and her own personality*'.

CONCLUSION

Twenty years have thus elapsed since the beginning of this chronicle, and we have indeed covered much ground from Isadora to Jean Weidt's Ballets 38, for example.

This route, both desired and endured, covered by the protagonists of this story, was influenced by many factors that included a number of socio-cultural conditions related to those economic and political imperatives that escape the control of the individual, belonging rather to the fate of the community.

The new dance that emerged depended upon the progressive rehabilitation of the body and the greater knowledge of the human being, body and mind. It took account of the recuperation of this body in its manipulated, exploited and materialized form. To the angelism of Isadora and her followers succeeded the raw violence of Weidt, to mention only these most extreme examples, the two being separated by some twenty years during which diverse and diversified influences infiltrated France, some tending to privilege dance conceived as a theatrical language, others as an educational practice, but both *expressing man*.

These two facets of dance, theatre and education, were sustained by theories of movement, which at the same time encompassed its working laws at the risk of rigidity, and yet widened the field of possible hypotheses and explorations – theories that came initially from the Dalcroze school, later that of Hellerau, and that of Laban. One hesitates to apply the term 'theory' to the *principles* of Wigman. Nevertheless, these principles played a fruitful role in the shaping of the story of dance at that time.

For twenty years the characters whose progress has been charted throughout this chapter dominated the scene. What a portrait gallery! Men and women outside the common run, creators and 'gardeners', in the sense in which Mary Wigman understood this term when she spoke of the pedagogy of dance. They cleared and ploughed the ground, and now their work, the pursuit of their vision must come to a more or less abrupt end, for we have arrived at the edge of an abyss: the outbreak of the war. This chapter has been concerned with the so-called 'inter-war years'. At this point dance lives on, sometimes stifled, sometimes, on the other hand, showing the way, and will later resume its true place and course in everyday life.

PART III

1945–1960

The Sowing Years

CHRONOLOGY

FROM VICTORY TO THE COLD WAR

DATES	EVENTS IN FRANCE	EVENTS ABROAD	CONTEMPORARY CULTURE IN FRANCE
1944	Landing in France. Oradour massacre. Creation of the Mouvement Républicain Populaire (M.R.P.). Maurice Thorez returns to Paris. First issue of *Le Monde*.		*Huis clos* by Jean-Paul Sartre. Creation of a directorship for Youth and Sport at the ministry of national education. Dance: Roland Petit, Serge Lifar, René Fenonjois, Janine Charrat.
1945	Women obtain the vote in France. Condemnation of Marshal Pétain. De Gaulle becomes leader of the government.	Yalta Conference (without France). Truman succeeds Roosevelt. Atomic bomb dropped on Hiroshima and Nagasaki. Hô Chi Min calls for insurrection.	Arthur Koestler publishes *Le Zéro et l'infini*. Robert Bresson shoots *Les Dames du Bois de Boulogne*.
1946	De Gaulle resigns. Succession of nationalizations. Foundation of the Congrès National du Patronat Français (C.N.P.F.). Success of the 4CV.	First general assembly of the United Nations. At Fulton Churchill refers to the 'iron curtain' that will divide the world into two blocks.	First Cannes festival First Avignon festival. José Greco and Boris Vian star at St Germain.
1947	Foundation of the Rassemblement du Peuple Français (R.P.F.).	Birth of the Kominform. Russia rejects the Marshall plan.	Jean Genet writes *Les Bonnes*. Albert Camus writes *La Peste*.

	Dismissal of communist ministers. Insurrection in Madagascar.		The Archives Internationales de la Danse organizes the choreography competition in Copenhagen. A gala brings together Lisa Duncan, la Teresina, the Loie Fuller ballets and Nyota Inyoka for the last time.
1948	Troops called in to suppress strikes.	Congress adopts the Marshall plan. Creation of the State of Israel. Blockade of Berlin. Tito condemned by the Kominform. Prague coup. Assassination of Gandhi.	Jean-Paul Sartre *Les Mains sales.* Jean-Louis Barrault stages Paul Claudel's *Le Partage de midi.* Maurice Druon writes *Les Grandes Famieles.* Hervé Bazin *Vipère au poing.* Roland Petit founds the Ballets de Paris. The Sakharoffs appear at the Théâtre des Champs-Élysées.
1949	Suppression of the High Commissariat of Food.	Signing of the Atlantic Pact. Constitution of the German Democratic Republic (G.D.R.). Proclamation of the German Federal Republic (G.F.R.).	Charles Dullin dies. Eugène Ionesco writes *La Cantatrice chauve.* Albert Camus writes *Les Justes.* Roland Petit stages *Carmen.* Simone de Beauvoir writes *Le Deuxième sexe.*

DATES	EVENTS IN FRANCE	EVENTS ABROAD	CONTEMPORARY CULTURE
1950	Adoption of the Salaire Minimum d'Interprofessionel Garanti (S.M.I.G.) (a guaranteed minimum wage). Léon Blum dies. Military defeats in Tonkin against the Viêt-minh.	Stockholm appeals for peace. Korean war.	*Clérambard* by Marcel Aymé in the theatre. Jean Cocteau shoots *Orphée* and Jacques Tati *Jour de fête.* American Ballet Company appears in Paris (Ruth Page and José Limón).
1951	Foundation of the European Community of Coal and Steel.	Mossadegh nationalizes Iranian oil. Armistice in Korea.	Gérard Philipe stars in *Le Cid.* Jean-Paul Sartre writes *Le Diable et le Bon Dieu.*
1952	Investiture of Antoine Pinay.		Creation of the Théâtre National de Paris. New York City Ballet appears in Paris. Keita Fodeba's African Ballets.
1953	Dismemberment of the R.P.F. First issue of *L'Express.*	Stalin dies and is succeeded by Khrushchev. Execution of the Rosenbergs. Settlement of the conflict in Korea.	Samuel Beckett writes *En attendant Godot.* *Le Loup* by Roland Petit with the Ballet de Paris. *Les Algues* by Janine Charrat. *Porgy and Bess* by Ruth Page. Jerome Andrews creates the Compagnons de la Danse.
1954	Defeat at Diên Biên Phu. Pierre Mendès-France	Rearmament of the G.F.R.	Simone Signoret and Yves Montand feature in *Sorcières de Salem.*

DATES	EVENTS IN FRANCE	EVENTS ABROAD	CONTEMPORARY CULTURE
	negotiates the independence of Indochina. Algerian uprising.		Simone de Beauvoir writes *Les Mandarins*. Françoise Sagan writes *Bonjour tristesse*. Martha Graham and company appear at the Théâtre des Champs-Élysées. Françoise and Dominique Dupuy restage Parade. Jean Serry in Chartres.
1955	Downfall of minister Pierre Mendès-France. Reservists appeal for Algeria.	Nikita Khrushchev recalled. Insurrection in Budapest.	Jean Cocteau admitted to the Academy. *Noces fantastiques* by Serge Lifar. Jerome Andrews, Jacqueline Robinson, Karin Waehner perform in Paris. The Dupuys appear at the Aix festival. The New York City Ballet performs in Paris. Raymonde Lombardin and Paul d'Arnot go on tour. A legal statute for choreographers is under consideration.
1956	Success of Pierre Poujade in the elections. Suez expedition.		Romain Gary writes *Les Racines du ciel*. Charles Autant-Lara realizes *La Traversée de Paris*. Formulation of a law regulating the teaching of dance.

| | | | Thomas d'Erlanger founds the École Supérieure d'Études Chorégraphiques (E.S.E.C.). Karin Waehner and Laura Sheleen establish the École Technique de Danse Moderne at the Association Française de Recherches et Études Chorégraphiques (A.F.R.E.C.). Maurice Béjart creates *Symphonie pour un homme seul*. Performances at the American Centre in Paris by the Compagnons de Danse, the Ballets Modernes de Paris, Françoise and Dominique Dupuy, Jacqueline Robinson, Karin Waehner and Laura Sheleen. |
| 1957 | Treaty of Rome. General Massu responsible for order in Algiers. Algerian war. | Launching of the Sputnik. | Albert Camus receives the Nobel prize. Emergence of the new novel: Michel Butor, Alain Robbe-Grillet, etc. Roger Vadim realizes *Et Dieu créa la femme*. Serge Lifar stages |

DATES	EVENTS IN FRANCE	EVENTS ABROAD	CONTEMPORARY CULTURE
			Chemin de lumière at the Opéra. José Limón appears at the Marigny. Janine Solane performs *La Belle au bois dormant* at the Palais de Chaillot. Jooss teaches at E.S.E.C.
1958	Investiture of Charles de Gaulle.		The American Ballet Theatre performs at the Théâtre des Champs-Élysées. Françoise and Dominique Dupuy win first prize for choreography in Aix. Karin Waehner founds the Ballets Contemporains.
1959	De Gaulle becomes president of the Republic.	Nikita Khrushchev visits the United States. The socialist party in the G.F.R. breaks with marxism.	The new wave. Jean Cocteau's *La Dame à la Licorne* is staged at the Opéra. Maurice Béjart produces *Orphée* and *The Tales of Hoffmann*. Birgit Cullberg in Paris. Latin American dancers.

I feel justified in grouping both the 1940s and 1950s in this third part of the book because of the obvious world-wide rupture in every aspect of life created by the Second World War. As a result of this break, pre-war events seem to belong to a distant era. During the war, except in certain areas, life faded into a kind of dimness. After the war, our story becomes one of many of our contemporaries.

The Return to Peace

France was deeply traumatized by the events of the war and the Occupation. It would be superfluous to recall here those sometimes peculiar events that coloured the behaviour and views of the French nation during the Liberation and the difficult years of recovery that followed, added to the usual problems pertaining to the resumption of peace. A whole kaleidoscope of reactions, aspirations and trends thus appeared that was made of heterogeneous elements: the search for and assertion of a national identity; the valorization of the cultural heritage; a spiritual renewal (in which the body also had its place); a lack of trust of anything resembling fascism; and perhaps also a certain uneasiness brought about by a more or less conscious sense of bitterness and guilt.

This could summarize the aspirations of the people to rehabilitate, to delete, to be reborn, to build.

[I returned to France in 1947. The beloved France of my happy childhood and adolescence, the France of which I had dreamed in my years of exile during the war. Aware of those six elapsed years that saw my development from adolescence to adulthood, during which my view of the world had no doubt changed somewhat, I found a Paris that had been transformed in relation to the memory I had of it. Above all, in the artistic and intellectual circles I frequented, I was struck by a kind of exaltation that emanated from the work of these individuals, and their judicious thinking, by the boldness of creativity, the circulation of ideas, the lively atmosphere and their fortitude in just coping with things.]

The years immediately following the war were in fact extremely fertile from a cultural point of view. It was as if a lid had been lifted after years of difficulties, both small or tragic, releasing tremendous energy. The context in which this took place was still difficult, however: the burdens of political and economic problems on both a national and an international scale, the absence of those who had lost their lives, the memory of the horrors, and the hardships of everyday life. Nevertheless, the overflowing vitality of youth sprang forth and manifested itself in a number of ways. It was a period of 'roaring years' all over again, years of which St-Germain-des-Prés became the symbol, the symbol of this fever of freedom, expression, pleasure and invention, combining philosophy (genuine or phoney), jazz, fashion, poetry and a new mores.

In contrast with the smoke-filled cellars of St-Germain-des-Prés were a number of other favoured moments and places, such as the evenings spent around campfires in which thousands of young people gathered together in order to seek to build a better world within the framework of socio-educational movements that were often spear-headed by actors or dancers. The resumption of this circulation of ideas and people opened up the country to a whole range of trends in every domain. These new trends, in whatever sphere of activity, did not arouse immediate enthusiasm or support, however; the immovable weight of conservatism, moral rigidity, and the power of the 'establishment' meant that it would take many years of struggling for ideas to gain acceptance that today pass unquestioned. But has it ever really been otherwise? It was particularly noticeable in this period in which an enormous dynamic creative force coexisted with a no less restrictive, confining and pusillanimous one. This was extremely apparent as far as dance was concerned.

The period of convalescence in France, as in the rest of Europe, came to an end during the 1950s, or rather, gave way to a state of growth and development that certainly did not pass unmarked by crises of both a national and an international nature: a growing change of attitude towards pre-war political, social, economic and cultural values; a withdrawal within nationalistic frontiers; the end of the Indo-Chinese and Algerian wars; the sketching of an economic Europe; a questioning look at the East; social unease and the jolts within the successive governing parties that culminated in the accession to power of De Gaulle and the founding of the Fifth Republic. Such crises did not prevent economic progress and expansion from occurring in France, however. This was the beginning of the 'Glorious Thirties': the modernization of industry, increased purchasing power, and a vast improvement in social policy. The young generation, 'the new wave', entered a new era of improved purchasing power and leisure. The older generation of great creators, such as Claudel, Matisse, Brecht, Dullin and Jouvet, disappeared from the scene and their mentors became instead Camus, Sartre, Malraux and Saint-Exupéry. The Church of France contributed to this renewal of ideas and activity with the liberal initiative of the Mission de France movement and working-priests.

Let us recall the situation that existed before the Second World War and list the resident and visiting practitioners of dance during this period.

In the field of classical dance:

- the Opéra and the Opéra-Comique, where Serge Lifar reigned supreme;
- the Châtelet theatre;
- the visiting Ballets Russes;
- similarly, the Ballets de Monte Carlo, of which Massine was the principal choreographer.

In the field of exotic dance:

- the much appreciated Spanish dance with Teresina, Escudero, etc.;
- Javanese, Korean and Japanese dances.

In the field of modern dance:

- native and immigrant dancers in line of descent from Laban, Dalcroze and Wigman: Mila Cirul, Julia Marcus, Ludolf Schild, Heinz Finkel and Marguerite Bougai, the schools and performances of whom were described in Part II;
- Jean Weidt's Ballets 38, Jean Serry's promising research and the serious pedagogical work of teachers such as Yvonne Berge and Hilde Peerbohm;
- the much loved visitors, such as the Sakharoffs and others, including Paul Swann, Alexander von Swaine and Ernestine Stodelle;
- the galas of the rhythmic dance schools, the lectures and performances organized by the Archives Internationales de la Danse, by the Tribune de la Danse...

And then war broke out. Like everything else, dance activity was reduced, perhaps more so than that in the other arts. France in particular withdrew into herself. Nevertheless, the following events may be noted:

- in 1941 Jacques Hébertot's 'Vendredis de la Danse' recommenced in his theatre on the boulevard des Batignolles, featuring Nyota Inyoka, José Torrès, Catherine Paul, Pierre Baruzzi, Madika and Julia Marcus;
- similarly, the Grand Palais resumed its programme of dance performances that included Janine Solane (*Les Potiers*), Teresina, the Ballets de Loïe Fuller and Marcelle Bourgat;

In 1942 and 1943 one heard of Ludmilla Tcherina, Lifar, Janine Charrat, Renée Jeanmaire, Roland Petit and René Fenonjois... 'moderns', hardly.

New Landscapes

Let us now consider the new landscapes in modern dance in France in the immediate post-war years, what grew there and what winds blew through it.

We must first of all set the scene and sketch the back-cloth against which modern dance obstinately pursued its own line of development. True, ideas were springing up on every front in a surfeit of creativity, but modern dance remained on the fringe in relation to the predominant trends and the approval of the public and establishment alike.

This was the reign, the heyday of Lifar at the Opéra (which continued from the period discussed in the preceding chapter in spite of a few jolts); of Roland Petit's Ballets des Champs-Élysées; the Grand Ballet du Marquis de Cuevas; Janine Charrat's Ballets de France and Maurice Béjart's Ballets de l'Étoile. Paris 'chic' still set the tone and neo-classicism was the principal standard against which every manifestation of dance was judged.

It is interesting to consider the programme of the annual gala of the Association des Amis de la Danse at the Théâtre des Champs-Élysées in February 1953, for example. This gala, entitled 'Toute la Danse,' brought together dancers principally from the Opéra and large classical companies (Cuevas, Nederland Opera), and the dances included, amongst others, Lifar's *Dramma per Musica* to music by Bach, Françoise Adret's *Apollon Musagète* (Stravinsky), Jaque Chaurand's *Tentation* (Leclair), Michel Descombey's *Frères humains* (Gershwin), Lycette Darsonval's *Rondo Capriccioso* (Saint-Saëns) and Léone Mail's *Quartetto* (Rossini). Only one modern work was included in the programme and that was *Jabadao* by Jean Serry to music by Georges Delerue in which Mila Cirul, Edith Allard, Georgette Watteau, Jacqueline Levant, Suzanne Rémon and Sadi Bazin danced.

Similarly, the report for 1951–52 as presented by Françoise Reiss in her book/chronicle *Sur la pointe des pieds* (Revue Adam, Paris, 1952), mentions productions, performances and visits by the Ballets des Champs-Élysées, the Grand Ballet du Marquis de Cuevas, the Ballets de Janine Charrat, the New York City Ballet (on its first visit), the Ballets de Marigny (Milorad Miskovitch), the Opéra (with Les Indes Galantes, amongst others) and the Opéra-Comique, of course. 'Outside of the classical line' are mentioned the Katherine Dunham Ballet, the Ballets of Latin America (J. Perez Fernandes), Carmen Amaya's Spanish Ballets, the Hindu Ballets of Mrinalini Sarabhai and Nyota Inyoka, and the Yugoslavian Ballets; and at the very end, with no detail, she refers to the recitals and galas organized by Danse et Culture.

Our Own 'Modern' Dancers

And what has became of our 'moderns'? The native French dancers who
made names for themselves during the years immediately preceding the
war resumed their artistic and pedagogical initiatives with renewed
vigour: Jean Serry in particular who aroused many vocations and
passionately broke new ground; Janine Solane; Marguerite Bougai;
Yvonne Berge and Hilde Peerbohm, to name but a few.

Amongst the modern dancers and choreographers from abroad
who settled in France during the 1930s there were, of course, a large
number of Germans and/or Jews, some of whom had disappeared when
the curtain rose on the new era. Some, like Jean Weidt, left the country,
whilst others such as Finkel, Schild and Wieskemann died at an early age,
leaving the torch to pass into the hands of their closest pupils: Françoise
Michaud and Dominique Dupuy, Raymonde Lombardin and Jacqueline
Levant, and Hélène Carlut, respectively.

Grafts

During the 1950s a number of other foreign artists came to settle in France
for various personal reasons, but doubtless attracted by the artistic
climate and the potential of budding creativity that existed there too.
These included Jerome Andrews, Jacqueline Robinson, Laura Sheleen and
Karin Waehner, the diverse talents of whom contributed to the development of dance in France. In the case of three of these, the influence of
Wigman predominated; however Laura Sheleen introduced techniques
that originated in America, especially that of Graham.

Very soon these personalities found themselves at the 'bridgehead'
within the French dance scene, working alongside artists of such ability
as Françoise and Dominique Dupuy, Anne Gardon and Olga Stens.

A number of other artists also came to work in Paris, including
Muriel Topaz and Edith Allard from America, Mara Dajanova and
Georgina de Uriarte from Argentina, Paul d'Arnot from Uruguay and
Gilberto Motta from Brazil. Some of these stayed for several years, which
was sufficient time for them to leave a deep-rooted memory, perhaps even
a mark. It is noteworthy that several of them came from South America, a
phenomenon that was to become increasingly common during the 1960s.

Turning Towards the Roots

It was during the 1950s also that a kind of return to the roots of European
modern dance – or rather a belated awareness – occurred. These roots

were not distant, either in time or space, but they had been somewhat neglected, as if hidden from view. We will consider here those summer schools that were organized in Switzerland after the end of the war by the Swiss Association of Professional Dancers and Gymnasts, and which took place successively in Macolin, Interlaken, Montreux and Zurich.

Great German masters such as Mary Wigman, Rosalia Chladek and Sigurd Leeder, whose reputations had spread to France in what appeared to be an underground way, and who, for obvious reasons, had been constrained to silence, taught there. Dancers eager for inspiration and knowledge flocked to work with them. These were times of extremely intense and fruitful study and encounters, and, moreover, many nationalities were represented there. For a large number of dancers who came from France, these summer schools constituted a high point, a pregnant moment in their careers, the memory of which remains particularly dear to them.

I should like to point out a related phenomenon that the specific orientation of this study may not allow me to discuss at length. There was a certain disaffection that occurred in *Germany* with regard to expressionist dance after the war. For whatever reasons, political, cultural, conscious or unconscious, there was a kind of 'void' that was filled to a certain extent by neo-classical dance and jazz. It was as though within its birthplace, expressionist dance seemed to have lost sight of its identity, and had a delay to make up for.

A sign of the growing importance of the phenomenon of dance in this period was the creation of new specialized reviews, such as *Toute la danse*, *Art et danse*, *La Danse* and *Danse et rythmes*. (Full references to these reviews are cited in the appendix.) Discourse about dance evolved towards a specificity that rested on parameters other than literary, musical or theatrical ones, or on classical dance alone. Certain writers and journalists made an effort, sometimes from actual dance experience, to understand the new principles at work, and they played a decisive part in the growing public awareness of modern dance. Their appreciation of those who sought new paths gave the latter moral encouragement and sometimes tangible help in promoting and disseminating their work. We may refer in the first instance to Dinah Maggie and the Association Française de Recherches et Études Chorégraphiques, but also to Jean Silvant, Pierre Michaut, Ferdinando Reyna, Lise Brunel, Delfor Peralta and José Atienza, Jacques Baril and Gilberte Cournand.

Trends of 'Culture for the Masses'

A very important and considerably far-reaching factor in the development of modern dance in France was the emergence of a movement based on 'socio-educational' premises, or 'popular culture', to coin a term current at the time. Often of left-wing political or religious (derived from scouting) allegiance, several organizations established during or after the war left their mark on the period: laboratories of ideas, nurseries of talents, a home of the spirit. These organizations shared the common aim of what I might be tempted to call 'moral rearmament', and preached the pursuit of authenticity, the opening out of the individual, creativity, and respect for nature, other people and permanent values. I would recall in this context the consideration I made in Part I of the emergence of this type of ideology and enterprise following a national or world crisis.

A document dating from this period may shed some light on this procedure; Michel Garnier wrote in *Faire des vivants* in 1947:

> 'This often unconscious tendency to rediscover unity through the dynamic equilibrium and constructive harmony of the individual as much as of society as a whole appears more and more frequently. Setting out from fundamental principles, it is manifested in the development of sport, camping and other open-air activities, and in the cultivation of a strong and healthy body that allows the possibility of rediscovering the value and joy of effort. This physical expansion constituted the first stage. The second, which is taking shape at present, appears to be one of psychological liberation. We are currently witnessing the emergence of educational groups born of the aspirations of the masses towards a living human culture.
>
> It was during their leisure hours that young people have often felt the need to sing to their own accompaniments, perform folk dances, act plays and tell stories or recite poetry whilst sitting round the camp-fire. They rediscovered a sense of festivity, the manifestation of collective joy, nourished by the contributions of those who possessed a rich means of expression. Good will and improvisation alone could not suffice to secure the acquisition of such means of expression. Artists and educators found themselves confronted by the problem of adapting their techniques to modern popular culture'.[1]

From this were born what might be called 'techniques of expression'.

Jacques Copeau and his Heritage

It would be impossible to discuss techniques of expression, theatre or dance in France from a historical perspective without mentioning Jacques Copeau.

In 1909 he founded *La Nouvelle revue française* with Gide and Schlumberger. In 1923 he created the Vieux-Colombier theatre and the company of the same name which included Jouvet, Dullin, Decroux, Jean Dasté and Suzanne Bing; he later established the École de Comédiens.

---

[1] *Faire des vivants*, collected authors (Édition de la Nouvelle France, Paris, 1947).

Copeau's doctrines led him to proscribe that theatre of convention or realism that was so dear to Antoine, and rather to draw inspiration from the concepts and techniques of acting and production advocated by Gordon Craig and Stanislawski. In the context of this more syncretic, poetic view of the theatrical act and event and a profound human dimension, the body (and the mask, which allowed a more intense reading of it) was called upon to play a much larger role, as were the pursuit of authenticity and inner necessity. For this reason, Copeau's work was not unconnected with the increasing perception of dance as an autonomous language.

The Vieux-Colombier was to exert a considerable influence on European theatre and on an entire generation of actors and producers.

This institution broke up in 1924. Copeau retired to Burgundy and, with a group of his disciples known as 'les Copiaux', he attempted to rediscover the sources of popular theatre: an adaptable travelling company, a deeply concerned team who performed before an inexperienced public. The Copiaux's mission was to inspire many other similar enterprises, such as the Compagnie des Quinze, directed by Michel Saint-Denis, and Léon Chancerel's Comédiens Routiers.

Copeau had numerous followers who were active during the period outlined in this chronicle, instigators of a genuine, living, poetic theatre, in tune with the public – *chargés de missions* in the policy of theatrical decentralization. Jean Dasté, Hubert Gignoux, Maurice Jacquemont, Olivier Hussenot and Jean Doat must be mentioned in this context, and these individuals will be referred to elsewhere because of their inclusion of dance as one of their principal concerns; dancers worked with them and drew inspiration from them.

The preoccupations underlying popular culture and the training in practices and techniques of expression became thus one of the directions taken by dance to flourish amongst a fraction of the masses. This phenomenon was regarded somewhat haughtily and sometimes even with a touch of anxiety by the professionals of dance – especially the well established ones, the mandarins of the stage. 'Dance-for-all' – a fine undertaking, might effectively imply the danger of a devaluation, a lessening of its technical demands, leading to any old thing and the view that anyone could become a dancer.

Not without reason, this anxiety still exists today, together with the view that everyone might believe that he can become a choreographer too. The entire phenomenon must be considered with discernment, and the *amateur* must be clearly distinguished from the *professional*.

[Dance is still not part of 'ordinary behaviour'. It continues to be considered as a rather special and extraordinary activity, an artistic or magical one. No one would take special note of a person who hums to himself or sings at a banquet! But if this same person began to 'move', or indeed dance, in the same circumstances, what would be thought of him then? That he were rather eccentric to say the least!

The average human being is expected to be able to handle a pencil, however clumsily, and draw something that illustrates a point or simply gives shape to an inner image. There is nothing unusual about this. But if this same human being began to make gestures or perform steps, 'honest passers-by would give them funny looks … '.

There are always discotheques!

Another phenomenon strikes me – that dance and music have always been associated with one another, as twin sisters. Thus they are most definitely in the innermost depths of man since the dawn of humanity. Nevertheless, they asserted their independence from the time when music became a developed language, codified in written form and therefore susceptible to autonomous development, both in structure and semantic. As a result, music never ceased to evolve over the centuries towards greater complexity, a thing of the mind, the heart and the senses, whilst dance in Western culture, on the other hand, remained more or less static.

The divergence between the paths followed by dance and music became conclusive at the end of the nineteenth century. Music ventured into unknown territory, breaking away from the old systems and forging new ones. Dance, for its part, continued to submit to the yoke of aesthetic and socio-cultural conventions.

It was not through its association with music but with the theatre that dance escaped from this rut. The approach of new dance thus followed that of new theatre in returning to the very roots of the expression of emotions and human condition, relying upon a more lucid consciousness of impulses and behaviour.]

The following sections provide some indication of the most important popular culture organizations, French institutions that did indeed leave their mark on the era and fertilize all the arts, theatre and dance in particular.

Travail et Culture (T.E.C.)

This was certainly the popular culture organization whose widespread influence, achievements and perenniality were the most remarkable. It would perhaps be appropriate to define the term 'popular culture' here since it has frequently aroused opposing stances. It was certainly a left-wing movement, but it must be remembered also that the connotations of belonging to a particular political party may differ from one period to the next. Common to almost all these organizations of popular culture, however, is an ideology that may be summed up in the following paragraph by Maurice Delarue, one of the founders of Travail et Culture, in *Éducation et culture populaire*, 1946:

> '*The endeavours of the present champions of culture to liberate art, science, thought and pedagogy ran symmetrically, or in parallel, with those of a youth and proletariat anxious to break free of their chains. Only a combination of the efforts of the proletariat and the younger generation on the one hand, with those of artists, educators and philosophers on the other in concerted action, only a reciprocal understanding between these, may ensure the rebirth of a culture which one will no longer need to qualify with the term 'popular' in order to give it its meaning, for it will then be understood that there is no genuine culture but that which proceeds from the shared impetus of an entire nation, fighting for the common cause of liberty*'.

Here are a few historical landmarks concerning individuals and events. Travail et Culture was established in 1945. Its aim was to '*create a board of studies whose function was to co-ordinate all the educational work with that of popular culture movements and to prepare the students and pupils of art schools for their roles as cultural promoters*'. Some of these founders had already played a part in the Jeune France association, established in 1940 and dissolved by the Vichy government in 1942; it was revived in part in 1943 by the Centre de Culture Populaire, which had as its principal activity the organization of courses in dramatic art and the distribution of literary data. (It is not without significance to recall that these organizations sprang up under the Occupation, and that the Resistance was occasionally active in them.)

Amongst the people responsible for Travail et Culture in its early stages were Maurice Delerue, Emmanuel Mounier, André Clavé, Jean Vilar, Jean-Marie Serreau, Jean-Marie Conty, Louis Pauwels, André Bazin, Pierre-Aimé Touchard and a number of other leading personalities. One of the first departments to be created was the C.I.D. (Culture par l'Initiation Dramatique) which was responsible for knowledge of the theatre, the education of the public, and contact between artists and the public. The C.I.C. (cinema), C.I.M. (music and dance, the latter trailing a little behind, as always!), and C.I.P. (plastic arts) followed shortly afterwards. Within these four sections Travail et Culture not only presented performances and lectures in various different settings (notably for students and workers), but also provided evening classes, courses, documentation and publications. Travail et Culture established itself in the provinces and North Africa also. In 1946 it co-founded the Centre

National de Documentation and, having installed its theatrical activities in the Maubel conservatoire, where Dullin also taught, it became one of the organizers of the Competition for Young Companies launched by Jeanne Laurent. The latter, who was responsible for music and performance at the ministry of national education, had been one of the key workers in the policy of theatrical decentralization since 1946.

The evening classes organized by Travail et Culture covered a range of cultural subjects, and the promoters during 1947 included Claude Martin, Roger Blin, Marcel Marceau and Charles Antonetti in the field of dramatic acting, and Jean Serry, Raymonde Lombardin and Marguerite Bougai in that of dance. This is a significant choice, for it represents modern dance exclusively.

The successive ups and downs of Travail et Culture form another story. In this context it is sufficient to note it as one of the places on the French cultural scene where expressionist dance could flourish and develop during these critical years, and as a meeting place for people driven by the same artistic and humanitarian spirit (Information extracted from *Travail et Culture – Éléments historiques*, 1986).

Education par le jeu dramatique (E.P.J.D.)

E.P.J.D., 'School of theatre – School of life', was established as a co-operative society under the impetus of Mytho Bourgoin and Jean-Marie Conty in May 1946 by the producers Jean-Louis Barrault, Roger Blin, André Clavé, Jean and Marie-Hélène Dasté, Claude Martin and Jean Vilar, who, for the most part, had been associated with the Travail et Culture team, and thus supported a certain popular culture ideology.

Rather than presenting a full exegesis, here are a few paragraphs presenting the school, dating from 1947:

> 'E.P.J.D. is not the product of intellectual theories, but of experience tried and tested on young workers and shown to be successful by men of the theatre, nurtured in the main on the ideas of Copeau and Dullin.
> The assimilation of techniques is necessary in the acting profession as it is in all professions. These techniques are indeed important, but, over and above technique in this profession more than any other, it is the instrument itself, the human being, that counts and makes such techniques possible and effective in order to induce in its pupils self-mastery in the interests of their personal creation. This is the principal aim of E.P.J.D... Many current methods of teaching are addressed above all to the intellect, whilst allusion to all feeling is reduced to a minimum. This natural sensibility must be rediscovered, and then refined and oriented: this is a school dedicated to the pursuit of the truth and sincerity necessary not only to the actors of the future but to educators too, as indeed it is to anybody, for it offers them the chance to be themselves and to take control of their own life.

These remarks entail some knowledge of the scheme of work of E.P.J.D. It aims first and foremost to provide an education in sensitivity through improvisation, together with an indication of the means of expression of this sensitivity, firstly through speech, by singing, which pitches the voice and enlarges its register, and then through attitude and gestures by means of appropriate gymnastics, relaxation techniques and dance. This education in sensitivity and its means of expression is completed by a study of the history of the theatre, the analysis of texts, courses in psychology, and lectures on theatre, cinema, music, painting and medicine etc.'.

Jacqueline Levant was responsible for the courses in dance. Maurice Martenot directed the relaxation classes, and Jacqueline Robinson, initially a student there, subsequently gave courses in drama improvisation.

A book entitled *Faire des vivants* (*To Make Living Persons*) was published in 1947 by the team within the framework of E.P.J.D. It covers in detail the aims, methods and socio-economic and cultural context of its teaching, together with its productions.

Like many private initiatives, E.P.J.D. was forced to close its doors as a professional school in 1951 through lack of financial support, although it continued to provide evening classes for some time. Until this date, it served as a melting-pot through which a large number of individuals who made careers for themselves either in the theatre, as actors, or as mime artists, dancers, producers and educators, passed – individuals working in the field of human adventure.

Spiritual Awakening

Within the framework of the spiritual awakening experienced by the catholic church in France, several initiatives saw the light of day, one of which had a bearing on the vitality of a growing movement towards authenticity expressed through dance. This involved an interpretation of liturgy through bodily expression, singing and dance, and the interest of certain ecclesiastics in the very phenomenon of bodily expression as an awakening of sensitivity and a sign or symbol of spiritual expression.

Amongst those organizations within the catholic faith that promoted research into and practice of bodily expression and dance, the following may be cited:

- the Mission de France, which undertook the provision of courses in bodily expression (including ones for the seminarists);
- Vie Nouvelle, a left-wing Christian movement established in 1947, derived from scouting. This movement sought a more natural, committed life, the ideal of which was the 'socially responsible individualism' and universality of mankind preached

by Emmanuel Mounier. It was in the search for this universality that, amongst the various activities encouraged by Vie Nouvelle, dance appeared as an instrument and path towards knowledge, expression and communal enjoyment. During the 1950s this organization (which is still in existence today), thus provided a social environment in which dance and bodily expression could be practised and understood.

Scouts

The particular vocation of the scout movement has always been to promote the complete man, on a practical as much as on a spiritual level, set against a background of loyalty to God, one's country and the community. Clearly, this type of organization will assert itself with even greater force when country, community or individual find themselves threatened, mocked or in danger. Thus, the scout movement emerged out of the war with renewed vigour and dynamism, and formed an ideal environment for the resumption of educational projects.

The female branch of the scout movement, the French girl guides, perhaps placed greater emphasis on 'artistic' concerns such as expression, creativity and aesthetics. The enormous activity of the guide movement in the field of expression, spear-headed by some remarkable individuals, was highly valued; traces of it remain not only in its direct spiritual legacy but also in a kind of contagiousness and the authority of its writings. The publications that emanated more or less explicitly from the French girl guides testify to the relevance and quality of its projects and achievements. One example, *Jours de vie, jours de fête*, published in 1961, was a work of combined authorship in which the section on dance and bodily expression contained a wealth of insights into teaching.

Cadences, a more or less monthly publication within the guide movement, must also be mentioned. Founded in 1944, this small review appeared for several years under the subtitle *Études et problèmes d'art et d'expression* and included Anne-Marie Debatte, Simone Piguet, Yvonne Berge and Hilde Peerbohm amongst its editorial team. It provided a most relevant ground for artistic and pedagogical problems relating to dance.

Expression through the Body

These 'expression camps' that flourished in the 1950s involving not only the scout movement but a number of secular movements also, gradually gave way to more specialized or technical and commercial courses.

In addition to the disciplines of community life and all forms of crafts, workshops were held in musical, graphic, literary, theatrical and bodily expression in these camps; thus the term 'bodily expression' in its most primitive, immediate and basic sense was born, often deviated, and became widespread. Naturally, it included the more clearly defined categories of dramatic action, mime and dance, but at base it simply implied improvisation and, ultimately, the staging of anything that could be expressed by the body, a form of gesture that resulted from an inner impulse. This was the common basis and point of departure of the disciplines and categories outlined above. In its crudest form, therefore, the spontaneous approach that was explored and widely practised by a large number of non-specialists, and in which convention was supposed to be banished and aesthetics relegated to the background, constituted an entirely new procedure. (Techniques of expression through the body may also be found much earlier in the work of Jacques Copeau at the Vieux-Colombier school, for example, but here they were aimed at a specific minority.)

It must be emphasized that, until this time, the improvisations of dancers had clearly been shaped by an overriding concern for aesthetics, whatever this might have been, and remained confined within the framework of a conventional vocabulary, achieving only an illusory freedom. Dance had to be beautiful and harmonious, if not graceful. Nowadays, of course, so much research and work have been carried out in the domain of the 'expressive body' that nothing can surprise us any more!

In this same period bodily expression, mime and dance witnessed a new and masterly application in the theatre. This was the age of Barrault's great productions, of Claudel's *Christophe Colomb*, Sophocles's *Œdipe*, produced by André Obey, and *Jeanne au bûcher*, staged by Georges Hirsch, in which choric movement occupied an important place.

It also saw Marcel Marceau's rise to fame, following in the footsteps of Etienne Decroux, and an increase in the popularity of the art of mime as both a theatre art and an amateur practice, in the hands of individuals such as Pinok and Matho, and Jacques Lecoq.

Modern dance tended to be referred to now as 'expressive dance' rather than 'free dance' as in the previous decade. ('Rhythmic' and 'harmonic' dance designated particular types that were of Dalcrozian, Duncanian, or gymnastic descent.) All the same, modern dance began to be taken a little more seriously both as a theatre art and an educational discipline. The work of psychologists, sociologists and other theorists encouraged thinking about dance, although still in a fairly discreet way, and about the body as a means of expression, its role within society and the very essence of movement itself. As a result, several 'historic' works appeared that included *Le Ballet contemporain* by Pierre Michaut, *Problèmes de la danse* by Maurice Brillant, works by Lifar, Reyna, Schaikewitch, and, more significantly. Janine Solane's *Pour une danse plus humaine* and Jean Serry's *Par le mouvement*. Laban's work was published in England and, in the field of psychology, translations of Freud and Jung appeared, together with the works of Piaget, Wallon and Reich that have since become classics.

Institutions that Foster Dance

The Archives Internationales de la Danse, following its eclipse during the war period, resumed its activities of lectures, demonstrations, performances and exhibitions perhaps on a slightly less prestigious, but nevertheless remarkable scale. Its library constituted a treasure-trove for researchers, and its director, Pierre Tugal, encouraged those young choreographers who had a real message to convey, through his advice and contacts and the putting at their disposal of the Archives's hall and reception structures. For various reasons, the Archives Internationales de la Danse barely survived beyond the 1950s.

An institution of great importance was Danse et Culture, established and fostered by Jean Dorcy. It provided a particularly dynamic means for the promotion and dissemination of dance (not so modern dance, it must be admitted, but this style clearly benefited from it, nevertheless, particularly during the following decade).

Similarly, although less widespread than Danse et Culture in the period and area it covered, but more effective and lasting in scope, particularly in relation to modern dance, was the Association Française de Recherches et Études Chorégraphiques (A.F.R.E.C.), founded by the critic and writer on dance, Dinah Maggie. It must be recalled that A.F.R.E.C. provided a meeting point for both local and immigrant modern dancers who were concerned with sharing their knowledge through a process of mutual enrichment, thus enabling a strong, lively and credible form of dance to take root in France. This occurred on every level: in the teaching of amateurs and the training of professionals; in the creation and dissemination of dance; and in the education and sensitizing of the public, that indispensable partner of the creator.

The places in Paris where 'new' dance could be performed and seen have already been discussed briefly. On the whole, we find the same places that continued to promote dance in an obvious hierarchy of notoriety, prestige or modesty, and above all, cost, with the addition of a few small theatres, such as the Poche Montparnasse, that dared to take the risk.

The dancers, whether soloists or members of the few private modern companies, were in general self-financed, but perhaps less extensively than in the past. A few projects, such as Jean Serry's large-scale open-air productions at Chartres, for example, were partly financed by official institutions.

It must be pointed out that certain associations, such as the A.I.D., Danse et Culture and the Théâtre d'Essai de la Danse, provided a framework in which dancers and choreographers could perform (by audition), without having to pay the costs. There were also organizations that sponsored performances and arranged meetings and competitions. These associations were rather conservative, however, and included the Association des Écrivains et Critiques de la Danse, the Association Française des Amis de la Danse and the Cercle Paul-Valéry, which promoted aesthetic studies in general, but in which dance occupied a certain position. The Jeunesses Musicales de France, which sometimes included dance in its didactic programmes, should be mentioned too.

Dance schools grew in number. Those dancers who were already well established in their careers had their own studios when possible, but there were some places such as the Salle Pleyel, the Wacker studio on the rue de Douai which is no longer in existence today, and the Morin studio on the rue du Bac, that hired out studios that took on an air of 'permanence' for certain dancers.

The position regarding the professional, legal and fiscal situation of the vast majority of non-amateur practitioners remained vague for a number of years. They lived from day to day, frequently unaware of these problems.

It was a fertile period nevertheless although the pioneers of modern dance had to fight hard in order that it might obtain its full right to existence. Little by little the seed was sown and this subsequently gave rise to a harvest, even if such a future did not seem obvious to the protagonists at the time. Let it not be thought that their cause was understood, in spite of the courage and fervour of certain individuals. There may have reigned amongst a 'happy few' an illusion of being recognized and understood, but this existed only as long as they remained together, at home as it were, for as soon as they ventured into the public arena the reality was less encouraging. Was it any consolation that the same situation had existed some ten or twenty years ago? Had things really remained unchanged? Audiences had increased in number, and the fighters had become a little less naïve and perhaps more aggressive.

With hindsight, the ignorance and resistance of the critics, and of the general public, bring a smile to the lips. Neither Martha Graham in 1954 nor José Limón in 1950 and later in 1957 were well received on their first visits to Paris, except by some of the more astute critics and a few members of the public who knew what to expect of the event.

I cannot resist the desire to quote Claude Baignères in *Le Monde* (June 1954):

> '*Martha Graham has combined in a vocabulary of unheard of richness formulas from classical dance, those of Jaques-Dalcroze and Isadora Duncan with those of the East, and knows how to blend and harmonize these diverse borrowings. How come that our enthusiasm sinks completely when these different elements are combined to constitute a performance? The music is extraordinarily weak and does not seem suited to inspire interesting choreographies; furthermore, the action unfolds with such a slow unchanging rhythm, the resulting impression is one of deadly monotony. Right now, Martha Graham reminds one of a painter who has discovered original colours and unusual brush strokes, and has written fascinating and revolutionary aesthetic treatises. All that remains is for her to create a masterpiece*'.

Oliver Merlin wrote also in *Le Monde* of 19 September 1957 concerning José Limón's performance:

> ' ... *with the exception of Emperor Jones, the show was distressingly worthless. Style and expressionism are indeed grand words for these rhythmic exhibitions, produced without scenery and in embryonic costume, in which the outlandish gives way to the awkward, to ungainly necks, fidgety hands and wriggling buttocks, the whole effect finally being one of solemn boredom. Limón's partners exert and writhe their bodies with the best will in the world. Nevertheless, they do take Parisians rather too much for Iroquoians*'.

Might it perhaps be taking too defensive a line to suggest that an indisputable atmosphere of bad faith reigned at this time? One need only take as an example and proof of this the article by Jean Dorcy, quoted in the appendix, which at the time caused a general outcry amongst the practitioners and defenders of modern dance.

The Birth of the Body

I entrust the task of concluding these reflections on the period 1945–1960 to Anne-Marie Debatte, one of the driving forces of these heroic years. Her account sketches the background, and the particular and varied context in which modern dance was then able to develop. It evokes most pertinently the state of mind that presided over human and artistic endeavour, or *one* of these endeavours at least, in the 1950s:

'Must we search for Masters?

Whence did we from our very childhood, discover this taste for movement, this desire, this union within us of Music, Silence and these great movements of the body, these images of outlines in space? This poetry gushing forth from underground rivers and rustling breezes.

The sound of imported jazz, the harmonies of Ravel and Erik Satie emerging from the wind-up gramophone, Mozart trios tentatively performed at family gatherings, all carried us away on unknown adventures. Summer holidays spent by the sea, recently cut hair style and the newness of wearing shorts. What freedom was promised us? The birth of the body, the birth of Bodies.

What did we care for these tutus from long ago, these shoe-clad feet, these timeless visions of the Ballets that we could only imagine through certain rather outdated picture books that bore no direct relation to our favourite games? . . .

The theatre of our teenage years smelt of wood smoke and was lit by the white horse of the moonlight. The reflection of the torches appeared in the lakes, and our voices echoed above the rocks. Our farandoles were fostered with silence and our dances sprang forth from the songs of many choirs. Our bodies learnt to feel from their breath in this perpetual dual encounter with the elements and the harmony of others. Those were our first theatres, even though in the winter we occasionally yielded to the temptations of the "real stage" where our intellectual friends raised us to the status of stars. Our unattainable models remained the Comédiens Routiers. They fulfilled our expectations of a communal theatre and of creation in which the body would play its part. Led by Léon Chancerel, they swept us along in the wake of those distant adventures of which our fathers spoke, those of Jacques Copeau, and of theatrical venture, spare, demanding and upright, free from approximation and histrionics.

Then France went to war, and we witnessed the tearing apart, the exile, the rupture and destruction of all our hopes and expectations; yet, the endless hope and expectation that one day everything could be rebuilt and our desire for freedom fulfilled. At age twenty, an uncertain future. This was the time of seeking for authenticity, of the deepest inner working of the body.

We felt the influence of teachers from abroad, of yoga and zen, and of the abstemious life. How should the inclination to express oneself be reconciled with the inclination to be true? Not even through the wish to break with academic conventions to which we were, anyway, unaccustomed; strangers to these techniques, these rites, we went beyond them to find the sources that inspired us.

Echoes of the work of Dullin and Barrault reached us and we lived on this as if it were our daily bread ... and we met Doat, Douking, and Jean Serry who had no desire to teach anything, except to share himself with us. Voyageurs du Rêve went on tour ... At the beginning of 1944, we became aware of the imminent collapse of Germany, yet we improvised all day and all night long ... we were intoxicated, unconscious, living only to express the new life that was to be ours, the new life we hoped would be pure, whole, clean. On the eve of finding ourselves free again, we felt that this freedom had always lived within us, leading us ever upwards.

I believe that in these troubled times, over and above what may have existed officially and reached us only from afar, without our being able to catalogue it, there also existed in France a very innocent intuitive trend that was to spread without noise, publicity, or desire for actual diffusion or methods. It was simply living, an expression of Life.

Living at last. Finding the physical, spiritual and intellectual means to live one's own life, the lives of the younger generation who had been entrusted to our care, and of those who had suffered so much during these terrible years. Inside this incubator we were finally able to witness the birth, the hatching out, of something different. Randomly nourished on books and rare but always exceptional discoveries, we could at last emerge from our own thoughts and meditations, exercises and experiments, and catch up on this time that had been stolen from our activity; we could declare publicly and to those fresh and excited youngsters who wished to follow us, that the body had its place in art other than as a statue in a museum, that it was not reduced to the role of a dummy or a target. What concern of ours were the models of others; were there any that existed for our own discoveries? We were born anew; we flew the flag of a different way of life. What did we know of sociology and its effect on the self? Little no doubt, but we nevertheless turned towards our fellows and to "teaching", eager to share, to make profound discoveries, not of schools or of knowledge, but of an exchange of experiences. The pursuit of the liberated body was opened up before us.

The opportunities provided by the post-war experimental theatres, the experiences of the return to sobriety, to purity of gesture and the taste for the rhythm of movement, the search for harmony between theatre and the expressive body, the poetry of gesture, reticence before the remnants of "artificial sumptuousness" from a disconnected past and the resurrection of freedom of expression, all that drew some of us to those waters on the fringe of text and silence, on the edge of music in this precious alchemy: I am referring to the choral bodily work that demands openness and sharing, to energies received and transmitted, to sustained attention to others, to the technique of balance and the breath that is the bearer of life, and to full mastery of the precision of the play of masks, amongst other requirements.

This kind of performance brought with it new hope, the fruits of which would be reaped later, and of which *L'Exode* (1945) by Jean and Marie-Hélène Dasté provided a good example. This work followed in line of descent from the Copiaux's *Jeu de la villle et des champs*, and Barrault's *Tandis que j'agonise* may perhaps have been a precursor too.

It is important, furthermore, to outline the most immediate applications of the legacy of the Groupe d'Art et d'Expression des Guides de France which, in 1942–43, in the free zone of France set up perfectly exemplary camps of dramatic expression, with Léon Chancerel, the Jolys, Yvonne Berge and Hilde Peerbohm. And then there were all these meetings of minds in the world of the theatre (Jean-Marie Conty, Charles Antonetti, the Frères Jacques and the Compagnons de la Chanson, the Voyageurs du Rêve and the Compagnons de Saint-Jean) and of dance (Finkel, Solane, Mallarmé, and later Jerome Andrews, Jacqueline Robinson, the Dupuys ...)

Neither must we overlook the encounter with those who led us towards a beautiful, living liturgy, and who were the first to help us to dance and sing and live it outside conventional norms.

Shall we ever know who was nourished by whom, or the sources at which they drank? Such mutually beneficial exchanges finally brought Dance into the world of Theatre and Theatre into the world of Dance – a single tunic that seemed only to tear itself into two, exalting the individual vanities of each, in order to reawaken the Living with even greater tenacity, to the marvellous utopia of Union.

(Anne-Marie Debatte to Jacqueline Robinson, 1986.)

THE ACTORS

Throughout the course of this chronicle it will become increasingly difficult to *catalogue* individuals, as derivations and influences become ever more complex. It will no longer be quite so easy as in the preceding chapters to claim that such and such a dancer is of Duncanian, Dalcrozian, or even Wigmanian descent now that we are two and sometimes three generations removed from our 'forefathers'!

Different parameters must inevitably be invoked. The new generation began to travel, both geographically (especially after the restricted and confined life led during the war) and doctrinally! Cliques became less closed perhaps, which was an excellent thing. Exclusive loyalty became less common, and the notion of a single master disappeared.

This phenomenon may entail a negative aspect in terms of approximative and superficial standards of training, even though the 'studio-hopping' that became widespread after 1970 had not yet begun to occur. During the decade we are about to investigate, the practitioners may be considered roughly as belonging to or influenced by:

- the French classically-based school, that of Janine Solane and Jean Serry, for example;
- the German-influenced French school of Jean Weidt, Ludolf Schild and Heinz Finkel;
- the newly arrived foreigners who soon established roots in France.

In any case, however, we are now concerned with a more recent history, that of the latter part of this half-century, and the majority of its actors are still amongst us today. Their work runs through the whole of this second half of our chronicle.

INSTITUTIONS

Jean Dorcy and Danse et Culture

[Modern dancers of my generation experienced mitigated feelings towards Jean Dorcy; and the least that may be said is that he returned them! His partisan enthusiasms often revealed only scorn for so-called 'free' dance, even though he held out his hand to more than one of us.]

The enormous role played by Jean Dorcy in the diffusion and understanding of dance in general, and from which modern dance benefitted, cannot fail to go unrecognized. The man himself cannot be dissociated from his chief endeavour, the organization Danse et Culture, over which he presided from 1947 almost until his death in 1978, and which leant him a certain omnipresence.

Let us consider the man first of all. Jean Dorcy came from a modest background and arrived in Paris in 1921, curious for anything of an intellectual nature. He spent some time at the Châtelet before discovering the theatre school attached to the Vieux-Colombier, directed by Jacques Copeau, and from which the 'cartel' of Jouvet, Baty, Dullin and Pitoëff came.

It was there that Dorcy met Etienne Decroux and became deeply interested in bodily expression. He married Anna Stéphan, from whom he learnt the fundamental principles of classical dance, and studied also with Lucienne Lamballe. During this period he worked as an actor in various places, and in 1928 he and Decroux founded Proscenium, an experimental theatre company and school with a very full programme that concentrated extensively on the body. Dorcy later separated from Decroux; nevertheless it was from these initial efforts that the French school of mime was born.

In 1934 Dorcy founded the Association des Écrivains et Critiques de la Danse, over which Rolf de Maré, founder of the Archives Internationales de la Danse, presided. Then Dorcy fell seriously ill and, like Jean Serry, fought against tuberculosis for many years, finally being forced to withdraw from his theatrical activities.

After the war, having in the meantime married the Spanish dancer Nora Rubio, who introduced him to Spanish dance, Jean Dorcy joined a group of theatrical promoters, men of the theatre who have already been discussed, and who founded Culture par l'Initiation Dramatique and, later, Travail et Culture (T.E.C.). The role of T.E.C. as a melting-pot of promoters and creators (as the Vieux-Colombier had been some twenty-five years earlier) has already been described. It was out of T.E.C., where he was entrusted with dance activities, that Dorcy founded Danse et Culture in 1947. He and Nora Rubio devoted themselves to this completely. Its chief aims were to promote and allow dance to be seen in the most varied and often culturally deprived places, and to help young dancers and choreographers make themselves known. During its many years of existence, Danse et Culture gave 740 sessions introducing dance throughout the whole of France and abroad, sometimes in association with Jeunesses Musicales de France. These took place at the rate of one per month in the Salle d'Iéna in Paris, which finally became their Parisian base. A whole network of communication was thus established, thanks to the faith and work of certain local people, such as Marie-France Babillot and her Maîtrise de Danse in Bourges, who provided Danse et Culture with an initial welcoming structure. Each session consisted of a lecture-demonstration, followed by a programme that was more or less related in a fairly eclectic way to the subject under discussion. According to this subject matter, classical dance for the most part existed side by side with character, Spanish, folk and neo-classical dance and mime, and finally, and somewhat against the grain, with modern dance. Within a single session, experienced artists and beginners were featured side by side in the most congenial way.

The association survived on members' subscriptions and the takings from its shows. The dancers did not receive any payment as a rule, but were guaranteed, over and above the satisfaction of working for a good cause, important publicity, adequate stage conditions, a highly motivated audience and the chance to be seen by the critics.

A pilgrim of dance, called the 'Apostle of Dance' by some, Jean Dorcy devoted himself body and soul to promoting dance with a passion that was typical of his character. Something of a visionary and a bit of a leprechaun, with his cap pulled down over one ear, his piercing blue eyes, bantering voice, rigid opinions and teasing irony; fiery, impetuous, demanding; at one and the same time a purist and a partisan, and yet always generous.

It would take too long to mention all the dancers and choreographers who passed through Danse et Culture during the twenty-five years of its existence in which almost two generations have written the course of the history of dance on its stages. After re-reading the programmes of these sessions, it may be assumed that almost everyone who was regarded as a professional dancer in France trod these boards, either as a choreographer or a performer. This provided a veritable documentary concerning the world of dance in the 1950s and 60s: recognized values, fresh hopes, reputations, fashions, passions, prejudices ...

A few names may be of interest, however. In the field of classical dance these included, Cyril Athanasoff, Olga Adabache, Claude Bessy, Janine Charrat, Yvette Chauviré, Roger Fenonjois, Maïna Gielgud, Attilio Labis, Noella Pontois, Claire Sombert, Nina Vyroubova and Violette Verdy. In the field of mime, there was Jean-Louis Barrault, Etienne Decroux, Marcel Marceau, Ella Jaroscewicz and Bella Reine, whilst the modernists were represented by Jerome Andrews, Paul d'Arnot, Marie-France Babillot, Mila Cirul, Raymonde Lombardin, Anne Gardon, Geneviève Mallarmé, Jacqueline Robinson, Suzanne Rémon, Olga Stens, Claude Stéphane, Jean Serry and Karin Waehner. Amongst the participants noted on these posters and programmes, it is interesting to read the names of Françoise Adret, Maurice Béjart, Yvette Bouland, Alain Davesne and Dirk Sanders, who continue to work in the field of dance in a way that they could not have foreseen at the time!

- The speakers were of no less renown: on 18 March 1954, for example, speaking on the subject of 'Diaghilev and the Ballets Russes' they included Alexandre Benois, Boris Kochno, André Lévinson, Nicholas Zvereff, Jean Dorcy, Pierre Michaut and Maurice Pourchet.
- The subjects discussed comprised 'Character Dances', 'The Unity and Universality of Dance', 'The Way in which Dance uses Music', 'Artistic Creation', 'Young Choreographers', 'The Languages of

Dance', 'Dance as a Social Phenomenon' and 'Dance and Cinema'.
Many of these lectures were given by Dinah Maggie. Since
discourse and thought on dance were not widespread during this
period, these lectures had a very useful and highly significant
didactic effect, in spite of occasional prejudices.

For many independent dancers without any other means of support,
Danse et Culture represented an ideal opportunity to display their work.
Over and above the little nucleus of frequently billed performers – the
dutiful demonstrators – it was for many dancers a stroke of luck! All the
more so since Dorcy was notoriously suspicious of modern dance in
general. As a journalist and critic, he had plenty of opportunity to make
his views known, and it is not surprising, therefore, that some modern
dancers harboured towards him the same hostile attitude ... He was,
nevertheless, forced to succomb to the rising tide of a new form of dance,
and to agree to the inclusion of its protagonists in his programmes.

There follow a few pearls from the pen of Jean Dorcy that have
passed down to posterity!

> – *'Go ahead! Do, preferably any old thing'*: this phrase, boldly stated
> by Dorcy, was aimed at the followers of free modern dance who
> had absorbed their knowledge from the German or American
> schools. The only dancers to escape this condemnation were those
> who had received a grounding in classical dance.
> – *'Wild running, the breaking of the rhythm between each movement,
> repeated tumbling, a vocabulary upon which they build psychological
> statements, no, he cannot bear all that'*, wrote Ginette Chabetay in
> *Jean Dorcy – Témoignages*, 1979.
> – And with regard to *The Green Table* in *Geste et jeu*, 1932: ' ... there
> is not an ounce of dance in the prized work, except for the brief moment
> in which the soldier seizes the flag and runs away in contretemps,
> coupés, jetés clumsily performed. The performers are to dance what a
> Percheron horse is to a thoroughbred'.

We must stop there since the shame falls ultimately on Dorcy himself,
blinded by his partisan passion. Nevertheless, it is no bad thing to recall
that it was against this kind of reaction that we 'pioneers' had to fight on
more than one occasion.

As a fitting conclusion to this portrait of Dorcy, I would like to
quote an aritcle by Dinah Maggie who supported and participated in
Dorcy's work. It is an old article that dates from 1949, but one that nevertheless provides a fair summary of the role played by Danse et Culture,
particularly within the context of this period:

Homage to Jean Dorcy, 'The Missionary of Dance'.

'In an earlier article, I touched upon the question of the "vulgarization" of Dance, an art that is still considered a luxury, and the devotees of which remain only the most privileged members of society.

It is clearly apparent that dance must find its place within culture in general with as much right as any of the other arts. Indeed, the art of dance, deriving directly from the instinct and requiring the intervention of no instrument other than the human body itself, ought to be more easily understood and accessible than any of the other arts to all beings who love beauty.

In dance, as elsewhere, it is to the enthusiasts, the persevering, the passionate ones, that the honour of fighting for a good cause falls. Jean Dorcy figures amongst these. He dedicated his life to making dance known and loved, and established himself as a sort of missionary of dance. In order to achieve his aim, he founded the group Danse et Culture over four years ago. This group was intended primarily for young people and workers, and its activities were demonstrated through shows, films and lectures on dance given by Jean Dorcy.

One may not agree with Dorcy's ideas on dance, his aphorisms and paradoxes, or his peremptory and often limited opinions. I would even go so far as to claim that it would be regrettable if his young audience accepted the dogmas of his religion as gospel truth. Nevertheless, one must pay homage to the efforts of this man who, living permanently on a tight-rope, and randomly gleaning a few meagre subsidies here and there from encounters with those who sympathised with his cause, succeeded in bringing a whole cultural group to life and in giving young people, through the quality of his shows, a curiosity and taste for dance. Thanks to Danse et Culture a large number of students and workers without the means to frequent the Opéra or grand ballet evenings have been able to see the greatest stars.'

(Dinah Maggie, *Combat* 5 August 1949.)

Dinah Maggie and Association Française de Recherches Chorégraphiques (A.F.R.E.C.) and the Théâtre d'Essai de la Danse

Dinah Maggie is one of the few people in this story to have contributed to the development of modern dance in France without being a dancer herself. She was certainly a character: enterprising and dauntless, what we might call a *fighter* today. As a critic, organizer and promoter, she displayed sure knowledge and redoutable energy. It was advisable to keep on the right side of her, as it were, for she could easily make or break reputations. Nevertheless, French dance owes a great deal to her.

Dinah Maggie was born in Paris in 1903, of Russian origin. Her father, a great scholar, had settled there towards the end of the century. Dinah followed a university career (letters and sciences) and worked in her capacity as chemical engineer at the Institute of Cancerology in the

Faculty of Medicine in Paris. She was later appointed to a position of responsibility at the ministry of industry, which she continued to hold alongside her 'choreographic' activities for a number of years. She was always impassioned by dance and studied as an amateur with Laban and Wigman, and with Dussia Bereska in Paris. She was also a musician and yoga enthusiast.

She was very active in the Resistance, and it was in this context that she met those who were to found the daily paper *Combat* after the Liberation. Forming part of this team, she began her career as a dance critic which she pursued constantly, either as a freelance, or, when *Combat* ceased to exist, at the *Quotidien de Paris*. Writing represented only one part of her activity in the field of dance, however. Dinah Maggie was a mobilizing force and could be found wherever anything of note was happening.

In 1948 a modest review entitled *Danse* appeared and existed for several years. Amongst the collaborators were to be found Pierre Tugal, director of the Archives Internationales de la Danse, the critic Ferdinando Reyna, Jeanne Ranay, the multi-talented Edmond Linval and Dinah Maggie.

In 1954 Dinah founded the Association Française de Recherches et Études Chorégraphiques (A.F.R.E.C.) and the Théâtre d'Essai de la Danse which served for a number of years as a laboratory and showcase for the new talents of young French and foreign choreographers. She was assisted most efficiently in this great enterprise by the Duncanian dancer Odile Pyros. An initial stage in the work of A.F.R.E.C. consisted of regular meetings, held in the studios of various modern dancers currently working in France, in order to discuss, compare, demonstrate and clarify in an informal way, their individual experiences and doctrines in an attempt to discover any basic or transmissible aspects that their diverse procedures might have in common. As Dinah quite rightly professed, '*working in an ivory tower can never produce edible fruit*'.

Jerome Andrews, Françoise and Dominique Dupuy, Anne Gardon, Jacqueline Challet-Haas, Raymonde Lombardin, Jacqueline Levant, Geneviève Mallarmé, Jacqueline Robinson, Laura Sheleen and Karin Waehner could all be seen regularly at these study sessions.

As a result of these initial efforts, the École Technique de Danse Moderne was created in 1956 under the aegis of A.F.R.E.C. The classes took place in the renowned little Studio 121 in the Salle Pleyel, and tuition was given in American techniques, especially the Graham technique, by Laura Sheleen, and Laban and Wigman techniques by Irma Specht and Karin Waehner respectively.

In 1957 A.F.R.E.C. organized a course in Essen taught by Kurt Jooss for teachers of physical education from the E.N.S.E.P., and every year, from 1958 on, the Théâtre d'Essai de la Danse organized at least one large performance followed by an audience debate either in the Apollo, the Comédie des Champs-Élysées, the Paris or the Récamier theatres. These shows were staged in extremely favourable conditions, made to be taken seriously. They provided an opportunity, moreover, for dancers to work under the direction of others from time to time, and this gave rise to fruitful exchanges. The choreographers had, of course, to pass an audition, and amongst those who presented works within this framework over the years were (in chronological order of their appearance on stage) Karin Waehner, Françoise and Dominique Dupuy, George Skibine, Michel Descombey, Joseph Lazzini, Susan Kaufmann, Jaque Chaurand, Geneviève Mallarmé, Rose-Marie Paillet, Norbert Schmucki, Gilberto Motta, Claudine Allegra, Annick Maucouvert, Fred Traguth, Christine de Rougemont, Jacqueline Robinson, Françoise Saint-Thibault, Aline Roux, Alberte Raynaud, Claude Decaillot and Pierre du Villard. So many well known names! Still, thirty years do not exactly make for ancient history, even though our traces are sinking into oblivion!

In 1962 Dinah set up the Tribune of dance critics which, at its outset, comprised herself, Marcelle Michel, Edmond Linval, Michel Hoffmann and M.J. Béraud-Villars, and later included Marie Brillant, Paul Bourcier and André-Philippe Hersin. The Tribune organized colloquia and debates on the contemporary dance scene which without doubt encouraged greater tolerance and understanding with regard to new forms of dance.

From 1963 A.F.R.E.C. took part in the dance section at the Biennale de Paris and organized performances and debates at the National Museum of Modern Art.

In 1971 Dinah Maggie organized the inauguration of the Espace Cardin.

Statistics indicate that between 1958 and 1968, the Théâtre d'Essai de la Danse staged 190 works by 93 choreographers, largely modern, and for 26 of these, it was their first work.

Dinah Maggie was also very active as a lecturer during the 1950s, especially at the A.I.D. and then for Danse et Culture with Jean Dorcy. In collaboration with Thomas d'Erlanger, she co-founded the École Supérieure d'Études Chorégraphiques which, at its outset, provided only a theoretical course, and, naturally, she ensured that classes in modern dance were taught there. She helped to launch the careers of certain dancers and choreographers, such as Karin Waehner, Michel Caserta, Pierre du Villard and Christian Conte ...

She continued to work professionally until 1982 when ill health forced her to retire from active life.

Dinah Maggie seemed to thrive on obstacles and enjoy over-coming these when she considered it necessary. Sidelight chronicles tell of calumny proceedings brought against her by a well known dancer about whom she had written rather harshly. The critic nevertheless carried the day.

It would indeed be interesting to read Dinah Maggie's innumer-able articles today. Occasionally sectarian, but more often shrewd, she recognized the direction in which dance was going, and in her own way, she fought so that it might enjoy full citizenship. Moreover, she wrote clearly and well, with a concern to inform and enlighten her readers, without falling into a certain literary complacency that is, unfortunately, all too widespread amongst present-day critics.

I will reproduce two of her articles below, the first for its historical value with regard to Graham, and the second for its poetic value in conveying the emotions she felt on seeing the Sakharoffs dance.

'The arrival in Paris of Martha Graham and her company threw the habits of dance enthusiasts into disorder. Some were transported with delight; others were shocked. But nobody remained indifferent in the face of this new form of bodily expression in which gestures lose their meaning and decorative quality, and become simply the means of direct communication between the hearts and minds of artists and spectators. In order to experience this communion, one must, from the outset, enter into a state of receptivity that is sometimes difficult to attain. But even those who, disconcerted or even repulsed by the first spectacle, attended the subsequent ones, felt in turn the persuasive spiritual force that radiated from these bodies schooled in an extraordinary technique, and seem to rely upon telepathy rather than expressing itself by means of a more or less easily understood vocabulary. As though one soul spoke directly to another through the mediation of transparent gestures.

Contrary to the opinions of those in too much of a hurry to pass judgement, Martha Graham's dance is not cerebral; it is a genuine reflection of feeling. The thought processes or anecdotal sources that affect the artist's sensitivity are no concern of ours. In fact, the arguments printed in the programme ought to be read only by those who, curious to know the genesis of such a passion, want to discover the spark that kindled it. Martha Graham reveals this passion in its raw state, independently of its causes. It is not important for us to know that Voyage nocturne, for example, was inspired by the myth of Oedipus and Jocasta. The more important aspect of the work is the emotions it expresses, those of the heroine who is both a wife and a mother, of the hero who is prey to his own inner struggles, and of the company of dancers who, like an antique chorus, amplify the resonance of the drama.

There is no human feeling that Graham cannot express. In order to translate all the nuances of such feelings, the performer must learn to master all his physical possibilities. The dancers of the company are able to make the slightest fibre in their body vibrate with control. They constantly direct the movement instead of allowing it to go its own way; they are able to release a muscle without loosing its feeling; their dance is a continuous breathing; one gesture always leads into another; a downward movement marks the start of an upward one, a contraction initiates a release; leaps form a play between space and the ground. The whole body is involved in the movement of a single finger. Each movement is unpredictable, like life itself; as it unfolds we think we can guess how it will end, but the body remains in an impossible state of equilibrium and sets off towards a new destiny with supremely controlled freedom.

Beyond the limits of a conventional aesthetic, Martha Graham carries us away on a journey to the source of all light at which the living truth may be found. Whether one is "for" or "against" her, the influence of her creative genius clearly extends even to those contemporary choreographers who are most opposed to her style. Consciously or unconsciously, the world of dance has received her message' (*La Danse*, July 1954).

It is important to remember that this article describes Graham's first visit to Paris, which effectively provoked extremely varied reactions, some of which were more than scornful. It is tempting to compare these lines by Dinah Maggie with those of Jean Dorcy in the famous article 'Les Danseurs populistes' (1955), cited elsewhere in this work!

The following extract from *Combat* (12 December 1949) was written by Dinah following a recital given by the Sakharoffs:

"Colloque Sentimental".
Why was it that, whilst in the grip of an indescribable melancholy, Verlaine's poem came to haunt me?

And yet there could be no mistake: it was definitely he, Alexandre, that wonderful painter of postures and costumes, who was there, his Pierrot-like smile spreading across his large oval face, his hands more expressive than words, his mind finely tuned to the music and gesture, and this inner concentration which, by its very stillness, left me with the imperishable memory of the most beautiful of dances.

But it was you, Clotilde, who was for us like a breath of spring, perfect happiness, a winged girl, a faun stretching out in the sun! How fortunate we were to find in the dances fashioned for the woman you had become, the calm fullness of your movements, the melody of your hips, of your arms stretched out towards the infinite, of your head extending the curves of your neck as it swooped down, the light and airy gliding of your steps, and that fluidity in the slow motion of which you alone hold the secret!

I would have liked only those who came to you, Clotilde and Alexandre Sakharoff, as if on a pilgrimage, to have been invited to your performance; for they alone might understand you and recognize through your metamporphoses, the perenniality of your art.

You have been called the poets of dance; but you might equally well have been called its painters or its sculptors or singers.

You have projected the reflection of your inner life onto your body and have inscribed your feelings in space.

You have spiritualized dance by freeing it from its earthly fetters.

Your names will remain imprinted on our memories as symbols of perfection and beauty'.

FRENCH DANCERS OF EUROPEAN DESCENT

Anne Gardon

[Of all the dancers who were active in Paris when I settled there in 1949, a small number captured my attention, and amongst these was Anne Gardon. A singular lyricism, unerring musicality, extreme refinement, a sense of line and a highly 'polished' presentation seemed to me to characterize her style. I learnt later that she had worked with Mary Wigman and understood certain affinities.]

Of Swiss origin, born in 1910.

She studied dance initially in Zurich in the Duncan – Laban – Wigman line and spirit.

Removed from dance for a time, she had the opportunity to travel widely, particularly in the East and Far East, and, perhaps unconsciously, she drew from these distant civilizations images that greatly enriched her own dance.

Returning to France, her first place of fall was Lyons where, in 1942, amidst the difficult working conditions of the war years, she began to give solo recitals with the pianist Germaine Montanier. It was during this time that Jean Serry saw her dance in Lyons and, observing in her person as well as in her work an embodiment of what he was himself seeking in dance, requested her collaboration for several of his creations. Thus, from 1945, she took part in *Danses bibliques* with the Compagnie de St-Jean (a newly constituted version of the T.E.C. team) at Puy-en-Velay. She became part of the little group of theatrical people who revitalized the French theatre after the war and instigated a policy of decentralization.

In 1946 Anne Gardon danced in the large-scale productions of Jean Serry in Bourges and Chartres, as well as in Paris, and collaborated in the performances given by Danse et Vie. At the beginning of the 1950s she went to work with Wigman at the Zurich summer schools that were such a revelation to the many people who flocked there to work with Wigman, Chladek, Jooss, Zullig and Kreutzberg, etc.

Anne Gardon then settled in Paris in a charming somewhat rustic house on the rue Victor-Massé. She taught and performed regularly in Paris in 'expressionist dance' recitals at the Vieux-Colombier, the Palais de Chaillot and the Comédie des Champs-Élysées. She appeared most often alone, but occasionally performed with her group or other dancers such as Suzanne Rémon and Georgette Watteau. She also appeared in the provinces and abroad. These recitals were eagerly awaited in choreographic circles for they were sure to contain many delights.

The dances that constituted her repertoire, brief pieces, dramatic or lyrical, were sometimes based on literary texts, and were often set to modern music by Debussy, Fauré, Ravel, Bartók, Tansman, Honegger, Messiaen and Jolivet. For many years Anne Gardon was able to rely upon the collaboration of musicians and Guillemette Boyer was her favourite accompanist on piano, percussion and ondes Martenot.

The titles alone give some idea of the nature of her dances: *Le Prince aux fleur de lys* (*The Fleurs-de-lis Prince*) and *La Porteuse d'offrandes* (*The Bearer of Offerings*), inspired by Cretan frescoes and set to Satie's *Gnossiennes; Au bord du Styx* (*On the shores of the Styx*) (Jolivet), *Le Gibet* (*The Gallows*) (Ravel), *Les Sons et les parfums* (*Sounds and Perfumes*) (Debussy), *Hécate, Ophélie, Le Néant* (*Nothingness*).

['I recall', I wrote in 1950, '*Le Perroquet* (*The Parrot*), set to music by A. Decaux, which emphasized the beauty of the dancer's body, clad in a short, close-fitting black velvet tunic; the bird's long tail that she held in her hand added to the play of lines in a happy combination of clear-cut, sculptural postures that were a delight to behold, set off by a perfect sense of musicality ... and the seduction of *Sieste*; her indolent grace and delicate sensuality'.]

Numerous writers have praised her: in *Plaisirs de France* Fernand Divoire wrote:

> '*in each successive recital she demonstrates a more noble richness, greater artistry and a heightened sense of communion – a movement that is very simple in appearance rises up, passes the foot-lights, enters the hall, and becomes imperial*', and in *Arts*,

Maurice Pourchet wrote:

> '*she plays with horror and masters it. The devil himself could not succeed in making her commit a single technical fault. She would dance the scalp to the tune of "Le Mois de Marie" without a wrong step or an ounce of bad taste*'.

A. Coullet-Tessier recalled *Les Fleurs du mal*, whilst Robert Charroux declared:

> '*her dances are like a magic spell. Any observer, one with guts and brain, must follow her, willingly or unwillingly, wherever she chooses to take him, whether it be pleasant or unpleasant*'. And for Fernand Divoire she still remains '*the most diverse and varied of all the expressionist dancers*'.

Over and above the dance recitals she gave regularly over a period of some fifteen years, Anne Gardon created dances for the theatre, particularly in collaboration with the producer Jean Doat. Amongst the choreographies she created with him are those for Gluck's *Iphigénie en Auride*

Plate 22 Anne Gardon, *L'Appel*. Photo: Paul Koruna.

at the Aix festival in 1952, Landowski's *Songe d'une nuit d'été* at the Cirque d'Hiver in Paris in 1953, and *Athalie* at the Comédie-Française in 1955 in a production by Vera Korène.

Anne Gardon taught at the Conservatoire International in the rue de la Pompe, the Russian Conservatoire and the Martenot school as well as giving private classes in her studio. She also worked with actors and singers who came to study with her.

She retired from the stage in 1955 and continued to teach for a few more years. It would seem that she wished to form a permanent group, but the difficulty of recruiting high-level dancers and the economic problems involved in such a project prevented her from realizing it.

Anne Gardon has occupied a mysterious place in the constellation of modern dance in France. She is of the same breed as the Sakharoffs and Olga Stens, a poet, a purist and a perfectionist. She seemed to offer the key to some dream-like world of finely drawn 'demons and marvels' and secret landscapes.

Anne Gardon is something of a magician.

Geneviève Mallarmé

French, born in Algiers in 1912.

Her family environment provided her with the opportunity to mix with artists and intellectuals from childhood. Geneviève Mallarmé received an initial training in drawing and engraving, studying dance (tap, acrobatics and expressive dance) as an amateur with Fernand Fonsagrive, who took charge of Georges Pomiès's group after the latter's death in 1933. In 1937 she worked as a costume designer with Jeanne Lanvin and continued to dance as an amateur with Janine Solane.

In 1939 war broke out and with it came the exodus. Geneviève Mallarmé settled in the Lot, where she met Pierre Tugal, director of the Archives Internationales de la Danse, who encouraged her enthusiasm for dance and guided her in her research. She returned to Paris after the Liberation, and worked with Alice Vronska. Like many other young dancers of the time, she gave her first recital at the Archives, going on to study classical dance with Yves Brieux but most of all and for many years, expressive dance with Mila Cirul who introduced her to the practices of the great German dancers.

She opened her school in Paris and performed regularly with her pupils. For her first group programme in 1955 she created *Jeanne* to music by Honegger, an ambitious work to which the critics were, as a whole, quite favourably disposed. In 1957 she was appointed to teach bodily expression at the Conservatoire d'Art Dramatique, a discipline that had never been taught there before. Geneviève Mallarmé preferred the term 'bodily expression' to dance, even expressive dance, in every case, perhaps out of a concern to go deeper into the motivation and essence of movement and the specific nature of modern dance, the inner quest, the personal gesture.

Definitely more a teacher than a creator or a performer, she has led some of her pupils, such as Françoise Saint-Thibault and Jean Bouffort, to the threshold of a professional career. Over and above her pedagogical knowledge, her pupils acknowledge their debt to her for initiating them to poetry, music and the graphic arts, and say that throughout her classes there reigned an atmosphere conducive to the stimulation of the imagination. Jean Bouffort wrote in a letter to me dated 1987:

> *'Particularly concerned with the type of perception we would today call kinaesthetics, she set me on the way to working with my body with sensitivity, economy and precision. She unleashed in me a spirit of inquiry and an understanding of what occurs in a moving body at a time when this was still considered a great mystery'.*

Raymonde Lombardin

French, born in Brussels in 1913.

From her childhood she studied classical dance under the direction of De Guistelle, star of the Théâtre in Brussels, and learnt the piano also. Subsequently, she studied at the Institut Supérieur d'Architecture et d'Art Decoratif, working especially on drawing and engraving with Joris Minne, where in 1937 she obtained its diploma with distinction. Throughout her career she continued to pursue this dual activity as a dancer and stage designer.

She came to Paris in 1940 and studied dance with various teachers: from 1941 to 1943 she worked with Marguerite Bougai and formed part of Yarmila Mentzlova's dance group, before spending a brief spell with Janine Solane.

From 1944 to 1945 she studied with Heinz Finkel and after his death spent a few months with Etienne Decroux. She continued to study classical dance with Nora Kiss and Nicolas Zvereff for many years and eventually jazz with Don Lurio.

We must consider in more detail the time that Raymonde Lombardin spent with Heinz Finkel for this was a decisive period for her personal development as well as for the continuation of Finkel's work, interrupted by his premature death. It was through him that Raymonde became aware of the doctrines and methods of Laban on which she based part of her own practice and teaching, particularly that which concerned the analysis of space and quality of movement. She rapidly became Finkel's partner and appeared in performances with him. On Finkel's death in 1946, she assumed the direction of the group he had formed, which included, amongst others, Manon Souriau, Annette Bleu and Paul Dougnac, who later became a member of Jean Weidt's Ballet des Arts. The group retained some of Finkel's works in its repertoire and included some by Raymonde Lombardin also. In 1949 she composed *Black Bill*, her first important group work, independent and thoroughly modern, and which seems to have made a strong impression on public and critics alike.

As early as 1941, whilst teaching at Jeune France, one of the first popular culture organizations to be created during the war, Raymonde met Charles Antonetti, actor, producer and teacher. Their personal and professional destinies became linked from then on and their careers must be discussed almost in 'tandem'. Antonetti said of Lombardin:

> '*I found in her exactly the type of person with whom it would be possible to effect the fusion between dance and theatre. We immediately began to work together and have not stopped since*' (letter to Jacqueline Robinson, 1987).

This rigorous collaboration occurred within the context of theatrical productions: Raymonde Lombardin acted and danced in, choreographed and painted the scenery for the plays that Antonetti produced during the 1950s, such as *Antigone, Macbeth, The Knight of the Burning Pestle, Richard III* and *Le Revizor*. The ballets, performed as part of Antonetti's productions, were integrated with the events on stage but were designed to be performed in public independently of the production.

This collaboration also took place on a teaching level. Both of them worked under the auspices of Travail et Culture, and Antonetti was appointed technical and educational adviser to a succession of ministers. As a result, from 1945 to 1976, both were made responsible for the training of coaches in popular education (Raymonde for dance, of course) through regular classes, courses and performances.

1945 also saw the opening of their studio on the rue Pelouze; it was known first as the Théâtre-École Perceval, centre for dramatic and choreographic training, and then as the Centre d'Études des Techniques d'Expression (Centre for the Study of Techniques of Expression), which also witnessed many activities. This was a time of intense activity for Raymonde, as it was for Antonetti. In 1950 and 1951 she went to Switzerland, like so many other French dancers, to take part in the summer schools at Macolin and Montreux, and felt a particularly close affinity with Hans Zullig *'because he focussed more closely on the quality of the movement itself and was more relaxed'*, she claimed, but perhaps also because Zullig, who had been a member of Jooss's company, had tried to effect a kind of fusion between classical and modern techniques. According to Antonetti:

> *'He found a complement to the discoveries of "free dance" in the classical tradition. There resulted from this a technique that was both strict and full of grace, demanding a rigorous and clear-cut performance and impeccable physical discipline ... that allowed the greatest freedom of expression without any aestheticism, or any pursuit of the bizarre or the unexpected'.*

Raymonde Lombardian denies having used classical dance in any way other than as a means of training, not allowing it to enter into the dances she performed in public, but how could she escape from the conditioning of a serious and long pursued training? This would tend to confirm that there were few modern dancers in France at the time who had total confidence in the modern techniques currently practised in order to achieve the desired level of virtuosity. It would perhaps have been up to the dancers themselves to change this state of things. It is certainly a clue to the reason why the general technical level of those who practised modern dance was not very high, particularly in comparison with the best classical dancers. This was probably an after-effect of the time when some of the earliest pioneers of free dance were more concerned to assert their freedom than to acquire the necessary technique to produce good results. Feeling took priority over form.

In 1951, at Macolin, Raymonde Lombardin met Paul d'Arnot, who had recently arrived in France. After having followed the summer school course together with Raymonde, Paul asked her to become his partner; this marked the start of the famous 'partnership' that was to last several years. Each one brought his or her own solos to the shared repertoire but their duets were based principally on South American folklore. To the autochtonous material provided by d'Arnot, Raymonde Lombardin contributed a sense of choreographic construction and scenic transposition. The result was a series of highly coloured, moving, naïve or spectacular pieces evoking the folklore of Peru, Bolivia, Argentina and Paraguay. The seductive music of these countries was beginning to become known and was rising to the top of the hit parades in Europe.

Paul d'Arnot and Raymonde Lombardin danced in France and abroad, and appeared on Swiss television, accompanied most frequently by the group Los Incas and the pianist Claude Pothier. In Paris they took part in the galas organized by Danse et Culture and Raymonde also performed in these alone with her own repertoire. Their collaboration came

Plate 23 Raymonde Lombardin, *Révolte*, 1949.

to an end in 1956. Meanwhile, in response to a request from Jean-Louis Barrault, Lombardin and Antonetti undertook the training of the actors of the Renaud-Barrault company in dance and mime. In 1954 Raymonde took part in the work of the A.F.R.E.C. (see 'Dinah Maggie and Association Française de Recherches Chorégraphiques (A.F.R.E.C.) and the Théâtre d'Essai de la Danse'). We often met in her studio in order to try to extract from our individual experiences a common doctrinal and methodological basis, and to try and create a 'French school' of modern dance.

Raymonde Lombardin also wrote about dance in several specialist dance, theatrical and educational reviews; her didactic remarks were always clear and shrewd.

Antonetti and Lombardin continued their training work until 1976, when they retired to the country. Their aims as teachers were always to *'produce dancers capable of acting, actors capable of moving, and educators capable of transmitting techniques'*.[2]

In this same text introducing their school we read the following lines on dance by Raymonde which I find significant:

> *'Dance is a constant invitation to "actions" engaging the mind and body, the feeling and the intellect at one and the same time. It is the development of an awareness of the relationships between inner and outer forms, these two extremes influencing one another mutually. These relationships result from the superimposition of several different rhythmic dimensions: the rhythm of the breath and of muscular tension and relaxation, internal or external musical rhythm, and the rhythm of the succession of forms.*
>
> *The involvement of the individual in this subtle interplay leads to a lucid perception of the dynamic inner relationships that convey and project the movement in space. It results in a "state of dance" that rules out merely decorative action'.*

Raymonde Lombardin will be remembered as a convinced and convincing dancer, an artist and an artisan. In conclusion, I would like to quote some of the views expressed by the critics on Raymonde Lombardin, which illustrate some of the opinions that were current in the late 1950s:

> — Maurice Pourchet in *Arts* emphasized *'her profound and lively sense of movement and colour, pantomime and dance ... truculent, mischievous and poetic, and that diversity of her imagination at once so French and yet so clearly refreshed by an American breath'.*
> — *'Supple and graceful, retaining her refinement in her very spontaneity, Raymonde Lombardin has created an individual style that is most*

---

[2] Jean Dorcy, *Témoignages*, collected authors (Nouvelles éditions touristiques et artistiques, Paris, 1979).

attractive. Clearly influenced by expressionism, she knew how to temper it and infuse it with greater poetry and lightness by incorporating it with the precise elegance of classical technique, the subtleties of Latin abstraction, an element of fantasy and at times all the charm of French fantasy' (*Toute la danse*, 1954).

– And Antonetti himself wrote: '*I know what it means to collaborate with Raymonde Lombardin: it means being constantly reminded of the demands of quality and precision, to the extreme point of the intelligence and the feelings'*.

Charles Antonetti

It is necessary to discuss Charles Antonetti's own career in a little more detail. Certainly, a considerable part of his activity took place within the context of the partnership described above, but he also realized a number of personal projects that contributed more or less directly to the spreading of dance.

Antonetti is French and was born in Paris in 1911.

He received his earliest theatrical training with Janine Solane in 1937, and then came greatly under the influence of Jean-Marie Serreau, taking part in his shows. His initial activities in theatrical teaching occurred within the Youth Club movement, and in 1940 he worked with Charles Dullin. In 1941, at Jeune France, Antonetti met Raymonde Lombardin, and the rest of this story is related above. In 1945 he worked with Etienne Decroux.

From 1945 to 1976 Antonetti was technical and educational adviser at the ministry of national education, and then at Jeunesse et Sports, and he trained teachers of popular education. He was also an instructor in dramatic art at T.E.C. He was later put in charge of the course in staging at the Institute of Theatrical Studies in the faculty of arts at Paris University III, and also of the course in oral communication in the faculty of law.

From 1950 to 1969 he was editor in chief of the review *Education et théâtre*, which provided a medium for the spreading of culture and served as an effective working tool. He wrote some half dozen works of a didactic nature on dramatic acting and production, certain ones of which were particularly relevent to dancers. He adapted plays from the repertoire and translated Stanislawski's *Building a Character*.

Antonetti's work was always directed towards the interests of dance, the language of the body, and his avowed aim was '*to bring Dance to modify the Theatre'*.

Jacqueline Levant

French, born in 1926.

Despite a rather brief and discreet career, Jacqueline Levant played an important part at a time when so many young people, enthusiastic and active in the French post-war cultural revival, were developing an interest in non-classical dance. She refers to *'the astonishing climate of 1945 in which I saw so many young men and women wanting to dance – and I was one of them!'*

Jacqueline Levant thus became involved in this popular education movement when she was still quite young. Trained initially in physical education guided by Jean-Marie Conty, who introduced her to T.E.C., she discovered dramatic acting, mime and then dance. It was there that she met the dancers Heinz Finkel and Ludolf Schild, in addition to actors Roger Blin, Jacques Dufilho, Claude Martin and many other remarkable men of the theatre. Finkel and Schild became her successive masters, but these associations lasted all too briefly because of their premature deaths.

She became a member of the Ballets Français Modernes, the little group created by Schild on his return from Algeria, and acted as his assistant when Schild himself grew progressively weaker as a result of illness. From 1945 Jacqueline Levant formed part of the team at E.P.J.D. where she was responsible for dance classes. She worked there until the dissolution of the organization in 1952.

[Arriving in Paris in 1947, I encountered Jacqueline Levant at E.P.J.D., where I enrolled as a student. I was delighted by the kindred spirit I found we shared as a result of the German training we had both, no doubt in slightly different ways, undergone, and I was impressed by her dynamism and ability to train, liberate and open up new vistas to these apprentice actors. Needless to say, we later shared other adventures.]

Like many other dancers in search of new horizons, Jacqueline Levant worked with Jean Serry and took part in his shows in Chartres, Grenoble and Paris. She remained a member of Serry's group until 1953. At the same time, from 1950 to 1952, she formed part of La Frairie, the folk dance group set up by Thérèse Palau and Jacques Douai. She was thus at the centre of those movements that sought to revive the cultural heritage, on the one hand this French dance that was gradually freeing itself from academicism, and on the other was firmly attached to its ancient and living roots.

Levant danced with the Ballets Modernes de Paris for three seasons from 1953 to 1955, and performed in many of the earliest choreographies of Françoise and Dominique who, in recognition of her very great abilities, cast her in important roles.

She retired early from dance, leaving the memory not only of a dancer of fresh vitality, capable of both humour and poetry, but also of an enthusiastic teacher who introduced many young people to dance and sought to guide them in their careers. She was a woman who marked out the furrows and sowed the seed for others to harvest.

Suzanne Rémon

French, born c. 1922.

Brought up in a family of musicians, Suzanne Rémon took her first steps (in rhythmic dance) with Odette Courtiade, after which she studied classical dance with the great teacher Atty Chadinoff who encouraged her creative gifts. She also worked with Préobrajenska and Egorova.

Suzanne Rémon maintains that: '*my life unfolded with one foot in sport and both feet in dance*'. Like many young people at the time, she took the City of Paris teaching diploma in physical education simultaneously with her training in dance in order to eventually insure her future. She thus taught both disciplines and was the first teacher of her younger sister Claire Motte. As an independent dancer, however, she went beyond the confines of her early training in order to experiment with a personal style in which she used contemporary music and speech.

It was during the 1940s that Suzanne Rémon met Jean Serry at the time when this pilgrim of dance was travelling throughout France on foot, spreading the word. She danced with him for several years in those memorable productions in Chartres and elsewhere that united most of the 'expressionist' dancers in France. She also gave 'joint recitals' with Anne Gardon, especially in 1955 at the Comédie des Champs-Élysées, and figured amongst those who returned to the roots of dance, attending the summer schools in Switzerland with Mary Wigman, Harald Kreutzberg …

Suzanne Rémon claims that she has been one of those '*bare-footed dancers, pioneers, who were often discredited*', and that as a teacher during the heroic period she had worked '*behind closed doors*'. Nevertheless, it was these pioneers who fertilized the French soil and took part in the ploughing and sowing of the land rather than in the harvest!

Claude Stéphane

French, born c. 1920.

She studied classical dance with Boris Kniaseff, and also worked with Heinz Finkel. She established her school in Paris in the 1950s. She performed solo or with her pupils and tried to reconcile classical and modern styles of dance. As it was, her dance was of an intimate character, with a touch of affectation, but from which a sense of poetry supported by real culture was never lacking.

Claire Markale, Michelle Lerondeau, better known as Michelle Blaise, who was to devote herself to traditional French dance, and Lola Valentin, who worked with Ludolf Schild and later with Jacqueline Robinson, numbered amongst her pupils. Lola Valentin taught dance in schools as a teacher of the City of Paris. She possessed a gift for theatre and sound educational approach.

Française and Dominique Dupuy and The Ballets Modernes de Paris

[When I finally settled in France in 1949 and surveyed the Parisian dance scene, knowing little outside of the world (and works) of Wigman and Jooss/Leeder, I did not at first sight see very much that seemed familiar to me. I was in search of cousins, French cousins. Was there anybody who might share my conception of dance, but who had been nourished on and was steeped in this French culture that meant so much to me? There was indeed, and here they were: Françoise and Dominique Dupuy and their Ballets Modernes de Paris – so French, and of an artistic level that impressed me to such an extent that it was not until later that I realized the struggles they must have had, and the tenacity with which they fought to impose their idea of dance in the face of an establishment dozing in the comfort of received ideas.

They played in every key, painted in every colour, and told stories in a frivolous as well as in a tragic manner. A whole kaleidoscope of scenes and characters created over the years remains in my memory: Françoise as Antigone, Dominique in *The Little Tailor*, the simple poetry of *Cants de Catalunya*, the frantic circular running of the couple in *Le Jour où la terre tremblera*, their serenity in *Epithalame*, the colours in *Paso*, the gags in *Apprendre à marcher*; and more recently, Dominique in *The Bird*, Françoise in *Ana*, and the magnificence of certain sequences in *Visages de femmes*. And it is not only their performances within the magical surroundings of the theatre that I remember, but also the hours of intense work in the studio, in classes and rehearsals, the endless discussions about dance, and the many young dancers seeking to grow through dance, to understand its very essence and, group after group, cohort after cohort, generations of students and dancers who came to study with Françoise and Dominique. Hours spent militating around various 'green tables', seeking within institutions and official organizations to resolve the thousand and one problems that confront the practice of dance, the lives of dancers, creation, dissemination and *tutti quanti*. All too rare hours of relaxation (for few worked as hard as they did), sitting in the sun, or around a well furnished table, or in dancing some more, a sardane perhaps, together, dance always within us.

This is what I have lived with Françoise and Dominique, sharing their joys and their worries, their hopes and their doubts, and that faith, and sometimes crazy energy that succeeded in overcoming every obstacle.]

The Dupuys belong to that rare breed of enterprising artists. A resourceful pair, they use their heads as well as their legs and their souls! Their fertile and bold imagination was unfurled not only in their works for the theatre, but also in the very real and sometimes discouraging domain of prospection, organization and conduct of the 'marketing' of dance. They were amongst the first to effect true decentralization of dance, taking it 'where it had never been before', into every cultural organization in France, first through performance, then through what today might be called promotion. Thence through a more far-reaching pedagogical activity giving courses of different types and with differing aims, both in France and abroad, and finally, the creation of a centre for professional training.

In addition to their ability to develop their own gifts as creators and performers, the Dupuys kept their eyes and ears to the ground in order to discover talent and worth in others. They possessed a certain skill for drawing into their orbit collaborators of recognized quality, and for discovering, stimulating or creating strategic situations that would promote the development of contemporary dance in France where it seemed to be much behind. This was certainly not achieved without difficulty, but their efforts paid off.

Françoise and Dominique: entirely French in their approach to dance, in spite of the inheritance from the German school they both received – received and asserted – but which they nevertheless integrated into their own approach. In the content and librettos of their early works, and in their choice of music and costumes, they often remained explicitly close to French, or Mediterranean cultural heritage. Equally close to folklore, or traditional music and dance at least, they appear to have shown a desire to go back to roots – roots of European or more distant origin, at all events, the roots of human nature. There was a search for a gesture or discourse that was, if not primitive, at least pristine. They flirted with archaism for this same reason. In their youth, they liked to use games, stories and legends, just as later they liked to exploit myths, as if it were necessary to assert a certain kind of innocence, whilst at the same time creating perfectly subjective lyrical or dramatic works.

This quest for the roots and valorization of the heritage was common to many artists of this period. It is a phenomenon already described elsewhere in this book, and a symptom of the revival of a need for national identity after the war and the occupation. We have seen other dancers, in particular Jean Serry, and organizations working in this context too.

So it was that Françoise and Dominique presented their first works, full of freshness and sometimes a kind of poetic tang. At first the critics did not know what to make of the taste that governed their artistic choices, and the Ballets Modernes de Paris were no doubt at first assimilated into other amateur or semi-professional groups that appeared at the time. This led Christine de Rivoyre, for example, to comment in 1955:

> *'It is nice and touching ... This couple of dancers deserve our sympathy. They have a taste for beautiful music, a love of their subject and plenty of ideas. But these ideas are not always clear, which causes a certain incoherence and disorder in their works',*

and Claude Baignères to ask:

> *'Why Ballets Modernes de Paris? Françoise and Dominique were indeed impudent in calling their company this. An aesthetic outmoded by some twenty years ... choreography without the slightest invention ... it is difficult to find in this wilderness anything remotely modern or Parisian; it even requires considerable goodwill to recognize it as ballet. Everything is dreary, mournful and dull, without soul and without character. Nothing happens of either a scandalous, moving or original nature' (Le Figaro).*

It would be difficult to slate them more strongly! And, we must not forget the attraction of anything remotely 'foreign'. The Dupuys, like other French artists, were hardly prophets in their own country; nevertheless, their individual and joint careers have spanned more than one chapter in the history of French dance. It was like a journey through changing landscapes, and evolving contexts that they themselves influenced in part through their stubborn toil.

Dominique was born in 1930 and spent his childhood in Paris in an environment that was receptive to all the arts. At the age of eight he was already learning dance with Jean Weidt and later with Doryta Brown. When war broke out Weidt went off to the army and Dominique left for the provinces where, as an adolescent and with the encouragement of his family, he had the opportunity to act. On his return to Paris, Dominique resumed his work with Weidt as soon as the latter was demobilized. He also acted in Dullin's company where he became acquainted and worked with Marcel Marceau, and studied classical dance with Olga Préobrajenska, Madame Illic and Nicolas Zvereff amongst others. It was at Weidt's class in 1946 that he met Françoise.

Françoise was born in Lyons in 1925, daughter of Marcel Michaud, art critic, gallery director and defender of contemporary art. Françoise grew up in an atmosphere of immense artistic richness. At the age of five she began to study dance at the Lyons Opéra, then took a course in Dalcrozian eurhythmics with Madame Birmelet and finally studied with Hélène Carlut (herself a pupil of Dalcroze and Rosalia Chladek in Hellerau). Throughout her adolescence, Françoise studied music with César Geoffray and painting with Albert Gleizes, proof of the multiplicity of her gifts and artistic training. Already, at the age of ten, the great art critic André Warnot said: *'She has dance inside her'*.

The war caused many artists to leave Paris, and Lyons benefitted from the presence of certain people with whom Françoise was able to work. She studied acting with Serreau, O'Brady and Jacquemont, for example, and classical dance with Youri Algaroff and Youra Lobov. At the end of the war she was encouraged by several people to go to Paris, where, like many others of us, she was supported by Pierre Tugal, director of the A.I.D., and also by Roger Blin. She worked with Marguerite Bougai, Nicolas Zvereff and Etienne Decroux and spent a brief spell with the Ballet des Champs-Élysées. Then she went to work with Weidt where she soon assumed the responsibilities of principal dancer and administrator.

From this time on, the careers of Françoise and Dominique became united, entwined. Reference has already been made to Jean Weidt, one of those refugees who came from Germany during the 1930s, and his Ballets 38 which was one of the few professional modern dance companies in France before the war. On his return from the war, Weidt founded the Ballet des Arts. Thus Françoise and Dominique took part in several of Weidt's new and extremely powerful choreographies, amongst which was *La Cellule*.

The success achieved by *La Cellule* in Copenhagen in 1947 was not repeated in Paris, and, discouraged, Weidt returned to Germany in 1949, leaving his dancers orphaned. Dominique and Françoise, now married, tried to form a group from the former pupils of Weidt (several of whom came from Hélène Carlut's company), Marguerite Bougai and Jacqueline Levant (who had worked as the assistant of Ludolf Schild, also a German refugee). Projects slowly began to take shape and rehearsals were organized. Faced with the difficulties of the enterprise, the Dupuys decided to abandon the idea of forming a company for the time being and created instead a duo known simply as 'Françoise et Dominique', under which name they worked professionally for a number of years. The early years

Plate 24   Françoise Dupuy, *La Femme et son ombre*, 1968.

were difficult ones, in which, as for all modern dance professionals, there was no question of joining a company. They had to work to earn their daily bread, however, so Françoise and Dominique also appeared in cabaret and music-hall, gave lessons, and participated either as performers or choreographers in various shows.

Once again they formed a group and began to give performances of their choreographies, which, for several years they continued to sign jointly. Already in 1954 *Parade* (Cocteau-Satie) and *Cants de Catalunya* figure in this repertoire and remained there for some time. 1955 was an important year which witnessed the creation of an Académie de Danse together with official approval (confirmed by the granting of a few small subsidies) of the existence of the Ballets Modernes de Paris which performed at the Marigny and Daunou theatres. The following decade saw Françoise and Dominique and the B.M.P. performing in Paris, on tour even into darkest Africa, and implanted firmly in the provinces, especially at the Grand Théâtre in Bordeaux.

In 1958 the English choreographer Deryk Mendel composed for them *Epithalame*, based on a quartet by Messiaen, which took first prize at the choreography competition in Aix-les-Bains. Messiaen subsequently withdrew permission for his music to be danced to and from that time on the work was performed successfully in silence.

Around 1959 Jerome Andrews showed particular interest in them and their work. Not only did he create choreographies for them, skillfully using their characteristic style and dynamism, but he also taught at their Académie. He was to have considerable influence on their artistic direction, pedagogical technique and approach. At this same time, Dominique made a serious foray into the field of jazz, in collaboration with Katherine Henry d'Epinoy, and they produced a number of dances in this style. It is perhaps also worth pointing out that, respectful of twentieth-century repertoire, Françoise and Dominique endeavoured to revive certain great works such as *Parade, L'Après-midi d'un faune* and *Jeux*.

In 1962, Françoise and Dominique founded the Baux-de-Provence festival and kept it going against wind and tide for seven years. Naturally, the B.M.P. performed there, but they also invited from abroad such groups as the Ballets de Susanna Egri, Serge Golovine, Etorki, Rita Devi, the London Contemporary Dance Company and Merce Cunningham (which was quite a risk at the time!). The activities of the B.M.P. spread to the provinces with seasons in Mulhausen (where they were the 'resident company') and Strasburg. In Paris, the Théâtre de l'Est Parisien (T.E.P.) welcomed them during several successive years, organizing a theatrical season devoted entirely to dance and thereby creating something of an innovation. They worked not only as performers, but also as

Plate 25 Dominique Dupuy, 1965. Photo: Georges Glasberg.

initiators, undertaking an extensive sensitization of a new public. The company gave over a hundred performances each year. This was a fertile time for the production of striking choreographies: *Incantations* (Jolivet), *Antigone* by Françoise, who played the role with great eloquence to the unanimous acclaim of the critics, *La Femme et son ombre* (Claudel/ Charpentier) by Dominique and *L'Âme et la danse* (Valéry/Koechlin).

In 1968, in collaboration with Lise Brunel, the Dupuys created a dance sector: A.R.C. (Animation, Recherche, Confrontation) at the National Museum of Modern Art in Paris. They presented fifteen performances there over two years, bringing together twenty-two choreographers from both France and abroad, such as Arlet Bon, Paulina Oca and Daniel Nagrin, for example, who were still relatively unknown in France. Similarly, they contributed to all the collective ventures in which modern dancers were involved in France: committees, debates, corporative actions such as those of the S.N.A.C. (Syndicat National des Auteurs et Compositeurs) and the A.F.R.E.C. with Dinah Maggie. They could be found on every barricade where it was possible to fight for the promotion and better understanding of dance and dancers.

In response to the growing demand for training of both an initial and a more advanced level, they created, in 1969, the R.I.D.C. (Rencontres Internationales de Danse Contemporaine), a diverse and penetrating educational venture that continues to organize courses and seminars of different types in France and abroad today. Then, together with Jacqueline Robinson, within the framework of the R.I.D.C., they founded a centre for professional training.

If I were to describe in detail the recent development of Françoise and Dominique, the B.M.P. and R.I.D.C., the artistic work and compositions of the couple, both solo and group, Dominique's creation of another focal establishment in the South of France, the work they undertook of both a private and official nature under the auspices of organizations such as S.N.A.C., the Association Technique pour l'Action Culturelle (A.T.A.C.), the Fédération Française de Danse and the ministry of culture, their successive periods of residence in various large French towns such as Reims, Vichy, Avignon, Bourges and Châlon, the 'Étés de la Danse' and other forms of courses, the swarming of their crew, their teaching and performances abroad, particularly in Italy, and the shooting of films and videos, I would easily go beyond the chronological boundary of this book. All this is well known and forms part of contemporary history.

Françoise Dupuy was without doubt one of the best dancers of her generation in Europe. It is not surprising, therefore, that several of the great choreographers created works for her, not only because of her refined technique and acute intelligence, but also of her enormous possibilities as an actress which enabled her to feel as much at home in a tragic or lyrical style as in a humorous one. The observer may simply be enchanted by the beauty of pure movement, or bowled over by its dramatic force.

As a result of their parallel and often combined careers, there may be a tendency to oppose or even compare the respective merits of Françoise and Dominique as dancers on the one hand and choreographers on the other. This is unfortunate but difficult to avoid. It must be emphasized that they are two entirely different and complementary personalities, as the success of their joint choreographies shows.

Reconsidering these independent creators in the last ten years, the individual qualities of each one and of what they learnt and developed from one another become obvious, as does what they themselves each *say* with their bodies, their mature spirit, and what they ask their performers to say.

For instance, Françoise, in her solo *Ana, non*, at one and the same time and with extreme subtlety, lays bare and fills gesture and form, thereby reaching the deepest place where all the nuances of human condition are expressed. In her group compositions this same type of simplicity, asceticism and precision in time and space seems to confirm Isadora's belief, quoted often by Françoise, that *'dance is an art that allows the human soul to express itself in movement, but it is furthermore the basis of a more supple, harmonious and natural conception of life'*.

Dominique has always been lighter and more whimsical, at once Pierrot and Harlequin. As a dancer, he brought a note of virtuosity and amusing poetry to their common repertoire. As a choreographer, he possessed less of a sense of form and architecture. Both his solo and group works often lose their impact through a tendency to superfluity, and it is regrettable that the indisputable force of his ideas and theatrical images are diluted by a lack of economy in their composition. His recent research has led him towards the 'deep' disciplines of yoga, the martial arts and Japanese techniques, and his latest solo works such as *Trajectoires* and *En vol* result from this attentive consideration of the hidden memories of the body.

It would hardly be possible to reconcile Françoise and Dominique with certain post-modern tendencies such as minimalism. They love the theatre too much and have too strong a sense of the theatrical, even the baroque. They are actors who have in all sincerity broken the strings that attached them to the subject. They were able to inhabit places, lay claim to and transform them. The same may be said of scenery and props, as if they were moulding their material and their environment until it became the very fabric of their dreams. All of this occurred well before their decisive encounter with Jerome Andrews, a magician in his use of fabrics.

Françoise and Dominique possess a natural flair for handling words and have written about dance either with a directly informative or didactic aim, or in a more lyrical way. Their words help to clarify further their aims and intentions. I will quote here a few aphorisms (poems?) that Dominique for his part calls *Visions de la danse:*[3]

The Paradise of Space

We are seeking a paradisiac space
and like others who have sought
an artificial paradise, we are taking
risks.
. . .
The reproduction of stereotyped movements
is a physical exercise during which
the dancer imitates a model.

Entry into the deep dance
is something different
here, there is no 'reference to'
But a journey inside the person.
One portrays one's own intimacy
Dancing thus becomes an unveiling.
. . .
Dance is a project. To project
a movement, it is at once
the ability to foresee, imagine and cast it out
into space; projecting it,
thanks to a tentacular body.
. . .
Adherence to the invisible and the unutterable is a
primordial condition of dance.
. . .
All movement is creation
it exists only because you do it.
. . .
In praise of space
there is in the relationship to space
not only the making of contact
but an act of love.
        It is a celebration'.

---

[3] Unpublished writings.

And by Françoise:[4]

> *Why dance?*
>
> *Indeed, why live?*
> ...
> *The dancer is the creator of*
> *the moment, who bears within him*
> *the whole world*
>
> *And his body is its privileged resonator*
>
> *This body,*
> *Instrument of precision*
> *made of ebb and flow is capable*
> *of gathering spent energies in order to*
> *use them in a unique current*
> *of strength, and of becoming an incomparable tool*
> *of communication.*
> ...
> *If we no longer dissociate*
> *either 'technique' or 'expression' in what is dance*
> *then we rediscover the rapture that comes*
> *from the bursting forth of the mental and physical powers of man*
> ...
> *The dancer is a man who*
> *works in public with his*
> *body. He 'offers it' publicly to view.*
> *One may offer it for favours*
> *or money.*
>
> *This has a name*
> *One may equally parade it*
> *before any ordinary human being*
> *But one may also offer it*
> *for a dialogue of love*
> *sacrifice*
> *and beauty*
> *for a dialogue that is humanly divine.*

[Since I wrote these pages, both Françoise and Dominique have been diversely and severally appointed to noteworthy 'official' posts. At the ministry of culture, responsible for dance, its role in education or as a performing art; then at the head of important institutions concerned with professional dance teachers' training. A most coherent furtherance of their respective talents.]

   In order to complete this sketch of their choreographic careers, it would perhaps be interesting to mention their principal works together

---

[4] *Ibid.*

with those musicians and scene painters who collaborated with them, and the dancers who formed part of the Ballets Modernes de Paris over the years: Jacqueline Séréville, Jacqueline Levant, Norbert Schmidt-Schaefer, Karin Waehner, Gayle Spear, Paul d'Arnot, Laura Sheleen, Edith Allard, Anne Nordmann, Jean Bouffort, Anne-Marie Gallois, Lucile Ellis from K. Dunham's company, Eliane Crevier, Anne Goléa, Norman de Joie, Françoise de la Morandière, Françoise Saint-Thibault, Katherine d'Epinoy, Brigitte Réal, Roger Ribes, Olga Stens, Michèle Nadal, Francine Lancelot, Anne Bedou, Tania Bari, Sonia Millian, Michèle Seigneuret, Jean Rochereau, Georges Tugdual, Jean-Jacques Béchade, Joëlle Mazet, Isabelle Mirova; and more recently: Danièle Talbot, Christine Gérard, Delphine Rybinski, Marie-France Delieuvin, Bernard Delattre, Brigitte Hyon, Bernadette Le Guil, Viviane Serry, Agnès Dravet, José Jaen Montalvo... An impressive list since each of these dancers have established their own personal career.

Extract From the Repertoire:

Joint Works

Date		Music	Stage Set
1954	*Paso*	Maurice Ohana	Pierre Philippe
1955	*Heidemarie von Dittmar*	Schubert	
1956	*Cants de Catalunya*	Catalan folk music	Albert Lenarmand
1959	*L'Arbre*	Alain Bermat	Etienne Martin
1963	*L'Âme et la danse*	Charles Koechlin	

Works By Dominique

Date		Music	Stage Set
1951	*Histoire du Petit Tailleur*	Tibor Harsanyi	Yves Bonnat
1961	*Mouvement en 3 mouvements*	André Jolivet	
1962	*Le Jeu de l'amour et du hasard*	Folk music	François Ganeau
1964	*Incantations*	André Jolivet	
1965	*Fragments*	Alexandre Tansman	Roger Stoffel
1965	*Le Mandarin merveilleux*	Béla Bartók	Pierre Philippe

1967	*Le Regard*	François Bayle	
1968	*La Femme et son ombre*	Jacques Charpentier	Pierre Philippe
1969	*En pure perte*	Philippe Capdenat	
1973	*Visages de femmes*	Ethnic music	Roger Stoffel
1976	*Le Bal des Gueux*	Bernard Liébart	Roger Stoffel
1977	*Objet-danse*	Denis Dufour	Roger Stoffel
1979	*Le Cercle dans tous ses états* (solo) (*Trajectoires ... En vol ...*)		Denis Dufour Marcel Robelin

Works By Françoise

1951	*Visages de terre*	Villa-Lobos	Pierre Philippe
1956	*Marinada*	Catalan folk music	
1965	*Sur la terre enchantée*	Alan Hohvaness	F. Dupuy
1966	*Antigone*	Jasuo Sueyochi	Modest Cuixart
1968	*L'Homme et son désir*	Darius Milhaud	Roger Stoffel
1972	*Le Manteau*	Tchen Jivane	Roger Stoffel
1975	*Eclats*	Jean Schwartz	Roger Stoffel
1974	*Comodulation*	Jean Schwartz	F. Dupuy
1979	*Danse en liberté*	Jean Schwartz	O. Faschino, L. Casaco, O. Franceschini

Works Composed for them

Jerome Andrews:

1960	*Le jour où la terre tremblera*	Carlos Chavez	Lucien Clergue
1967	*Capture éphémère*	B. Parmegiani	
1968	*Le masque de la double étoile*	Francisco Semprun	

Deryk Mendel:

| 1958 | *Epithalame* | Olivier Messiaen | Imai |
| 1961 | *Apprendre à marcher* | Ivo Malec | R. Acquart. |

THE GRAFTS

Jerome Andrews *by Delphine Rybinski**

[When I was in Montreux in 1952, I attended one of Mary Wigman's summer schools, although ill health prevented me from actually taking part. Amongst the numerous pupils present, one man in particular fascinated me. He was already mature and displayed incredible technical mastery and a completely individual and compelling style of movement that I considered somewhat over passionate (was it romantic or expressionist?) – in short, he was someone who could not go unnoticed. 'Who is he?' I asked. 'An American ...'.

A few months later, in Paris, I went to a show organized by Danse et Culture in which one striking, flamboyant, moving dancer performing short, marvellously constructed pieces, such as the *Acteur, Pierrot* and *Œdipe*, stood out clearly from the rest of the programme. Consulting my programme, I saw that he was one Jerome Andrews. I rushed into the wings, and with tears in my eyes, spluttered out my thanks and asked him if he taught in Paris. 'Come and have a cup of tea with me tomorrow ...' came the reply.

Leaving his dressing-room, I suddenly realized: 'It's the same American I saw at Mary's summer school!'

And that was how it all began – the installation of Jérôme in Paris, the increasingly widespread radiance of this colourful character who belonged to the race of 'stars', his growing influence on dance and dancers in France. During these years I learnt so much from him ...]

American, born in 1908, died in Paris in 1992.

When Jerome Andrews arrived in France for the first time in 1936, he already had a long career behind him.

He was born in 1908 in Plaistow in the State of New Hampshire, of a carpenter father and a mother who wished to awaken him to all the arts, allowing him to choose his own direction. His education and the artistic climate in which he was brought up were thus of the richest kind. This was the era of 'fancy dancing' on the toes or barefoot in the kitsch style of 1914 to 1922; however, already in his own conception of dance he had begun to renounce purely decorative performance. Isadora Duncan danced her *Marseillaise* and opened up the relationships between the

---

*Delphine Rybinski: dancer and teacher. The course of her career led her from Anne-Marie Debatte to Jerome Andrews, via Françoise and Dominique Dupuy and the Ballets Modernes de Paris. She explored theatrical paths as well as those of aïkido. Her choreographies were of a very personal and lyrical style.

body and soul. At the same time, those dancers who might be called the phenomena of the time emerged onto the scene: Ruth St-Denis, Ted Shawn, and other personalities such as Maud Allen, renowned in both London and Berlin.

From his earliest years, Jerome Andrews studied fancy dancing as well as salon and classical dance at the Cornish School in Seattle, before going on to study with Ruth St-Denis and Martha Graham, and taking composition courses and music with Graham's own musician, Louis Horst. He worked with Doris Humphrey, Hanya Holm and Margarete Wallmann (of Wigmanian descent), perfected his knowledge of classical dance with Olga Préobrajenska, Léo Staats in Paris, and the Italian Albertieri. He also studied the ethnic dances of Mexico and Africa, and Hindu, Chinese and Japanese classical dances, evidence of the richness of his studies.

His earliest stage experiences began in Los Angeles and New York, with the creation of short and extremely personal compositions in which he performed as a soloist in various cabarets and theatres:

> '*Andrews is a dancer of rare grace and subtlety. He has the imagination and spirit to transform his poetic and affective ideas into dances*', wrote Joseph Arnold (*American Dancer N.Y.*)

His impact was noted at the Pasadena Playhouse, then at the Théâtre Habima, and between 1930 and 1937 he also made a brilliant solo career for himself at the Radio City Music Hall in New York.

> '*Andrews is an amazing dancer and a superb acrobat; his best works are those that simply reveal his corporal ability. He developed leaps that are as interesting as they are dangerous*' (*Lenard dal Negro N.Y.*).

He thus became a star, displaying a virtuoso talent, but also a particularly expressive physique. John Martin, the great American critic, devoted a page to him in *America Dancing* (1936), a work that has since become a classic, hailing him as one of the greatest 'hopes' of the young generation:

> '...*He is technically superb and moves with admirable fluency...such potentialities as his are not to be found every day in the year*'.

He studied and danced with the ballet-master Ivan Tarassof from Diaghilev's company, with Léonide Massine, Doris Humphrey, Ruth Page and Graham, as well as at the Jooss-Leeder school in England. Finally and above all, Mary Wigman, whom he met in 1951, having already seen all her performances in the U.S.A., turned his entire life and work upside down. He said of her:

> '*My first encounter with Wigman dates from fifty years ago. In this New York City theatre where she danced for the first time in America, everything I had seen, heard or learnt previously, was turned upside down. Later, I studied at the*

Plate 26 Jerome Andrews, *Oedipus*, in 1951. Photo: Paul Kehren, Nice.

*Wigman school in New York, under the direction of Hanya Holm, and then
finally with Mary Wigman herself in her school in Berlin.*

*There, new shocks completely transformed my idea of what the study of dance
could arouse in the theatre as much as in the human being. Through her actions
on stage and the knowledge and inspiration she revealed in her teaching, she
showed us that the "poetry of the human being" was the real instrument of
dance, extending beyond styles or countries'* (November 1973, concerning the
death of Mary Wigman).

Jerome Andrews then realized what his own aims as a dancer were:

*'It was Wigman who made me take the decisive step towards the understanding
of "technique". From this moment, all the excellent teachers I had known came
back to me in a flash, showing me what they had learnt by experience rather
than through any system ... Now, the greater part of all that has settled within
me and I try to pass on to the up-and-coming generations something of what I
have learnt, and also what each individual might alter in his quest for his own
style of dancing, so that all this experience might take a new direction for the
dancer. In this way the fruit of all the experiences of past and present dancers
may find its place in the development of the débutant, from feeling to shaping
it into form'* (extract from a lecture by Jerome Andrews).

At the age of thirty-two, a serious foot accident led Jerome to meet Joseph
Pilates, a former circus hand, who practised the re-education of the body
using 'machines'. As a result of his work with Pilates and with these
instruments, Jerome Andrews developed a refined skill based on the
opening of the joints through tactile sensitivity and consciousness of the
points of support, a true preparation for dance. He was invited to teach
with Pilates for two years during 1944 and 1945, and Hanya Holm was
one of his first pupils.

Much research into Eastern philosophies and different types of
yoga finally completed the training of this dancer whom the French
public were to discover during the 1950s: a choreographer, performer and
marvellous teacher who imparted the constant development of his work
through his intuition and knowledge, with a perpetual opening to
question.

Jerome Andrews's earliest Parisian encounters in the 1930s were
those with Mistinguett and Maurice Chevalier. He performed *Rhapsody
in Blue* at the cabaret Le Colisée, and divided his time between Paris and
London, where Sigurd Leeder, Kurt Jooss's 'right-hand man' in England,
was choreographing *Prometheus* for him. In 1936 he danced at the Gaîté
Lyrique in the same programme as Julia Marcus from the Wigman school.

When Andrews returned to Paris after the war, Pierre Thiriot
wrote of him:

*'Every expression of his body may be perceived beneath his light costume as
much as on his expressive face. Highly artistic and sympathetic to the public*

from his very first movement, it appears that we might expect great things both of himself and of his ideas'.[5]

And Paris indeed appreciated his solos: *Macbeth, Le Mendiant, Le Pierrot, Esquisses japonaises, l'Acteur* and particularly *Œdipe.*

Helen Dzermolinska, editor of the *Dance Magazine of New York,* wrote in 1951:

> *'When you watch Jerome Andrews dance, what do you see? The mocked and scornful lover, the prisoner shaking the prison bars of his own heart with his bleeding stumps, a beggar and the raucous, hollow sound of his flapping wings, the whims and arrogance of this comic fellow, the actor.*
>
> *What have we here? It is a terrible shock, like falling from a mountain top in a dream, or as enchanting as soaring above the earth on the wings of a dream. It is yourself that you see and gather in the silence of your heart. It is the shock of recognition'.*

Anthony Anderson had already claimed in the *Los Angeles Times* in 1927:

> *'I believe that Jerome Andrews is extremely original. So original that he disturbs and creates a kind of uneasiness amongst many members of his audience. And his work is as masculine as it is original'.*

These two reviews, written thirty years apart, mutually enhance one another, for although, in a way, not speaking of the same dancer for the process of change he underwent was so great, they express more or less the same impressions.

Having established his first company in California at the age of twenty, he went out to found Les Compagnons de la Danse in France in 1953. The company included amongst its members Jacqueline Robinson, Renate Peters, Saul Gilbert, Karin Waehner and Solange Mignoton. In this period, he composed *Rencontre* to music by Erik Satie, in which he was partnered by Olga Stens. In 1955 Laura Sheleen, Noëlle Janoli, Muggi Egger and Michèle Husset joined him for a while.

In 1964 the Théâtre du Tertre and in the following year the Vieux-Colombier welcomed the Jerome Andrews Dance Company and its repertoire. Jerome Andrews and Noëlle Janoli presented *Une âme morte danse avec un ange,* and Roger Ribes, Dominique Paul-Boncour, Renée and Fernanda Karmitz, Hélène Herba and Danièle Ménassol joined the company. Between 1965 and 1970 Jerome composed three striking works, *Le Jour où la terre tremblera, Capture éphémère* and *Le Masque de la double étoile,* for Françoise and Dominique Dupuy, brilliant, intuitive performers.

---

[5] *Pierre Thiriot in Toute la danse* (December 1953).

'When it is a question of creating a dance', Andrews said, *'there are two possibilities:*

> *to choose that which creates an effect (which is a formidable and very advanced stage in the art of composition in a thousand ways), or one may prefer dance that is a development of the knowledge of all these things in relation to the personal knowledge of yourself and beyond yourself, of your instincts and dreams, and give shape through a chain of acts the clear meaning of your spirit. Unfortunately, we have become such perfectionnists in the intellectual, functional and so-called realistic aspects of the discipline that we forget what are the keys to it'* (lecture, 1975).

Through inner necessity and the demands of this 'meaning', which for Jerome Andrews meant listening to the fundamental and organic nature of movement, he strove to make his dancers discover their own thematic desires.

What is an inner *meaning?* No language can give a truly satisfying definition.

> *'When one makes a movement, this movement possesses its own life-blood just as it has its own colour and skin, and these things cannot be explained in words. It requires a teacher to say: "No" or "Again" or "Not like that ... ". And after a thousand times, the person feels that he can go no further ... But he has got there without realizing and the meaning is found. At the outset, one makes the mistake of looking for an intellectual support through the exteriorization of movements and this is incorrect'* (lecture, 1979).

He was not a choreographer from whom one learns choreography. Dance was not, for Andrews, a series of forms or a prescribed and stylized investigation, but rather, he attempted to discover within each one of his dancers a movement of their inner being in relation to their creative potential.

> *'There is an internal structure in the form of the movements that produces the desired form. In spite of one's very precise and correct conceptions, each individual possesses a unique sense of integration that is peculiar to him. He must be given the opportunity to come to terms with his experience and his material'* (lecture, 1975).

Ode, first danced in 1970 by Jerome himself, Noëlle Janoli and Jérôme Rachell, is an excellent example: with each successive performance, the circular motion of the three dancers seemed like a new creation, and yet the precision of the structure and the very intentions of the movements could each time be recognized.

An adventure of the mind and body in space, an adventure of the relationship between the dancers, which lie in an awareness of the consciously lived moment with all the demands of its fluctuations.

'Movement is something that lives in the heart, it is ephemeral, it cannot be specified, it passes' (1969).

Jerome Andrews called this type of dance in which the human being seeks to discover his primary self 'deep dance'. It requires preparatory work of the most demanding nature.

In his understanding of technique, he naturally emphasized the notion of physiological discipline, and of psychological and spiritual disciplines too, but above all he placed an emphasis on the intuitive discipline through which play was integrated as an essential path to dance; he treated each of these disciplines with care so as to avoid blurring the actual stuff of dance or of the body, the instrument that has to be appropriately tuned.

Jerome Andrews's originality lay in his ability to make constant connections in his teaching between an infinitely precise and scientific knowledge of the functioning of the body and the intuitive and sensitive experience of the dancer. The practice of technique always takes into account the inner animal and the instinctive being.

After spending several years as the assistant of Alyse Bentley, whose method, known as 'Motor Mental Rhythmics', used fabrics and other objects to teach rhythm to children, Jerome Andrews developed this work, especially that with fabrics, large, heavy cloaks and a whole variety of ribbons and bands etc. Unlike his contemporary Nikolais who used these types of objects principally to create plastic effects and to satisfy a theatrical vision, Andrews accorded greater importance to the movement experienced by the dancer in relation to the actual stuff, so that he may fill the space within and around him, and the fabric become rather like the very stuff of life itself.

This approach encompasses all the technical notions of weight, resistance, suspension, impetus, turning, leaping, falling ... together with an extraordinary approach to the use of costume in relation to the movements of dance. To allow the unconscious to come into play, to seek to penetrate the inner nature of each act, Jerome Andrews nevertheless did not in any way go to work with a psychoanalytical discourse. He spoke to the creator in each one of his pupils, and it was through his quest for the magic of movement and the constant exaltation of its ecstatic content that his work arrived at an ethical stance that was close to the purified paths of zen.

Finally, it may be claimed that he was amongst the first to have introduced into the mind of the French dancer the notion that dance and music might have a dialectic relationship.

Jerome Andrews held a unique position in the evolution of contemporary dance in France, standing, as he did, completely outside the fashionable products of the American stream, and those who worked with him certainly realized that he approached dance in its most fundamental aspects.

Remaining faithful to the principles of Wigman, who maintained that diplomas only existed to encourage beginners, he allowed each person to develop in his own way, without 'safety nets'. Having always sought to avoid the systematization of a school, Jerome Andrews nevertheless led two or three generations of dancers towards the pursuit of expressionist dance. Whilst marking out its own path, the French school of contemporary dance, exemplified by Françoise and Dominique Dupuy, as well as other teachers, followed the tradition of this style which in certain respects aimed to perpetuate Wigman's vision.

Jerome Andrews's progression from the little boy he recalled dancing in the morning dew in California ('*It amounted to more than mere technique*') to the brilliant dancer of the Radio City Music Hall, later transformed by his Wigmanian conversion, and ultimately the seeker striving towards the understanding of essential freedom, was an unique one.

His creative work, research and teaching turned him into a figure to whom many people flocked in order to seek a revelation of the meaning of life through dance. Lovingly close to Mary Wigman, he was one of the best examples of that generation of artists who were fascinated by the relationship between mind and body, and who developed through their art not the codification of a style or method, but the art of dancing and a profound sense of humanism.

Jacqueline Robinson *by Geneviève Piguet*

Of English origin, born in 1922.

Jacqueline Robinson's most immediately striking features seem to me to be her universality and humanism in the philosophical sense of the word: her aim to expand the human being.

On a choreographic, pedagogical and literary level, her extremely rich work may be linked with the effulgence of the Atelier de la Danse which she founded in 1955, influencing several generations of dancers and choreographers, and which she still directs today.

I first discovered the Atelier de la Danse in 1959 through a performance that took place in the avenue Junot. From the outset one could sense the breath of a new spirit and the smouldering of the fire within that boiling pot of a studio in Montmartre. The novelty of the dances, their intensity and deep physicality opened up a whole new world to me. Each one of the dancers retained her individuality, whilst demonstrating the same fervour and quality of movement. As for Jacqueline Robinson

herself, she was exactly the kind of person I was looking for, not only as
a contemporary dancer, but as a complete artist, an artist whose open-
mindedness and general musical and artistic culture bore no relation to
the stereotype of the 'dancing-girl': a pair of legs and no brain, not much
understanding and still less in the way of ethics.

Jacqueline's imaginative use of the body, her art of production,
and profound sense of musicality took me straight back to my own
theatrical and musical roots. For it was through music that Jacqueline
Robinson, like myself, came to dance.

An anecdote she liked to tell illustrates perfectly the mentality
of the time and the divide that separated our youth from the new
generation.

As a refugee in Ireland during the war, her first job had been to
teach dance in a supposedly progressive 'Bridgidine' convent. She was
approximately twenty years old, and her pupils were aged between
twelve and fifteen.

> '*After my first class, for which I wore a long skirt*', she recounted, '*I was
> summoned by the Mother Superior. "Miss Robinson, I have heard that you
> lifted your skirt, revealing your legs, which, furthermore, were spread wide
> apart". (We were doing second position pliés.) "You cannot possibly do that
> here!". Torn between hierarchy and pedagogy, and so as to avoid having to lift
> my skirt, I got ready to give my second class in a short tunic. Would this be
> considered decent? Dressed thus, I appeared before an areopagus of nuns who,
> startled, conferred with one another, and pronounced that there could be no
> question of bare legs, even ones that were kept together. What was to be done?
> "Well! Give your class in your coat and skirt!" the Mother Superior declared.
> After a term in coat and skirt, the bishop decided that there would be no more
> dancing classes*'.

This non-too-distant world is difficult for us to imagine.

Jacqueline did have the privilege of growing up in an environment that was filled with art and culture. Born in London in 1922 of an
English father and a French mother, a singer, who took Jacqueline to
concerts, the theatre and exhibitions from an early age, she was educated
alternately in France and England. Her upbringing was completely
bilingual and placed an emphasis on artistic training: music at the École
Normale de Musique in Paris and eurhythmic dance with Yvonne
Redgis. In 1938 she entered the department of professional training at the
École Normale de Musique and studied piano with Yvonne Lefébure.

In 1939 the war forced her to leave Paris. She continued her
musical studies in Dublin and also took a course in history of art at the
university. It was there that she found her destiny. She met the dancer
Erina Brady and became her pianist. Erina had been a pupil of Wigman

in Dresden, later danced in her company, and had left Germany to open the Irish School of Dance Art in Dublin. Jacqueline discovered the world of contemporary dance and choreographic research, and she took lessons as an amateur. Then, making a sudden decision to change her course, she took the professional training course and obtained the diploma closely modelled on that of Wigman's school. At the same time, she continued her studies in the history of art at the University of Dublin and was awarded a diploma and a scholarship which enabled her to continue her studies.

In 1946 she attended a course in London with Sigurd Leeder, Jooss's favourite partner, and on her return to Paris the following year she began her theatrical studies at E.P.J.D., a most eminent place at that time, under the directorship of Jean-Marie Conty and Mytho Bourgoin. She danced with Jacqueline Levant there and also worked with Ludolf Schild. She danced in the company established by Mila Cirul (a colourful character who was also Wigman-trained), and thus took part in the choreography competition organized by the Archives Internationales de la Danse in Copenhagen. Then, she gave her first recitals in Paris. She made her first real débuts as a solo dancer in England in 1948 when she opened a studio in Nottingham. Attached to the municipal theatre as a choreographer and teacher of movement to the actors, she could boast some three hundred pupils at the end of the first year! She created solos, went on tour, and scored a huge success:

> '… *Jacqueline Robinson has about her an air of dedication to the dance, and draws her audience into the rhythm and the music with the command of the truly great artist'* (Nottingham Journal, 1947); 'Her style is both wide-ranging and delicately nuanced, and is characterized by a contagious fervour, an intelligence of gesture and a remarkable sense of musicality'* (Paris, La Danse, 1949).

She chose to settle permanently in Paris for personal reasons. Love, marriage and motherhood (she had four children, which was unusual for a dancer) all influenced her career without interrupting it.

Jacqueline Robinson returned to E.P.J.D., this time in order to teach drama and improvisation, and later created Dance Workshop which became the Atelier de la Danse. She met all the modernists of the period: Jerome Andrews, to whom she owes a great debt, Françoise and Dominique Dupuy, and Karin Waehner. She became acquainted with the latter at one of Mary Wigman's summer schools in Switzerland. In Wigman, Jacqueline found her 'mentor'; everything she had imagined of Wigman's genius was confirmed and she was utterly fulfilled. After that first experience, she never missed a course and spent the winter of 1957 in Berlin with Mary who showed such affection towards her that the two corresponded regularly until Mary's death.

Plate 27 Jacqueline Robinson in one of Mary Wigman's classes, 1953. Photo: Boog, Zurich.

'Jacqueline was more Wigmanian than Wigman herself', asserts Karin Waehner, Jacqueline's colleague throughout the 1950s. *'It was this common heritage that immediately bound us together in our work'*. Karin evokes Jacqueline's warm and generous friendship on her arrival in Paris:

> *'The Atelier de la Danse was my refuge, my home, my family. I owe Jacqueline the deepest gratitude for her welcome, without mentioning the work we did together, the exaltation of creation, the rehearsals and discussions and the confrontation of our two personalities: this very opposition of our characters enriched our research; it was rather like the combination of fire and water or day and night, and as a result of this confrontation* Judith et la nuit *was created. There was* Le Seuil *too, both pieces being set to the music of Francisco Semprun.* Le Seuil *was a kind of life experience. In it Jacqueline portrayed the character of an over-protective mother from whom I had to cut myself off in order to pursue my own way in life. It was a very powerful and significant piece of choreography.*
>
> *With hindsight, it may be said that the field of dance was well and truly ploughed by our generation. There was plenty to do, and as we all needed to support one another; it was very important for us to find a human and artistic home'.*[6]

This 'human and artistic base' found its point of anchorage in 1957 with the establishment of the Atelier de la Danse in the avenue Junot in Montmartre, where it remains today. For Jacqueline Robinson, who already had some sixty solo, duet and ensemble dances to her credit, the big creative burst began with the Atelier's first company which brought together under her direction several independent soloists, such as Birgit Lundin from Stockholm, Patricia Fabri from Florence and Françoise Saint-Thibault from Paris.

Two years later I became part of the first professional ensemble of the Atelier de la Danse which consisted of five dancers, all from different backgrounds: Monica Schade-Pagneux, a former Wigman pupil, the Canadian Blondine Albert, Françoise Saint-Thibault and myself, both from the same Burgundian roots, and the young Annie Gallois, who trained at the Atelier school. The repertoire included a wide range of works. The colourful palette in the manner of the naïve painters she used in *Danseries pour Noël*, to music by Ferdinand Piesen, seemed to underline the quasi-austere choreographic writing of *Lamento* (Vivaldi), a trio in black and white, with its both sober and sensuous architecture, the pure lines of which called to mind the strain of a gothic arch and the solidity of stone. The joyful *Carnaval nocturne* (Boccherini) threw into relief the magical aspect of the enchanted atmosphere of *Chants de Majorque* (Semprun).

---

[6] Unpublished interview with Karin Waehner.

Chant rituel, described by Marcelle Michel in *La Danse* in 1953 as a *'haunting and terrific work of the highest calibre'*, was followed by *Cantique pour la terre*, based also on the music of Semprun, a striking work of a mythical and primitive nature, with bold movements and costumes – tights painted onto the actual body of the dancers by Maurice Lang.

I would like to emphasize in passing the pioneering nature of our early performances. I recall one in particular, *Cantique pour la terre* in Poitiers, at which half the audience booed and whistled whilst the other half applauded and shouted bravo! The dance concluded with a perpetual circling movement. Amidst the general chaos, we spiralled round and round, waiting for the lights to go down, but nothing doing! The audience became more and more agitated and we all began to feel quite sick. Jacqueline gave a signal for us to improvise a fall and when everybody was lying on the floor, the stage-manager, having finally understood the situation, closed the curtain. The audience continued to shout; it was all very exciting and invigorating! The audiences of the avant-garde today are too docile. Fearing that they may seem to be behind the times, they indiscriminately swallow everything that is offered to them.

Jacqueline's choreographic works followed one after another; amongst the most important ones of this period were *Les Illuminations* (Rimbaud-Britten) of 1963, hallucinated and baroque in its dream-like quality and different from her usual style. 1965 saw the creation of the solos *Le Jardin clos* (Daniel-Lesur), and *Nocturnos*, to poems by St Jean de la Croix and music by Semprun, about whom I shall speak further on.

Rites was created for us in 1967, based on authentic ethnic music. It is one of those dances that cuts across all time because of the universality of its themes as much as its sensual, bare, limpid and clear writing. *Rites* appeared so timeless that when it was recreated in 1986 as a tribute to Mary Wigman for the Biennale de Danse in Lyon, it did not seem at all dated. Daniel Dobbels wrote of it:

> *'this dance condenses within it all the finest tensions that surround it discreetly and which may be described as elemental – the breathing of air, the flowing of sparkling water, the dark, all-consuming colour of the fire that the bodies conjure up and attenuate for the benefit of the audience ... dance at the most secret of its powers – sobriety of all fertility ... '.*[7]

I remember the 1960s as a period of intense activity: all those rehearsals, the sweat, the laughter and the tears that they brought with them, the enthusiasm and excitement of the new works and the stage-fright we

---

[7] Daniel Dobbels, introductory text to *Rites* (Catalogue-programme for the Biennale Internationale de Danse in Lyon, 1986).

experienced began within the Atelier. Respectful of our individual personalities, Jacqueline knew what she wanted and what she could ask of us. When I think back to this time, the studio in Montmartre seems something of a magical place, with its open space between the bars and under the loggia from which exotic instruments hung, the den where the grand piano stood, space that was just waiting to be filled or, better still, like a kind of luminous, water-tight bathyscaphe made to plunge into the unknown, into the process of imaginative creation. This in turn manifested itself publicly in the form of shows, galas and tours. The Atelier never ceased to provide a place where painters, musicians and journalists from all walks of life could meet for performances, concerts and exhibition; it was a kind of 'bateau-lavoir' of dance.

How many artists from different disciplines could be named amongst those who have cast anchor in the Atelier de la Danse at one time or another? There were the dancers/choreographers from abroad (Mara Dajanova, Brigitte Garsky, Raden Mas Jodjana, Roemalaiselan, Edo and Liong Sie and Gilberto Motta); the theatre or stage producers (Jean-Pierre Brodier, Nikos Athanassiou and Guy Bousquet); painters (Basil Rakoczi and Maurice Lang); the dancers who taught there (Jerome Andrews, Atty Chadinoff, Bella Reine, Laura Sheleen, Katherine d'Epinoy, Elisabeth Robinson, Jacqueline Challet-Haas, Françoise and Dominique Dupuy, Francine Lancelot and Susan Buirge); and the musicians, (Francisco Semprun, Ferdinand Piesen and Michel Christodoulides.)

At the same time as pursuing her stage career, Jacqueline also took charge of the school for children, amateurs and professionals. She was the first to offer a full three-year professional training in contemporary dance. We received a multi-disciplinary training under Jacqueline's direction and that of guest teachers.

Jacqueline herself claims not to know which excites her the most: creating or teaching. She has always tried to avoid teaching according to a certain style or codifiable 'technique', and in this respect she remains faithful to the philosophy of her master, Mary Wigman. On the contrary, she seeks to develop in her pupils an aptitude for using *neutral* material, each according to his desire. This neutrality does not imply indifference, but rather observation, rigour and subtlety. She has always been very strict about actual commitment, the personal investment of each individual in the slightest movement, the smallest sensation that may be experienced and brought to life. *'Sensory pleasure and the delights of the spirit'*.

The following extracts are taken from a number of different articles:

'What use is an instrument if it has no music to play?

Plate 28 *Cantique pour la terre*, 1959, choreography by Jacqueline Robinson, music by Francisco Semprun. From left to right: Patrizia Fabri, Birgit Lundin and Françoise Saint Thibault. Photo: Associated Press.

Above all you must listen to your inner truth, follow the internal logic of what you want to say and are discovering. Exclude the showy. Distrust superfluousness. Question the necessity of everything you do. You must reconcile boldness with rigour: boldness of content with strictness of form. The absolute specificity of what you have to say and the absolute clarity of the discourse. Do not be content with approximations.

... Dance must be met with respect; in teaching, any intervention must be made with the utmost delicacy. You must guide without interfering, arouse the demands of truth, clarity, precision, generosity and that imaginative additional dimension known as theatre ...

... Freedom comes through knowledge; quality is acquired only through strictness. Raise yourself above the everyday; we have lost a little of our original divine nature ... '.

The most remarkable aspect of Jacqueline Robinson's work has undoubtedly been her teaching of children, even those as young as three. Dance became a complete, all-round education. She knew how to awaken a child's curiosity and inspire his imagination, confidence and motivation. She could inspire both freedom and strictness at one and the same time. She opened to those children an approach towards their everyday life (family, school, the immediacy of the body) and other forms of knowledge, modes of expression and communication, a judicious blend of discovery and reflection that developed in them sensory, intellectual, affective and social awareness, a balanced state of being manifested in their creative endeavours.

Amongst the children who studied at the Atelier de la Danse were Stéphanie Roussel and Christine Gérard, well known today as dancers and choreographers. Christine had been brought to the Atelier by Françoise Saint-Thibault who had immediately recognized her potential amongst all her pupils. She was fourteen years of age. *'For me'*, she said, *'dancing class was the highlight of the week. I lived for it. My training at the Atelier was a sort of long-term incubation period, a magical time in which I merely had to exist, breathe and feel, and learn to listen to my body and move with music, space, time and the other dancers. The struggles and difficulties would come later. At the Atelier there was no urgency or rivalry, everything was assimilated in an intuitive, unconscious way, offered without favouritism or prejudice and suffused with a nourishing aspect. Jacqueline did not impose any physical rules or definitive form – we had to find these within ourselves. We never felt as though we were being forced into anything, or thwarted. She made us feel the vital necessity of dance, the importance of elemental subjects and the sense of the sacred. Her teaching allowed us to go to the limit of our experiences, however clumsily. At the Atelier my personality was well and truly formed and became indelibly marked. Even now, as a choreographer, I try to find dancers who were trained at her school, for in them everything is strongly in evidence without deformation or obstruction'.*

L'Ensemble de l'Atelier de la Danse came gradually to be replaced by young dancers from the Atelier school, who formed the following groups:

Le Thyrse (1963) with Anne Lecouvreur, Marie-France Frisch, Marie-Béatrice Robert, Anne Le Rolland and Isabelle Lemarchand;

Le Zodiaque (1968) with Christine Gérard, Alexandre Witzman, Madeleine Fajon, Anne Mulliez, Borghild Dudde, Delphine Rybinski, Philippe Henry and Marie-Odile Langlère.

For this group, Jacqueline Robinson produced *Terre d'exil*, to music by Theodorakis, a sort of freedom manifesto that characterized this period of 'commitment' in her career. Christine Gérard remembers it with emotion:

> *'Terre d'exil was a fundamental dance concerned with death and revolt, with the earth giving way, and bottomless pits in opposition to the living roots to which we must cling'.*

A film of this dance, shot in the rocks of Fontainebleau, was made by Alain Lartigues.

For *Le Zodiaque,* Jacqueline also produced *Fortuna*, a fresco inspired by Tarot cards, with costumes by Basil Rakoczi and music by Carl Orff. The medieval stylization of this piece did not preclude sado-masochistic violence and, in contrast to this violence, Monteverdi's *Magnificat*, gave a feeling of fullness and feminine serenity.

The ritual aspect is a constant in Jacqueline Robinson's work: she invents a kind of sensual liturgy in which meditation assumes a physical form and the rhythm of celebration becomes organized in time and space ... a sense of the sacred and the 'inner dimension' of dance, of which the poems of St Jean de la Croix (and now 'La Sybilla') are an illustration. P. Lafaille wrote of her:

> *'Tall and hieratic, she shines with the quiver of life; for her the word is made flesh and movement'*, and the composer Daniel-Lesur claimed *'she is not a dancer who moves to music, but a musician who dances music, and rediscovers its original pulse. Her whole body is spiritualized by the skillful economy of the forms it creates and transfigured by the meanings it assumes'.*

A brief decline in activity for health reasons in 1978 allowed Jacqueline to pursue other opportunities; she returned to music and her writing career. She had already published several collections of poems and numerous articles and didactic works on dance which, in a clear and practical way, provide a mine of information for student dancers and choreographers. These works include *Les Cahiers de l'Atelier de la Danse* (an irregularly published review), *L'Enfant et la danse* (1975), *Introduction au langage musical* (1979), *Eléments du langage chorégraphique* (1981) *Danse, chemin d'éducation* (1993) and a translation of Mary Wigman's *Language of Dance* (1986), and Doris Humphrey's *The Art of Making Dances* (1990) and John Martin's *Modern Dance* (1991).

She also worked in journalism for a time and, as dance critic for several reviews, she seized every opportunity to widen the debate and give her work a didactic focus. The following quotations are chosen at random:

> *'Some have claimed that music resides in silence and poetry in the inexpressible. Out of these paradoxes a fundamental truth seems to emerge: that is, it would be wrong to try to say too much, do too much or give too much to the observer, throwing him into a state of confusion and denying him access to the secret and mysterious voices of art. This dancer often rushes into the movement; she is not lacking in technical skill, but her movements have no density in space ... which is the very material of the dancer; this living sculpture cannot be achieved in a vacuum. It requires conscience and an almost tactile sensibility towards this essential matter which must in turn dominate or be dominated by the dancer, from a linear as much as from a dynamic point of view ...'.*
>
> *'... It is not enough to have an all-consuming theme in one's heart, or even to possess a more than honourable physical technique; one still has to create a work. Not a monument, that is to say, – let us not be too ambitious – but an object whose architecture and structure are solid, logical and functional. I use the word "object" deliberately, for we need objectivity, objectivity that does not imply indifference or artifice but the possibility of considering the work in its own autonomy and form ...'.*

In addition to her literary activity, Jacqueline Robinson is an active militant and enjoyed a close association with various organizations that aimed to promote dance: the Syndicat National des Auteurs et Compositeurs, the Fédération Française de Danse of which she was president from 1978 to 1982, the R.I.D.C. and the Conseil Supérieur de la Danse.

I believe that through the inner nature of her artistic approach Jacqueline Robinson creates within us an echo of the invisible, this fourth dimension in which the human being moves when confronted by the mysteries of mind and matter.

Laura Sheleen

[In the thirty years or more in which I have known Laura Sheleen, she has never ceased to fascinate me. So many different trains of thought, experiences, disciplines, modes of existence and action, and elements seem to join together in her work and personality. She is a multiple being, in search of unity. She is a paradox of mysticism and pragmaticism, opacity and transparency. She is of the earth and the moon; she analyses like a geometrician and dreams like a poet. She cannot even be called an 'eclectic', since her various skills are only combined in order to disentangle the essential from the universal.]

American, born in 1926.

Who is Laura Sheleen today? Someone who tries to place man in possible harmony, who seeks to rediscover the great cosmic laws that govern life and treats others with love and exigency (for them), a scientist and an artist, a person who recalls the period of her life in which she was predominantly a *dancer* and now believes that *'You have to make a choice; I do not want to be imprisoned in a machine. I would prefer to die in my garden'*. Laura Sheleen elaborated what she calls the 'mythodrama', the whys and wherefores of which she presents in her book *Théâtre pour devenir autre*.

What path did she take, then, and what has been her specific contribution to the development of modern dance in France?

Laura was born in 1926 in Battle Creek, Michigan. She relates in an interview with Jean Serry:[8]

> *'At the time when everything was in turmoil in Europe, the war brought hoards of people to America who continued to pursue there the work they had begun in Germany or France. This applied also to dance. I discovered dance when, at the age of fifteen, I went to see a ballet. Straight away I wanted to dance. Everyone tried to dissuade me since I was "too old", but I waited patiently for seven years.*
>
> *At twenty-two, I said "too bad, I will never be a ballerina, but I will at least be a dance teacher". And I left for New York at the precise moment when Martha Graham, Doris Humphrey and José Limón were at the height of their careers. I was able to profit from their teaching and worked with Balanchine and other classical teachers; but, curiously, the memory of them that has remained with me is not of their steps or their style, but of themselves, their artistic personalities, which went far beyond dance itself. As for dance steps, well now, I've had quite enough of those!'.*

Her training may have been belated; it was certainly eclectic. Beginning in Detroit where she studied classical and modern dance, she then went to New York where for eight years between 1947 and 1954 she worked principally on modern dance, successively and sometimes simultaneously, with the New Dance Group (with Mary Anthony, Jane Dudley, Sophie Maslow and William Bales), in Graham's company (with Graham herself, Robert Cohan and Helen McGehee), José Limón, Merce Cunningham, Jean Erdman and Louis Horst; in addition, she studied classical dance with Balanchine and Alexandra Fedorova, and acrobatics. Thus she became familiar with a variety of techniques.

---

[8] Laura Sheleen, interview with Jean Serry in *Danse et enseignement* (Dijon, 1977).

In 1954 Laura Sheleen received from the American Theatre Wing the most important scholarship awarded to an American dancer in order to pursue her research into the functioning of the human body as an instrument of artistic expression (she had already obtained a diploma from the New York Board of Education).

She arrived in Paris in 1955 and became acquainted with the modern dance scene, which was, as we know, rather limited. Affinities were perceived, doors opened for her and Laura came to play a part in several of the artistic and pedagogical adventures of the time.

She was very beautiful and as a dancer created an impression through her inner quality and meticulous concern with form. She was Olympian in style; some people found her cold. In everyday life she appeared mysterious, contained and poised. As a teacher, her principal contribution was of a Grahamian style that was barely known in France, and, in addition, tremendous analytical rigour in a number of technical domains, such as the exact placing of the body with a concern for the awareness and knowledge of the correct kinaesthetic working. Also, knowledge and awareness of directions in space, studied in great detail, of energies and time. Laura based her research on Laban's systems which once again proved to be an extraordinarily fertile source in which the geometrical aspect is underscored by the symbolic and cosmic aspects.

Laura's proposals were immensely clear and subtle on both a technical and a stylistic level. She had already begun to show an interest in the psychological aspect implied by the act of dancing and one could read between the lines of her teaching that interest in therapy through movement that was later to become her principal concern. Dance professionals were enriched by her teaching in terms of precision and rigour, whilst amateurs in search of themselves found a guide. Over the years, Laura increasingly came to assume this latter role, abandoning work directed towards the professional stage.

Although Laura worked in various countries, Paris became her home port. As a dancer, she was a member of the Ballets Modernes de Paris for a time, and in 1956 took part in its performance at the Théâtre Daunou, most notably in *Visages de terre*. Later, she danced with Karin Waehner, having landed up at the famous Studio 121 in the Salle Pleyel, where she also met Jerome Andrews and Ludolf Schild's heirs, Nadia Schild and Jacqueline Levant, who helped her enormously to establish herself in Paris. Karin and Laura performed together for a few seasons and both composed choreographies. Laura created the duo *Dumki*, to music by Dvořák.

Dinah Maggie showed an interest in Laura's work and established for her and Karin the École Technique de Danse Moderne under the auspices of A.F.R.E.C. Its courses were held initially at the Studio 121, then at the École du Mouvement (Schild's base) and finally at Rose-Marie Paillet's studio.

From 1956 to 1959 Laura taught in Finland, Germany, Switzerland (at the famous summer school, where she took over from Mary Wigman who had now transferred her own summer school to Berlin), and finally in Sweden, where she was responsible for professional training at Lia Schubert's School of Contemporary Dance and the Ling Institute for Gymnastics.

In 1960 Laura returned to Paris where, for some years, she pursued a threefold career as a dancer, choreographer and teacher. She founded a school, the Centre de Recherche dans l'Art et la Science du Mouvement, which based its teaching on a penetrating study that went beyond dance in many respects, and witnessed increasing success. She also taught at Jacqueline Robinson's Atelier de la Danse, where she was a permanent staff member in the department of professional training for many years. She was, moreover, invited by numerous dance organizations to teach courses.

She organized joint performances in which other dancers and choreographers took part, out of her concern for their confrontation and mutual enrichment and for greater public awareness. She organized a series of evening performances at the American Centre; in 1963 'The Body in Movement' that brought together works by Katherine Henry d'Epinoy, Monica and Jean Pagneux, Laura Sheleen and *Les Illuminations* (Britten/ Rimbaud) by Jacqueline Robinson; then in 1964 at the Montparnasse theatre with Françoise Saint-Thibault; and finally, on a regular basis with her own company under the auspices of the Théâtre du Geste, an association that she founded in order to *'unite with artistic and educational purpose, people who loved (and practised) mime, dance and stylized movement'*.

Amongst her most striking ensemble pieces were *Incantation* (Hovhaness), *Aquatique, Paysage irréel* (Boucourechliev), and *Visions fugitives* (Prokofiev).

Simultaneously with her work in the field of dance and the theatre, Laura Sheleen explored the field of psychotherapy. She went from psychiatric hospitals to universities and other specialist groups, studying every aspect from physical education to 'artistic kinaesthetics', psychosociology to socio-dynamics, psychophysical functions, rehabilitation. Thus she learned and taught, in an attempt to fathom the implications, applications and meanings of movement, and to observe its physical and psychic mechanisms and their interdependence. She became closely associated with (and subsequently married) the psychopedagogue Jacques Dropsy, a specialist in the areas of teaching through movement and group therapy, whose method, known as 'psychotonus', was expounded in his book *Vivre dans son corps,*[9] published in 1973.

Then came the moment of choice between the uncertainty (she might herself have said vanity?) and stress of the professional dance world, and research and therapy. Laura chose the latter and became even more deeply involved in it: *'I am not interested in making money by giving performances'.*

She studied analytical psychology (Jung), group work and psychodrama (Moreno); from 1976 to 1986 she collaborated with the Groupe Français de Sociométrie founded by Anne Ancelin Schutzenberger, and the Fritz Perls Institut für Gestalt Psychologie in Düsseldorf. The list of places, people and organizations with and for whom she worked both in France and abroad is indeed impressive!

Taking one step further along the path indicated by Jung, Laura added to, or rather confirmed, within her work, a spiritual (mystic, metaphysical?) dimension. She leant towards the sacred traditions of zen, Sufism, animism and fundamental Christianity, and from these deciphered, penetrated and assimilated the common foundations of humanity, the 'collective unconscious' that forms part of the cosmos and with which every individual is imbued.

Laura Sheleen currently lives in the rural Yonne where she continues to refine her research. She never ceases to work, both there and elsewhere, with groups in which *mythodrama* has become her speciality. The course of Laura's career enables us to shed some light on this term she coined and through which the progression from dance studio and stage, costumes and masks, to the symbolically determined domains in which such therapeutic rituals are at play may be seen. Everything she sought to achieve and realize throughout her career fell exactly into place. In no way did her work become scattered as her ardent supporter Gilberte Cournand feared, who wrote about her in 1965:

> *'so many diverse activities run the risk of dissipating Laura Sheleen's energies; her teaching must soon be seen to reveal its results and her young disciples ensure its continuation in order to guarantee the well-being and enrichment of all those who find in dance spiritual forces as well as physical equilibrium'.*[10]

There was in fact no scattering but rather convergence, and it takes a whole lifetime to achieve that.

What exactly was her contribution to French dance? At the time of her arrival in France, there was a need for her particular analytical,

[9] Jacques Dropsy, *Vivre son corps* (Édition E.P.I., Paris, 1983).

[10] Gilberte Cournand in *Art et danse* (Paris, 1966).

Plate 29 Laura Sheleen, 1956. Photo: Associated Press.

subtle and rigorous (some might say almost fanatical) approach towards certain elements of choreographic language, to complement the specific and individual contributions of those practitioners already at work who were more inclined towards pure theatricality, or musicality, spontaneity, abstraction, or one or other of the thousands of facets of dance. Moreover, Laura had the ability to mobilize the energies around her and inspire in others the spirit of creation and enterprise.

There is no shortage of texts by Laura Sheleen to which one may refer. She has been sufficiently explicit with regard to the aims of her work. We may recall *Théâtre pour devenir autre*. There is also a short article entitled 'Espace, temps et structuration symbolique' which appeared in December 1983 in the review *Art et thérapie*, and pinpoints her current preoccupations:

> 'No human gesture is indifferent. It is a sign ... Dance, choreography, mime and the theatre of images all demonstrate the art of signs par excellence: non-verbal communication, iconic expression through images ...
>
> I have been concerned with the problems of body – space – time – imagination and communication for thirty-five years now. I have explored them through dance, research into functional movement, Jungian psychotherapy, Moreno's psychodrama, the theatre of the image and the movements of handicraft workers as well as through research into symbolic objects and gestures and the use of theatrical techniques for the exploration of the self by means of masks and corporal actions ...
>
> What the practice of dance, and Laban's conception in particular, brought to me personally was the vision – and the experience – of being able to become a multi-dimensional being, conscious of my own evolution in a multi-dimensional universe. Ideally, such a multi-dimensional being would, by analogy, be a solar being, capable of functioning in each and every one of the directions and dimensions associated with it. It would be capable of assuming solitude (or solartude) which implies that becoming a "sun" is to achieve a sense of uniqueness. It is, therefore, to be one, and alone ...
>
> Laban has taught us his principle of the four directional categories. Setting out from this construction of space, it is by dividing up space and then organizing it that one may conquer it. I exist. I occupy a sphere of approximately one cubic metre of which my independent movements make me master. My centre of gravity – my inmost physical being – is situated at the heart of this structure; and it is from this centre that Laban's dimensional categories spring ...
>
> – The so-called cosmic directions: the two apparent movements of the macrocosm and microcosm in relation to the sun (with it: clockwise; against it: anticlockwise)
> – The so-called absolute directions: ...the poles from zero to infinity (down towards the centre of the earth – upward vertical thrust, infinity).
> – The so-called personal directions ... phylogenetic ... these belong to me: my right, my left, in front of me and behind me. Within "my" threefold dimension of past, present and future, "my" temporal notions of orientation in space and

time appear: I am the present … the future lies ahead of me. The past is behind me.

When the dancer dances for himself he expresses his individual mythical space. When he dances for other people he creates resonances in collective mythical space. Thus he transmits the promise of an archetypal mutation: the passage from the whole of chaotic space-time to controlled space-time. Myths and rituals also express this.

I find great difficulty in accepting the idea that a movement may not have any meaning. Its directions alone are meaningful. Movement for movement's sake, like art for art's sake, seems to me to be a sign of autism, of a determined refusal to communicate, and of shutting oneself off in a narcissistic universe. The tendency to believe that a dancer's movements are self-sufficient, without affective or imaginative meaning fails to satisfy me. Every dancer has the right to choose this option. But the "receiver" of any movement "designed to be seen" will, nevertheless, consciously or unconsciously, seek to decode the signs of a conscious intention, or those springing from the unconscious of the dancer. Having caught this message, he will in turn weave his own projections'.[11] (Extracts from Laura Sheleen, 'Espace, temps et structuration symbolique', 1983).

Karin Waehner

[I met Karin Waehner in Switzerland in 1953 at one of Mary Wigman's summer schools. This blond girl, at once ardent, generous and shy, in whom there existed an extraordinary combination of athletic strength and modest delicacy, captured my attention from the very start. She was trying to establish herself in Paris, where I had been for only a few years myself, and during the following season we naturally met again. Thus began our years of adventures.]

Of German origin, born in 1926.

Karin Wachner was born in Silesia. It is no doubt significant that her mother was a keen follower of a movement that was much in vogue in Germany at the time, which encompassed naturism and the practice of gymnastics, especially the Mensendieckian method. (This method still underlies some practices similar to 'gentle gymnastics' in the United States today). Anxious to provide her daughter with a 'serious' training, whilst complying with her desire for movement, she enrolled Karin in a school of Dalcrozian-type gymnastics in Dresden. But this failed to satisfy

---

[11] Laura Sheleen, 'Espace, temps et structuration symbolique' (in *Art et thérapie*, no. 8–9, Paris, December 1983).

Karin, who was thwarted in her impetus which was of another kind. Indeed, her colleagues found her quite bizarre!

In this isolated, bloodless Germany, torn asunder by war (the year was 1946), Karin and her mother travelled to Leipzig where Mary Wigman had settled. Wigman had become a sort of outcast and was put under surveillance following the advent of Nazism; her art was decreed degenerate and her school and company in Dresden were dissolved. Karin and her mother thus began a journey that led them to spend three months in a labour camp and cross borders illegally, before arriving on Wigman's doorstep like a couple of vagabonds, as Karin described them, and being admitted straight away to observe an improvisation class. Karin says:

> 'Even now when I relive that moment ... after everything I had experienced, the moment I saw Mary, I knew I had to go and work with her'.

There followed years of training in the most unusual circumstances:

> 'It was an exceptional time. We lived with Mary as if on a remote island, from dawn till dusk. The world was in ruins around us, but all this misery helped us to concentrate on our work'.[12]

Thus, there were only a few pupils, and all shared in this great moral and material poverty, hunger and cold, but also experienced a feeling of faith and a burning passion for work that were greater still. Three years of apprenticeship followed for this young steed who was pawing the ground, at the same time drawing nourishment from and rejecting what the 'master', then at the height of her maturity, had to offer in her very exacting, yet sensitive and poetic teaching. Karin, filled with impatience to 'get going' and the desire to take off on her own, acknowledged that Mary Wigman never failed to encourage her to discover herself as an individual and realize her full potential.

On completing her studies in Leipzig, she left for Argentina to join her brother. She was free at last, eager and away from home; however, she was unable to adapt to the Latin temperament. She seized every opportunity to work, notably with Renate Schottelius, to teach and perform.

It was there that she met Marcel Marceau who revealed to her a language that she perceived to be close to her own. She returned to Europe, convinced that she would find the ideal artistic environment in Paris. On Marceau's advice, she worked for a year with the great mime artist Etienne Decroux, who offered her a place in his company. But she chose ... dance!

---

[12] Karin Waehner, unpublished interview with Jacqueline Robinson (1986).

Having settled in Paris, Karin made the acquaintance of those people who were most favourably disposed to the understanding and appreciation of her work – few in number, it must be emphasized. She has said time and time again how like a desert France was at this time as far as modern dance was concerned, and complained of the lack of understanding not only of the public, but of dance students also. It is possible that she may have suffered an unconscious ostracism. Each one of us had a different experience of this period according to our own personal stakes, the opportunities provided by our immediate environment and our differing circumstances.

Karin received a warm welcome at the famous Studio 121 in the Salle Pleyel where Ludolf Schild, Jacqueline Levant, Jerome Andrews and many others had taught, including Merce Cunningham during his first visit to Paris in 1949.

Karin and myself then worked with Jerome Andrews, who, like us, had only recently settled in Paris himself. This work was of both a technical and a personal nature that moved us deeply. Later, in 1953, we joined with him in founding the company Les Compagnons de la Danse. At the outset, the company comprised, in addition to the three of us, Renate Peter, Solange Mignoton, Saul Gilbert, Jean Serry, and subsequently many other French and foreign dancers who had in general been taught by Jerome.

[I served as Karin's pianist for the creation of several of her solo works, the most memorable of which were *Carrefour* (Kessler), *Le Jardin secret* (Bartók), *Devant la porte* (Mussorgsky) and *L'Attente* (Granados), works that might be described nowadays as expressionist or romantic. I would simply say expressive, direct, economical, and without doubt innocent in relation to the dance of today!

I composed many solos too, and we sought mutual enlightenment in one another. How many hours must we have spent dancing, rehearsing and discussing! We also composed a number of duets, sometimes calling on composers who were interested in dance as we conceived it. Our favourite musical collaborator/colleague was Francisco Semprun.]

Semprun wrote several pieces for Karin, among which was *L'Appelée*, a dance that led Lise Brunel to write in *Danse et rhythmes* in February 1959:

> '*L'Appelée based on music by Semprun, achieved such a degree of perfection that day that it tore at my heart strings as if I had seen a sight of rare intensity and great beauty*'.

[Semprun composed *Judith et la nuit* and *Le Seuil* (*The Threshold*) for us. *Le Seuil*, which received numerous performances, explored the relationships

Plate 30   Karin Waehner, *Extase* in 1962.

between mother and daughter – tenderness, possessiveness, jealousy, rebellion – and ended up with the daughter's departure. We liked this dance very much as it corresponded to our different temperaments: Karin was smaller, more excitable and livelier, whereas my own gestures were broader and full of contained violence. We complemented each other.]

> '... *I awaited the combination of Karin Waehner and Jacqueline Robinson with a certain amount of unease: their opposing personalities complemented one another perfectly in their dance Le Seuil*' (L. Brunel, *La Danse*, 1956). '*In their performances, they present dance like priestesses impassioned with devotion. And since they have something to say, their works are engaging and make one want to follow them attentively*' (A. Tys, *Le Soir*, Brussels, 1955).

Like the majority of interesting modern dancers of the 1950s and 60s, Karin appeared within the framework of two institutions that did much to further the cause of dance.

On the one hand, Danse et Culture, the driving force behind which was Jean Dorcy, and the Théâtre d'Essai de la Danse, under the aegis of Dinah Maggie, on the other. Dinah Maggie gave Karin Waehner her unconditional support and facilitated her rise to fame. She observed in Karin '*an intimate correspondence between what is intended and what is said, between the structure, intensity and rhythm of a gesture and the spirit that inspires it*' (*Le Quotidien de Paris*).

In 1954 Karin was invited to take part in the huge shows staged by Jean Serry in Chartres; they made several duets together. She also spent a number of years as a dancer and choreographer at the Ballets Modernes de Paris under the direction of Françoise and Dominique Dupuy, and in this capacity she created *La Terre promise*, based on negro spirituals, for the company in 1966.

Karin soon began to attract as much attention as a teacher as she did as a dancer. Everything she had learnt from Mary Wigman – lucidity, rigour, impassioned generosity – that nourished her as an artist, assisted her teaching. What, then, was her own contribution? An almost reckless enthusiasm, bursting energy and physical and emotional demands that were far removed from the practices of other established dancers and teachers of the time, practices which did not lack a certain degree of affectation and in which bodily control sometimes proved insufficient. She soon began to give lessons that rapidly grew in popularity and finally became institutionalized, firstly, within the École Nationale Supérieure d'Education Physique, where her teaching influenced a whole generation of 'gym teachers' who were becoming converted to contemporary dance, and secondly, at the Schola Cantorum in 1960, where, under her influence, modern dance was able to penetrate this august temple of music. Karin's rarely waning ardour, her total conviction and unbelievable

Plate 31 Karin Waehner and Jacqueline Robinson in their choreography *Le Seuil* in 1954. Photo: Iliesco, Paris.

energy stirred up enthusiasm and created shocks in certain quarters, but above all it opened the way for contemporary dance and the many guises it was to assume.

The encounter that had the greatest impact on Karin in that period (1956) and opened up new horizons to her was that with Laura Sheleen, for it was through Laura that she became acquainted with American techniques and styles. More instinctive than rational, more a romantic than a classicist, Karin was less at ease with the formal problems of dance. Laura Sheleen taught the Graham technique with an infinite degree of elegance and mathematical precision. The formal beauty of her work as a teacher and choreographer was somewhat cold and distanced, but it nevertheless demonstrated enormous clarity and subtlety. This formal (corporal and structural) mastery impressed Karin deeply and she succeeded in drawing inspiration from it in her own most recent work. Their collaboration was, on the one hand, pedagogical, and on the other, artistic. Their most notable composition was *Dumki,* a duet based on Dvořák's *Trio in E flat,* a lyrical and admirably written piece, warm and yet cool in its expression and of great linear and rhythmic clarity.

Another fruitful encounter was that with the musician Paul Arma who composed several scores for her, including *Ani Couni,* an invocation to the sun in the form of an ensemble piece based on a song theme from Nevada, the lighter *Images,* and particularly successful *L'oiseau-qui-n'existe-pas,* a solo work that was at one and the same time virtuosic yet bare and heart-rending.

> 'Karin Waehner remains one of the best representatives of this art form. Her ballet *Ani Couni* ... commands respect on account of its incantatory style, construction and profound gestural technique' (François de Santerre, 1966).
> '... *L'oiseau-qui-n'existe-pas* presents an unforgettable vision of a bird that still haunts our memories and fills us with nostalgia' (Marcelle Michel).[13]

Karin was, like many of us, impressed and inspired by the choreography of José Limón who came to Paris in 1957. She found herself, quite logically, much closer to his language and way of thinking than she could ever have been to Graham's.

During the summer of 1959 she left for the United States to work with Graham at the summer American Dance Festival at Connecticut College. She worked there with Louis Horst too, from whom she learnt much. This great teacher and musician and close collaborator of Martha Graham, exerted an influence, either directly or indirectly, over the entire American dance world and had one great speciality: the teaching of

---

[13] Marcelle Michel in *Le Monde* (10 March 1980).

choreographic composition. (His works *Preclassic Dance Forms* and *Modern Dance Forms*[14] are models of clarity in the analysis and synthesis of these specific problems and their relationship to the other arts.) It might indeed have been the inspiration gained from her study of primitive art with Horst that led Karin to compose *Discours primitif* (1959), using drums from the Bahamas and spectacular masks, in which she herself portrayed the sorcerer, engaged in dialogue with a quartet. Precision and legibility of form, an archaic yet personal style and a note of humour all contributed to the realization of a delightful work! There followed in *Terre promise*, referred to above, a more lyrical work that demonstrated a kind of return to the sources of expression.

Karin's company, Les Ballets Contemporains de Karin Waehner, was established in 1958 and consisted initially of the most able of her pupils. It later attracted dancers from both France and abroad. Karin returned to the United States several times, first in 1960 when she worked with José Limón, in whom she found a kindred spirit and then to New York in 1966. For some years the American influence remained apparent. Certain critics spoke of her 'intellectual' method. If this were true, it could only have been a passing phase, an isolated moment in her development, for her innermost nature was far removed from intellectualism.

Lucile Rossel stated in Les Saisons de la danse (1978) that

> 'Karin Waehner's dances are highly structured and lucid in the presentation of their intentions and their realization. The ability to speak with such an authentic voice is proof of meticulous work and a lively and flexible sensibility ...'.

For over twenty-five years Karin Waehner pursued her dual roles as a teacher and director of her company, creator and pedagogue. She assimilated various influences, adopted a more abstract language, flirted with the avant-garde, experienced many ups and downs, had health problems, taught throughout France and abroad, composed for her company and went on tour. She was a 'charger' who tried to pursue simultaneously both sides of this twofold career dedicated to dance. She received due acknowledgement of her talent in 1982 when she was offered a chair in contemporary dance at the Conservatoire national de La Rochelle, the first official school to open its doors in this way to a discipline that had long seemed either revolutionary or nonsensical. A more recent event marked, or rather confirmed, a turning point in Karin's artistic career, however. *'I reject the idea of sudden change'*, she declared. *'In the life of a choreographer, there are phases, tendencies, influences, but then one must discover oneself without these influences and inspirations being excluded'*.

---

[14] See the general bibliography at the end of the book.

During the 'Paris-Berlin' exhibition of 1979, the director Pierre Dufonds asked her to choreograph some dances in a style appropriate to a film on expressionism. She hesitated at first, feeling out of her own cultural territory. Robert Wiene's masterpiece of expressionist cinema, *The Cabinet of Dr Caligari* (1920), was suggested to her. She was bowled over by it, finding in the gestural language of the film something that struck a familiar note with her: '*bold, untransposed gestures ... open/closed ... black/white ... everything/nothing*', gestures that had perhaps been suppressed in her earlier 'periods/styles'. From this moment she had the courage to speak out, to allow a vital and emotional language to come into play '*without too much interference from the intellect!*' Faced with undoubted anti-German ostracism in those post-war years in Paris, could it be that she repressed everything that characterized her artistic temperament, the particular culture from which she originated and the education she received on account of the past? The shock of 'Paris-Berlin' was so great that it gave her renewed inspiration and enabled her to discover herself and, in a way, reconcile everything that belonged to her childhood and youth with her present experience and maturity.

> '*I believe that I am now capable of transposing everything I have learnt, everything that I am*'.

She recently stated:

> '*I have always worked with symbols that manifest themselves in a realistic way and which may be understood immediately by the observer or simply felt ... I would like to pursue this line of contrasts between realistic theatrical moments and choreographic moments transposed from real situations*'.

She claimed to rely heavily upon her dancers and to create her dances from their improvisations, with all the risks that implied:

> '*It's exciting! The dancer does not reproduce a sequence, but draws on his own experience: ultimately it is not "my" but "our" choreography! It takes a long time to arrive at a precise gesture in space, time and expression – it requires much love and practice*'.[15]

Karin never stopped composing for her company, and since 1979 she has produced *Les Marches* (1980), *Sehnsucht* (1981), *Changement de quai à Poitiers* (1983) and *Dernière page, déchirée* (1985), *Exode* (1986) which she composed in memory of Mary Wigman for the Lyon Dance Festival, and for various soloists, *Sehnsucht 2* (1989), *Celui sans nom* (1990), *Journal intime* (1994). Today she is ever active, teaching in France and in other countries with unfailing passion.

---

[15] Karin Waehner, interview with Jacqueline Robinson.

Muriel Topaz

American, born in 1932.

Although Muriel Topaz spent only a brief period of time in France, she nevertheless contributed to the development of contemporary dance there. She later held a position at the very top of the international professional ladder as director of the Dance Division at New York's prestigious Juilliard School and is a world authority on Labanotation. Currently she is a dancer, writer and editor of international standing.

She began her training in dance with Hedy Kaufmann, a pupil of Mary Wigman, later pursuing her university studies at the Juilliard School with Martha Graham and Antony Tudor. It was there that she met the composer Jacob Druckman and they married whilst still students. She arrived in Paris in 1954 and worked with Jerome Andrews, Karin Waehner and Marguerite Bougai, to whom she paid great homage. *'I arrived'*, she claimed, *'at a critical moment in the history of French dance – a moment of awakening and a crisis of conscience. It was extremely enriching and I felt that I had something to offer'*. What she 'had to offer', in addition to what she had to *say*, was a unique sensibility, technical knowledge and great clarity of approach to the subtleties and precision of the very substance of dance.

Muriel Topaz was offered numerous engagements, but after a year she returned to the United States where she pursued her career as a dancer and choreographer and devoted herself to the study of Laban's notational methods. She notated scores of many of the great works of the modern repertoire by Balanchine, Graham, Tudor, Limón, Jooss, Robbins and Sokolow, and also wrote several didactic texts.

She returned to France for various lengths of time as a dancer and choreographer and later as a specialist in notation. She enjoyed a close relationship with Dinah Maggie and, in particular, was a guest lecturer at E.S.E.C. (École Supérieure d'Études Chorégraphiques) where she gave some of the early classes in Labanotation in France, at the invitation of her colleague Jacqueline Challet-Haas, the pioneer of Labanotation in France.

[I remember one particular piece that she choreographed in 1955 for Les Compagnons de la Danse, directed by Jerome Andrews. This was *Les Innocents*, based on Henry James's novel *The Turn of the Screw*, set to music of Schoenberg, in which Jean Christiaens, Noëlle Janoli, Solange Mignoton, Karin Waehner and I danced. I recall the pleasure I obtained from dancing under her sensitive and intelligent direction.]

Paul d'Arnot

Uruguayan, born in 1922.

Paul d'Arnot first trained in Uruguay then in Argentina with some of the great European teachers who had settled there during and after the war. So he came to work with Harald Kreutzberg and the Sakharoffs. He was a member of several companies, most notably in Buenos Aires, and appeared as a soloist in numerous countries across the continent. At the same time, he carried out research into the folklore of various Latin American countries.

Paul d'Arnot arrived in France in 1951 where he drank at the European sources of modern dance. He attended summer schools in Switzerland where he worked with Wigman, Jooss, Kreutzberg and Zullig, to name but these, and it was there that he met Raymonde Lombardin with whom he formed a 'duo' that enjoyed enormous success in France and elsewhere over a period of five years. In addition, he studied classical dance with Lubov Egorova.

He led a very active life in Paris and was rapidly adopted by everyone on account of his rather unusual qualities: his physique, like an aristocratic 'gaucho' and his ability to pass from as subjective and subtle a work as *Le Gibet* (Ravel) to the popular dances of Argentina and Peru. He was both a costume designer and a scene-painter, and made his own costumes for his choreographies.

In 1956 Paul d'Arnot joined the Ballets Modernes de Paris. He danced with Françoise Dupuy in her *Visages de terre*, a role that suited him particularly well, and remained with the company until 1959. During that year he created a dance for them entitled *Altiplano* based on traditional Latin American melodies. In the same year he toured extensively with the group Los Incas with whom he collaborated willingly, for the Jeunesses Musicales de France.

Paul d'Arnot left France shortly after to return to Uruguay. He created a profound impression in France, not only on account of his 'exoticism' and the seduction of the Latin American dances (it was not until some years later that this music became widespread in Europe and the flutes of the Andes could be heard resounding in every corner: in this respect Paul d'Arnot anticipated fashion!), but also on account of his own strikingly moving dances which, it might be said, were considered to be tinged with expressionism.

Plate 32   Paul d'Arnot and Françoise Dupuy, *Visages de terre*, 1957.

Edith Allard

American, born in 1927.

An exquisite dancer who spent several years in France and established a discreet yet stable career there, leaving behind her a memory of particular charm. It was an unusual feature for this period that Edith Allard, a pure and noble interpreter of the classical repertoire, was able to become an equally convincing interpreter of modern dance in the hands of modern choreographers. ('*I am condemned to be a perpetual soloist!*', she maintained, on account of her diminutive figure.)

It is worth pausing for a moment to consider Edith Allard's career both in France and in Europe. Her path is indeed exemplary since she passed through every available channel, providing a kind of overview of dance in France at the time. Fanatical about dance from childhood (she paid homage to Mary Vandas, her first teacher in Chicago), she took professional lessons at the School of American Ballet and was later employed at the Chicago Opera in the Markova-Dolin company. She also danced at the Radio City Music Hall. It was at this time that she met Jerome Andrews who already gave her a glimpse of a different kind of dance. She began to dream of Paris:

> '... Jerome was instrumental in an indirect way for my going to France. I studied with him in Chicago the Pilates system ... I was definitely a Swan Lake and Sylphide thinker. One can say that Jerôme sowed the seed! Then the Paris Opera ballet came to New York – it was around 46–47 – their first tour abroad after the war – I remember the picket lines in front of the City Center where the company appeared – against Lifar who was accused of collaborating with the Germans. Anyway – this was a revelation to me – I saw Chauviré dance in Mirages and I felt that was the way a dancer should dance and decided then and there that I must go to France! ... At the time I was working at Capezios part time – anything to pay for my classes ... started to save my sous for the trip ... a scandal in the family! of course, but I went! I travelled with one suitcase and intended to stay three months which turned out to be eleven years! I did not know a soul in Paris but once at Studio Wacker* – I got into the Ballets Russes with Colonel de Basil – rehearsed for several months but the company abandoned before we ever went on tour – so it was to find a new job! Went to one of those open auditions at the Châtelet and got a job for about a year in one of those operettas – was even given the title of Premier Sujet and replaced the Première Danseuse on her day off – coming from the States this was all so new for me – who ever heard of titles there? ...
>
> Through one of the dancers in the company I started going to class with Zvereff whom I loved very much – here I met Olga (Stens) and other friends which are still in my heart! She was also instrumental in my work with Dorcy

---

* A complex of studios on the rue de Douai, now converted, where the classical masters Préobrajenska, Egorova, etc. taught.

with whom I danced for years ... Jerome landed in Paris and we worked together again – rehearsed a few dances but were never performed ... years of uncertainty but I was learning so much! ... ' (extract from a letter to Jacqueline Robinson, 1987).

Edith Allard appeared in one company or another during these years:

- in 1953, in Jean Serry's group, most notably in *Jabadao*, in which Mila Cirul and Jacqueline Levant amongst others also danced;
- in 1954, Edith danced in *De la berceuse au chant de la victoire*, choreographed by Lilian Shapiro and re-staged by Olga Stens, in which Jérôme Andrews and Karin Waehner also danced;
- in 1959 she became part of the Ballets Modernes de Paris and created the role of Lilith in *L'Arbre* by Françoise and Dominique Dupuy;
- during the same year she danced for Gilberto Motta in *Surréalisme 2001*.

From the 1960s on, Edith Allard's professional career became more eventful and itinerant; she appeared as a dancer in various festivals throughout France and toured extensively as an actress in Françoise Sagan's play *Le Rendez-vous manqué*. She attracted notice in Sweden (which eventually became her home port) and was employed as a solo dancer in Malmö and later in Gotheburg. There followed a series of engagements as a dancer and teacher:

- a year at the National Theatre in Tel-Aviv, three at the Ballet de Lyon, and seven at the Stockholm Opera;
- periods as a 'guest teacher' at La Scala, Milan, the Royal Ballet School in London, Stockholm University and the Avignon festival, etc.

Edith Allard lives in Sweden today where she teaches, notably in Ivo Cramer's company, and recalls with emotion those early years in Paris in which she shared in the struggles of the 'marginals' of dance.

Katherine Henry d'Epinoy

American, born in 1933.

This rather unusual artist and remarkable dancer formed part of the constellation of modern dancers in France for several years. Her long red hair, pale complexion, big dark eyes and wiry body that radiated energy, created a distinct image. She made a deep impression on and was an inspiration to many of those who were closely associated with her and who worked with her.

Her recent retirement to California and the subsequent lack of any direct contact with her have made it surprisingly difficult to obtain any precise information about Katherine's career, in spite of the close professional and social links she had with many people.

She was an unpredictable character who could have made a leading career for herself as a dancer, choreographer or teacher.

Born in the United States in an apparently rural environment, she attended Martha Graham's dance classes at the time when Yuriko taught there. Graham's style influenced Katherine greatly – too greatly, some have said, believing that, as a choreographer, she had something much more original to say than she revealed. She also studied jazz with Luigi and practised this style with finesse and elegance. She began to study dance therapy in California in the 1950s, and for several years she worked with the mentally ill in a psychiatric asylum.

Katherine Henry d'Epinoy arrived in France in 1961 and became assimilated quite naturally into the group of modern dancers active at that time, principally within the orbit of the Dupuys. She took part in several 'collaborative ventures' as a performer, teacher (the Graham technique and jazz), and choreographer. She was most continuously active as a member of the Ballets Modernes de Paris. It was through contact with her that Dominique Dupuy became interested in jazz, and in 1963 Katherine and Dominique created *Jazz Out* to music by Dave Brubeck, that remained in the repertoire for many years. Other experimental works followed in which they tried to integrate the idiosyncratic style of jazz with that of classical dance or with the spirit of modern dance. In 1964 an event entitled 'the influence of jazz in ballet', to which Katherine contributed several choreographies, was created for the Théâtre de l'Est Parisien, directed by Guy Rétoré, in which the Dupuys were responsible for the dance section. It was also under the banner of jazz that she appeared within the framework of A.R.C. at the National Museum of Modern Art.

This was only one side of her activity, however. She took part in several of Françoise and Dominique's creations with the Ballets Modernes de Paris and danced with them on and off for a number of years. She established links with other groups or companies, performed the lead role in Jacqueline Robinson's *Les Illuminations* in 1963, and collaborated with Laura Sheleen and Roger Ribes amongst others. She also created solos of a very personal nature; particularly striking were some of the duets she composed with her guitarist-singer partner.

She taught courses both in France and abroad in various institutions and centres including the American Centre, C.I.D. and R.I.D.C., and

Plate 33 Katherine Henry d'Epinoy and Laura Sheleen. Photo: Philippe Fresco.

also taught privately in Paris. She was very demanding as a teacher, as she was of herself, and *'pushed people to their limit'*, extracting from them everything of which they were capable, as Poumi Lescaut, who claims to owe a great deal to her, maintains. This heightened sensibility that characterized Katherine was a source of great richness, but also of suffering.

Katherine Henry d'Epinoy later took part as one of the leading dancers in the Châteauvallon festival. She shared a bill with Françoise and Dominique Dupuy (three remarkable soloists!) in which choreographies by Jerome Andrews and Deryck Mendel were also featured. Then in 1972 she presented some pieces there with her group which comprised Jean Jarrell, Poumi Lescaut and the American Lyn MacMurray amongst others, sharing the bill with Pinok and Matho and Kathakali dance.

In 1975 she taught what she called 'Body eyes through dance' at the Studio du Marais. She made a few further appearances in various places throughout France before returning to California, leaving a trail of nostalgia behind her.

Gilberto Motta

Brazilian.

He probably received his training in Buenos Aires or Mexico, the principal channels or seats of modern dance in South America.

He arrived in France in the late 1950s. An excellent dancer, original choreographer and scene-painter, he soon became integrated and was rapidly adopted by one and all. He danced in the companies of Karin Waehner, Rose-Marie Paillet and Jacqueline Robinson, and for several years was one of the 'stars' of Dinah Maggie's Théâtre d'Essai.

The first work that he presented in France in 1959 was, in fact, *Surréalisme 2001*, for which he made the costumes and produced the scenography himself, based on a score by Lalan (a female composer of Oriental origin who was much appreciated by the modern dancers with whom she worked at the time). This spectacular, grotesque, comical and terrifying piece witnessed huge success; Edith Allard, Nita Klein, Françoise de la Morandière and Jacqueline Robinson were featured amongst the performers.

In 1960 Gilberto Motta presented *Bachianas* (Villa-Lobos), choreographed for the Ballets Contemporains de Karin Waehner, and *Signes* (Claude Laloum) at the Théâtre d'Essai, and, in 1961, *Tryptique* (J. Bondon) and *Panneaurama* (F. Semprun) with his own group of which Annick Maucouvert was a member.

Gilberto Motta left France during the 1960s.

Régine Drengwicz

Of German origin, born c. 1927.

> She received her earliest training in dance with Mary Wigman, and later with Harald Kreutzberg; she became a teacher at the Wigman school in Berlin in the 1950s and created her first choreographies. Karin Waehner invited her to Paris in 1962 and took her on as a member of the Ballets Contemporains. In 1963 she appeared in pieces by Karin Waehner and Sara Pardo. She presented her own dances at the Biennale de Paris and was employed for two years as Karin's assistant at the Schola Cantorum. She then worked with Yuriko and became associated with René Deshauteurs. Before leaving France, she taught contemporary dance at the Popard school. As a teacher, she appears to have had a certain amount of influence and introduced a number of young people to contemporary dance.

It is difficult to name all the practitioners from abroad who settled and worked in France. However, it is appropriate to mention some of these. For example:

> — Trudi Kressel, a Viennese who studied with Chladek in Hellerau-Laxenburg, and then with Wigman in Dresden in the early 1930s. She lived in China and the United States before opening her studio in Paris where she taught and directed a group;

> — Paula Padani who also studied with Wigman in Dresden. She left Germany in 1935 and danced and taught in Italy, Greece and finally Israel, where she established an important school. She settled in Paris with her artist husband and pursued her career as a dancer and teacher there. She continued to teach non-professionals in the Wigman tradition;

> — Alice Ostrowski, who also studied with Wigman in Dresden, took part in several theatrical projects and taught in Berlin before settling in Paris. After the war she resumed her pedagogical activity in Clermont-Ferrand, where she founded the group Danse Nouvelle. A pioneer in this region (a rare enough fact to be worthy of pointing out), she upheld and promoted modern dance there. She died in 1985.

IN THE LINE OF JANINE SOLANE

Rose-Marie Paillet

French, born in 1924.

Her career was typical of those of many dancers of her generation: higher education (was it this factor that gave these women, and few men, a certain intellectual maturity and general culture, particularly in comparison with the youth of the next generation to enter the dance profession?), followed by the discovery of dance, an initial training in classical and/or eurhythmic (Dalcrozian) dance with Janine Solane, and finally an intuitive progression towards a less arbitrary, more personal style of dance.

Rose-Marie Paillet effectively followed this route: philosophy and three years studying medicine during which she also pursued her studies in dance.

[I became acquainted with Rose-Marie Paillet when I returned to France in 1947, eager to meet other modern dancers with whom I could empathize. I was struck by her charm, her tall, slender figure, blond hair, and a certain harmonious quality and somewhat haughty sensibility that were true poetry. The style and vocabulary she employed at the time (very Solane-classical/natural) seemed then alien to my own experience and conception of dance, however.]

She has described her own development in the following terms:[16]

'Jaques-Dalcroze revealed the world of music and its relationship to expressive movement to me as a child at his Institute in Geneva. Kurt Jooss and the performance of his Green Table in Geneva in 1933 were also a revelation and created in me the desire to become a dancer. I was eleven years old. In Paris, Suzanne Blancpain, a student of Lisa Duncan, initiated me to Isadora's style and gave me a grounding in the classical technique. I studied with her for ten years, at the same time as pursuing my secondary and university education.

In 1947 I returned to the Maîtrise de Janine Solane where I stayed for three years from 1947 to 1949. Janine's personality fascinated me. She was a musician, Isadorian in inspiration and influenced also by Kurt Jooss. From her I gained experience of the stage, an awareness of the responsibility of the artist in creating roles and a pedagogical training [Rose-Marie created the character of Time in the *Grande Passacaille*]. *I was, nevertheless, seeking my own identity* [at this time Rose-Marie composed *Le Coeur*, a somewhat striking and individual solo using a sound track constructed from heartbeats].

In 1950 I opened my own independent school and pursued my training in classical dance, which I considered at the time to be indispensable to me. In 1953

---

[16] Rose-Marie Paillet, letter to Jacqueline Robinson.

I spent a year in the United States in Boston where I presented my repertoire; it was there that I witnessed Graham's method of teaching and saw José Limón dance. On my return to Paris, I met Karin Waehner, Jerome Andrews and Jacqueline Robinson. On Jacqueline's advice, I took part in one of Mary Wigman's courses in Berlin (at which Jacqueline Robinson, Karin Waehner and I performed a trio). This encounter with Wigman forced me to question everything I was doing and seek to free myself from received influences and discover a new and less classical vocabulary for the expression of the problems of our age. As a result, I went to work with Karin in her first company'.

Rose-Marie Paillet thus played a part in the individual and collective adventure of the emergence of modern dance during those epic years of the 1950s and 60s. She appeared as a dancer and choreographer with Jean Dorcy at Danse et Culture, and under the auspices of the Théâtre d'Essai de la Danse (Dinah Maggie), where her most notable performance was of *Visages intérieurs*, an ensemble piece to music by Bartók. She appeared both as a soloist and with her company in France and abroad, and, for a while, she collaborated closely with Helga Kimpel, another German in the Wigman line.

Rose-Marie has always been a most generous person. She welcomed into her lovely studio many French and visiting foreign colleagues, including Karin Waehner and Laura Sheleen, within the framework of Dinah Maggie's educational project which aimed to create an advanced, multi-disciplinary school of contemporary dance. Juan Carlos Bellini taught the Humphrey-Limón technique there later, to mention only these few.

From the 1970s to the present day, a period which, strictly speaking, lies outside the boundaries of this chronicle, Rose-Marie Paillet has continued her work, teaching in her school and for other organizations such as the Fédération Française de Danse Classique et Contemporaine, of which she is currently president of the contemporary section, composing new works for her group Les Ballets Modernes de Rose-Marie Paillet, and for the students in her school.

Throughout her career Rose-Marie has passed through numerous stages (or overcome numerous obstacles?) from the mannered, but entirely musical and structured classicism of Janine Solane, to the influence of various contemporary trends, whilst still maintaining her own style characterized by a sense of measure (atemporal classicism) and a vibrant sensitivity. She has stated:

'I think I can say that, for me, Dance has above all been a quest for truth and a hymn to life. Art and life have been intimately bound up in the desire to share in this quest. In my teaching I have tried to transmit this personal creative spirit that, in my opinion, can alone ensure that dance remains alive'.[17]

---

[17] *Ibid.*

Denise Blanc-Raillard

French, born in 1925.

Denise Blanc-Raillard has pursued her career as a dance teacher and choreographer in her native city, Marseilles, since 1953. At the age of ten, the world of dance was revealed to her by the Sakharoffs, and during her adolescence she studied physical education, the Popard and Dalcrozian techniques of dance and acted in the theatre. It was at E.N.S.E.P. that she discovered the 'classical-natural method' of Janine Solane, with whom she was later to work and obtain her diploma.

From 1953 Denise Blanc-Raillard promoted a school of 'expressionist dance' in Marseilles, which later became the Centre d'Enseignement de Danse Éducative et Culturelle. Over the years this centre became known throughout the region as a place where specialist training in the teaching of children could be received.

During the 1960s, however, Denise Blanc-Raillard regularly attended courses and became acquainted with different techniques, particularly within the framework of the C.I.D. She associated with people such as Karin Waehner, Laura Sheleen, Jacqueline Robinson, Jerome Andrews, the Dupuys and Susan Buirge and took part in their adventures. She met her childhood gods, the Sakharoffs, again in 1966 and worked with Clotilde in Paris and Italy. Denise Blanc-Raillard was a member of the first team of the Fédération Française de Danse and assumed responsibility for numerous pedagogical projects. She summarizes her own development in the following terms:

'It was my encounter with the Sakharoffs at the age of six that made me decide to make my career in dance. Exercises in suppleness, the "breaking in" of the body and an introduction to rhythm were all given to me later by Margaret Gray, following the Popard and Dalcrozian methods. The local dramatic company helped me to discover gestural and vocal expression ... the possibility of expressing myself with my whole body and of bringing different characters to life filled me with excitement.

Due to my great interest in natural elements, Janine Solane's "classical-natural" method seemed to respond to my deepest aspirations: the soul and the breath united in movement ... The connection between the spiritual and the natural was important, indeed essential, but it was strongly bound to a sense of earth and space, the return to the original primordial soil of life, a vital source of energy – all this was revealed to me by Karin Waehner. This approach, together with the work of Mary Wigman, was a source of new growth.

Throughout the various courses I attended, I often received the impression that one seeks for what one has already found. All these influences became absorbed deep within me, which explains why a specific label could not be attached to my own school of dance.

My only concern was to dance in a true way. Dance as a means of expression and communication became a necessity for me. Ensemble and solo pieces allowed the inexplicable to spring out forcibly in spite of itself.

The exploration of space seemed inexhaustible to me; this voluminous canvas is essential and indispensable. My exploration of Laban's icosahedron opened up new possibilities and this theoretical knowledge confirmed my feeling, my "raw substance".

Where does dance originate? What is dancing? Why do we dance? How do we dance? These questions must be asked on every level. Familiarity with the history of dance and the knowledge that, like all the arts, it evolves through time, seemed important to me. For this reason, and wishing to provide the public with an opening to contemporary dance, I organized and promoted illustrated lectures in educational establishments, youth clubs and socio-cultural centres, and such like. But it was also necessary to respond to the demands to provide dance teachers, whence the need to train these future teachers in order to avoid the notion of "anything goes ... ". I continued unremittingly to pursue my choreographic research and maintain a pedagogical approach, whilst taking care to preserve the essential message: that Dance is above all an Art'.

Marie-France Babillot

French, born in Bourges in 1928.

She was introduced to dance in 1943 by Janine Solane after receiving an initial training in physical education and the award of an instructor's diploma from the Fédération Sportive de France. She remained with Solane for four years, took part in her shows at the Palais de Chaillot, and bore the mark of her influence for many years to come. *'This dance has shaped my body and my heart'*,[18] she says, and recalls the richness of the 'artistic immersion' of music, painting and sculpture in which Solane plunged her dancers.

In 1949 Marie-France established the Maîtrise de Danse in Bourges along the lines of Solane's work. This was to be her home port for many years and was the base from which she carried out her teaching and creative work. She met Jean Serry there in 1951 and collaborated with him in numerous performances in Bourges and elsewhere. It must be observed, as stated above, that both Solane and Serry based their work, albeit in very different ways, on an adaptation of classical technique and vocabulary. It was quite natural that Marie-France Babillot should follow this same, almost inevitable course that was followed by so many young French dancers of the time who were seeking something other

---

[18] Marie-France Babillot, letter to Jacqueline Robinson.

than the traditional classical way without straying too far from familiar paths. Solane and Serry represented important stages in the development of French dance, and their teaching was sought by a whole generation of dancers. Marie-France thus belongs to this well established trend in France, hybrid, half-way between tradition and modernity, which attracted so many. It was doubtless a necessary transition and served to soften the impact of an entirely new language.

In 1954, however, Marie-France Babillot encountered modern dance through Karin Waehner, with whom she was to work for several years. The years that followed were particularly productive ones in terms of contacts and performances. She worked with Mila Cirul, Olga Stens, Jerome Andrews, Françoise and Dominique Dupuy, and in Jacqueline Robinson's company; she attended a summer school with the Sakharoffs in Sienna, became associated with the research of several modern groups, and appeared with her school in various different contexts, most notably that of Jean Dorcy's Danse et Culture; she was awarded numerous prizes (La Scène Française), and taught not only in Bourges and its district, but also in Paris.

She settled in Châtenay-Malabry in 1965, leaving her sister Claire* to run the school in Bourges where Marie-France nevertheless continued to teach and perform successfully for many years. Today, at her school, Joie de la Danse, in Châtenay, Marie-France pursues important work in teaching and the sensitizing of the public, particularly in educational institutions associated with research in musical pedagogy.

Marie-France Babillot has been a genuine dancer; her ardour and vitality went far beyond the often rigid and conventional stylistic frame in which she cast her choreographies; precise, musical work, though perhaps sometimes timorous.

Similarly, she is a sincere and devoted teacher, dedicated to her idea of dance and to her pupils. As a choreographer and promoter, however, she might perhaps have gone even further had she freed herself completely from a certain degree of conformity. She is, nevertheless, a fine example of this generation of French dancers who were concerned with liberating the art of dance and bestowing upon it a human warmth, without losing an entirely classical sense of balance and moderation.

---

* Claire followed a similar path to Marie-France, working also with Karin Waehner; she attended courses with Mary Wigman in Berlin and then, in 1951, with Graham and Limón at the Connecticut College. She too is currently employed as a teacher at Parly-II and has an authentic talent for choreography in a more innovative style than that of her sister, choreography that allies a sense of form with poetry.

Titane Saint-Hubert

French, born in Clermont-Ferrand in 1933.

Passionately fond of dance from her childhood, Titane studied classical dance and Popard rhythmics in various provincial towns according to the movements of her family. In 1951 she went to work with Janine Solane, first as a student, then as an instructor, and finally as principal dancer in her company, the Théâtre Chorégraphique de France. Titane thus took part for a number of years in the Solane company's shows and tours.

On receiving her diploma from the Maîtrise Solane in 1955 she opened her own school in Clermont-Ferrand. Then, conscious of the need to widen her experience of dance and become acquainted with new approaches, Titane continued to study and familiarize herself with different styles such as classical and contemporary dance, jazz, mime and yoga. The palette of her creative and pedagogical work thus became all the wider and her school one of the foremost regional ones in France. Over the years, Titane Saint-Hubert revealed genuine choreographic gifts as director of the semi-professional company she established in Clermont-Ferrand in 1975. She also possesses a number of qualities common to many of the female choreographers of her generation: a wide musical and artistic culture, a sense of balance and formal harmony and a genuine and refined sensibility, qualities that were indeed highly valued and cultivated by Solane and which all her former pupils claim to owe to her. Alongside these qualities, however, there is also a certain limitation doubtless stemming from the same source and to which I referred earlier: a certain mixture of refinement and grandiloquence that today appears mannered. One would have liked to have shaken these talented people, daring them to cast off this *'bon chic bon genre'* aesthetic, and assert themselves with more audacity and rigour.

THE INDEPENDENT ONES

Olga Stens

Of Russian origin. Born c. 1918, died in Paris in 1985.

Olga Stens was, in a way, the 'princess' of Parisian modern dance between 1955 and 1975. Aristocratic, capricious, romantic and Slavonic! She was a highly colourful character. Her father, a rich Ukranian landowner, was killed at the start of the Revolution. Olga and her mother fled the country in incredible circumstances and arrived in France in 1920. Like so many other Russian refugees who settled in Paris, they experienced great poverty, but also solidarity. Whilst retaining her Russian roots, Olga became a true Parisian, dreaming of art and dance. In the face of maternal opposition, she asserted her independence at the age of sixteen and went to study classical dance with another Russian refugee, M. Delsov, and later with Boris Kniaseff and at the Russian Conservatoire directed by Serge Lifar.

A knee injury forced her to quit dance for three years, after which she made a brief appearance in cabaret. This was followed by a series of fruitful artistic encounters with Nora Kiss (classical dance), Nicolas Zvereff who led her further and introduced her to character dance, Mila Cirul, with whom she discovered expressionist dance, and, a little later, with Jerome Andrews. She also studied dramatics with Vitold, and the Uruguayan Paul d'Arnot became one of her favourite partners.

Olga Stens always described herself as a modern dancer (that is, as creating her own choreographies using a new vocabulary for each new work). She also performed Nijinski's *Danse de l'élue*, reconstructed by Zvereff, and used and performed 'character dance' with unusual elegance and intelligence. It would perhaps be useful to recall what is meant by 'character dance' for it is held in much less esteem today than in the past. As a form of theatrical stylization of folk dances, chiefly from Central Europe, Russian, Spanish and Polish dances and other mazurkas, it was used to particularly good effect for over a century in the great classical ballets, such as *Sleeping Beauty* and *Nutcracker*. It may be said to represent the exotic branch of classical dance. Olga Stens perfected a thorough technical method that, as well as a firm foundation in classical dance, included a detailed study of the different steps, rhythms, and specific details of stance and gesture appropriate to each folklore, moreover emphasizing expressivity.

She tried to approach the authentic sources of these folklores and worked with native specialists on Georgian, Indian and South American dances. Her characteristic perfectionism and remarkable stage presence turned the dances of this type she composed and performed into real pictures, a kind of invitation to travel, through *Danse tartare*, *Mazurka*, *Images de la Russie ancienne*, and the unforgettable *Simhas Tora*, a hassidic interpretation of religious extasy, evoking many subtle and delightful images.

Olga Stens worked with Mila Cirul for a number of years, first as a dancer in her company (she took part in the famous *Chemin de la vie* that Mila presented at the 1947 A.I.D. competition) and then as her favourite performer and collaborator in the field of teaching (these two rather eccentric women, both Russian, refugees and artists were made to collaborate). They produced dance concerts together and some of the independent dancers of the time, such as Jean Serry, could be found working alongside them.

Plate 34 Olga Stens and Jerome Andrews, *Rencontre (Encounter)*, 1955. Photographic montage by Etienne-Bertrand Weill, Paris.

Around 1952 Olga met Jerome Andrews who took her to Mary Wigman's summer schools. Olga was deeply impressed by the latter. Olga and Jerome partnered one another for a while and left in their wake the memory of *Rencontre,* a miraculous dance to the music of Erik Satie, and over the creation of which it seems Wigman herself presided! A man and a woman stand in opposite corners of the stage. They come together, touch, and go back again three times; from the first light touch to the incandescent lifts and slow separation, there is an extreme economy of means. The stark austerity of Satie's music is reflected in the sobriety of the dancers' black velvet and pearl grey muslin.

Olga also took part in the performances given by the Compagnons de la Danse, which Jerome Andrews directed from 1955 to 1962, and Jean Dorcy frequently engaged her for his performance/demonstrations within Danse et Culture, either to demonstrate character dance or as a modern dancer. Jacqueline Robinson also invited her to dance in the various group recitals she organized during the 1960s.

As early as 1952, Olga Stens had shown an interest in reviving court dances. At this time such work as Francine Lancelot's in decoding the choreographic scores of the *'grand siècle',* the age of Louis XIV, such as those by Feuillet and Pécour, for example, was not as widely known as it is today. Owing to her wide culture, musical intuition and profound knowledge of the classical school, Olga was able to reincarnate these dances, and her *Indifférent,* based on a painting by Watteau and a gavotte by Lully, was truly a small masterpiece of delicacy and refinement.

Refined and highly strong, a true thoroughbred, Olga Stens possessed a rare theatrical presence. Although her output was relatively small, each one of her dances was meticulously crafted. Each striking detail had its place within the totally controlled structure. One may recall the thrilling and magical image of the sphinx crouched on top of a pedestal in *L'Enigme éternelle.*

Olga Stens hardly ever showed an interest in ensemble choreography, except for her adaptation of the American Lilian Shapiro's *De la berceuse au chant de la victoire,* a choreography in the Jewish tradition which portrayed *'Jewish life, the joy of family life, love cruelly interrupted by war, and the heroic struggle of the believers'.* This work was performed in Paris in the Salle Gaveau in November 1954 and received critical acclaim as an important modern ballet. In addition to Olga Stens, other dancers resident in Paris such as Jerome Andrews, Edith Allard, Karin Waehner and Roger Ribes, all took part in it.

Olga Stens ceased dancing around 1965 and devoted herself to teaching, mainly character dance, in her studio in the Salle Pleyel, at the Centre International de la Danse, and courses both in France and abroad.

She was closely associated with the activities of Jacqueline Chaumont within the framework of her school as much as in the federation she established. She was also technical adviser to the Ballet de l'Ile-de-France.

Ever faithful to her characteristic sense of dignity, Olga displayed much courage at the end of her life, alone and fighting against the cancer that was ultimately to lead to her death in 1985.

Has she justly been credited with the place she deserved in the contemporary French dance scene? The facilities she enjoyed at the height of her career may not always have worked to her advantage, however, in the sense that she was not taken sufficiently seriously. She was, nevertheless, a sincere and refined artist.

Geneviève Piguet

French, born in 1921.

Geneviève Piguet belongs to that family of dancers who come from the theatre world, which explains in part her aptitude for staging and concern for striking detail as a choreographer.

Born in Beaune into a large family in which the arts, music and drama occupied an important role, Geneviève began by studying piano, solfège and harmony at the Dijon conservatoire. She experimented with theatre and 'body expression' within the framework of a company of dramatic actors that grew out of the girl guide movement and was known as 'Le Jeune Poulailler' in homage to Jacques Copeau's 'Vieux-Colombier'. In 1943 this initial homage to Copeau, who had at that time established himself in the Beaune region with his Copiaux, developed in a way that was to be a revelation to Geneviève. She took part in the *Miracle du pain doré*, staged by Jacques Copeau to celebrate the 500th anniversary of the Hôtel Dieu in Beaune:

> *'this was a miracle for me'*, she wrote to Jacqueline Robinson; *'working in it, I met all the artists who were to set me off on my career: Jean and Marie-Hélène Dasté for the theatre, Jean Serry for dance, and Joseph Samson, precentor of Dijon cathedral for singing'.*

Geneviève Piguet subsequently pursued her training in singing (she has an unusual and deep contralto voice) with Samson in Dijon; she took part in dramatic art 'camps' where she studied dance with Anne-Marie Debatte, Hilde Peerbohm and Yvonne Berge. Settled in Paris in 1945, she devoted herself more extensively to singing and became a member of the Compagnons de la Musique (which was later to become the Compagnons de la Chanson). She continued to dance with Anne-Marie Debatte, and also with Hilde Peerbohm *'whose remarkable teaching not only restructured my*

*spinal column, but gave me physical foundation that was to serve me for the rest
of my life'.*

In 1950 Geneviève Piguet worked with Janine Solane and took part
in the creation of *La Belle au bois dormant* and other performances and tours
given by the company as a dancer and occasionally as a singer. For some
years she combined singing and dancing, sang in several of Jean Dastés
productions at the Comédie de St-Etienne, and danced for Janine Solane,
Anne-Marie Debatte and especially Jean Serry, to whom she acknowledges her great debt. It was with him that she took part in the creation
of those memorable performances in Chartres of *La Geste médiévale* and
L'Autre île that united acting, choric movement, dance and music.

1958 marked a turning point in Geneviève Piguet's career: she
took charge of the Maîtrise de Danse in Rouen, which had been a branch
of the Solane school directed by Mimose Méry. From then on, she spent
part of her professional life in Rouen, where she developed her pedagogical method – which always included a basic classical training – and
where she could put to good use her gifts as a choreographer. At the
same time she worked for several years as a member of the choir at the
O.R.T.F. and as a dancer at the Atelier de la Danse in Paris. She was thus
involved in the creation of a large number of Jacqueline Robinson's
choreographies, and in various performances in Paris and the provinces.

[The many rich and fertile moments of our work and shared
adventures have been described elsewhere. Geneviève brought to the
company her feeling for the theatrical, her musicality, and, more specifically, her individual style which could be intense and sombre like an
antique tragedy, or rugged and earthy, then suddenly an unexpected detail
might change everything in an almost surrealistically humorous way.]

Geneviève sought to free herself of the stylistic traits and mannerisms she had acquired from Janine Solane (particularly the *'hanchée'*
position) and attended courses on which she worked with Yuriko, Anna
Mittelholzer and Walter Nicks. Until about 1970 she continued to work
jointly as a singer and an actress in various productions, including
L'Orestie by Barrault and Béjart's *La Neuvième Symphonie*. It was in Rouen,
however, that Geneviève Piguet was able to demonstrate the extent of her
skill as a choreographer. Over the years, she was able to free the Maîtrise
de Danse from the classical/Solane image it had assumed in its infancy,
and direct her students along a more resolutely modern and creative
path. She produced some remarkable choreographies with the children
(and adults) at her school, and it may be presumed that in a different
context and with different human resources, she might have gone even
further. She produced quite sophisticated works insofar as the treatment

of the contents, in general meaningful, was full of allusions, literary and musical references, and strange, poetic or droll juxtapositions. Her imagination might have slipped into incoherence had it not been controlled by her preoccupation with form and musicality and visual effectiveness. Those who took part in the elaboration and realization of these significant pieces, regardless of whether they subsequently became dancers or not, were enriched by the experience. Artistic enterprise coincided here with pedagogical project.

Geneviève Piguet also taught in Paris under the auspices of various different institutions, and in particular she led workshops in creation and initiation to music. She also worked as a pedagogical adviser.

Geneviève Piguet's creative talents extend into the literary domain too, and she has written short stories, tales and poems in which that world of dreams and of slightly shifted reality, similar to that revealed in her choreographies, comes to the fore.

The very range of her skills (which had as a result a certain dispersion) no doubt prevented Geneviève Piguet from assuming the place she deserved amongst the leading rank in professional dance circles. This in no way detracts from her contribution as a dancer, choreographer and teacher.

Frédérique Franchini

French, born in Algeria in 1926.

Throughout the highly cultured environment of her childhood in Sousse, Tunisia, Frédérique received a full artistic education that included piano, dancing and painting lessons. Returning to Tunis after the war in 1946, she completed her studies and became an art critic with the local press. She then went to Paris and studied at a school of journalism. At the same time, she pursued her study of dance, working with Claude Stéphane for a time, and then with Janine Solane, performing in the latter's shows in Chaillot. She also studied theatre with René Simon and at the E.P.J.D. where she studied dance with Jacqueline Levant.

During the 1950s, she lived through many of the adventures of the early days of French modern dance – Jean Serry's great shows; courses at Studio 121 in Pleyel with Jerome Andrews, Karin Waehner, and Françoise and Dominique Dupuy, amongst the first cohort of students of the E.S.E.C.; and she studied classical dance with Egorova and Tikanova.

Frédérique Franchini began teaching in 1956 at the Schola Cantorum, where she worked for a year, and opened her own school in 1959. Like so many others, she too formed a semi-professional dance group, for which she produced choreographies in various frameworks, such as Dinah Maggie's Théâtre d'Essai. Her most notable performance there was of *Les Agriates* (1960), to music by Varèse, for which she also produced the costumes and scenery. Her personal style at this time tended towards a certain preciosity but revealed a true feeling for visual effect. She was interested in the cinema too and produced several short films about dance, in addition to working at the Service de recherches de l'O.R.T.F. during the 1960s.

In her creative work as in her teaching, she acknowledges a distinct Asiatic influence stemming from her close links with Indochina, where she had lived, and absorbed something of its culture. She speaks of it as 'amazing'.

She has recently become involved in literary activities whilst still maintaining her school and staging performances with her pupils. Frédérique Franchini has also featured amongst the 'militants' of dance, taking part in the toil and struggles to gain recognition for choreographers and the promotion of dance.

Antoinette Guédy

Born in 1927, daughter of Jacqueline Chaumont.

She received a somewhat eclectic education which included the study of music, dramatic art and, of course, dance. She studied classical dance with Jacqueline Chaumont, early and character dance with Olga Stens, and folk dance with Pierre Goron. She also attended several courses abroad. After a few years on the stage as an actress, Antoinette Guédy turned to teaching and succeeded in integrating the various disciplines in which she had herself been trained. She taught in the studios of Jacqueline Chaumont and Olga Stens as well as in a number of other institutional frameworks.

She was amongst the first to work with the mentally sick and developed her own method of dance therapy.

She is currently artistic director of the Ballet de l'Ile-de-France and teaches history of dance, specializing in court dances, at the Dance Conservatoire of the Ville de Paris. Antoinette Guédy has continued Olga Stens's work in character dance since the death of the latter.

Roger Ribes

French, born in 1931, died in 1994.

His initial vocation was painting, which he studied at the Institut des Arts Décoratifs, and it was not until 1953 that he discovered dance, his first mentors being Jerome Andrews and Mila Cirul. Although he was trained principally by Andrews, Roger Ribes also studied with Geneviève Mallarmé, Jacqueline Robinson and the Dupuys, in whose respective companies he also danced. He became Jerome Andrews's assistant and created his first ensemble pieces for Andrews's company. He was also a member of the Ballets Modernes de Paris (Dupuy) for several years, and shared in several of their adventures.

Roger Ribes appeared in various contexts over a period of twenty years. He experienced experimental theatre with Marc d'O, and later with Bulle Ogier, and explored jazz with the musician Michel Roques, and subsequently with Dominique Dupuy and Katherine d'Epinoy. These three dancers/choreographers combined forces in an attempt to integrate jazz with modern dance, and, amongst other works, they created *Jazz Out* (Brubeck), which remained in the repertoire of the B.M.P. for many years.

As a choreographer Ribes participated in the Paris Biennale in 1967, and at the A.R.C. shows held in the Musée National d'Art Moderne in 1968. He created his own group and formed a duo with the dancer Michèle Husset. In 1971 he took part in *Trois à danser* with Françoise and Dominique Dupuy, a piece that was performed amongst other venues at the Hébertot theatre. He taught, both privately and in various institutions, such as the University of Vincennes and the Rencontres Internationales de Danse Contemporaine.

He left France in 1975 and settled in Venice where he continued to perform and teach. He died there in 1994 after a long illness.

THE EDUCATORS

Hilde Peerbohm *by Marie-Madeleine Cosnard, Paul and Annelise Galland* (*Hilde's daughter*), *Monique Golhen and Régine Le Bourva*

Of Dutch origin (1905–1979).

Hilde Peerbohm was born in Düsseldorf on 7 February 1905. Her father's work as a Dutch merchant involved frequent family removals from the Netherlands to Belgium and Germany. From her childhood, she benefitted from an education that was already considered 'modern', and attended courses in eurhythmic dance. She received her secondary education at a boarding school in Wiesbaden run by English nuns. These instructresses were remarkably receptive to artistic and cultural influences. Her parents, on the other hand, were firmly opposed to their daughter's wish to make dance her chosen career and rejected it with scandalized incomprehension. She nevertheless enrolled on the Dalcroze course and studied piano at the same time for six to eight hours a day for almost eight years, reaching a high level of performance. Confined to her paralysed mother's bedside for long periods, the piano became her confidant and music her second language. Improvisation came as easily as breathing to her and, instinctively, she practised what has since been called 'music therapy': *'I capture the tonality of a person'*, she explained later, *'and through successive modulations, I try to develop him according to his needs, whether these be for dynamic movement or relaxation'.*

After her mother's death in 1930, Hilde Peerbohm decided to finance her studies of dance herself, working as a trilingual secretary, first in Germany and then in France. From 1934 to 1938 she attended Rosalia Chladek's course in Vienna, and took the gymnastics teachers' diploma in Stuttgart. The war prevented her from embarking on her chosen career and it was not until 1946 that her professional activity really began. This involved teaching eurhythmic dance to children and expressionist dance to adults, and creating choreographies and shows in collaboration with Yvonne Berge.

The ensuing years, until 1959, were one of intense activity for Hilde Peerbohm. Her creative skill and adaptability allowed her to respond to many different demands and she worked within the framework of the French girl guides' team, concerned with 'expressive activities', directed similar work in the adult movement Vie Nouvelle, ran courses for the children and teachers at the Montessori school in Paris and for specialist teachers at the Institut de Psychopédagogie Appliquée in Créteil, and carried out research into ergonomics ... In Paris, her weekly classes were attended by groups of adults and young people, and she spent part of her summer holidays teaching courses both in France and abroad. During this time so rich in discoveries and fruitful in terms of shared creation, Hilde Peerbohm developed her own method of teaching. Her preoccupation was to allow each individual to express himself through dance. She could not stand anything that was affected, maudlin or overdone. She gave a preliminary training, a sort of way into movement, in her initial concern to implant movement into the authentic expression of the body. In this way, a distinct, autonomous and coherent discipline that she was perhaps the first to call *'travail corporel'* (body work) was born.

From 1954 there grew around her a research team that was totally involved in this bodily work. It entailed the analysis of received teaching in order to structure and transmit it with a certain rigour. Thus the objective basis of a method of teaching which had its roots in personal experience and creative intuition was established, and study and thought on an anatomical–physiological, psychological, philosophical and spiritual level became deeper. This collaborative work continued after Hilde Peerbohm's death.

From 1952 to 1962 Hilde Peerbohm promoted training centres for instructors in 'body action' in Switzerland and then in France, and in the summer she ran courses in the faculty of educational sciences at Sherbrooke University in Canada. Until her death, she lived and taught near Rennes, giving regular private classes and numerous courses and sessions. Both convents and monasteries asked her to promote sessions on a corporeal approach to contemplative life.

She died on 26 July 1979 at the age of seventy-four, whilst preparing for a course. Suffering from cancer for ten years, she had managed to keep up her activities, thanks to a personal therapeutic method based, on the one hand, on a carefully planned diet, and cellular oxygenation, linked to the intensive practice of body work, on the other.

Hilde Peerbohm never wished to restrict her ideas to dance and movement alone. Her research focussed on the very 'Laws of Life' themselves, and the sequence 'Breathing–Concentration–Movement' formed the essence of her body work from the start. She inherited from Rosalia Chladek's teaching the demand and the technical precision of 'correct movement', and became acquainted with Zen as a result of her encounter with Karlfried Graf Dürckheim. Not being attached to any particular theory, she was intensely receptive to the traditions of both the West and the East.

> '*Bodily expression sets out from the theory that we are virtually the whole world, that we have within us everything in the world ... Casting off my own identity, I concentrate on the thing I want to become until it alone exists in my place. I become a rock, a flower, a bird. Everything has to take root in the deepest part of my being.*'

Her enthusiasm did not stop at the embodiment of objects, but carried her further still, beyond, to what is therefore the inner self. It was whilst dancing one day that she had a revelation of the divine Gift, and this experience affected her for the rest of her life. She was always careful not to transmit this inner richness in the form of 'lessons' or 'recipes' or 'models' ... out of respect for the richness of each individual. In her teaching she was both tolerant and demanding: the student was warned that he would have to take responsibility for himself and control of his own 'vital capital'. These demands, which often seemed rough and severe, were also able to combine with the expression of life within her, a smile, a burst of laughter.

It is difficult to assess the importance of an individual like Hilde Peerbohm especially as hers was hardly a 'showy' career. Over and above her acknowledged choreographies, she succeeded in revealing the way to personal creativity to a large number of people, whether their discipline be dance, the plastic arts or music, and above all in the art of everyday living, of which Hilde herself was an amazing example to all.

Hilde Peerbohm's entire teaching method may be summed up in a phrase that she used herself to describe dance: to gently guide the disciple towards the most secret and best aspects of himself in order to *'EXPRESS THE LIFE WITHIN HIM'*.

Yvonne Berge

Of Swiss origin, born in 1910.

From 1924 to 1927 Yvonne Berge was a boarder at Elisabeth Duncan's famous school in Salzburg, where she received the broad education outlined above (see 'Elisabeth Duncan'). In 1929 Raymond Duncan summoned Yvonne Berge to Paris to teach at the Isadora Duncan Memorial School he had recently established on the rue de Grenelle, and when he set up his Akademia, rue de Seine, Yvonne went with him.

In 1930 Yvonne Berge left Raymond Duncan and began to give her own classes. Nevertheless, she remained in close contact with the direct heirs of Isadora: Elisabeth, with whom she spent every summer, in Salzburg and then in Prague, and the Duncan group in New York.

In 1935 she married a physiotherapist and together they opened a studio on the rue de Bellechasse, which was to serve as a hub of intense activity for some years. Yvonne Berge also gave recitals in Switzerland and at the Archives Internationales de la Danse, the Vieux-Colombier and the Salle d'Iéna in Paris, both with her pupils and in collaboration with other artists such as Lily Laskine and later with Hilde Peerbohm. Her partnership with the latter was to last eleven years and was so productive that their names were often associated. She also claimed to owe much to Fée Hellès.

In 1940 she and her family settled in St-Germain-en-Laye. Throughout the war she taught in various different contexts: Secours National, Vie Nouvelle and in a religious community in Switzerland, and in the late 1960s she taught at the school of the Marigny Theatre and collaborated with Jean-Louis Barrault. Her school in St-Germain-en-Laye became a centre of widespread influence until the present day. Yvonne Berge has also maintained regular contacts in Switzerland, in particular with the Jaques-Dalcroze school in Geneva and teachers in Lausanne.

Yvonne Berge is first and foremost a teacher – her own choice, and in this respect she remains faithful to the ideals of the Duncans:

> *'Isadora hoped to get the whole world dancing, and bring dance into the street. This view has oriented all my work and distinguishes it from that of my colleagues who train dancers. I have created many works too and have danced in ensembles and as a soloist in Paris, Munich, Vienna, Berlin and Prague. But in the end the teaching took over, and in answering the students' needs I had to go beyond dance to discover the deepest meaning of this procedure'.*[19]

From this point of view, Yvonne Berge drank at many different sources and studied various disciplines: medicine and physiotherapy with Boris Dolto, psychology with Carl Rogers, the techniques of relaxation with Gerda Alexander, of rhythm with Rosalia Chladek, and philosophy with Dürckheim. *'In this way'*, she says, *'the foundations of the method progressively took shape, thanks to my experience with pupils of all kinds, ages and different backgrounds.*

> *From what I see, great confusion reigns in the minds of most people. The type of dance that is seen on stage is a performance reserved for the stars whom dance students think they have to imitate in order to appear like them. But the concept of being on the stage (a concert performer, one might say), has nothing whatsoever to do with the type of dance the Duncans presented, that is, a basic culture accessible to everybody, and a fundamental education for youngsters from the earliest age.*

> *As for the teachers, they are entrusted with opening wide these doors to the youth of today, so that they might "dance their life". The teacher's task is to release the natural movement of each individual through play and exercises that take into account sensory receptivity (which is virtually excluded from current teaching). This cannot be achieved by juxtaposing techniques gleaned by attending numerous short courses on which one might pick up ideas. This sort of patchwork study is no use at all. There is no organic link. I am trying to clarify all this so that one may feel better in one's self; one's movements, in space, and with others, independent and creative'.*[20]

Yvonne Berge summarized her beliefs in her book *Vivre son corps* (Edition du Seuil, 1975) which has been translated into English, Italian and Portuguese, proof of the widespread international renown of her rich and fundamental work. Another book, partly an autobiography, and further describing her approach to dance, has been recently published: *Danser la vie* (1994).

---

[19] Yvonne Berge, letter to Jacqueline Robinson.

[20] *Ibid.*

Phyllis Drayson

Of English origin (1911–1974).

Phyllis Drayson's earliest training was in psychopedagogy, according to the Montessori* method. She taught initially in Belgium and then in Paris where she directed the Montessori centre for some ten years.

In 1944, having established another Montessori centre in La Bourboule, she met Jean Serry who introduced her to dance. On returning to Paris in 1945 she devoted herself to dance and worked with Malkowski and later with Yvonne Berge and Hilde Peerbohm. She opened a school of dance in Toulon in 1946, and in the late 1950s she met Janine Solane whose musical work impressed her deeply.

Phyllis Drayson also contributed to the introduction of expressive activities to the French girl guides. The sidelights on history tell how she, with her pupils in Toulon, and Hilde Peerbohm with hers in Paris, conceived and rehearsed 'by correspondence' throughout the winter in order to combine the two groups in a perfectly executed dance that formed the high point of a pilgrimage to Lourdes. She continued to teach in Toulon until she too died of cancer.

Phyllis Drayson was an eclectic who never denied her diverse influences and defined the character and filiation of her work in the following way: eurhythmic dance (Dalcroze, Malkowski) – classical/natural dance (Solane) – contemporary dance (European schools and Martha Graham). She appears nevertheless to have been most profoundly interested in 'gymnastics' as a means of providing a complete training for the human being. In this respect she belonged to the same family as Yvonne Berge and Hilde Peerbohm, to whom she was actually very close. She was also an accomplished musician, practised hatha yoga, and was widely cultured. All that, together with the experience of her Montessori work with children, enriched her research into the teaching of movement.

Phyllis Drayson belonged to that group of educators who devoted themselves chiefly to the harmonious development of the human being through movement and dance.

On her death, the work of her school was continued by her pupil, friend and assistant, Alberte Midière, who still teaches there today in the Phyllis Drayson tradition.

---

*The Italian Maria Montessori (1870–1952) was a doctor, anthropologist and teacher. She initiated a pedagogical method that achieved worldwide fame. This method emphasized above all the cultivation of the senses, the development of memory, and advocated the active freedom of the child.

Mireille Fromantel

French, born in 1914, died in 1991.

Mireille Fromantel without doubt played a key role in the development of modern dance in France after the war. This role may perhaps have
gone unrecognized by a number of dance professionals, but the work she
undertook throughout her long career (admittedly within the institutional framework of physical education) had obvious consequences.

She entered the École Normale Supérieure d'Éducation Physique
around 1935, but within the world of the E.P.S.* her passionate love of
dance remained constant, and whilst working as a student and then a
teacher at the E.N.S.E.P.[†] she studied dance, principally with Dussia
Bereska (and therefore in the Laban tradition) and Malkowski, familiarized herself with Dalcrozian eurhythmics and made an assiduous study
of classical dance for a while.

In 1938 she went to work with Janine Solane and became a dancer
in her company. She appeared as a soloist under the name of Myrtille
Romane in the creations of this period, namely *La Pastorale, Passacaille* and
La Fugue, and she taught children at the Solane school. Mireille Fromantel
also developed an interest in folklore and learnt through actual fieldwork
various regional dances of France.

She wished to integrate all this experience of dance with the
training of sportsmen and future teachers of physical education. Thus, as
early as 1945, courses in 'eurhythmics', folk dance and later 'free' dance
in the Solane style, representing the French school, began to take place at
the E.N.S.E.P.

Mireille Fromantel never stopped learning, training and gathering
information in order to become a better communicator of her ideas. After
the war she worked with Jooss and Wigman at the summer schools in
Switzerland, and with Graham and Limón in New York; she also kept up
to date with all the ventures and opportunities available in France. In
addition, she sought to provide a theoretical education at the E.N.S.E.P.
that consisted of pedagogical studies, music and the history of dance, and
was one of the first to try to identify and define the new trends in modern
dance as they were applied in France. She contributed to the dissemination of Karin Waehner's work. Many of her pupils subsequently made
their careers in dance and movement theatre. Mireille Fromantel was a
genuine pioneer and conducted her work through all these stages from
the initial clearing of the ground to the final flowering.

---

*Education physique et sportive.

[†]Ecole nationale supèrieare d'e'ducation physique.

Anne-Marie Debatte

French, born in Normandy in 1918.

Her father was an architect who had destined his daughter for a career in the fine arts. As an adolescent, however, Anne-Marie Debatte developed an interest in the theatre and also became deeply involved with the scout movement. The perils and confusion of the war showed her new paths. In a former chapter of this book she outlines the most decisive encounters for her during these years of discovery:

> *'in 1942, Jean Serry and his break away from all classical structure – Jean and Marie-Hélène Dasté and their work with the mask technique (in the line of Jacques Copeau); in 1944–45, Yvonne Berge, Hilde Peerbohm, Phyllis Drayson and their psychophysiological research – Finkel, Weidt and Schild on a course at T.E.C. – in 1950–55, Janine Solane and her musical knowledge – folk dance with Miss Pledge and Thérèse Palau'.*

By 1945, however, Anne-Marie Debatte had already established in Lille her group 'Les Cantarelles', both a choreographic company and a cultural association that was recognized by the national education system as early as 1947. In its early years, the company was made up entirely of women, but later became mixed:

> *'The membership of the company was renewed many times but its spirit of invention remained constant – that of a communal dance theatre with an original expressive style. It made use of the talents and personality of each individual, and was based on Jacques Copeau's demands for "the avoidance of approximations and quackery", "amateurs" in the original sense of "those who love", artists at the service of the work from the setting up of the scenery or lighting, to the performance of the theatrical action without a star'.*[21]

Around 1951 Anne-Marie Debatte opened a school of dance and body expression in Lille itself, which, over the years, branched out to Roubaix and Tourcoing. She tells of the joyous and heroic beginnings of their activities and early existence in Lille in the following way:

> *'How does one rouse an entire province? We returned to ours nourished by all the differences and riches we came across quite at random during our wartime adventures and we simply had to make it! Modestly we dug and sowed the seed in schools, amongst youth movements, the bourgeoisie and the working class alike; obstinately and without respite, we sought to express our regained freedom, to create places and centres where life would be dance, and dance would be life; where music would be heard and cast to the very depth of vibrant bodies; where silence would be the ally of musical movement; where choral singing would show how dance could also be choral; where celebrations could again*

---

[21] Anne-Marie Debatte, information document issued to the *Cantarelles*.

become the creation both of one and of all, provided that the body as well as the heart had been prepared for it.

At a time when dancing and singing had gone out of fashion, we danced and we sang in gardens, in factories, in schools, at fairs and in churches, in old peoples' homes and hospitals, in taverns and châteaux, and, during our much curtailed holidays, in frontier regions and distant provinces. Always penniless, we were unaware that one could obtain subsidies – they did not exist anyway at that time – and we held firm to our amateur status, reserving our professionalism for the pupils in our classes.

Visiting-cards: teachers of dance, music and body expression – a new term – and in our spare time dancers and musicians for the love of our art. Our repertoire combined Rainer-Maria Rilke, Claudel and Debussy, the fables of La Fontaine, the songs of our friends, Jacques Douai, Francine Cockenpot, the folk dances of France and elsewhere, and our inventions to the music of Jacques Ibert, Stravinsky and J. S. Bach. Laughter and prayer, fantasy and drama, mime and poetry ... Nothing could stop us – we were ready for anything. Preparing our juniors over the years to follow in our footsteps in order to succeed us; seeking to find ourselves so that we might help others do the same. And once more, as during the war, we were nourished by courses, which were few and far between in this period, costly, involving setting out at dawn and returning at nightfall. These meetings were rare, precious and exceptional'.[22]

It was during this period of the 1960s that Anne-Marie Debatte, and the Cantarelles often with her, attended courses in Paris, learning from and absorbing what other dancers and choreographers had to offer. Anne-Marie Debatte claims to have learnt much from Geneviève Mallarmé, Jerome Andrews, Jacqueline Robinson and the Dupuys.

[I personally remember having welcomed groups of Cantarelles on my courses at the Atelier de la Danse on several occasions, and I recall with pleasure their fervent attention, musicality, receptivity and generosity, the serious and joyful nature of their dance – a special breed. This quality is to be found in those dance artists of today who first belonged to the Cantarelles, such as Delphine Rybinski, Christine Bastin, Blandine Calais (also a remarkable physiotherapist), and Andrée Lamotte who now directs retired Anne-Marie's school, 'Danse Création' which has become one of the important centres for contemporary dance in France.]

'Our province thus began to dance without the need of a tutu or the accompaniment of academic ballet music, and in a way that did not give the children the roles of ballerinas from the opera or music hall.

For certain of our student festivals, the Lille opera house opened its "sacred" doors to our undertakings: stories that we danced to, movement theatre, mime and choral dances. We inaugurated dance holiday camps and tours with thrilled adolescents. With increasing joy, hundreds of young people gathered around us or we went out to them in traditional institutions, various youth or adult

---

[22] Anne-Marie Debatte, letter to Jacqueline Robinson.

movements such as Vie Nouvelle, technical schools, workshops, and the growing number of youth clubs and research groups. In 1968 a large studio was built in the heart of the metropolis. We are happy there, surrounded by gardens, in a clear, sunny, comfortable and welcoming place. I wanted it to be a home and a place where festivities and meetings could take place. A place where poetry, music, dance and painting would meet, as well as being a place of work. This does not prevent numerous classes from being held in various parts of the province too nor our young aspiring teachers of the living body from taking care of these faithfully year after year, as though the spirit that had presided over the birth of this venture never stopped sowing its seeds.'

Anne-Marie Debatte's achievements were truly remarkable. Should she be placed amongst pedagogues of movement (or *through* movement), or amongst theatre directors, or dancers and choreographers? Whatever she does and has done in the past, she leads her followers, be they students, dancers, audiences, with undeniable conviction and charisma, towards an opening of the mind, a sense of fundamental unity, and a quality of demand, a sense of responsibility that has a spiritual dimension.

She never wanted to be treated as a theatrical 'professional' in the sense in which this is usually understood, nor that the Cantarelles should be considered in this way either, for fear no doubt of losing a certain dimension and quality that were important to her. But it cannot be denied that Anne-Marie Debatte was indeed a professional in the various aspects of her discipline. Her reputation as an animateur in the true sense of the word and a teacher beyond compare, must not lead us to forget that she was also a choreographer who had a particular talent for choric movement and large-scale group effects. Music and architecture and the dramatic pertinence of gesture are all apparent in her work. Anne-Marie Debatte's greatest productions included *Les Témoins de la onzième heure* (by Jean Debruyne) at Notre Dame de Lourdes in 1964 and *Fille de Roi* at the Porte de Versailles in 1967, composed for a large assembly of young people. Amongst the ensemble choreographies Bach's *Magnificat* is characteristic of her ample, clear and luminously intelligent style.

As a result of the excessive centralization of dance in Paris (until recently), it appears that those who worked in the provinces did not receive the attention, respect and recognition they deserved. Anne-Marie Debatte perhaps succeeded in constructing something in the north of France that she would not have been able to achieve in Paris, precisely because of the singular conditions that prevailed there: competition, fashion, dispersion, illusions. Who knows?

Anne-Marie Debatte has expressed herself not only through dance and the theatre, but also writes in a relevant and stimulating way. It is to be hoped that one day her many writings will be collected together and made public.

FROM DRAMA AND MIME

> *'There have always been enthusiastic, patient, fervent and meticulous individuals who have dreamt of translating the soul's passions and the picturesqueness of life through the movements of their body alone, that truest of all expressive instruments, neglecting and disdaining words, which have the privilege of being able to lie'* (Alexandre Arnoux).[23]

Bella Reine

[Bella Reine does not truly belong to the family of 'modern dancers', and therefore features only indirectly in this chronicle, but as a woman of the theatre and movement she created perfectly achieved works within a clearly defined framework, and had a definite influence as a teacher. I was one of her students and performers and owe a great deal to her in the fields of dramatic acting and the sense of 'timing'. I also had the privilege of sharing numerous recitals with her in the 1960s until 1973.

She was already famous well before the war; but her renown as a teacher in France became increasingly specific after 1947. It is on this account that she is included amongst the actors of this period in this chronicle.]

Of Russian origin, born in 1897 in Lithuania, died in Paris in 1983.

Bella Rein (the 'e' was added in order to gallicize her name) was born in Dvinsk in Lithuania, the youngest child of a large family in which artistic activities were held in high esteem. She studied classical dance and acrobatics in Leningrad, and theatre with Stanislawski for three years. She embarked on a career as an acrobatic dancer and married the painter Bogerianoff. They left Russia in 1923 and settled in Paris. Like many emigrants, they experienced years of extreme poverty, and Bella suffered from ill health. Once cured, however, she began to make a name for herself and gave several recitals with the dancers Paul Pétroff and Serge Vladimiroff.

In the early 1930s Bella Reine created *La Buveuse* after the painting by Toulouse-Lautrec, which brought her much fame and was performed throughout her entire career. Not strictly dance or pantomime in the usual sense of the terms, it evoked a character through gesture and

---

[23] Alexandre Arnoux, preface to Marcel Marceau's programme in Paris, 1951.

physical presence alone in a marvellously timed dramatization that was staggering in its aptness (Divoire referred to it in 1935). Following this, Bella created a whole series of solos inspired by characters from paintings by Daumier, Renoir, Degas, Picasso and Chagall, to mention only these, which aroused much enthusiasm. The characters she so vividly brought to life were often derived from Russian or Jewish folklore also, or, in perfect contrast, from late nineteenth-century Paris – tender, tragic, disquieting or satirical figures – a highly individual art that earned her the respect and friendship of artists from all spheres, such as Serge Lifar, Francis Carco, Guillot de Saix, Maurice Chevalier, André Breton and Philippe Soupault, and the collaboration of musicians such as Henri Sauguet, Henri Cliquet-Pleyel (who served as her accompanist until his death in the late 1960s), painters and costume designers such as Georges Annenkov, Gontcharova and Karinska.

Her Parisian career was interrupted by the war, however. She managed to reach the United States where she collaborated in the summer schools at Jacob's Pillow, Connecticut, organized by Ted Shawn. Although she could have remained in New York and pursued her career there, she had grown firmly attached to France in spite of her strong Slavonic character (she had become a naturalized French citizen in 1929!), and returned to France in 1946.

Bella Reine then became associated with the developing 'young theatre', popular education and with the struggle for due recognition for 'body expression'. She worked in particular with the team at the E.P.J.D. and revived some of her solos in recitals. She also created new ones based on literary sources and once more enjoyed the collaboration of musicians, painters and writers. She staged productions (mostly adapted from Russian authors), taught and wrote. Until her very last years, she was in charge of the theatre chronicle in the Paris Russian periodical. Amongst other things, she wrote a series of moralizing and excruciatingly funny articles entitled 'Je hurle ... ' ('I scream ... ') that consisted of ironic commentaries, a biting criticism of facts and attitudes in the world of art and so-called contemporary culture.

She also taught in Zürich for several years at the famous 'Bühne Studio', where Maria and Peter Schell featured amongst her pupils, and in 1963 she returned to teach at Jacob's Pillow. Her courses, wherever they were held, attracted actors, dancers and mimes who found with her a basic and rigorous training in dramatic acting in the spirit of Stanislawski. Her pupils included Marina Svetlova, Oleg Briansky, Nicolas Bataille, Jean-Paul Cisife, Pierre Frag, Gabriel Blondé, Patti Swann, and Jacqueline Robinson.

In 1971 the cultural division of the Foreign Office sent her on an official mission to Japan where she gave a series of performances and courses that scored an enormous success. During this same period she made several films with Nicolas Bataille (based mainly on her own repertoire).

Paul Mourousy wrote of her with great sensitivity:

'Bella Reine is not a "character". She is a true and honest expression of human existence. She does not dance, she does not speak, or sing or act. She communicates the contradictions, imponderables and questions of the entire universe. This respite from hearing sharpens the acuity of sight and the observer may delight all the more in a single gesture, a shadow or merely a raised finger. A miracle of speed, order and concision within diversity'.[24]

Etienne Decroux

French, born in 1898, died in 1993.

If Etienne Decroux cannot be described as one of the founding fathers of modern French dance, he can at least be made an honorary 'uncle'.

He succeeded in bringing a vast public and a large number of theatrical practitioners to the discovery of a new dimension of the expressive body. He revealed, awakened, analysed and systematized an entire language and in a way fertilized the land for future generations. His influence on French movement theatre (and dance too) was indeed very important and it is possible that this influence persists in a diffuse and completely unconscious way amongst the young choreographers of today.

Etienne Decroux was an individual of great character. Born into a modest family in Boulogne-sur-Seine, he lived until his death in the house built by his father, a mason with a liking for comic opera and 'café-concert'. In his youth, Etienne Decroux dabbled in various professions and served as a nurse during the First World War. He later became a member of the anarchist group in Romainville. Curiously enough, it was his militant activities that led him towards dramatic art: anxious to perfect his skill as an orator, he enrolled on a course in elocution at the Institut Philotechnique. From this time on, curious about things of the mind, he organized poetry readings in his own home; he developed an interest in the surrealists and became initiated into music. He married a singer called Suzanne, who worked with him throughout his career.

In 1921 he entered the school attached to the Vieux-Colombier directed by Jacques Copeau, with the same aim of reinforcing his personal impact. The school gave lessons free of charge in exchange for

---

[24] Paul Mourousy in *Art et danse* (Paris, November 1963).

duties, and the pupils were often called upon to serve as extras in Copeau's productions. Decroux met Dorcy there, a student like himself, with whom he had much in common.

It was Copeau's work with masks (which naturally emphasized body espression) that awakened Decroux's interest in what was to become the centre of his life: body acting. Decroux later maintained that he regretted having called his method 'body mime' since the word mime evokes *Pantomime*, whilst 'body acting' is much wider in its implications.

Etienne Decroux completed his training with Copeau and when the Vieux-Colombier was dissolved in 1924 he followed him to Beaune as a member of the Copiaux. He was then employed by Dullin in the troop at the Atelier Theatre. He worked as an actor there (Maria Casarès and Jean-Louis Barrault were amongst his young companions) and Dullin encouraged him in his research into 'body acting'. Barrault tells in *Souvenirs pour demain* of the working sessions to which they both devoted themselves, Barrault following Decroux's experiences all the way:

> '*We soon became accomplices embarking on a quest for a new type of mime. Decroux was the real searcher. He possessed the genius of selection. He let nothing pass. I improvised before him and he selected, classified, retained and discarded. And then we would start all over again. In this way the famous "walking on the spot" took us three weeks to devise: imbalance, counter-poise, breathing and the isolation of energy. Thanks to him, I discovered the infinite world of the muscles of the human body. Its nuances and its alchemy. Decroux's genius lay in the rigorous nature of his approach. But this rigour ended up by being oppressive*'.[25]

Etienne Decroux remained with Dullin for ten years and his reputation grew. During his career as a 'speaking actor' which lasted several decades, he took part in numerous productions, worked in radio and appeared in no less than thirty-five films. At the same time, he refined his work on mime, acted, produced, composed completely textless pieces, gave lectures and taught. One of his most successful pieces dating from this period was *Les Trois âges*, which represented the fundamental human conflict between man, nature and the very substance of life itself. This piece, transmitted by Decroux to his last students, seemed to evoke Butoh in the eyes of the young audiences of today.

During the war Decroux laid low since his political opinions made him suspect and he harboured 'undesirables' in his own home. Once the war was over, he resumed his activities with renewed vigour, principally in the field of performance, in which he made numerous tours, and also in teaching. He could be counted as one of the 'masters' of a number of

---

[25] Jean-Louis Barrault, *Souvenirs pour demain* (Le Seuil, Paris, 1972), p. 72.

Plate 35   Etienne Decroux in *Le Menuisier*, 1940. Photo: Etienne-Bertrand Weill, Paris.

theatre folk: Jean-Louis Barrault, Marcel Marceau, Charles Antonetti, the Frères Jacques, Eliane Guyon, Raymond Devos, Jean-Marie Serreau, Pinok and Matho and Jessica Lange, to name only these, not to mention his son Maximilien.

In the late 1950s Decroux was invited to teach at the Actor's Studio in New York where he was welcomed as a true master. He also taught at the Piccolo Teatro in Milan. This immense activity gradually diminished and it was only in 1986 that Etienne Decroux gave up teaching.

According to his closest associates as well as Decroux himself, there was a whole world between his early experiences, which he described as 'gym for actors', and the teaching of his later years, which was in a sense multidisciplinary, both wider in scope and more ascetic. It is hardly surprising that successive generations of students, some thirty years apart, were influenced by him in different ways. Corinne Soum,* to whom I am indebted for much of the information about Etienne Decroux included here, and her husband Steven Wasson were his last 'assistants'. She described the methods of working at the school: a three-year training at beginner, intermediate and advanced levels; then one might hope to rise to the status of 'assistant'. This meant living with the master, sharing his daily life, helping him, preparing the new pupils for him, rehearsing at seven o'clock every morning (without any warm-up) and being under his critical eye all day long. For everything was a matter for learning and perfecting, from the attention accorded to the body's appearance and verbal expression to the spiritual and intellectual nourishment that was constantly offered.

Etienne Decroux's work (research, creation and teaching) followed a similar path to that of the pioneers of modern dance: a return to sources, the quest for 'virginity' in the face of a priori aesthetics, listening to and seeking out the expressive body in all its nakedness (inner, if not actual!). Decroux's early work – like that of the dancers Laban and Wigman etc. – was without either text or music, in the starkest of styles. Later, he integrated music and text as completely independent partners within the structure of the work with his concept of body acting.

Etienne Decroux has always been somewhat distrustful of dancers (in spite of his admiration for classical and character dance which

---

* Corinne Soum received her initial training in movement at the Popard school. Steve Wasson studied literature at university in the United States. After spending five years together working with Decroux, they opened their own school, the École de Mime Corporel et Dramatique de Paris, and founded a company, the Théâtre de l'Ange Fou.

he practised all his life). With the exception of Kurt Jooss who found favour with him, he harboured a constant prejudice against German expressionist dance.

He was a single-minded person, a great spirit, somewhat despotic, and a great artist, if a little excessive, according to those who were close to him. He was a prolific writer and the manuscripts of hundreds of lectures and articles on dozens of subjects (phonetics was one of his fields of investigation) remain to be explored. His *Paroles sur le mime* (Gallimard, Librairie Théâtrale, 1963) has become a classic of its kind.

His son Maximilien is his worthy successor and the most loyal upholder of his father's approach (principles and methods). He currently teaches at the Marcel Marceau school.

Jacques Lecoq

Born in 1922.

Since 1956 he has directed his internationally renowned school.

He was led to this achievement first by training in sport and physiotherapy, the discovery of the theatre with Jean-Marie Conty (see the chapter on E.P.J.D.) in the post-war period, followed by a spell with Dasté in Grenoble, and the discovery of Copeau's principles and mask technique, then eight years in Italy during which he became acquainted with the commedia dell'arte and the choruses of Antiquity, and also worked at the Piccolo Teatro in Milan.

Constantly seeking the infinite possibilities of body language, Jacques Lecoq wrote to Jacqueline Robinson in 1977:

> 'I believe that I have freed mime from the ghetto in which it had become enclosed and have opened it up to the theatre and dance and to itself. I have also sought out movements to accompany the music of today with Schaeffer and Berio. I still deplore the narrow tracks to which the particular aestheticisms that seek to define the genre are keeping. It is for this reason that the school is committed to the movements of life and nature as a fundamental reference, enabling each creator to express his part in them at a more or less basic level. After the initial silence, the use of voice, the approach to texts and objects are added. The school has followed the fashions of the time, the cries, the gesticulations, the body in paint, in sheets, on cushions: people crushed bananas or ate them in front of us, then one day they presented them to us. Fashion ... ?
>
> But the school remained true to itself. A continuous line grew ever deeper in the memory of our bodies, made of light and substance, space and sound, rhythm and colour, that enriched our gestures, attitudes and movements.
>
> This journey hither and thither, from the evanescent to the fundamental, strengthened our ideas, defined them more clearly and implanted them in that common ground where all men are akin'.

Marcel Marceau

Born in 1923.

He studied decorative arts and enamelling at the Limoges conservatoire. After the Liberation, Marceau went to Paris where he became a pupil of Dullin and Decroux, and joined the Renaud-Barrault company. From 1947 he devoted himself to the revival of mime, founded a company, created the celebrated character 'Bip' and went from one success to another, achieving the world-wide fame for which he is known today. There are plenty of texts devoted to Marcel Marceau to satisfy the interested reader.

IN THE DUNCAN LINE

Madeleine Lytton

Of English origin, born in 1921.

Madeleine Lytton was born in France into a family of artists and intellectuals. She began her dance studies as a child with Lisa Duncan and for ten years took part in the performances Lisa gave with her pupils in Paris and elsewhere. She was amongst those of whom our old friend Fernand Divoire wrote in 1935:

> 'In their turn, they picture that eternal youth, filled with shining harmony, and that pure sweetness which brings deep happy tears'.

From the beginning, through Lisa, she learnt Isadora's technique and some of her dances. Again, Divoire wrote of Lisa's pupils:

> 'If the students are talented, these dances awaken in them the gift for creation, for those movements that are born of a supreme sensitivity bring into being further sensitivity'.[26]

Madeleine began her independent career in London during the war and danced with several ballet companies. She studied classical and character dance, and was later to study modern dance with Jerome Andrews. She was equally interested in medieval and renaissance dances and did considerable research in that field. Upon her return to France she collaborated for a while with Jean Serry and in 1952 took over Lisa Duncan's school.

For many years she taught, performed as a soloist and with her group in a wide repertoire, but chiefly in that of Isadora, or in an

---

[26] Fernand Divoire, *Toute la danse* (Édition Saxe, paris, 1935), p. 67.

Isadorian spirit, including evocations of Antiquity and the Middle Ages. She also staged works for sundry theatrical and musical events and toured in many countries.

She has run her own school in Paris since 1965 and remains today one of the truest heirs of the Isadorian tradition, passing down in her turn the true spirit of Isadora's approach to dance. She has, in that context, done much research, lectured, written, and taken part in staging and film making, both in France, European countries and the United States, and continues this activity today.

Odile Hamelin-Pyros

French, born in 1921.

From 1932 to 1950 Odile Pyros was successively a pupil, instructress and dancer with Lisa Duncan. Over the years she thus took part in the shows, recitals and tours of Lisa's company. After the war, she took great care of Lisa herself.

From 1958 Odile taught independently and in 1959, on the establishment of the Association Française de Recherches et d'Études Chorégraphiques (A.F.R.E.C.) – Théâtre d'Essai de la Danse, by Dinah Maggie, Odile Pyros became general secretary (see 'Dinah Maggie and Association Française de Recherches Chorégraphiques (A.F.R.E.C.) and the Théâtre d'Essai de la Danse). She was thus at the centre of this venture that did so much to promote dance during the 1960s.

She continues to teach in the Duncan tradition today (sometimes in collaboration with Madeleine Lytton), anxious to preserve this tradition intact and develop its most powerful aspects.

CONCLUSION

And so the curtain falls on this third act of our chronicle. When it rises again there will be no change of scenery, nor any new characters immediately: 1960 as such serves only as a punctuation mark here.

We are growing acquainted with the principal actors. We know pretty well to which family they belong and something of their characters and achievements. We have noted the innovators and the traditionalists.

Some have caused more of a stir than others, but the more discreet have been no less influential; some have been obsessed by an inner dream and have been first and foremost creators of works, whilst others have preferred to devote themselves to helping their fellow beings to develop through dance; some have placed their abilities at the service of dance and dancers, whilst still others have dedicated their pen to the same purpose.

And, come wind, come weather, these actors of the sowing years worked for the future. Many of them have lived to witness the flowering season. They have also seen new characters come on stage, new tendencies develop and new institutional devices come into operation. From all of this they have drawn satisfaction or alarm, bitterness or reward.

But we must not forget the public! Audience and actor, for the public plays an essential role and evolves too. It does not always follow; it is thrown into confusion by the innovators and becomes cold or aggressive. It may even be led unawares along the easy trail of fashion, a phenomenon that is on the increase. But the public is beginning to show a certain amount of discrimination and open mindedness, particularly in the case of the growing number of people who are becoming acquainted with dance 'from the inside', through amateur practice.

And so the season of manifold flowering has arrived.

PART IV

1960–1970

The Flowering Years

CHRONOLOGY

SETTLEMENT OF THE COLONIAL PROBLEM, RECOVERY AND CREATION

DATES	EVENTS IN FRANCE	EVENTS ABROAD	CONTEMPORARY CULTURE IN FRANCE
1960	First French atom bomb. Creation of the new franc.	Independence of black African countries. Great Britain launches the European Association of Free Trade.	*A bout de souffle* by Jean-Luc Godard. Henry de Montherlant, René Clair and René Huygues elected to the Académie Française. Karin Waehner teaches modern dance at the Schola Cantorum. The Ballets Modernes de Paris and Ballets Contemporains appear in Paris. Dance-music-theatre festival at the Atelier de la Danse.
1961	Putsch of the generals in Algiers. Slaughter of Algerians in Paris.	Yury Gagarin becomes the first man in space. Construction of the Berlin Wall. John F. Kennedy elected president of the United States.	Creation of the Biennale de Paris. Alain Resnais directs *L'Année dernière à Marienbad*. Promotion of dance on television by Lucienne Bernadac. *West Side Story* at the Châtelet. Rosella Hightower establishes the Centre

Dates	Events in France	Events abroad	Contemporary culture
			International de Danse in Cannes
1962	Evian agreement. Return of Algerian-born French citizens to the capital. Georges Pompidou becomes Prime Minister.	Cuban missile crisis.	Yves Robert produces *La Guerre des boutons*. Jean Guéhenno and Joseph Kessel elected to the Académie Française. Paul Taylor in Paris. Dance is introduced into the university sector following the creation of the Jean-Sarrailh Centre. The Dupuys found the Baux festival.
1963	De Gaulle refuses Great Britain entry to the Common Market.	Assassination of John F. Kennedy.	Death of Jean Cocteau and Edith Piaf. Roland Petit creates *Les Chants de Maldoror* with the Ballet National Populaire. Founding of the Paris International Festival of Dance (Jean Robin).
1964	France recognizes the Republic of China.	Leonid Brezhnev replaces Nikita Khrushchev. Riots in the black ghettos in the United States. Founding of the P.L.O.	Marc Chagall repaints the ceiling of the Opéra. Jean-Paul Sartre refuses the Nobel prize. Philippe de Broca creates *L'Homme de Rio*.

DATES	EVENTS IN FRANCE	EVENTS ABROAD	CONTEMPORARY CULTURE
			Jacques Demy creates *Les Parapluies de Cherbourg*. Alvin Ailey Dance Theatre in Paris. Merce Cunningham appears at the Théâtre de l'Est de Paris.
1965	Re-election of de Gaulle.	First Chinese atom bomb.	*La Folle de Chaillot* at the Théâtre National Populaire. Roland Petit stages *Notre-Dame de Paris* at the Opéra. Passing of the law regulating dance teaching.
1966	France leaves N.A.T.O.	Cultural revolution in china.	*Les Paravents* by Jean Genet at the Odéon. Merce Cunningham and company perform at the Paris festival. Michel Descombey founds the Ballet Studio at the Opéra.
1967	Close result at legislative elections.	Six Days War in Israel.	Television broadcasting in colour. André Malraux writes *Les Antimémoires*. Creation of the Orchestre de Paris. Founding of the National Centre of Contemporary Art.

DATES	EVENTS IN FRANCE	EVENTS ABROAD	CONTEMPORARY CULTURE
			Tutankhamen exhibition.
1968	May '68. Grenelle agreements.	Student revolts in Europe. Assassinations of Robert Kennedy and Martin Luther King. Mobilization against the war in Vietnam. Prague Spring. Willy Brandt becomes chancellor.	Creation of Art-Recherche-Confrontation (A.R.C.), dance section of the National Museum of Modern Art. Yuriko's first teaching visit.
1969	Resignation of de Gaulle. Election of Georges Pompidou.	First men on the moon. Richard Nixon becomes president of the United States.	Founding of the Théâtre Français de la Danse. Brian McDonald and Félix Blaska are billed at the Ballet Théâtre Contemporain. Birgit Cullberg and Company perform at the Paris festival.
1970	Death of de Gaulle.		Eugène Ionesco elected to the Académie Française. Michel Tournier awarded the Goncourt prize for *Le Roi des Aulnes*. Merce Cunningham at the A.R.C. Alvin Ailey and Viola Farber perform at the Paris festival.

Sowing years and flowering years... An engaging metaphor indeed, but it must not lead us to imagine that these events were connected in an entirely linear way, and in any case, from the 1960s onwards, this linear progression was interrupted in economic, social and cultural spheres as much as in the specific field of dance.

This process, which was already under way in the 1950s, became more rapid ten years later. After the war, the need to assert and strengthen human, social and national roots became apparent and the sense of continuity was held in greater esteem. Once this need had been satisfied, other phenomena came to the fore.

Social Changes

Before considering events in the field of dance, it is more important than ever to take the social context into account. We must recall that we are at the height of the 'Glorious Thirties'. The particular enthusiasm discussed above that characterized certain ventures, initiatives and trends of thought and that served as a binding and driving force throughout the post-war period had grown much weaker. The country had been rebuilt. Modern economy was being established alongside many new technological discoveries and as a result a number of social changes took place and a new middle class began to emerge. But it did not yet possess economic, political or cultural power. The members of this rising class, young obviously, had their own primarily cultural demands. The interaction between social change and artistic possibilities, and the profusion and diversity of the mechanisms linked to this social explosion, had rarely been more effective.

Amongst the forms that these cultural demands took (the ecological or anarchist movements, the rising tension towards the paroxystic crisis of '68 are but some of these), is it not surprising that there should have been a renewal of interest in matters relating to the body – the expressive body? Could it be that these new social classes, having so far failed to obtain political, economic or cultural power, would deny the concept of a purely productivist or monetarist body and consider (consciously or otherwise) the body as 'the last place to which one may lay claim'?

The new values that sprang from this awareness of the body, in addition to the changes in certain social laws concerning the body and sexuality came into play. One of the most important aspects was perhaps the complete reversal of the respective roles of men and women as a result of increased access to birth control.

The 1960s witnessed a real change in the field of culture and became a turning point in which the dialectical relationships between technological innovation and symbolic and ideological changes were linked as never before. From that time on it became apparent that art in all its manifestations would undergo similar changes – changes in finality, aims and means, with artists coming from new social strata, with a new form of cultural heritage, different aspirations and a *consumer* audience for whom the old ways and aesthetic values would no longer hold the same importance, meaning or justification as they might have done a generation earlier. New stakes and desires and different criteria would, for want of references, come to the fore amongst this new audience.

This term 'reference' brings us back to the notion of linear progression. We see beginning to emerge in this period a process that was to become increasingly widespread in the ensuing decades: together, the progressive loss of both collective memory and historical consciousness, and, as a result, the disappearance of references. The instant, instantaneity, took its place alongside the 'sense of the phylum' to such an extent that we were witnessing a progressive shift in the very nature of artistic production, which would no longer be an aesthetic process but a socio-cultural one. Were we then experiencing an epistemological rift? It seemed likely.

The socio-cultural climate had definitely changed. Dance would inevitably take new turnings as a consequence of various phenomena.

The Rights of the Body

As I have suggested above, the body began to make its own demands, but these were in the line of continuity established by those activities that had already been rehabilitated, revalued and practised since the beginning of the century, such as gymnastics, sport, and bodily expression, activities that aimed to promote the integration of the complete human being.

During the 1960s sport witnessed a remarkable upsurge – in schools, as a leisure activity, as a rallying-point for the community, and as a 'market' also. It soon fell into the hands of state- or para-state controlled organizations, and thus became in part 'institutionalized'. Sport mobilized both people and investments, and played an important part in the design of daily life. The body was at the centre of all this.

The same was true of gymnastics, partially assimilated into sport through its emphasis on 'athleticism' – and underlying both practices was competition and everything that this implied from an ideological point of view... The body found expression, moreover, in the many different forms of gymnastics – school gymnastics, therapeutic gymnastics, women's gymnastics, etc. – some of which were institutionalized.

The body was seized upon by intellectual disciplines also and it became a favourite object for consideration amongst sociologists, psychologists and philosophers... It passed through the filter of psychoanalysis, structuralism, anthropology, phenomenology... A number of texts appeared in France (either in French or in translation) by authors such as Paul Schilder, Herbert Marcuse, Henri Wallon and Melanie Klein, who included the body in their field of investigation, and amongst the titles published at this time may be listed *The Hidden Dimension* by Edward Hall (1966), *Cinq méditations sur le corps* by Jacques Brosse (1967), *Dictionnaire de la danse* by Jacques Baril (1964), *Anthropologie du geste* by Marcel Jousse (1969) and *Les Structures anthropologiques de l'imaginaire* by Gilbert Durand (1969), all of which have become classics.

At the point where the physical and social activity represented by sport and the intellectual speculation surrounding the body meet, dance may perhaps find its place as both an individual and a collective practice, and as an aesthetic venture with all the production/consummation dialectic that this implies. This problem is certainly not new: it had always existed; but during the 1960s it came out into the open. Dance emerged out of the darkness. *Modern* dance began to loom out of the shadows at the risk of receiving many blows!

From this moment on we may begin to speak in terms of a market. The dawning of the consumer society is upon us. The practice of sport has become a market with its own infrastructures and by-products: venues, coaching, apparatus, accessories, clothing, information, advertising, investments and profitability. The same occurred, although perhaps more slowly, in the case of dance: its infrastructures and by-products were somewhat similar. Markets for dance as a leisure activity and as a form of education also were established, without mentioning that provided by stage performance. This valorized body demanded to be looked after, adorned, kept in good working order, and even spoilt a little – so many different aspects in which industry and commerce were to become engulfed.

Dance teachers profited from this new demand: for anyone who sought to become aware of what may be termed 'psychosomatic' or of the 'body and mind', or the underlying implications of bodily expression and attention to finer feelings, rhythm etc., dance responded to the need for the 'more than physical'. And it was not just any kind of dance either, but preferably that which laid emphasis upon the concepts of awareness, expression and creativity: that is, modern dance.

The Institutionalization of Dance

The most notable phenomenon in France during the 1960s as far as dance was concerned was the interest shown in it by the public authorities and institutions. These either created or provided centres for performance and/or teaching, or took charge (through subsidies) of existing activities, be they the creation of venues and structures, or the promotion of individuals or enterprises and works of art. This form of intervention already existed as far as classical dance was concerned, but it was completely new in relation to modern dance.

It would indeed be quite justifiable to question the extent to which these various initiatives were concerned with 'pure', authentic *modern* dance. Seduced by novelty, contaminated by the spirit of the times, and experiencing, albeit in a somewhat confused way, the need for renewal, the decision-makers, choreographers and dancers closest to the key positions (and therefore within the circles of the Opéra or well known ballet companies), praised and claimed to create or practise contemporary dance. But in spite of this, they did not abandon their attachment to classical traditions and remained conditioned, perhaps unconsciously, by an academic approach. Their modernism was, in many cases, only superficial. Neoclassicism was not what it strove to be. The severing of this umbilical chord was gradually achieved through the will and tenacity of certain clear-sighted individuals, and through the arrival on the scene of a new generation who were rather more iconoclastic and untainted by the influences of the past. All this was not achieved easily to be sure: the purists of contemporary dance experienced much difficulty in imposing their work within the framework of an establishment that was not prepared to take risks, and it was only at the cost of stubborn fighting, many defeats and strategic readjustments that it slowly began to gain an audience.

We will see below the way in which contemporary dance came to penetrate certain institutional organizations, such as the universities and the École Normale Supérieure d'Éducation Physique. Various private initiatives that saw the light of day in this decade were mentioned in the preceding chapter: the Baux festival founded in 1962; the dance sector of the A.R.C. at the Museum of Modern Art in 1968; the dance seasons at the Théâtre de l'Ouest in Paris and later at the Théâtre de l'Est under the direction of Guy Rétoré, due largely to the efforts of Françoise and Dominique Dupuy who were gradually establishing their credibility. We must also mention the performances and debates organized by Dinah Maggie within the framework of A.F.R.E.C. and the Théâtre d'Essai de la Danse, and the numerous galas at Danse et Culture in which Jean Dorcy had to invite modern dancers to perform.

There was a growing number of halls in Paris that willingly opened their doors to modern dance, including the Salle d'Iéna, the Maison de la Chimie (neither of which function as theatres today), the Théâtre des Champs-Élysées and the Hébertot, Marigny and Daunou theatres, without mentioning the little local halls, cinemas and, of course, the studios of certain individuals.

It was also at this time that official dance companies were created, either at the direct instigation of the ministry of culture, or funded by the public authorities, with the aim of promoting new tendencies. These were principally the Ballet Théâtre Contemporain and the Théâtre Français de la Danse, which will be considered in more detail below.

It is appropriate to pause here for a moment in order to reflect upon the presence of Michel Descombey at the Opéra, for the role he played there had many important consequences: a child of the Opéra himself, he was appointed ballet-master there in 1963 – a somewhat surprising appointment in view of his known fondness for new aspects of dance. He sought to create an opening for modern dance within this bastion of classical ballet and in 1966 succeeded in founding the Ballet Studio there, a little nucleus of creation that brought together dancers in an experimental vein... As a choreographer, Descombey created pieces that were strongly criticized. Amongst those who took part in the work of the Ballet Studio were Jacques Garnier and Brigitte Lefèvre, who we will meet again later in the context of their Théâtre du Silence; then Michel Caserta, Richard Duquesnoy, Jean Guizerix and Wilfride Piollet amongst others. The Ballet Studio was to become the Groupe des 7 and then the Jeunes Chorégraphes de l'Opéra, which achieved a certain recognition at the 1970 Avignon festival. Meanwhile Descombey left the Opéra, expatriated to Mexico, and it was with the arrival of Carolyn Carlson in 1973 that the next shake-up came.

Festivals

Amongst the enterprises that saw the light of day in this period, the Paris International Festival of Dance, created at the instigation of the Paris council in 1962, by Jean Robin, must be mentioned. This annual festival, held at the Théâtre des Champs-Élysées, still exists today. It was definitely a prestige operation that drew on the participation of recognized talents, such as opera companies and big international companies with secure financial resources, that were guaranteed to attract large audiences. However, it also provided an opportunity to launch and evaluate new up-and-coming talents from both France and abroad, and it was as a result of this festival that Paul Taylor (1964), Merce Cunningham (1966) (this was not his first visit), Nikolais (1968), Alvin Ailey and Viola Farber (1970), and Birgit Cullberg (1969) met with applause.

The big French companies did not appear there, but a few companies that could be described as semi-modern: the Opéra de Marseille

(Joseph Lazzini) in 1983; the Ballets de France (Janine Charrat) in 1964; the Ballets de Marseille in 1967; the Ballets de Strasbourg (Vladimir Skouratoff) and the Ballets Modernes de Paris (Dupuy) in 1968; and finally, the Jeunes Solistes de l'Opéra in 1969. These were the only French companies that appeared in the programmes given at these festivals during the 1960s. Later, in 1975 and 1977, the 'Forum' took place as part of the festival, more modest and experimental with a wider participation by contemporary companies or soloists. On reading these programmes one might think, with the exception of the Ballets Modernes de Paris, there were no modern companies in France. Those that did exist had perhaps not yet reached the same standard or degree of professionalism as the international companies, either in terms of technique or of production? They obviously lacked financial resources, but they also had little opportunity to perform and thus to learn and consolidate their skills.

A further official cultural initiative in which contemporary modern dance featured was the Paris Biennale (which first took place in 1959). This 'occasion where all forms of aesthetic expression for the young generation could meet on an international scale' provided a stage for the performance of theatre and dance for artists under the age of thirty-five. The Théâtre d'Essai de la Danse became associated with the festival in 1965 and amongst the choreographers programmed were Laura Sheleen, Aline Roux, Annick Maucouvert, Teresa Trujillo and Karin Waehner. That same year also saw the independent participation of Francine Lancelot, Muriel Jaër, the Argentinian choreographers Arlet Bon, Paulina Oca, Graziella Martinez and Sonia Sanoja, who will be discussed in more detail later, and the Studio d'Essai de l'Opéra. The particular vocation of the Biennale was to provide an opportunity for new artistic developments to be seen. It was therefore not surprising to find more avant-garde choreographers and dancers there than were featured in the more conventional programmes of the Paris Festival of Dance.

Companies and Schools

There already existed during this decade a number of thoroughly modern groups (can they really be called companies?) variously modest, discrete, competent, whose work no longer remained completely in the shadows.

The Ballets Modernes de Paris, created in 1955 by Françoise and Dominique Dupuy, were without doubt the most professional of the French modern companies. The Ballets Contemporains de Karin Waehner were of a similar standard and came into existence in 1958. Jerome Andrews directed the Jerome Andrews Dance Company (formerly the Compagnons de la Danse), Laura Sheleen the Théâtre du Geste and

Jacqueline Robinson the Ensemble de l'Atelier de la Danse (later to become Le Zodiaque).

Some of these companies were relatively short-lived – assembled under the direction of a choreographer passing through Paris, or for a specific choreographic event. But as our chronicle unfolds, we will see how some groups really took off.

The experiences in connection with teaching and professional training in university and sports environments have already been mentioned. Thus the Schola Cantorum, that venerable institution of music education, opened its doors to modern dance in 1960, inviting Karin Waehner to teach there.

The Centre International de la Danse (C.I.D.), a private organization established by certain modern dance fans, of whom Mireille Delsout was one, began its policy of widespread dissemination and training in 1964. The methods of working at this time tended to favour large-scale short courses held both in Paris and the provinces. These courses were given by experienced teachers and were attended by many people; for example, the eleventh course at Vincennes in 1969 attracted some 500 participants!

It was within this setting amongst others (the American Students' and Artists' Centre was a favorite one) that various foreign practitioners came to teach and it was through them that American techniques spread throughout France. The C.I.D. was, nevertheless, eclectic in its choices and promoted several dance disciplines. It is interesting to note some of the principal great dancers and teachers who taught there regularly during the 1960s in addition to the 'adopted' French ones such as Karin Waehner for modern dance, Atty Chadinoff for classical dance and Lutys de Luz for Spanish dance:

- representing the Graham school were Yuriko, Helen MacGehee, Bertram Ross, Mary Hinkson, Anna Mittelholzer and Noémie Lapzeson;
- from the Limón school, Betty Jones, Fritz Ludin, Lucas Hoving and Ruth Currier;
- and later, Walter Nicks, Dorothy Madden and Clotilde Sakharoff, etc.

The arrival of these various remarkable persons was a decisive factor in the development of modern dance in France and it created an opening, a diversity, a stronger know-how and a depth of artistic conception. Moreover, in addition to their intrinsic qualities and virtues, they came from a foreign land: from this America, thought to be the cradle of modern dance, the Eldorado in which the young hoped to go and acquire technical and artistic richness. It is in no way to belittle the impact of this contribution to say that many young French dancers of this period were so profoundly affected by it that they lost consciousness of their European roots and of their specific 'Frenchness' that had barely been drawn upon. This tendency became even greater at the beginning of the 1970s with the arrival of still more Americans who were to create shock-waves in the world of dance. These included Susan Buirge and Carolyn Carlson to name but two. The efficiency of the Americans, if one may be so bold as to call it that, and their seriousness and knowledge was, however, something of which French dance was no doubt in need.

Some private schools offered a high standard of tuition. These included:

- Françoise and Dominique Dupuy's Académie, attached to the B.M.P., which, in 1969, became the Rencontres Internationales de Danse Contemporaine (R.I.D.C.);
- Jacqueline Robinson's Atelier de la Danse, which was one of the first schools to provide a full professional training in contemporary dance;
- the École Supérieure d'Études Chorégraphiques, founded by Thomas d'Erlanger in 1956, which aimed to provide a theoretical and aesthetic education in dance and included in its curriculum a course entitled 'Principles and Aesthetics of Modern Dance', taught by Dinah Maggie;
- the schools founded by those persons referred to in the preceding chapters, whose reputations were now confirmed, both in and outside Paris, such as those of Anne-Marie Debatte in Lille and Hélène Carlut in Lyons, who ran active centres of modern dance, and others now entering the scene.

We should perhaps digress a little at this point to consider the axis between Paris and the provinces. Naturally, the capital attracted the majority of dancers from abroad, who, in the previous decades, had brought modern dance to France. Paris was considered the home of the avant-garde in everything.

It was not until the 1950s and 60s that genuine cultural decentralization was achieved, in music and theatre as well as in dance. This procedure shook the provinces somewhat, for they undoubtedly suffered from an inferiority complex, in spite of the presence of a number of first-rate specialists in several large or medium-sized towns.

On an amateur level, modern dance gradually gained ground. Besides the schools mentioned above that were of course open not only to professionals, dance spread through youth clubs, lay groups and organizations derived from scouting, such as Animation Jeunesse (an extension of the Centre d'Expression des Scouts de France, created in 1955, under the direction of Georges Dobbelaere, and the principal driving forces behind which were men of the theatre, Jean Bouffort and Philippe Henry. Their aim was to provide technical education for social workers).

A Digression on Folklore

I would like to mention here what important work was done in the specific genre of folk dance. Outside the realm of modern dance, to be sure, but I feel there is a kinship in these two kinds, these two approaches insofar as both tend to return to original sources. The work and principal realizations of folk dance specialists in France occurred simultaneously with research into bodily expression. It is not surprising, therefore, to find at the forefront of modern dance certain individuals who made a detour into folk dance. (Admittedly, this detour occurred less frequently in the 1960s than in the previous decade, but traces of it remained.)

As early as 1947, Jacques Douai, the delightful singer and poet in the French tradition, and Thérèse Palau, his dancer wife, were working within the sphere of T.E.C. and E.P.J.D. They created La Frairie, a group that travelled throughout France and abroad, performing traditional songs and dances. Ethnologists might claim that their material was not authentic; theatre folk claimed that it was a judicious staging of a heritage that was not initially intended to be 'performed'.

Jacqueline Levant and Jean Bouffort, to name but two, began their careers, which were subsequently to turn towards modern dance, at La Frairie, of which both speak with emotion. In 1961 La Frairie, its creators encouraged and aided by the public authorities, became the Ballet National de Danses Françaises. It seems that their aim was to create a company similar to those spectacular ones of Eastern countries that had witnessed such rapid success, and that could proffer the treasures of the French heritage in a more theatrical way.

As a twofold concern, the Ballet National ran a school, Chants et Danses de France, which also trained teachers. In the school's prospectus, published in 1963, we may read the following paragraph, which I find interesting to compare with the observations on social changes and culture at the beginning of this chapter:

> ' … *To prepare for this profession (of promoter)*, which was itself invented not long ago, in order to meet the needs created by new living conditions connected*

---

* There is no exact term in English corresponding to '*animateur*'. Approximately, and according to the context, it may refer to or designate a teacher, a social worker, one who directs creative activities …

with technical progress, and the demands of an increasing public avid to quench its thirst for knowledge and culture'.

The Ballet National remained in existence for several years until the death of Thérèse Palau. Two of its best dancers, Michel and Michelle Blaise, took over the direction of the Compagnie Populaire de Danses Françaises, and other groups were created too.

Competitions

From around this time a modern dance section was included in some dance competitions. This was so in the case of the Scène Française, a competition for children and young amateurs that frequently served as a springboard for young people embarking on their careers. The principal event in this field was without doubt the creation of the Bagnolet competition by Jaque Chaurand in 1968. Bagnolet rapidly became a necessary transit for young choreographers, the place where one had to go in order to test the temperature and make prognoses concerning the health and future of both French and foreign dance.

The year in which the Bagnolet competition was founded is a symbolic one; occurring after the crisis of '68, it represented an accumulation of the diverse aspirations that arose during the decade and marked a period in which young creators, quite rightfully, sought to make their own voice heard.

The 'Militants'

In 1965 a number of dancers, choreographers, teachers and practitioners from all disciplines met with the aim of regulating the profession and, in particular, of establishing a state diploma in dance teaching. As I write these lines, twenty-two years later, this diploma is still in gestation.* Nevertheless, this step was a symptom of the time. It pointed to a new attitude amongst practitioners who were now more aware of the role of dance, of its very definition, its place in society and, indeed, of *their own* place in society. It was a sign that dancers could think for themselves and take over responsibilities. It was a time of round table discussions and ministerial commissions, reaching common ground and bitter quarrels, wars between factions and fruitful partnerships, hopes and paltriness, but at least it gave a large number in the profession the opportunity to

---

* A law regulating the profession was actually decreed in 1989. Today, in 1995, the state diploma for dance teachers in France is compulsory.

confront ideas and doctrines and to be put with their backs to the wall. As a result of these efforts many records were written, and the Conseil National de la Danse was founded, under the presidency of Marcel Landowski, an organization which, like many of this type, witnessed a brief spate of enthusiastic activity and then fell into dormancy. Likewise, it provided an opportunity for various structures of a corporate nature to consider the specific problems of dance and attempt to find solutions. We should note the significant work carried out under the aegis of the Syndicat National des Auteurs et Compositeurs (S.N.A.C.) with its choreographers' section to which we owe the recognition of the choreographers' statute (the choreographer as *creator*), which represented a major victory in both symbolic and real terms.

The Syndicat Français des Acteurs also had a dance branch. Two federations saw the light of day:

- the Fédération Française de Danse Classique et Contemporaine, which was the result of the various restructurings of syndicate organizations; in 1967 it introduced a contemporary dance section under the presidency of Jacqueline Chaumont;
- and the Fédération Française de Danse, d'Art Chorégraphique et d'Expression Corporelle, founded in 1969, which emanated from the Centre International de la Danse. This second federation was predominantly modern in outlook, and became important over the years for its function and the work it carried out. These two federations are known today as the Fédération Nationale Inter-professionnelle de la Danse and the Fédération Française de Danse respectively.

Everything Changes

I have so far referred only to the social context and the new structures that conditioned contemporary dance (from this point on I will use this term which gained official recognition by the sundry ministries in 1965). We must now consider the evolution of this type of dance during the course of the decade, and its technical and aesthetic developments in relation to the preceding period.

The social changes referred to above clearly produced new ways of thinking amongst professional dancers, particularly those of the new generation; these new modes of thought concerned not only their approach and relationship to the material and finalities of their art, but also their relationship with their pupils.

The whole colour and tenor of the language surrounding dance changed progressively, related to a more scientific and sometimes "scientistic" approach. The training of dancers became more rigorous and included more and more frequently an introduction to anatomy, physiology and psychomotricity, whilst a higher level of technical performance was demanded too. The material of dance in its most fundamental form was dedramatized whilst its aims and doctrines were stated in a more abstract form. We no longer heard the lyrical, even sentimental exaltation of the virtues of dance as either an artistic or an educational activity, as in previous times. For sure, the total being, harmony, balance and freedom continued to be extolled, but without the capital letters with which these noble concepts used to be embellished.

It was not only the form, technique and gestures of dance that changed, but its very content. Young choreographers revealed less of a tendency to treat universal subjects. Their discourse was more personal, more immediate: the relationship of individual bodies. It was as if this body were gradually freeing itself from the restrictions imposed by tradition and the tyranny of music, narrative, spatio-temporal architecture and censorship of every kind. This body, which was no longer necessarily glorified (either by expressive discourse or by the conventional accoutrements of the theatre), was to find itself in a state of phenomenological nudity. Movement would become self-sufficient and give rise to new parameters. The concepts of classical structure were gradually being eroded. This process was for the time being only a distant outline on the horizon, but its presence was felt forcefully, brought about by everything that had happened during this decade.

American Influences

The introduction of American techniques in France (in particular the Graham but also the Humphrey-Limón techniques) played an important part in this change of approach. Indeed, the Americans, greatly in advance of Europe in the field of dance at this time, and more pragmatic too, brought clarity and definition to the components of movement, an analysis of motor phenomena, through their specific technique. The particular movement vocabulary they proposed opened up new horizons in the theory and practice of dance. (This type of analysis could have been achieved earlier, through Laban's doctrines, but France was not yet ready to take them in.)

The French, with their frequently Cartesian nature, found in the American techniques satisfaction in their need for semantic landmarks. It was Graham's technique that was absorbed the most eagerly, precisely because it could be codified and become a vocabulary in its own right. This phenomenon was not peculiar to France. The success of this technique, which could also be regarded as a *style*, lay in part in its latent, and *ipso facto* reassuring academicism.

As early as the 1950s, Laura Sheleen had introduced the Graham technique, but to a relatively small number of people. Then in the 1960s several renowned American dance teachers came to France and, through giving courses, influenced a growing number of dance enthusiasts. In addition to those already mentioned in connection with the C.I.D. courses, Winifred Widener and Katherine Henry d'Epinoy taught at the American Centre. The American influence made itself felt in other ways too: the visits of Paul Taylor's, Nikolais's, Cunningham's and Alvin Ailey's companies, for example, were all events that aroused mistrust or disapproval in some quarters and enthusiasm in others. Through each of these choreographers a new universe, a new aesthetic and a new theatrical language were revealed.

Then there came a time when young dancers began to travel abroad to study and a number of these went to the United States to complete their training with Graham, Cunningham, Limón, Dunham or Ailey, according to their inclination. Returning to work in France, impregnated to a greater or lesser degree with American choreographic culture, they continued to teach in this vein.

Jazz dance infiltrated France at this time too, and was sometimes erroneously classed as modern dance. This was yet a further new influence that was firmly upheld by several eminent practitioners, such as Walter Nicks, Matt Mattox and Katherine Henry d'Epinoy.

The Wave from Latin America

France came under the influence not only of dancers from North America but of those from Latin America too. We must recall that during the war a number of modern European dancers had taken refuge in South America, especially Argentina. They, as it were, founded a family there, and a new generation of native dancers demonstrated their creative originality, spirit of initiative and seriousness of intent.

During the 1960s several dancers and choreographers came to Paris, some of whom are still there today. Others simply passed through but nevertheless stayed long enough to leave a tangible influence. They formed a nucleus within the French dance community where they taught and employed French dancers in their choreographies. They will be discussed in more detail below.

Multiplication

On considering this decade it is striking to note a kind of multiplication of dance.

Be it lineage or not, grafts, cuttings; the metaphor is not important; we were indeed witnessing a flowering – a flowering of wild, or hybrid or hot-house plants, annuals or perennials, and so on ...

There was much dancing and much to see and learn, discover and develop. Nevertheless, we are still confronted with a generation of pioneers, for contemporary dance was far from having acquired automatic citizenship in France.

[Throughout the 1960s my generation fought all the more vigorously as the situation began to show signs of improvement and the horizon no longer seemed so blocked. We were eager to shake those strongholds of conservatism. With what youthful ardour did we too for a moment place our faith in the cultural revolution of '68!

I can picture us now at the Sorbonne, filing along, with great seriousness, to sign our allegiance to the Comité Révolutionnaire d'Action Culturelle (C.R.A.C.) ... We dreamt of grand projects that would give shape to so many discoveries and possibilities for creation and dissemination. In search of our own truths, we proselytes imagined great changes.

I can see us also at the Conservatoire National on the rue de Madrid, giving lessons in contemporary dance, free of charge, of course, to the students of this worthy institution that was rather strict at that time, happy to have the opportunity to awaken new hopes and new demands in them.

I recall us plotting a march on the Opéra (in imitation of the occupation of the Odéon); dreaming of accosting, of violating ancient customs and of founding a new city in which dance would blossom through work and creativity.

I can picture us too sitting around various green tables, discussing doctrines, teaching, priorities, rights and duties.

The memory of moments in which we experienced a tremendous sense of solidarity in the face of a great cause that we were prepared to support with all our might lives on in my mind. And then, when all this feverish excitement had died down, daily cares came to the fore again. But something of this desire to build remained, and today we are a little closer to the realization of our dreams of those days ... but nothing is ever simple and other problems have arisen!]

Youth and Vulnerability

There existed at this time several reviews of dance (see Appendix). The most friendly and 'sympathizing' of these in my opinion was *Danse et rythmes*, founded and edited by José Atienza. This review was for a time bilingual (French/Spanish). Amongst the regular contributors, Delfor Peralta, an Argentinian man of the theatre, possessed a good understanding of the specific problems and essence of modern dance and of its development in France. The passage quoted below was written a little before the decade in question, but it nevertheless seems entirely relevant. It deals with 'Youth and modern dance' and appeared in July 1959 (*Danse et rythmes*):

> 'The greatest strength of young people – especially if they are artists – lies much more in what they are destined to become than in what they are now. Indeed, one of the principles of this review is not to applaud what young dancers are doing today but to spur them on to hard work and rich and complex research, to give them ideas and open doors for them.
>
> It is undeniable that many young dance artists today seem, in a way, blocked, compared to their predecessors, many of whom – one need only mention Martha Graham, Mary Wigman, Dore Hoyer, Hanya Holm, Clotilde Sakharoff, Harald Kreutzberg and Agnes de Mille – show a renewed and surprising freshness and vigour.
>
> The same is true in all artistic disciplines. In the case of Picasso or Bunuel as with Mary Wigman, this renewal is the result of a vocation, yes, and talent, but above all of many long years of discipline and vivifying experience that will build a trustworthy stock, the contents of which bear the mark of quality, strength and personality. They did indeed present their early works, but their later ones provide a convincing illustration that "youth" (or any other similar designation) is not an end in itself, but a means; that above all youth is not a justification. If you are young and someone like Rimbaud, for example, you can revolutionize literature, but if you are a Minou Drouet or Françoise Sagan* any demonstration of talent is merely a wager that must be proven in the future, a stage that, instead of making us look to the artists' past work forces us to anticipate their future development. Neither classical nor modern dance escapes this law. Modern dance is facing a very definite danger.
>
> Let us again take an example from painting. To a solid training, demanding effort, patience, time and work, over and above talent, many young people prefer to take that shorter and more spectacular route towards abstract painting. Very often the choice of the easy way conceals a lack of a real calling. I do not mean to imply by this that modern painting is easy, but it cannot be denied that nowadays it has become difficult to discern genuine worth from false claims, that modern art constantly takes advantage of the moment, whether to exalt or fight against it, and that, attracted by this attainable goal, learning to draw, for instance, may seem a hard task and one that will be of little use in the future.

---

*Well known literary 'prodigies' of the time.

But modern dance was not born yesterday and in countries where it is a reality, as in the United States, for example, the danger is less great: a certain maturity amongst the audience, diverse but clearly defined characteristics (for modern dance is just as rigorous as classical dance, "nothing demands more rigour than the mastery of freedom") and the existence of definite values make it much easier to distinguish genuine renewal from improvisation, ambition from pretentiousness. In France, the doors remain barely ajar to dance as an expression of our time. It is here, in this international centre of art, that modern dance is most vulnerable. Let no-one be deceived: the discipline of modern dance – spiritual and physical – must not support false values, for the public – even though it drew a blank on Martha Graham and José Limón, and even though it continues to consider the incontestable art of Roland Petit as "modern" – cannot recognize itself in these values any more than it can see itself in those whose meaning is already out-dated.

It is important that modern dance should not start out with the faults of old age: over-confidence, a lack of modesty and an absence of self-criticism. No point in trying to close doors that are already closed: this would be a waste of time and energy and, in the best of cases, would delay still further the arrival of the new expression in dance of which theatrical art, especially in the Old World, is so greatly in need.

To conclude, I quote a phrase by René Clair: "The true avant-garde is that which carries on regardless without taking the trouble to turn round to see if anyone is following it", a phrase that may be useful for the future development of young dancers; and to end, an anecdote attributed to the writer Jorge Luis Borges: in order to justify a mediocre literary work, someone said of its author: "He's still young". To which Borges replied: "Well then, may he soon grow up". An anecdote that I hope will apply only to the past of these young dancers'.

Delfor Peralta

THE ACTORS

A number of problems confronted me in presenting the actors of the 1960s. How should I choose from the ever increasing number of those who ought to be included? And how should I introduce them, under what collective designation? These problems were all the more pronounced since, during this last decade lines of descent became distinctly blurred.

Moreover, the majority of those who will be discussed are still active today. Some of them have taken unexpected directions. According to the convention adopted in this book, they appear in our chronicle from the moment they begin to gain a reputation in the line of work they assumed at the time.

INSTITUTIONS

The Introduction of Dance into Parisian Universities
by Mireille Arguel

This little episode in the history of dance in universities, although an epiphenomenon localized within the Paris academy, nevertheless reveals a certain institutional and socio-cultural context, and reflects the mentality of the period, and the hidden or open conflicts that came to light as a result of the attempt to institutionalize a physical and artistic activity such as dance. This period 1962–1974 began with the creation of a centre and an interuniversity dance establishment, and ended with the inauguration of the first university diploma in dance.

The Jean-Sarrailh Centre in Paris was a sports complex, opened in 1962, for students from different Parisian faculties and certain high schools. The students had to be registered either with the sports association of their faculty or directly with the secretariat of the sports centre in order to practise certain physical activities such as rhythmics, dance, keep-fit, gymnastics, judo and swimming. These activities were organized by the management of the centre and were overseen by physical education teachers contracted by this interuniversity complex. In a way, this structure was in competition with the university sports associations which charged subscriptions of varying rates for each activity depending upon the faculty and the type of activity chosen, whilst the courses provided by the centre were free.

When the centre was opened in 1962, a few courses in modern and rhythmic dance were set up and already aroused a great deal of interest. From 1964, five women teachers, holders of the C.A.P.E.P.S.* in dance and experienced professional dancers, were employed by the centre to provide instruction in dance at all levels. They were Annick Maucouvert (modern), Anne-Marie Constant (classical), Mireille Arguel (modern, jazz and contemporary), Colette Chaussonet (rhythm and movement, gymnastics preparatory to dance), and Denise Hubert (folklore, within the framework of the sports association of the faculty of arts). It was around these women that the practice of dance in universities developed. They aimed above all to share their love of dance as an art form, but also to use it as their preferred means of achieving a modern physical education, of training dancers for the creative workshops,

---

*Certificat d'aptitude au professorat d'éducation physique et sportive.

providing everybody with access to an introduction and training in dance and sensitizing future audiences to this art.

Between six and ten lessons were offered every day, representing different styles and levels of practice:

- preparatory level – rhythm and movement;
- beginners, immediate, advanced and very advanced levels;
- composition and choreography workshops.

This system gave rise to several new ventures:

- a course entitled 'dance for all' that did not lead to any professional qualification but aimed to provide a deeper knowledge of dance, to produce informed amateurs;
- a more specialized training: semi-professional, even professional, for some students;
- a research initiative: research/action, artistic research, choreographic research (performance) and scientific research.

This interuniversity system was based on an interdisciplinary method of dance teaching. Every student who wished to continue his studying for several years was required to practise classical dance and at least two branches of contemporary dance (Graham, Limón, new tendencies) and jazz, in order to acquire a richer and more diverse expressive palette. Each university year ended with a presentation of the work of the choreographic workshops. These performances were given before an audience of students, teachers, university administrative staff and those representatives of the ministry of youth and sports who defended this teaching against the sectarianism prevalent in sport sectors where sport and dance were supposed to be opposed.

The attendance figures increased from year to year, and in 1970, 1500 out of the 2500 students who registered at the beginning of the year were following courses regularly and assiduously. Out of the total 1500 annual participants, the student population practising dance at the centre was 98% female. However, the males, who represented only 2% of this total, seemed especially motivated since they formed 20% of the very advanced class in contemporary dance and the choreography workshops. Almost all the boys who were taught on these courses became professional dancers or dance teachers. It is a remarkable fact that a large number of both male and female students re-registered in their faculty just so that they could continue to study dance, some of them even staying for ten years!

Some of the dancers who went on to make a name for themselves took their first steps at the centre. These included Jean Rochereau,

Georges Tugdual, Marie-Christine Georghiu, Anne-Marie Reynaud and Nicole Ledain. Others, such as Linda Mitchell, who were already dancers, came to the centre to profit from its teaching which gave a new dimension to their knowledge of dance, especially in the field of pedagogy. Numerous students of physical and sports education (at Paris V – faculty of medicine – institute of physical and sports education) came to obtain a more advanced qualification in dance in terms of both technical level and choreographic research; some of them took part in the works of Annick Maucouvert's contemporary dance group or at Mireille Arguel's university choreographic workshop. In 1971 and 1972 the latter group won the second and first prizes respectively at the Ballet pour Demain competition in Bagnolet. These groups were not afraid to compete with the private sector of the dance world.

The establishment of both qualitative and quantitative dance teaching on such a large scale within the framework of sport (in which the majority of male colleagues cast a scornful yet interested glance in the direction of '*this girlish practice*' that they considered to be encroaching upon their territory!) was a pioneering task. We also had to struggle against the prejudices of the cultural milieu of dance which was at the time very classically oriented and looked unfavourably upon the appropriation by these teachers of physical education and sport, these non-professional-dancers, of an artistic discipline to which the dance establishment claimed exclusive rights. Moreover, the principal teaching offered by the centre was in modern dance which, in the aesthetic climate of this elitist culture, did not enjoy much prestige or status before 1970. Only the university environment seemed to welcome us. In this struggle to promote a bodily and artistic activity accessible to all students, our weakness lay in the fact that we belonged to the world of sport. Our strength, however, lay in the great interest our activities aroused and in the fact that our attendance rates and numbers of participants were higher than those of any of the student physical sports activities; indeed, our numbers were so high that we had to draw up waiting lists in order to avoid over-subscription: 80–100 students per beginners class and 40–60 for the intermediate ones! We had at this time the disconcerting impression that we were becoming a factory of dance. It was essential to preserve the quality of the teaching at all costs.

Although 1968 was a period in which the majority of teaching was thrown into question, the crisis did not affect dance at the centre, this seat of novelty, techniques and creation from which the discussion of ideas was not excluded. From 1971, all teachers appointed by the centre or employed by the former faculties were compelled under Faure's law to choose a university to which to be attached, which created a certain institutional upheaval regarding this system of dance teaching. The teachers distributed themselves amongst the universities Paris-I, II, IV, V and IX and became increasingly dependent upon the Services Universitaires des Activités Physiques et Sportives (S.U.A.P.S.) or the Département d'Éducation Physique des Sports et des Loisirs (D.E.P.S.E.L.) at Paris-III. (This new ruling affected me personally at Paris-III, new Sorbonne, where I was involved in the founding of the D.E.P.S.E.L., and in proposing the creation of the first university course in contemporary dance teaching.)

Indeed, the quality of the classes, which attracted more and more students, the possibility of self-development through different techniques of dance and of pursuing these practices, together with research, choreographic creation and scientific research, carried out in these fields over several years, plus increasing student demand, led me in 1974 to work on a university diploma in contemporary dance teaching, combining research and teaching, technique, creation and pedagogy. The dean, Las Vergnas, president of Paris-III, was most appreciative of the work carried out at the Jean-Sarrailh Centre and encouraged the founding of this diploma as a logical result of the influence and efficiency of this inter-university home of dance.

This project took account of the internal constraints of Paris-III and foresaw the possibility of a double course which would enable dance students who failed in the dance course to transfer to a different one. An initial survey conducted amongst the thousand or so students practising dance at the centre enabled me to predict the enrollment of some forty candidates at the start of the term in October 1975, not including the applications that were flooding in from other regions of France.

This course instituted a three-year training based on a renovation of the pedagogy of dance and movement in general; it laid emphasis upon a programme of research in the field combining teachers and students, entitled "Operation of pedagogical research with a view to elaborating a new pedagogy of contemporary dance in its diverse specific technical aspects". This programme included a practical, technical and choreographic part consisting of a range of styles, plus workshops; a theoretical part (anatomy/physiology, psychology, sociology, music, history of art: dance, theatre, music, painting, etc., legal studies, notation of movement), and a pedagogical part, both theoretical and practical.

Although the various committees of Paris-III encouraged the creation of this new course, it was the group of teachers of the physical education department (sportsmen) who prevented the realization of the project. The departmental committee considered it to be an elitist operation, at a time when the dominant trend was towards more universal activities, freedom of expression, non-technical ideologies, and more 'democratic' activities, such as tennis and boxing! Moreover, the involvement of professional dancers in this new training scheme was considered unfavourable, revealing a definite corporate block. And yet, how enriching this association between professionals in the fields of culture and education might have been to such a course. Only the research programme, approved and funded by the science council, materialized and gave rise to a publication *Danse et enseignement Quel corps?*

It was this first university diploma in dance, however, that served as a detonator to Jean-Claude Serre, who based his diploma project at Paris-IV on the potential of students who had spent many long years of training at this interdisciplinary seat of dance that was the Jean-Sarrailh Centre.

It is interesting to compare the Jean-Sarrailh Centre project with the creation of the Groupe de Recherche en Expression Corporelle (G.R.E.C.) at the Toulouse Institut Régional d'Éducation Physique in 1968. *'The impetus came from J.B. Bonange, a teacher of physical education for men: this fact is not insignificant, since all too often, following the predominant socio-cultural model, bodily expression is associated with activities that are regarded as feminine ... From the very first issue of Cahiers du G.R.E.C. a question arose: should physical education students not have studied the dimensions of the expressive body during their training? Be it only for the purpose of testing their mode of conduct in a pedagogical relationship ... The physical education student, although trained to a high degree in the knowledge and mastery of his body, seems to discover an unfamiliar body. It must be said that the G.R.E.C. was perceived by the institution in a more or less fanciful way: a political group, a secret, mystical, spiritualist sect. Would bodily expression upset physical education?'* (extract from *Expression corporelle – langage du silence* by Claude Pujade-Renaud, 1974, E.S.F.).

The Growing Presence of Modern Dance in Physical Training Centres *by Mireille Arguel*

Modern dance was introduced into the École Normale Supérieure d'Éducation Physique for girls in Châtenay-Malabry for the first time in 1958. This noteworthy initiative made this period from 1958–1960 a crucial one in the evolution of the conception of bodily movement and gave rise to the first group of contemporary dancers employed in both a professional artistic company and a national institution of education as physical education teachers. Aline Roux and Mireille Arguel belonged to this first generation of physical education teachers-cum-modern dancers, and were followed closely by Annick Maucouvert in 1961.

It was at the instigation of Mireille Fromantel, teacher of rhythmics and dance at the École Normale Supérieure, and under the influence of Marie-Thérèse Eyquem and Denise Truc who had recently returned from a visit to the United States and Sweden where they had discovered a different kind of movement vocabulary and bodily training, that there arrived at the École Normale an ardent and passionate young woman who radiated strength and energy through a new use of the body as she danced. This bounding will-o'-the-wisp who projected herself in space with strength and suppleness, power and feline agility, and who sculpted three-dimensional space, arousing both emotion and astonishment was Karin Waehner. Her performances stimulated the enthusiasm of future teachers of physical education and launched more than one career. From this dancing elf arose the first sense of aesthetic emotion related to the discovery of modern dance, the same aesthetic emotion that was first expressed by Mary Wigman and brilliantly conveyed by Waehner her pupil. This intrusion of modern dance into the field of physical education and sport brought about a veritable revolution in the physical culture of the time, the concept of movement and the moving body, and set in motion within this school a current of thought and research into bodily expressivity. Over and above the motions of entertainment, the formal and analytical exercises of our gymnastics, designed to develop muscles and suppleness, co-ordination and the mastery of a mechanized body (in the bio-mechanical sense only of the motion of a body machine), there appeared another quality of movement constructed from dynamic forces and varied forms, a new way of moving, living through one's body and dancing.

At this time dance existed in the training of teachers of physical education under the label of 'rhythmics' only and it was exclusively for women! Rhythmics and dance: the fusion and confusion of the two was important. However, with Mireille Fromantel, totally involved in the theories of Delsarte and Laban, the notion of dance came into existence – the spirit before the letter: dance lived. At this time the teachers' certificate in physical education consisted of two parts and was still governed by the official instructions of the decree of 28 March 1945, which was modified in 1954 and then in 1956 with regard to some of its tests, of which rhythmics was one. The 1954 decree introduced rhythmics into the physical tests of the first part of the certificate in the form of *"sight reading of a simple rhythmic series and its realization in movement."* Rhythmics was defined in this period as a musical and not a gestural component since the movement realization served to illustrate the rhythmic series. In 1956, however, institutionalized rhythmics changed its meaning and became a form of physical exercise based on a musical support. It consisted of *"a short and simple series of physical exercises and skipping combined for a few bars following a rhythm played on the piano. It is recommended that one should ensure good general sense of balance of the body and check the placements of the lower limbs, respect the musical structure (phrase, rhythm) and translate the essential character of the theme – representing martial music by strong, well defined gestures, for example – and avoid the teaching of a too specific technique, for this often leads the student to the exclusive use of steps, whereas the aim of the examination is to reveal a sense of rhythm and not technical attainment".*

In the examination itself, candidates were given a choice between two pieces of music of different character; the chosen piece was then played to the candidate three times and she had to improvise or compose in front of the jury and present the translation of the designated music into gesture. This examination was already veering towards dance in view of the importance accorded to the expression of gesture in relation to musical character and the techniques of the period. Rhythmics drew its inspiration from Dalcrozian 'eurhythmics', Irène Popard's harmonic gymnastics, and Malkowski's principles of expression through movement, or illustrated a musical phrase through the use of classical steps.

The different regional centres of popular and sports education and institutes (attached to a faculty of medicine) provided preparation for the first part of the certificate of physical education (which served also as the entrance examination to the École Normale Supérieure d'Éducation Physique et Sportive) and training for this examination; this reflected in large part the teacher's own concept of rhythmics and dance, and involved a great heterogeneity of candidates according to location (the Dijon centre, for instance, with Annie Garby, was orientated more towards dance in the line of Malkowski, whilst others placed greater emphasis on Dalcrozian rhythmics).

At the École Normale rhythmics evolved into dance. We learnt dance there and received alongside it a musical and rhythmic training with Mlle Gervais, a teacher at the C.N.M.S. We took courses in both classical and expressive dance. The latter bore the mark of Solane and was influenced by the principles of Delsarte and Laban; after 1958, it demonstrated the influence either of mime with Monique Bertrand, modern dance with Karin Waehner, or a combination of the two.

Throughout this period, the official documents concerning the preparation and recruitment of future teachers of physical education retained the term 'rhythmics', but in reality, dance was changing. In 1960, for example, whilst the best results in the physical education teachers' training course were awarded for performances of modern dance that already revealed a highly elaborate technique and spirit, the official texts still spoke of a rhythmics examination.

It was not until the decree of 12 December 1966 that the term 'Dance' appeared unmistakably amongst the subject choices for the classification examinations of the physical education and sports teachers' training certificate.

It was to take a further ten years for the official texts to correspond to what was actually taking place, both in the preparation of physical education teachers and during the entrance examination for the recruitment for women teachers, namely the experience of classical, modern and later contemporary and jazz dance. And one may indeed measure the time-lag between these official instructions that fixed the tendencies of the time in a sort of out-of-date map and the irresistible impetus of the innovatory trends due to the enthusiastic and creative pioneers who established a new trilogy – body – space – time – and a new dynamic in teaching. Alas, it is never easy to be a prophet in one's own country. The intrusion of modern dance into the field of physical education and sport and its subsequent spreading was the result of a long and sometimes painful struggle.

The institution of physical education and sports has always maintained an ambiguous relationship with dance. This bodily and artistic activity was profoundly different from the rhythmics of the period. For one thing, its relationship to modern music, interaction with a musical partner, percussion, voice, sounds was different. Its forms and gestural dynamics were completely different from those of classical dance, which had become totally engulfed in pedantic and mechanical technicalities, removing all substance from dance. If at the outset, however, a new gestural technique emerged, very soon the aims of this practice of dance diverged from the educational aims. The doctrine of the time in physical education and sport, changed not in any conscious or voluntary way, but because the 'subversion' came about logically through the nature of the proposed bodily and artistic activity itself. This new technique revealed an art of movement that was different from that practised in France at the time of perfecting the body–machine in order to provide increased mechanical efficiency; the new art substituted this image for one of a sensitive, inventive body, a human body.

In 1959, under the impetus of Monique Bertrand, a newly appointed teacher of rhythmics at the École Normale Supérieure, a new approach to movement through mime was introduced, based on bodily expression. This bodily expression adhered to and attempted to analyse the fundamentals of movement through the new practices in dance but also through mime, under the influence of Decroux, for example. This approach corresponded more closely to the needs of the students at the École Normale Supérieure, who were athletes rather than dancers.

Some tried to build their argument in defense of dance on an opposition between dance and sport. Did such an opposition between dance and certain sports really exist in terms of technique? For my own part, my training as an athlete led me to deny any such opposition. My specific skills as a high jumper in the mastery of the take-off and suspension, helped me to make rapid strides in modern dance. Conversely, having become a professional dancer at the same time as a top athlete, I had at that time only my technical lessons in modern dance to give me all the thorough training I needed, and in this I found a dynamic that approached that of the running and jumping of the athlete.

Bodily expression took its form and drew sustenance from classically constructed, analytical gestures as much as from the techniques discussed above. The whole fundamental relationship between the body, space and time was thus called into question. In fact, through the teaching of structured gymnastics and a rhythmic method based on the technical elements of academic dance, a body somehow fragmented began to emerge corresponding to a particular formal aesthetic. The relationship between music and movement was an elementary one and was all too frequently reduced to a collage of steps based on the musical rhythm; personal expression was, moreover, all too often treated as 'a nicety' added to the performance of a classical technique, the demands of technical perfection of which proved completely inappropriate to the physique of athletes ill-prepared to assume this gestural language.

On the other hand, recourse was made to Malkowskian free dance, passing through the 'diverted' classicism of Solane. This alternative was an interesting one to specialists in the field of movement and a thought-provoking one too, but it revealed more problems than it solved concerning the acquisition of dance techniques. The 1960s were a melting-pot in which new questions relating to the body came to light and in which there was a reconsideration of the expressivity of the body. These questions arose both in the sphere of physical education, on a fundamental level, in which bodily expression aimed to prepare the human being for all subsequent physical activity of a more specific nature, and in the resolutely artistic sphere of modern dance training. Depending upon the particular interests of the physical education teacher and his or her artistic bodily culture, this bodily expression assumed new forms whilst remaining faithful to the definition currently put forth by the École Normale Supérieure: "*a fundamental activity preparatory to sports and non-sports activities (dance, mime)*", before coming to signify the systematic gestural manifestation of emotions, feelings, pulsations or sentiments, an aesthetic trend which then became preparatory to dance and mime, if not actually synonymous.

Little by little, however, a psychologizing tendency began to set in, taken over from psychoanalysis and political ideologies of a marxist turn that perverted the initial, relatively simple idea and altered the course of bodily expression. Bodily expression became a charger, the new Trojan horse (the aim being to destabilize and call into question the institution of physical education and sport, and traditional physical education), of splinter groups referring to Freud, Marx, Reich etc.

The institutional relationships between bodily expression and dance, which were all too often confused with one another, thus became rather strained. The general inspectorship of physical education and sport grew concerned over the efflorescence of different trends ranging from a completely laisser-faire attitude in the name of spontaneous creativity (an unfortunate misinterpretation of Carl Rogers's concept of non-directivity current in 1965–1967) to the assertion of a bodily and artistic practice that was as demanding as the rigorous practice of a sport, but which had cultural overtones of a feminine activity (graceful, light, indeed superfluous) and ultimately was unconsciously considered as frivolous or as straying from the doctrinal path marked out for teachers of physical education. This confusion of genres posed serious problems, even a matter of conscience, within the institution of physical education and sport. As far as the world of sport was concerned, dance was useless, to be totally rejected. The classical dance world was itself wholly opposed to both modern dance and everything that emanated from sport and physical education.

During 1958–1960 the École Normale Supérieure in Châtenay-Malabry became a real incubator of a whole new creative tendency, a new form of physical education and the place in which a new dimension of the art of dance through modern dance emerged. This privileged haven of serious thinking, thanks to the open-mindedness of three women: Mme Surrel, headmistress of the school, Mireille Fromantel and Monique Bertrand, teachers of theory and dance, made possible the development, over and above ideological, corporate and other conflicts, of a new conception of rhythmics, dance and human movement, with all the possible implications of these in the field of physical education. The after-effects, if not the delayed tremors of this development may still be felt today, some thirty years later!

[The description of these events by Mireille Arguel tends to confirm the difficulties in gaining recognition for modern dance during these years that I have indicated elsewhere. Not that modern dance did not exist at that time. We have seen that during the 1950s and '60s there were already numerous practitioners of no small significance at work, bearers of new ideas of an artistic as much as of a pedagogical nature. It is nevertheless surprising to note with hindsight, and as Mireille Arguel clearly points out, that whilst we were working so ardently in our own studios ... understood by our loyal supporters, the institutions were so far behind in both spirit and letter with regard to the intense actual practices. Karin Waehner succeeded in opening a few doors, first at the École Normale Supérieure and later at the Schola Cantorum. These events tipped the balance both symbolically and effectively towards the full rights of citizenship for modern dance for which we were fighting.]

The Ballet Théâtre Contemporain

Within the scope of a policy that aimed to bring about the decentralization of dance, a scheme for attaching dance companies to existing Maisons de la culture* was devised. This scheme was soon abandoned, and was only to come to fruition several years later with the establishment in various towns throughout France of the companies we know today.

   The first company of this type was the Ballet Théâtre Contemporain created in 1968 on the initiative of Jean-Albert Cartier. The Ballet Théâtre Contemporain was initially attached to the cultural centre in Amiens, at that time under the direction of Philippe Thiry, and was later transferred to Angers. Ten years later, Angers became the stronghold of the Centre National de Danse Contemporaine, and Jean-Albert Cartier left for Nancy where he founded another ballet company. The Ballet Théâtre Contemporain was to provide a focus for many hopes placed in the future of dance, particularly modern dance. During the first year, dance weekends were held that aimed to sensitize both the public and professionals. Françoise Adret was the first ballet-mistress and promoter. During their Parisian season and on tour, a repertoire was born that provoked mitigated responses from the critics and public alike.

   Various choreographers created works for the Ballet Théâtre Contemporain, including:

- Félix Blaska, who was later to venture more definitely into the field of contemporary dance. He sought to escape the influence of neo-classicism and to deepen his knowledge of American techniques and ways of thinking. He went later to work with Martha Clarke formely a member of the innovative Pilobolus dance company) and became a member of the Crowsnest Trio;

---

*Institutionalized cultural centres in various cities.

– Michel Descombey, who created several noteworthy works. He was ballet-master at the Paris Opéra from 1963 to 1969 and, turning towards new perspectives in dance, he attempted to create an opening within that venerable institution. He succeeded in establishing the Ballet Studio there in 1966, a little nucleus of creation, that anticipated the Groupe de Recherche Chorégraphique de l'Opéra de Paris (G.R.C.O.P.). Finally he went abroad;
– Joseph Lazzini, ballet-master at the Marseilles Opéra from 1959 to 1969;
– and later Dirk Sanders, Jean Babilée and Françoise Adret, etc.

It seems to me that the choreographers who gave their works to this company (and other similar ones) were not genuine moderns – neither total converts nor adequately trained in modern dance. The same was no doubt true of the performers. It seems surprising that as late as 1970 the company still did not provide any classes in modern dance. Over and above the foreign choreographers who were invited (Paul Sanasardo, John Butler and Brian MacDonald, for example), the French choreographers belonged for the most part to the neo-classical* movement, influenced by Roland Petit, Maurice Béjart and Janine Charrat. This was a phenomenon peculiar to this period, namely the confusion that existed between works in the neo-classical style (that were still based on the classical tradition and relied heavily on the actual staging) and the point of view of modern dance, the perpetually renewed vocabulary of which gives back its autonomy to pure movement. In the words of the great American critic John Martin: *'modern dance is a point of view!'*.

In *Histoire de la danse en Occident*, Paul Bourcier wrote of the Ballet Théâtre Contemporain:

> "Its founder, the art critic Jean-Albert Cartier, wanted to make it a place where a synthesis of all the contemporary arts could occur. Each ballet was to be entrusted to a team comprising a choreographer, a musician and a designer chosen from amongst first-rate creators. The first programme – Danses concertantes (choreography: Félix Blaska; music: Stravinsky; scenography: Sonia Delaunay); Salomé (Lazzini, Miroglio, Claude Viseux); Déserts (Descombey, Varèse, Groupe de Recherche d'Art visuel) – is evidence of his aims.
>
> But we must still observe the constraints of this system: firstly, the financial cost; secondly, the need to weld into a totally coherent team artists who were often unknown to each other; and finally – and most serious of all – the risk of falling into aestheticism, and of giving pre-eminence to form. To take up Diaghilev's

---

* The term 'neo-classical' designates in France what is frequently considered as 'contemporary ballet' in the U.S.A.

formula and try to bring it up-to-date was, unless used with extreme clear-sightedness, to run the risk of making the same mistakes as he did".[1]

And Jacques Baril wrote in February 1968 in *Les Saisons de la danse:*

> *'Our choreographers apply themselves more to creating an atmosphere by means of stage and sound effects than through the stuff of bodily expression. It is regrettable that what is not expressed through movement should be so by means of theatrical effects. The dances seek to be eloquent, and all the more so when their subject is obscure. The effects achieved through the deliberate use of all kinds of artifices impress the public who are no longer able to distinguish the theatrical from the choreographic work. Some claim that the age-old use of the human body as the sole material limits and reduces the possibilities of bodily expression. This is not so. It is obvious that our 'young' choreographers, bereft of essentially choreographic inspiration, like to compose works for particular occasions. In order to achieve this, they employ procedures that are alien to specifically bodily expression, vain distractions that adorn the scenic presentation of the ballet. They elaborate digressions around or on a theme. Their gestural inadequacy is compensated for by visual and auditory ornaments.*
>
> *It would appear that this weakness is the result of a restricted vocabulary, frequently limited to knowledge of a single school: the traditional school'.*

The Théâtre Français de la Danse

Created in 1969, the Théâtre Français de la Danse was set up with the assistance of the ministry of culture. Its direction was entrusted to Joseph Lazzini following his departure from the Marseilles Opéra. The aim was to create a dance company on a par with the Orchestre de Paris, and therefore an organization of some prestige. It was installed in the former Gaîté-Lyrique and would have served as a kind of Maison de la Danse, offering work, premises, an archive unit, and a meeting place. It would appear that the first performance witnessed a mixed success; connoisseurs of contemporary dance had become more demanding and the realizations of the Théâtre Français de la Danse did not fulfil the expectations that this ambitious project had aroused. It was, alas, another case of infant mortality and the initial project of the Théâtre Français de la Danse was never resumed.

The Théâtre des Nations

Firmin Gémier had already suggested the idea of a theatre of nations as early as 1922! It was in 1948 that, under the auspices of U.N.E.S.C.O., in which Jean-Louis Barrault was one of the key workers, that the Institut

---

[1] Paul Bourcier, *Histoire de la danse en Occident* (Le Seuil, 1978), p. 304.

International du Théâtre was born, and this was followed in 1957 by the Théâtre des Nations which functioned at the Sarah-Bernhardt in Paris until 1970. It was also under the auspices of U.N.E.S.C.O., and as a sister organization of the Institut International du Théâtre that the International Dance Council was established in 1973, under the presidency of Jeannine Alexandre-Debray and Kurt Jooss, later of Bengt Haeger and currently Milorad Miskowitch.

The Théâtre des Nations included dance in its programming, thus enabling foreign companies practising different styles to become known in Paris. Over the years, the groups that performed there were, amongst others, the American Ballet Theatre, the Japanese Classical Ballet, the Budapest Opera (ballets to the music of Béla Bartók), the Indian National Theatre (with dance), the Stockholm Opera (choreographies by Ivo Cramer and Birgit Cullberg), the Ballets of the Warsaw Opera, Jerome Robbins' Ballets USA, the Ballets of Haïti, the Ballet du XXᵉ Siècle (Béjart), the Berlin Opera (choreography by Dore Hoyer), several Latin American Companies, the Paul Taylor Dance Company, the Inbal Dance Company of Israel, and the Merce Cunningham Dance Company. In addition to the performances, there also existed the university of the Théâtre des Nations, directed first by Albert Botbol and then by André Perinetti; this offered a course of theoretical and practical studies, and lectures on theatre and dance. The only dance performance that appears to have been given within this setting was one by Sara Pardo in 1962.

The Châteauvallon Festival

This project was born in 1965 as a result of the meeting between Gérard Paquet and Henri Komatis in a country house in a valley in Provence. Year after year the house was fitted out and the activities multiplied, including performances (theatre, dance, variety, music, cinema), exhibitions, didactic events, courses and congresses, on an international scale. Today, Châteauvallon is the home of the Théâtre National de la Danse et de l'Image.

Dance featured there from 1966, on a modest scale at first, and then more extensively as the location and projects grew in size and scope. During these years, the closing ones of our chronicle, Françoise and Dominique Dupuy, Katherine Henry d'Epinoy (both as a soloist and with her group), Kumari Malavika, Pinok and Matho, the Ballet-Théâtre Rusillo, the Ballets Félix Blaska, the London Contemporary Dance Company, the Théâtre du Silence, the Alwin Nikolais Dance Company, and many traditional dance companies appeared there. Today it is both big international companies such as Martha Graham's, as well as the up-to-date young French choreographers, who make up the basis of the institution's vocation, along with a new emphasis on the image.

Art, Recherche, Confrontation at the Museum of Modern Art

In 1966 a section known as Art, Recherche, Confrontation (A.R.C.) was created at the National Museum of Modern Art (quai de Tokyo). The aims of this section were to present artistic events (exhibitions, concerts, performances, debates) centred on contemporary research within an educational perspective, and to stimulate confrontation between public and artists. Dance was represented from 1967, and its promotion was entrusted to Françoise and Dominique Dupuy and Lise Brunel. It provided an opportunity to sensitize the public to styles and approaches it had not experienced before, to introduce little known artists to Paris and to instigate events relating to dance, often in conjunction with other artistic disciplines. Unfortunately this initiative lasted for only a year and a half, mounting performances at the rate of one per month (except for 'Museum Events' by Merce Cunningham in the 'Horspace' exhibition in 1970, and Claire Markale in the Duvillier exhibition in 1972, added to the regular programme).

The experience seems to have been cut short due to a lack of resources in terms of equipment, staff and adequate structures. It was too important an enterprise to remain on a voluntary basis for long. Nevertheless, the following events took place there: 'De la Perse traditionnelle à l'Iran moderne' (dance and music); Daniel Nagrin's first Paris recital; appearances by Jerome Andrews, Karin Waehner, Françoise and Dominique Dupuy, Barbara Pearce, Anna Mittelholzer, Dora Feïlane, Katherine Henry d'Epinoy, Paulina Oca, Igor Fosca, the mimes Claude Dedieu and Gérard Lebreton . Sessions were also held on the subjects of "Dance and Musique Concrète" with Jerome Andrews, Françoise Dupuy, Paulina Oca and Karin Waehner, "Choreographies based on the same score" (Jerome Andrews, Dominique Dupuy, Katherine Henry d'Epinoy, Deryk Mendel, Paulina Oca, Barbara Pearce, Roger Ribes and Sonia Sanoja) and "The intervention of chance in choreographic creation" (Arlet Bon, Jean Dudan, Annick Maucouvert, Sara Pardo). Sara Pardo featured within the context of a Rauschenberg exhibition, moreover, and Graziella Martinez appeared in improvised performances. The A.R.C. brought together the avant-garde of the plastic arts and music (concerts and debates of the greatest interest). It is indeed a pity that contemporary dance was not able to remain within this congenial framework.

The Bagnolet Competition: Ballet Pour Demain *by Nathalie Collantes*

In the Paris of 1969 new dance had created its own history with its dancers, choreographers and even its theorists, but there were still very few opportunities or places for young creators, longing to show their work on stage. It was in Bagnolet, in a specially equipped gymnasium, that a choreography competition came into existence on the initiative of Jaque Chaurand, a fugitive from the Opéra and a dancer, choreographer and great lover of novelty. Christened 'Ballet pour Demain', this annual meeting comprised, in its first year, five groups or schools; twice that number participated in 1970. Over the years this figure continued to multiply. In spite of the spirit of the time (1968 was not long past), this competition was supported first and foremost by the town and then, from 1979, by the state.

At the outset, Jaque Chaurand created this competition in order to help young choreographers and their groups perform on stage and to promote French dance. The problem was not unknown to him, for he took part as a choreographer in the initial session and was awarded first prize. The following year's winner, Aline Roux, did not yet fall into the categorization that in 1971 divided the candidates into amateurs and professionals. In 1972 no prizes were awarded to professionals, whilst in 1973 four prizes were awarded (D. Fielden, Jean Pomarès) and for the first time the prize-list included a foreigner. (In 1979 there was a prize awarded by the ministry and amateurs were excluded from competing).

Above all, the organizers wished to facilitate communication between dancers and choreographers, and among choreographers themselves. The Bagnolet competition attracted those who performed contemporary dance (the 'professionals') or those who should do so (the 'officials') and the Parisians, who made a real event of it, a festival of dance. And so, Bagnolet became a place where contemporary dance enjoyed full rights of citizenship, where choreographic talents were both demonstrated and predicted, and where the stakes became increasingly important.

FRENCH DANCERS, NOMADIC AND SEDENTARY

Françoise Saint-Thibault

French, born in 1927.

Before devoting herself totally to dance, Françoise Saint-Thibault obtained a university degree in psychology and studied art, receiving the diploma in architecture and interior decorating from the École Nationale Supérieure des Arts Décoratifs in 1951. She was also a musician.

It was in Paris that she began to study dance initially with Geneviève Mallarmé, Jerome Andrews, the Dupuys and Jacqueline Robinson. She then followed courses abroad with Mary Wigman, Kurt Jooss, Fred Traguth, Yuriko and the Sakharoffs, and finally went to America where she took lessons at Martha Graham's school and studied jazz with Walter Nicks and Alvin Ailey to whom she never ceased to refer.

During the 1960s she became a member of the Ballets Modernes de Paris (Dupuy), the Ensemble de l'Atelier de la Danse where she formed part of a very active trio with Piguet and Robinson, and the Théâtre du Geste (Sheleen). She naturally took part in the performances organized by Danse et Culture (Jean Dorcy) and the Théâtre d'Essai de la Danse (Dinah Maggie). In 1967 she founded her own company consisting of seven dancers and an actor who performed her own choreographies. She created a work for herself and her partner entitled *Le Geste et la voix*, a dance to contemporary poetry, that was performed throughout France, abroad and on television for many years. This genre or type of work suited Françoise Saint-Thibault's lyrical, bold and rational personal style well. Her choreographies were enriched by her attention to musicality (whether in relation to music, text or silence) and by her choices in the domain of plastic arts. Her many talents served her well!

She also began to teach during the 1960s , giving lessons in provincial schools and organizing introductory courses in modern dance for teachers and promoters. She was appointed as a teacher of contemporary dance at the Institut de Pédagogie des Arts Chorégraphiques (I.P.A.C.) in 1972 and finally opened her own school in 1977. As in the majority of cases, the relative eclecticism of her training has not, when all is said and done, prevented her own teaching from being summed up in terms of a few basic principles:

> "To fight for the recognition of dance as an activity of prime importance in the life of each and every human being, and not as an exceptional activity, reserved for a privileged few.
>
> To prove that in all forms of education, the training of the body through movement, or, better, through dance, is of prime necessity, and that technique is not an end in itself but a means of building the human body as an instrument and giving it meaning. For over and above technique on every level, it is a matter of finding the purity of true movement and freeing the creative energies through the perfect mastery of healthy, strong, supple, controlled and beautiful body".

Noëlle Janoli

French (1932–1983).

A rather mysterious woman. Noëlle Janoli, who departed from this world all too prematurely, had an elusive quality and was at times an enthralling dancer.

She received her first lessons in dance in Toulon with Phyllis Drayson and went on to study with Janine Solane and subsequently with Malkowski in Paris. In 1954 she met Jerome Andrews and became his pupil, assistant and partner. She created several dances in this period that remain in our memory, including the duet *Rencontre d'une âme morte avec un ange* which she performed with Andrews, her own solo *Salomé* (Xenakis), and the trio *Ode*, an unaccompanied work, with Andrews and Jérôme Rachell (Noëlle continued to work in the field of dance in silence).

In 1971 Noëlle Janoli and Jérôme Rachell, her companion and, likewise, a pupil of Andrews opened the Atelier de la Baleine, which became a seat of creation and teaching. They also organized performances there in which Jerome Andrews and his pupils frequently appeared. Noëlle's great solos, those tremendously powerful works based on Goya, such as *Le Cri*, *No hubo remedio* and *La Maya*, date from this period. She took part in several joint performances and appeared at the Avignon festival.

Illness forced her to withdraw from active life and she died of cancer at the age of fifty-one. (Jérôme Rachell died shortly after too.)

Françoise Julliot de la Morandiére

French, born in 1932.

Following studies in philosophy, psychopedagogy and music, Françoise came to dance through socio-educational work promoting active methods. She taught at the well known new school, La Source, and from 1953, having become increasingly involved in dance, she went on to study, principally with Karin Waehner and subsequently with Jerome Andrews, Laura Sheleen, Raymonde Lombardin and Mary Wigman. She thus found herself in the melting-pot in which contemporary dance developed in Paris. She took part in various dance performances for choreographers Jerome Andrews, Karin Waehner and Jacqueline Robinson amongst others.

On receiving a scholarship in 1959, she left for the United States where she worked successively with Martha Graham and José Limón, whose technique made a particularly deep impression on her. She went on to work with Mary Anthony and Louis Horst, and taught in New York, particularly in educational spheres. On her return to France in 1964,

Françoise de la Morandière danced with the Ballets Modernes de Paris (Dupuy) for several seasons and created *L'Aube naîtra de ton flanc* for them. She founded her own school, the Centre de Danses Contemporaines, in Paris in 1967, where she taught children. Her own earlier training had prepared her well for this sound and sensitive undertaking. She formed a dynamic team with Marianne Menessier, Anne Minot, Emmanuelle Lamy and Christine Lenthéric amongst others who collaborated in the research and choreographic and pedagogical productions of the school.

Françoise also found time to dance in the companies of Katherine d'Epinoy and Michel Caserta and she returned to New York from time to time where she worked with Merce Cunningham. From the 1970s on, Françoise de la Morandière was to become increasingly involved with institutions such as the Fédération Française de la Danse whilst continuing to develop her own personal work and her own school where she taught pedagogy and choreography in particular. She became more and more interested in socio-cultural problems on the one hand and everything concerning the analysis of movement, kinesiology and physiotherapy on the other. She has written several articles on these subjects.

Eclectic yet rigorous in her range of skills as in her spheres of interest, Françoise de la Morandière has nevertheless continued to pursue the course she had embarked upon as a result of her training with José Limon:

> "the Humphrey-Limón technique has always appealed to my body, heart and mind on account of its liberalism and philsophy. It is also particularly well adapted to needs of amateurs, offering them a place of their own where they may find what they are looking for, where they are not mixed with professionals or neglected in their midst, and where their needs, potential and aims in coming to dance may be satisfied. Kinesiology and the body work it entails was discovered in the United States some years ago, but was not yet at that time a subject for a full course of study in France. Since then such a course has come into existence and, thanks to Odile Rouquet, I became assiduously and passionately involved, discovering for myself ways of extending its use still further in terms of my own body and of dance and choreography. These possibilities, of which I was already aware, became deeper and more refined on a purely physical level as much as on an artistic, human and spiritual one".[2]

Claudine Allegra

French.

Claudine Allegra would not approve of being labelled either as a classical or a contemporary dancer. Although steeped in classical culture

---

[2] Françoise de la Morandière, letter to Jacqueline Robinson (1986). (The majority of quotations in this chapter are taken from interviews or letters from the person in question to Jacqueline Robinson.)

and competence, she is, in my view, nonetheless related to the contemporaries, for she has dared to say what she wanted in the way that she wanted and has not been afraid to invent. For these reasons she is included here.

Her early career was in a certain sense typical: an irresistible calling for dance, which was opposed by her family; musical studies at the Schola Cantorum; and a training in harmonic gymnastics with Andrée Joly; a brief spell with Janine Solane; studies in classical dance with Nina Tikanova, Nora Kiss, Tatiana Granzeva and Raymond Franchetti. At the beginning of the 1950s Claudine Allegra was appointed teacher of classical dance at the Schola Cantorum, a first sign that this institution was beginning to acknowledge dance (we should recall that Karin Waehner was to introduce contemporary dance there in 1960). Claudine Allegra claims to have learnt a great deal from this experience and to have gained the courage to dare further. She was, moreover, greatly influenced in this period by her work as a choreographer with Xavier de Courville and Jacqueline Casadesus and their Micropéra, a small but important venue for opera theatre. Similarly, she claims to have learnt much from her collaboration with Lasry and Baschet, creators of 'sound structures', a rich complex of electronic instruments.

Claudine Allegra presented her choreographies within various settings, the Théâtre d'Essai de la Danse amongst others. These works included *Intermezzi* (Rossini) and *Prélude métallique* (1959) with 'sound structures', and *Illusionis Amica* (1960), in which the critic Marcel Schneider noted a certain *"boldness, odd poetry and amusing discoveries"* (*Combat*, 16 June 1960). Indeed, it is perhaps these qualities that characterize Claudine Allegra's personal style. She also worked as a choreographer in television and cinema and founded the Ballet de Chambre with Stéphanie White and Sophie Lessard.

After 1971 Claudine Allegra's choreographic career really took off: she won first prize at the Bagnolet competition in 1971 with A. Ludwig, became ballet mistress and choreographer at the Grand Ballet Classique de France (Lyane Daydé), and created choreographies for Rosella Hightower at the Marseilles Opéra, the Ballet Théâtre Contemporain, soloists at the Paris Opéra and the Madrid Opera. Her pedagogical activity that has always included, even at the outset, the impulse to create, the teaching of improvisation and composition, should not be forgotten either.

Isabelle Mirova

French, born in 1935.

Isabelle Mirova has been described as a *'protean dancer'*, which is perhaps a reference to the many characters she has created or performed, masked or unmasked, human or animal, sorceress or tramp. For she has indeed experimented in many fields and these have enriched her teaching and creative work.

She was brought up in Marseilles in an artistic family; she studied music to quite an advanced level and rhythmic dance with Marguerite Caspari, a Dalcrozian who, from her base in Marseilles, had made rhythmics known. Isabelle's vocation was decided: theatrical studies in Aix and subsequently in Geneva, and a classical dance training with Boris Kniaseff, inventor of the 'barre a terre'. She became his assistant and remained with him for five years.

In 1958 Isabelle Mirova went to Paris; it was there that she discovered modern dance through Jerome Andrews, Françoise and Dominique Dupuy and Yuriko, as well as jazz, African dance, primitive dance and above all mime, studying for three years at the Jacques Lecoq school. There she met Isaac Alvarez. She and Alvarez went on to create Les Comédiens Mimes de Paris, a group that remained extremely active and creative until Isabelle's departure from Paris in 1969. During this time, Isabelle Mirova also worked in Jacques Lecoq's company, and subsequently in the Ballets Modernes de Paris (Dupuy) and the Jazz-Ballet in combination with musicians and the dancer Roger Ribes. Over the years, Isabelle Mirova sought to expand her dance education: she became initiated into Indian and Balinese dance. Having made a study trip to Bali in 1973, she composed *Danse-Image de Bali* in 1974. She explored other disciplines too, such as hatha yoga, t'aichi and Gerda Alexander's 'eutony' – testimony indeed of the diversity of her sources and resources. During her early years in Paris, whilst teaching within the framework of the Rencontres Internationales de Danse Contemporaine and the Centre International de Danse, she developed a wider palette, choosing to focus on dramatic acting/mime, or the relationship between music and movement, or jazz or inner equilibrium.

In 1969 Isabelle Mirova opened a school in Marseilles taking over from her first teacher, Marguerite Caspari, now deceased. The many activities that occurred there led to the creation in 1976 of La Triade – a group that works tirelessly in the spheres of creation, training and promotion through dance, theatre, music, and the graphic arts. Isabelle experimented with street performances for children. She performed in such places as the disused quarries in Baux-de-Provence, and has brought movement/theatre to hundreds of other venues.

Claude Decaillot

French, born in 1938.

Claude Decaillot was brought up in Mâcon in a family of musicians. She studied piano and classical and rhythmic dance. At seventeen, she began to study medicine in Lyons whilst continuing her dance and music studies. She also became involved in the university Theatre for which she produced her first choreographies (Goldoni and Brecht). In 1958 Claude Decaillot gave up medicine (commenting nevertheless on the immense enrichment she had gained from these years of study) and went to Paris. She entered the Popard school and was initiated into contemporary dance by Gilberto Motta, who introduced her to the Schola Cantorum. On leaving the Popard school, she entered the Schola where she studied music, modern dance with Karin Waehner and classical dance with Atty Chadinoff.

At the same time she continued to teach in Lyons, commuting between the two every week for four years. During this time she discovered jazz with René Deshauteurs and also the Graham technique. With other artists in Paris she founded Actuel, a working group directed towards creation and research that included dance, theatre, the plastic arts and the audiovisual. But wishing to establish firmly contemporary dance in Lyons, Claude Decaillot gradually began to devote more time to her activities there: information, promotion, training, creation, supported by local personalities, journalists, teachers and directors of cultural organizations. She finally settled there.

She took part in various multidisciplinary creative activities in the region together with Gabriel Cousin and Catherine Dasté, to name but these. In May 1968 for the Théâtre d'Essai de la Danse at the Récamier theatre in Paris she produced *Moulinologue*, and in 1971 she spent some time at the London School of Contemporary Dance. She was appointed technical and pedagogical adviser in contemporary dance at the ministry of youth and sports. Claude Decaillot never stopped producing works, just as she never stopped learning. She continued to study different styles of dance, particularly with Betty Jones, (Limón technique), and subsequently with Jean Cébron,* Bella Lewitzky and Walter Nicks amongst others. She also followed a university course in musicology.

---

*Jean Cébron: French, born in 1938. Son of Mauricette Cébron of the Paris Opéra. He made his career outside France, working in London with Sigurd Leeder, and established himself as a soloist. He became a member of the Ballets Jooss in 1964 and taught in Germany at the Folkwangschule in Essen and also with Palucca in Dresden. He was thus closely linked with the emergence of new German dance, especially at the Tanztheater with which we are now familiar through Pina Bausch amongst others.

1973 was a lucky year for her which saw the creation of the Théâtre Pied-Nu in collaboration with Annie Legros and Lila Nett, and the school, Théâtre du Mouvement. Finally, the securing of permanent premises enabled her to establish not only an education centre but also a place where the public could be invited to shows, debates and films. Claude Decaillot succeeded in attracting dancers and choreographers to the centre for performances and courses. That same year she set off on an expedition to Mali with the University of Lyons in order to study the content and structures of Malinese dance, and during her stay there she worked as a choreographer for the Malinese National Ballet. She also had the opportunity to work in other countries such as Italy, Tunisia and India (in the province of Kerala where she studied Kathakali song and dance), and learn a little of their cultures.

Nourished by this range of experiences and inspired by her desire and ability to undertake new ventures and break new ground, Claude Decaillot was extremely active in the field of creation as much as in those of teaching and promotion. Various institutional responsibilities were entrusted to her:

- in 1969 she became one of the founders of the Fédération Française de Danse et d'Art Chorégraphique;
- she was one of the promoters in the creation of the A.D.R.A. (Association Danse Rhône-Alpes) which prefigured the Maison de la Danse of Lyons that took over in 1980, becoming the important institution that we know today;
- she features in radio and television broadcasts, carries out cultural activities with various bodies such as universities and local communities, creating choreographic productions for the Théâtre des Jeunes Années in Lyons as well as for the Maison de la Danse, and continues to work in liaison with "national education" and "youth and sports" institutions.

Claude Decaillot cannot be separated from the work she carried out in Lyons with the Théâtre Pied-Nu. This work was fully integrated into the daily life of the community, exploiting new relationships with space, locations and the public (street performances, for example, in Perrache station in 1981), information and practice in schools – playing with all sorts of experiences: today dance-climbing.* Claude Decaillot herself says:

---

*A combination of dance movement and climbing techniques practised and performed in such venues as buildings, walls, rocks etc.

*"I have always been deeply interested in dance and the body, space and the
environment, every potential audience and every 'individual' concerned either
directly or indirectly with the body; this is why I have always continued to work
with amateurs as well as professionals in every context".*

A characteristic feature of Claude Decaillot's personality is expressed in
the presentation of her 1974 piece *Gun*:

*"React!
In a world in which violence is born of fear, defence or stupidity, in a repressive
society that tries to force us into a mould that does not respect human dignity,
we must react without hiding our heads in the sand".*

Dora Feïlane

French, born in 1938.

She studied dance in Paris, briefly with Janine Solane, and
classical dance with Atty Chadinoff and Tatiana Granzeva. She also
studied contemporary dance with Jerome Andrews, Laura Sheleen and
Karin Waehner. Her private life often took her abroad. Thus, at the
beginning of the 1960s, we find her in Palma de Mallorca where she
worked with Nadine Lang, a pupil of Laban, who encouraged her to
develop her own personal language, and then in Dakar where she danced
alone and began teaching. Returning to Paris in 1964, she continued her
training and became a member of the Ensemble de l'Atelier de la Danse
directed by Jacqueline Robinson. In 1966 she took part in the Théâtre
d'Essai de la Danse, and in 1967 founded her own company, presenting
her choreographies both in Paris and the provinces. Several encounters
that were decisive for the rest of her career date from this period: first of
all with Yuriko and Mary Hinkson, with whom she studied the Graham
technique which she has always favoured above all others; secondly, with
Fée Hellès who gave her much support; and finally with the composer
Marcel Frémiot who became her chief collaborator.

The particular course of Dora Feïlane's work was, then, the correspondence between various artistic disciplines: graphics, movement and
sound. From 1971 she settled in the South of France, obtained the state diploma in re-education through psychomotricity and opened a centre in Aix-en-
Provence where she pursues her creative and pedagogical work today.

Aline Roux

French.

Her early training was in physical education; she was immediately drawn to dance, however, and pursued an eclectic training in classical,

modern dance and jazz. Aline Roux was a member of Karin Waehner's company for ten years and acknowledged her great debt to Waehner, as well as to Yuriko for the Graham style, Walter Nicks for jazz and Andrej Glegolski for classical ballet. From 1965, the prolific Aline Roux presented her choreographies for group and solo at the Théâtre d'Essai de la Danse (Dinah Maggie), Danse et Culture (Jean Dorcy), the A.R.C. (National Museum of Modern Art), the Scène Française competition, the Spoleto festival and Harmonie de la Danse; in short, she followed the usual itinerary of young choreographers twenty years ago. She, too, made the pilgrimage to America, where she continued her studies at Kansas State University. In 1970 she founded her own company, Rhythme et Structure, created ballets, some of which were awarded prizes (*Volutes* in Cologne, *Psalmos* in Bagnolet), and toured in France and abroad.

Aline Roux's work has sought to reconcile very different aspects of dance: a creative approach with the use of a conventional vocabulary (the vocabulary and style of a kind of modern dance allied to those of jazz); a predilection for subject-matter of a mystical or Christian content and connotation; together with a taste for entertainment, sensual and playful, and a touch of show-biz a disconcerting mixture. She herself claimed that:

> *"my years of teaching and choreographic research produced in me an individual style that emerged from the three types of dance that I regularly performed (classical, modern and jazz)".*

Annick Maucouvert

French, born in Bordeaux in 1938.

Attracted to dance from childhood, Annick Maucouvert, like many young people of her generation, went through the channel of physical education guaranteed to give a certain professional and financial security. She trained initially at the École Normale Supérieure d'Éducation Physique and studied dance with Karin Waehner and Gilberto Motta. She then worked amongst that wave of Latin American dancers referred to above who were in regular contact with Karin Waehner. In 1962, having decided to devote herself entirely to dance, Annick Maucouvert went to America where she continued her studies in New York with Graham, José Limón and Merce Cunningham, and then to Essen where she worked with Kurt Jooss.

On her return to Paris she became active within several settings, including the companies of Gilberto Motta, Yuriko and Graziella Martinez successively. She appeared as a choreographer and independent dancer at the National Museum of Modern Art and the Paris Biennale amongst other venues, and was awarded third prize at the Cologne competition.

Since 1963 Annick Maucouvert has also pursued an important career as a teacher. She became involved in the Jean-Sarrailh Centre project and was appointed contemporary dance teacher at Paris-V. She thus featured amongst the pioneers of dance in universities. She herself maintained:

> *"It is always difficult to look back upon one's past, for, with time, values change. Two periods were very important for me: 1962 in New York, where I was nurtured on modern dance, particularly during my studies with Graham, and to where I regularly returned, as if by compulsion. Then May '68 in Paris, a time that enabled me to bring new ideas to and restructure the teaching of dance within the university, for at that time dance classes amounted merely to a study of technique. I began to increase students' awareness of the value of "workshops" by supporting all my technical classes with a choreographic workshop that emphasized creativity and the art of choreography".*[3]

Annick Maucouvert also taught, always in the Graham tradition, at the Centre International de la Danse alongside visiting teachers from across the Atlantic such as Yuriko. She directed courses in the provinces and abroad. Towards the end of the 1960s Annick Maucouvert worked with painters and sculptors as well as musicians, took part in productions, and made the acquaintance of Richarth Sosa (a former soloist at the Montevideo Opera) with whom she founded a dance company in 1969. Sosa and Maucouvert sought to lead their company towards a way of collaborative work in which each member would play a part in the creation, oriented towards a search for expression rather than formalism. As Lise Brunel wrote at the time concerning *Reportage*, composed in Latin America:

> *"Turning away from abstraction, props and modernism, Annick Maucouvert and Richarth Sosa tend towards a kind of new realism that is sometimes harsh, sometimes lyrical".*

In 1970 they made a long tour of Latin America and in 1974 participated in the founding of the National Ballet of Zaire... The diversity of experiences (which she is still pursuing today in other far-away places) has enriched Annick Maucouvert's pedagogical and artistic work within the university environment, where, in 1980, she established the René-Descartes dance company.

She has also written numerous articles on contemporary dance teaching.

---

[3] Annick Maucouvert, letter to Jacqueline Robinson (1987).

Plate 36 *Quel temps*, choreography by Suzon Holzer. Photo: Pierre Fabris, Paris.

Suzon Holzer

Swiss, born in 1939.

During her youth in Switzerland, Suzon Holzer studied music and also dance in Moutier with Yvonne Morf, to whom she says she owes a great deal and held in high esteem. (Educated at Hellerau-Laxenburg, Morf appears to have been a modest and spirited character, and a teacher beyond compare). Suzon Holzer recalls her emotion as a child on seeing the Sakharoffs dance, and the confirmation of where dance can reach on seeing the Ballets Jooss and Mary Wigman in Macolin (visits organized by Yvonne Morf).

Suzon came to Paris where she undertook professional training in dance and teaching. She studied choreography with John Butler, Dorothy Madden, Lucas Hoving and Carolyn Carlson, and also went on study trips to Germany and New York. She became a member of the Ballets Contemporains de Karin Waehner and took part in Yuriko's first tour in France. She performed at the National Museum of Modern Art, the Cité Universitaire and the American Center. Later she studied choreography with Lucinda Childs, video with Merce Cunningham, scenography with John Davis and 'body meteorology' with Tanaka Min.

From this abundance of sources, Suzon Holzer drew a knowledge that made her own teaching a synthesis:

> *"To place movement in space: and time. In space: working one's body – a basic technique deepened through the visualization of the skeleton and energy lines in order to obtain on an intellectual level a precise and subtle bodily image. Time is rhythm and music. The study of phrasing, attacks and different rhythmic combinations in order to obtain infinitely varied qualities of energy translating by means of their rhythmic and motor precision the states that are specific to the poetics of dance".*[4]

Suzon Holzer's teaching and choreographic career began just at that moment at which our chronicle draws to a close. We should simply note that from 1973, when she composed *Ménage ton manège* for the Ballets Contemporains de Karin Waehner, it was obvious that she would be a prolific choreographer, both for herself and other dancers and companies. She took part in avant-garde demonstrations such as the experimental music festival in Bourges and recently 'Tous en scène'.

She is also known as a specialist in the relationship between music and dance and provided numerous classes and courses on this subject in collaboration with the recently deceased musician Francisco Semprun who, as a composer, was particularly sensitive to movement. Today, in addition

---

[4] Letter to Jacqueline Robinson, 1987.

to her activities as a dancer and choreographer, Suzon Holzer teaches dance, choreographic composition and 'dance and music' in the dance course at the Sorbonne, and regularly runs courses in Switzerland and Belgium. She has lately become a specialist in Matthias Alexander technique.

Her style, in the field of teaching as much as in that of creation, is subtle and refined.

Renate Pook

Of German origin, born in 1942.

She initially studied music and medicine before developing an interest in dance at the Folkwangschule in Essen where she took the full course from 1963 to 1966. She took part in the opera-ballet *The Fairy Queen* (Purcell), one of Kurt Jooss's last important choreographies (in which Pina Bausch danced the leading role). She then spent a year with Lola Rogge in Hamburg working for a teachers' and dancers' diploma, before arriving in Paris in 1968. Naturally Renate Pook met Karin Waehner there and many other contemporary dancers such as Suzon Holzer, Kilina Cremona and Linda Mitchell. These four women formed a group known as 'Ouverture', which performed, toured and attempted to sustain its activities over a certain period.

After gaining experience in the fields of teaching and creation, Renate Pook worked at the Théâtre National de Strasbourg where she taught within the setting of the École d'Art Dramatique which was to become her principal home port. During the years that followed (which exceed the boundaries of this chronicle), Renate Pook established a career primarily as a dancer and choreographer. She appeared with the Rhine Ballet Company, Michel Caserta's company in Vitry, Dominique Bagouet's company in Montpellier and Hideyuki Yano... She also created numerous works, mainly solos for herself, and is today a prolific creator of choreographic projects of an individual as much as of a collective nature.

Renate Pook describes her teachers (whom we have already met in this chronicle) and pays homage to them making them seem immediate and alive.

"Kurt Jooss, first of all, by no means just a technician nor a strict or doctrinaire teacher, but an impassioned and exciting musician in the way that he led us to surrender to the life within the music, within this curve or that leap.

Lucas Hoving: a man of such generosity, and a musician too, human in his demands, yet demanding of the human.

Yuriko, a teacher who remained faithful to the spirit of Martha Graham, whilst everything about her was so Japanese.

> *Rosella Hightower who, at fifty, sits on the floor amongst the pupils in her class introducing Graham technique, putting aside that pride with which some artists are so filled.*
>
> *Gret Palucca: an old yet very young woman with such strength in her apparent frailty.*
>
> *Rosalia Chladek: a great, indeed very great lady, not at all frail, of such perseverance in her research into the functioning of movement and an 'analytical' mind of such calibre that she was difficult to accept since she was so demanding, a character who was, wrongly, all too little known in France.*
>
> *Pina Bausch, who I was able to watch secretly when I was a little pupil at the Folkwangschule and who represented for me the personification of the soul. Her progression towards a kind of choreography that lay completely off the beaten track did not surprise me in the least".*

Renate Pook declares further:

> *"the essential, such as the real influences, confrontations and most intimate events in our lives, is hidden between the lines. But of these things we speak all the more clearly within our works which often exist only in the memory of those few people who saw them and in our own memory – an endless process of "becoming" in which no moment is the same as the next and passes unnoticed like time itself"*[5]

Poumi Lescaut

Born in 1945.

She was attracted to dance from her early childhood in Brussels. She began her first "serious" studies at Rosella Hightower's school in Cannes, then, returning to Brussels, she danced with the Ballet du XXᵉ Siècle during the 1965–66 season. In 1967 Poumi Lescaut arrived in Paris and worked in various different disciplines: theatre, music, graphic arts. She met Katherine Henry d'Epinoy with whom she worked and danced for several years, notably at the Châteauvallon festival in 1972.

She then created her own company. Her early choreographies (at the Sigma in Bordeaux and the Opéra Comique) were, she says, anguished, like an exorcism. It was then that she embarked upon a spiritual quest, making several journeys to the East and spending much time in India where she was initiated into yoga. Returning to Paris, she changed her path and pursues creative work (sacred dance) and teaching (a synthesis of the different techniques she had studied) that aim to discover the *"cosmic conscience of being"*.

---

[5] Letter to Jacqueline Robinson, 1987.

Anne-Marie Reynaud

French, born in 1945.

She studied philosophy and gymnastics in St-Etienne. In 1966 Anne-Marie Reynaud went to Paris and studied at the Popard school *"in order to gain rapid entry to the profession"*. She worked there with Régine Drengwicz and discovered contemporary dance. She soon began to teach at the Maison pour Tous on the rue Mouffetard, that melting-pot of young artists in whose company she began to widen her interest in the other arts, a fertile collaboration that was to influence the future direction of her career.

Anne-Marie discovered the Graham technique and style and went to London to further her study at the London School of Contemporary Dance, where she met Carolyn Carlson. Returning to Paris in 1974, she became a member of the Groupe de Recherches Théâtrales at the Paris Opéra where she took part in seven productions. In 1976 she created Le Four Solaire with Odile Azagury, a group based around the multidisciplinary aspects of dance. From that time on, Anne-Marie Reynaud's activities went from strength to strength: she created performances within various structures; initiated cultural demonstrations; made films; and established roots in Nevers in Burgundy. All this is well known today. She is one of the most enterprising choreographers of her generation.

THE SCHOLARS

Michèle Nadal

French, born in Saigon in 1928.

A dancer, actress and "researcher", she was an eclectic artist who first studied classical dance with Pierre Conté and Nora Kiss, and subsequently modern dance with Kurt Jooss. In 1950 she danced in Léonide Massine's company, appeared as a soloist with the Ballets Jooss in 1952–1953, and became a member of the Ballets Modernes de Paris in 1956. She also worked in Italy for Aurel Miloss, already a well known choreographer in Berlin before the war.

Michèle Nadal developed an interest in the notation of movement; obviously in a position to have acquired a thorough knowledge of Pierre Conté's system, she also studied Labanotation with Albrecht Knust in Essen. During the 1960s she formed her own company and gave performances which had a slightly didactic flavour, indicated by their titles: "From folklore to ballet", "From sacred dance to jazz", "The development of steps in French dance", "Modern rhythms – Aspects of

contemporary dance". She collaborated with Pierre Conté on his choreographies as well as in the vitally important work in the definition, use
and dissemination of his method of notating movement.

She was, moreover, a writer, and published reports and articles
on various subjects in the specialized periodicals of the time. As an actress, Michèle Nadal appeared with the Grenier-Hussenot company, the
Branquignols, and at the Comédie de St-Etienne with Jean Dasté. In 1960
she created the role of Chen-Té Choui Ta in *The Good Person of Szechwan*
at the Théâtre National Populaire. She featured in films (Renoir's *French
Cancan* amongst others), and produced didactic films with Pierre Conté.

In 1969 she was appointed as a teacher at the National Conservatoire of Dramatic Art in Paris. Today, she gives lessons and courses in the
notation of movement and in social dancing within the framework of
various organizations and is currently engaged in work of a methodological and pedagogical nature. She is, in a way, a historian of dance, but not
simply in a theoretical sense, for she has experimented with and experienced different styles of dance, including classical, of course, but also
European modern dance according to Jooss and Miloss. She appeared in
the television production of *Marie Curie* in the Loie Fuller style, and also
French folklore, music-hall and dance scenes in classic theatrical works.
Indeed, she has always shown remarkable openness and curiosity towards
different aspects of dance which she passes on to those who work with her.

We must briefly consider Pierre Conté (1891–1971) in this context.
His work was also of a multiple nature and in this respect Michèle Nadal
mirrored the concerns of her teacher. The film producer Jean Painlevé
wrote of him:

> "*A genius of threefold allegiance, gestural, musical and scientific, Pierre Conté
> demonstrated, as never before, the closeness and universality of the bonds uniting
> Sound and Gesture, Music and Dance. His system of notating movement is the
> logical, straightforward and obvious consequence of this unity of views which has
> always been lacking from the disciplines and Art of Movement. This synthetic
> view places the French system amongst the rank of great discoveries*".[6]

Pierre Conté was in fact a choreographer, composer (occasionally writing
the music for his own ballets), teacher and theorist. He invented the
'French system of notating movement', and his work began to be known
during the 1930s; it was not until 1952, however, that *La Danse et ses
lois* (published by *Arts et mouvement*, a review for which he was also
responsible) appeared. This work, of a philosophical and somewhat
doctrinaire nature, deals with the fundamental physical and structural
relationships between dance and music. He also published *Technique*

---

[6] Pierre Conté, *La Danse et ses lois*, preface (Art et mouvement, 1952).

générale du mouvement and worked with an ethnological choreological approach on French cultural heritage, including folk dances, court dances and nineteenth-century social dances. Similarly, he made a collection of French traditional music and wrote a number of works in this field, of which *Danses anciennes de cour et de théâtre en France* was one.

Pierre Conté was also concerned with the problems of physical education and sport, the role of movement in education, and popular education.

Francine Lancelot

[I owe some of my greatest joys to Francine Lancelot, not simply those of an enchanted observer, my eyes, ears, heart and mind revelling in her creation and recreation of dances of the past, but those of a simple human being dancing as her forefathers used to do.

She took me by the hand, as she did so many others, and led me through the time-honoured yet ever new repository of traditional songs and dances. From Brittany, Auvergne, Provence, the Balkans, so many worlds in which to discover our primitive roots, and to which Francine had such easy access, and with such veracity that her whole body seemed to take on a new appearance. She sang and danced, and through her all the freshness of the world seemed to communicate itself to us, her enraptured companions.

She also initiated me to the subtle universe of baroque dance, an experience I will never forget for it was both personal and intimate, and yet overflowing with the richness of a tradition susceptible of metamorphoses.

Francine personified all of this with astonishing intuition and precision. The various twists and turns of her exceptionally rich career seem to have been necessary stages in her development towards her present position, rooted in the earth and yet moving within the complex and ambiguous refinements of court dance with equal success.]

French, born in 1929.

Francine Lancelot was born in Montpellier into a rather strict university environment. She spent her early childhood there and took piano lessons. During the war life was very quiet; then, in 1944, the family moved to Paris. Francine continued her education there and studied dance with Malkowski and Madika and also learnt classical dance. At the age of eighteen she decided, against her parents wishes, to become a dancer, and she left her family home and security. These were difficult years for her during which a combination of circumstances led her to Berlin where, in 1955, she worked with Mary Wigman and Tatiana Gsovsky. On her return to Paris in 1957 Francine Lancelot went to study with Françoise and Dominique and joined the Ballets Modernes de Paris with which she took part in several performances. It was there that she met Michèle Nadal. During this same period her quest for knowledge led her to study dramatic art, mime and acrobatics.

In 1959 she worked as a dancer at the Atelier theatre and took part in Mayakovsky's *The Bedbug*. She met Pierre Conté and Michèle Nadal again there, learnt Conté's method of notating dance, discovering with enthusiasm the principles of movement notation. In the ensuing years, Francine Lancelot belonged to Jean Dasté's troop at the Comédie de St-Etienne (following her experience at the Atelier where she, Nadal, Conté and the company were engaged for *Le Bourgeois gentilhomme*). Dancer, choreographer, actress and singer in turn, she acquired there a degree of professionalism in many subjects. She took part in the celebrated production of Brecht's *Caucasian Chalk Circle* amongst others, and created a children's show entitled *Les Musiques magiques*.

It was in St-Etienne that Francine discovered and was totally entranced by traditional dance, revealed to her by a Yugoslavian group from Sarajevo. Nevertheless, in 1962, she returned to Paris and, as impassioned as ever, embarked upon a period of intense activity:

- she danced and created choreographies for various events and institutions, including dramatic centres, exhibitions and the Paris Biennale in 1965;
- she became involved in the contemporary music research group directed by François Bayle and Bernard Parmeggiani;
- she founded the company Choreia 3 with Claudie Jacquelin and Christiane de Rougemont;
- she gave lessons in various locations within educational organizations;
- she continued to study Dunham technique with Christiane de Rougemont, Indian dance and yoga with Malavika;
- and in 1964 she was assigned to a research post at the Museum of Folk Arts and Traditions. She made a collection of traditional dances of France for the C.N.R.S.,* and worked with the dance ethnologist Jean-Michel Guilcher.

In 1969 she obtained a master's degree at the École Pratique des Hautes Études on Feuillet's (1675–1730) choreographic notation, and in 1973 she received a Ph.D. for a thesis on "The Farandole and its Societies".

---

*Centre National de Recherches Scientifiques.

The years from 1967 to 1977 were thus predominantly devoted to research, principally into the history of French dance from the fifteenth to the eighteenth centuries, including village, town, court and theatre dances, and the relationships between these dances and their evolution. Francine Lancelot may add to her many identities (dancer, actress, choreographer) that of choreologist. She is not simply a bookworm or scholar; she is a dancer, creator and teacher. As an actress, she certainly knew how to get inside her characters and those societies of olden times. As a result, she was able to teach and transmit to others what she had herself discovered with such passion, as much in the field of traditional (folk) dances as of court dances and the beginnings of classical dance.

This remarkable heritage was thus brought to the attention of a whole section of the dance community, who were now able to rediscover the feeling and meaning of deeply rooted dance, as well as enter the world of the baroque. Francine Lancelot taught within various frameworks such as schools and associations, some particularly prestigious: the Paris Opéra school; the Rencontres Internationales de Danse Contemporaine; the Institut de Musique et de Danse Anciennes; the Centre International de Recherches Musicales et d'Animation Régionale in Saintes; the Sorbonne and Paris-IV. Viviane Serry, François Raffinot and Christine Bayle were amongst her first pupils to become specialists.

It was certainly no coincidence that this (re)discovery of a choreographic heritage by diverse specialists should have occurred more or less simultaneously with that (although perhaps a fraction earlier in the latter case) of early music by a number of musicians in both Europe and America and by a wide audience. The baroque became fashionable. But is there not an apparent need here for a return to roots? Not to ideal, universal and inexpressible sources (as had occurred in the field of dance several decades previously), but to a particular moment, a great moment in the history of Western civilization in France.

The curtain falls on our chronicle precisely at the moment when Francine Lancelot enters the third period of her career (*"balanced between the university and the stage"*, as she describes it), a period that is so rich, perhaps subject to the unexpected, but nevertheless exemplary. We must recall the creation of the company "Ris et Danceries" directed by herself and François Raffinot, and her superb choreographies for the Paris Opéra, Rudolf Nureyev, Wilfride Piollet and Jean Guizerix, for *Atys* and other works by Lully. Furthermore, her vast production of research, articles, books and data of all kinds concerning baroque dance has undoubtedly made her "the" authority in this field.

Muriel Jaër

French, born in London in 1930.

Muriel Jaër was born into a remarkable family: her grandfather, Fritz Blumen, was a pupil of Liszt; her grandmother, Jeanne Bucher, owned a famous art gallery and promoted contemporary art; her father, André Cournand, was awarded the Nobel prize for medicine; and her aunt, Eva Daniel, was an actress in Pitoeff's company. She thus grew up in the most favourable of environments for the encouragement of her own artistic talents.

Muriel received her first intensive training in classical dance in New York. Then, after settling in Paris, she began to call this early training into question and seek in other artistic and scientific disciplines the physical and spiritual laws governing movement. She wrote:

> *"... by concentrating on the transformation of my instrument, developing a skeletal frame that breathes, and making the muscles servants rather than masters, in the belief that technique should not be an end but a means of expressing feelings, I gradually came to reject what I had learnt".*

Nevertheless, Muriel Jaër studied contemporary and Oriental dance with Elle Foster, Djemil Anik, Jerome Andrews and Princess Jodjana, drawing from each what would contribute to the synthesis for which she was searching; she was influenced by other artists and thinkers from both East and West. Sri Aurobindo, with whom she went to "seek" in Pondicherry, was one of these. This fundamental research led Muriel Jaër to pursue her work in different directions: artistic/creation and teaching. In all of these she aimed to find Resonance, the name she gave to her dance group and method.

Muriel Jaër began to attract attention as a dancer/choreographer at the beginning of the 1960s. She performed alone mostly, but occasionally with her group, and always in collaboration with Eastern or Western musicians and artists from different disciplines and traditions. Since 1965 she has presented programmes of dance, music, poetry and projected illustrations in France, India and various European countries. She has also appeared in several television broadcasts, be they about music, the East and psychology as well as dance, and collaborated in festivals of contemporary and Oriental music. All this is evidence of her great eclecticism and the fact that she appears to have discovered what is common to human and spiritual essence through apparently very different forms of art and expression.

[The first time I saw her, in a piece to music by Varèse, I was struck by the formal intelligence and absolute musicality of her dance; sober, serious and lyrical. I had never seen anyone like her before.]

Muriel Jaër was also highly successful as a teacher of expression therapy within various frameworks, in particular the St Anne psychiatric hospital. She directed a number of courses in France and abroad. But it is in her studio above all that even now she continues to refine her understanding of what she describes as *"the fundamental laws of movement"*, and to militate in favour of her ever new findings. Her endless questioning has led her to constantly push forward in her pursuit of the essential. She is currently researching, and transmitting, a knowledge of respiration that is as subtle as it is fundamental: the respiration of the bones.

Should Muriel Jaër be regarded as a "mystic" of dance? Her work is certainly imbued with spirituality, Eastern rather than Western, but it is by no means vague. This quest and concern to convey the essential has not prevented her from realizing her own potential as an artist-creator and giving the audience through her stage performances something similar to that which she offers her pupils.

She once wrote:

"How important it is to learn to relax and breathe deeply concentrating our efforts on the elimination of all trace of the 'self' and of personal habits, thought, desire and will. Stillness reveals the secret of the dynamism involved in effort and the liberation of spontaneity. The source liberates the reality of the innermost depths of the soul, made manifest through movements born of absolute necessity. When the whole being surrenders itself in this way, body, heart and mind experience the rapture of unconditional abandonment. Dance thus fulfils its sacred mission and transmits its spiritual message, radiating a pure resonance of beauty, light and peace that reverberates within ourselves and throughout the world".

Claude Pujade-Renaud

French, born in 1932.

Following her initiation to classical dance, Claude Pujade-Renaud worked with Janine Solane and took part in the company's performances, whilst training to become a physical education teacher and taking a degree in philosophy. She discovered modern dance with Karin Waehner in 1957 and attended her classes. She went on to work with several teachers in Paris, including Laura Sheleen, Sara Pardo, René Deshauteurs (jazz) and Susan Buirge at the Atelier de la Danse. She also attended summer schools, in 1965 at Connecticut College, with José Limón and Betty Jones, Martha Graham in New York, and subsequently in Cologne and at the London School of Contemporary Dance. Along with dance, she also studied mime for a number of years with Etienne Decroux and later with Pinok and Matho.

Since 1959 Claude Pujade-Renaud has sought to introduce modern dance into the framework of physical education and the training of physical education and sports teachers; she was put in charge of the teaching of dance and psychopedagogy at the I.R.E.P. in Paris. Throughout these years of study and discovery, she also worked as a choreographer, and her *Passages* at the Théâtre d'Essai de la Danse in 1968 left the memory of a work of discrete intensity and elegant choreographic writing. Indeed, she came increasingly to base her teaching on composition and creation and also studied parallel disciplines, such as relaxation.

In 1970 Claude Pujade-Renaud resumed her university studies and graduated in 1974 with a thesis entitled "Narcissism and Communication in the Teaching of Dance". Together with Daniel Zimmermann, at the University of Vincennes she directed a course on "dance and karate" and, in 1981, again with Zimmermann, she obtained a Ph.D. for a thesis on non-verbal communication in schools and in dance. Claude Pujade-Renaud currently teaches the science of education at the University of Paris-VIII and pursues a literary career as a novelist.

Her didactic works are the fruits of the rich and varied practical experience of a dancer/choreographer nourished at many sources, as well as of the penetrating views of a teacher, views that affect numerous disciplines relating to dance (psychoanalysis, sociology, linguistics). She has published *Expression corporelle, langage du silence* (E.S.F., 1974), *Danse et narcissisme en éducation* (E.S.F., 1976), *Le Corps de l'enseignant dans la classe* (E.S.F., 1983), *Le Corps de l'élève dans la classe* (E.S.F., 1983) and *L'École dans la littérature* (E.S.F., 1986), works of a didactic nature.

The following paragraph is an extract from *Expression corporelle, langage du silence* which seems to me to summarize all the fantasies, claims, expressions, practices and trends of both that period and this.

> "... *Myths of the body. In order to answer once and for all this question of the body's alibi, may we recapitulate the various ideologies transmitted through bodily expression and parallel techniques?*
> ... *The body as a substitute for a lost nature*
> *A substitute for religion*
> *An archaic, primitive body*
> *A child's body, spontaneous, happy and innocent*
> *An instant body. Drained of its past history*
> *A smooth body, devoid of all opacity*
> *An authentic body, revealing the truth of the matter*
> *A liberated body. Liberator. Deviant. Revolutionary.*
> *An antidote to the word? A universal and democratic language*
> *An immediate body? A tangible, unquestionable reality.*
> *The body as a means of healing.*"[7]

---

[7] Claude Pujade-Renaud, *Expression corporelle, langage du silence* (E.S.F., 1975), p. 119.

Jacqueline Challet-Haas

French, born in 1934.

Attracted to dance from her childhood, Jacqueline Haas was unable to devote herself to it fully until she was a student preparing a degree in philosophy and German and studying at the School of Oriental Languages. She then began training in classical dance with Alexandra Balachova, and subsequently with Atty Chadinoff, herself a pupil of Olga Preobrajenska and a wonderful teacher whose teaching (which I have myself experienced personally and held in great esteem) was both extremely penetrating and most far-reaching. Jacqueline Haas describes this teaching from a technical point of view:

> *"For many years Atty Chadinoff has been concerned with working on the basic placement of the dancer in order to enable him to acquire, through a series of floor exercises inspired by yoga postures, a solid and balanced technique; and she has achieved this without ever losing the smallest particle of that poetic impetus she possesses so instinctively and which she is able to communicate so intuitively".*[8]

Jacqueline also studied with Preobrajenska and Lubov Egorova, discovering through them the purest and most refined form of classical dance.

In 1956 Jacqueline Haas became a student at the recently founded École Supérieure d'Études Chorégraphiques. There she was introduced to Kinetography Laban through the teaching of Dinah Maggie and developed a deep interest in the subject. In 1957 she saw José Limón perform and this revealed to her a whole new world of dance. Two events then occurred that were to influence the rest of her career: in 1958 the first lessons in Kinetography Laban (given by Diana Baddeley) took place at the school and Jacqueline Haas was to be the first and most enthusiastic student of this method. Then, in 1960 and 1961 she went to the Folkwangschule in Essen, with the desire of turning towards roots, as it were, studying dance with Kurt Jooss and notation with Albrecht Knust, who had been Laban's closest collaborator, particularly in the field of notation.

On her return to Paris, Jacqueline Haas became involved in multifarious activities. She never abandoned classical dance, which she went on to teach with both strictness and generosity. She studied modern dance with Laura Sheleen in whose group she danced in 1963. She also took part in the activities and work of several modern dance groups, in particular at the Atelier de la Danse. But above all she sought to introduce Kinetography into the consciousness of French choreographers. She

---

[8] Jacqueline Challet-Haas, *La Danse – son enseignement aux enfants* (Amphore, 1983), p. 11.

became a teacher at the E.S.E.C. (Ecole Superieure d'Etudes choré-graphiques) where she taught the theory and practice of various subjects, including psychopedagogy, the pedagogy of classical and modern dance, analysis of the principles of dance and Kinetography Laban, which she was later to teach at the University of Paris-IV. She taught classical dance for several years as Atty Chadinoff's assistant and then opened her own school in the Paris region.

Over the years Jacqueline Haas has come to be regarded not only as a specialist but as an authority in the field of Kinetography Laban or Labanotation as it is called in certain parts of the world. (It is important to remember that Laban's system of notation is not only an extremely logical, lucid, exhaustive and reliable code for the transcription of movement, but that it implies and rests upon a subtle analysis of every component of movement and thus constitutes a fruitful discipline in itself, whatever the style of dance).

As an expert member and subsequently vice-chairman of the International Council of Kinetography Laban (I.C.K.L.), Jacqueline (now 'Challet-Haas') was led to carry out and apply her research on an international scale. It is research that, by the very nature of Kinetography Laban, encompasses a wide field, for the range of the systematic proposals embodied in Laban's method is such that it makes for a development of the conceptualization and practice of movement involving subjects as diverse as pedagogy, therapy, aesthetics and the preserving of works.

Jacqueline Challet-Haas still pursues her work as a dance teacher along with that in the dissemination, application and teaching of Labanotation, which she pursues at the Conservatoire National Supérieur de Paris. She is currently president of the Centre National d'Écriture du Mouvement (C.N.E.M.). (We should not forget that several other systems of notating movement, including those of Conté and Benesch, exist in addition to that of Laban). She is a woman of great integrity and sensitivity, a philosopher as much as an artist, who has written a number of works of a didactic nature which are well on their way to becoming classics. These include *Manuel pratique de danse classique* (Amphora, 1979), *La Danse, les principes de son enseignement aux enfants* (Amphora, 1983), *Manuel élémentaire de cinétographie Laban* (E.S.E.C./C.N.E.M., 1962/1981), and *Manuel complémentaire de cinétographie Laban* (C.N.E.M., 1975/1985) as well as numerous articles and courses on the principles of dance and psychopedagogy. She has also translated Laban's *The Mastery of Movement* into French.

She trained many movement notators and, of course, notated extracts from classical, modern and traditional dances herself; she has also collaborated on various projects with other researchers.

Jacqueline Challet-Haas expresses bitter regret today that notation was not used more frequently or more readily in the 1950s and 60s, and even the 1970s. Had this been otherwise, many works of the best French choreographers might have been preserved for posterity. (The practice of notating scores of dance works was used much more widely in England and the United States). Today the problem is resolved in part by the use of video, but this proves inadequate. In order to recreate a work, the ideal is an association between image and score.

Very few dances from thirty years ago survive today. They remain a hazy recollection in the memories of a few people. At the time, Jacqueline Challet-Haas, anxious to preserve our work, begged some of us choreographers to let it be notated. We were either not sufficiently concerned or too busy preparing for the immediate future; we never found time to do so. Perhaps we were also so unsure of the value of our work that we dared not imagine that it was worth the trouble of preserving at the cost of such hard work (setting up a camera is easier, practically and morally). Would it be Utopian to dream that one day dancers will be able to read the score of a dance in the way a musician reads a musical score, and thus acquire precision, clarity, objectivity and culture, and finally save time in his training?

Mireille Arguel

French, born in 1936.

Mireille Arguel is a fighter, who has had to contend on more than one occasion during her career with the inertia or hostility of individuals and institutions with regard to modern dance. She is, moreover, an indefatigable researcher. She began her career by training as a primary school teacher at the École Normale in Le Bourget and at Les Batignolles where, in 1955–1956, she carried out experiments in rhythm and movement in nursery schools. She then entered the École Normale Supérieure d'Éducation Physique where she practised classical and rhythmic dance and also took lessons with Malkowski.

In 1958, at the instigation of Mireille Fromantel, who taught dance at the same school, she worked with Karin Waehner. Waehner revealed to her a whole new conception of dance, that of Mary Wigman. From that time on, Mireille Arguel sought throughout her entire institutional career to *'reconcile technique and creation through the teaching of this activity (dance), and all my work – technical, didactic and scientific, became determined by my concern for the renovation firstly of a form of teaching movement that had all too long been confused with technical training, and secondly of a practice of dance that had all too often been designated a priori individualist, even narcissistic. In this way I issued a series of challenges that penetrated to the very heart of the institution of physical education and sport'.*[9]

During these crucial years at the turn of the decade (1950–1960) in which modern dance was beginning to take root in France, Mireille Arguel also perceived dance through the eyes of a dancer. She worked within the École Normale Supérieure d'Éducation Physique where a deeper level of thought concerning bodily expressivity and dance was beginning to develop under the impetus of Mireille Fromantel and Monique Bertrand (Pinok). She also joined the Ballets Contemporains de Karin Waehner, whose assistant she soon became, taking part during several seasons in the creations, performances and tours of the company. Within this new organization, she became aware of other views and styles of dance and other techniques including 'primitive' dance, José Limón's technique, and jazz with Fred Traguth. She was then invited to work with Kurt Jooss in Essen, where she discovered Martha Graham's technique with Yuriko, and a different style of jazz with Luigi.

Amongst the dancers who formed part of the Ballets Contemporains at this time (1960–1964), Ingeborg Liptay, Fritz Ludin, Patrizia Fabri and Aline Roux all pursued stage careers, and Mireille Arguel was the only one who chose to remain within an institutional setting and promote the development of a new form of movement within the field of physical education in an attempt to establish dance. She thus continued to work within the domain of national education and over the years devoted herself to a series of activities that were all directed to this end: fieldwork, technical, practical and theoretical approaches, and studies of a sociological and aesthetic nature. The following chronology highlights some of the landmarks in her career:

> –1964–1974: teacher of physical education. It was this period that saw the birth of the Jean-Sarrailh Centre. We should recall that at this time Mireille Arguel also directed the Atelier Chorégraphique Universitaire de Paris, which won prizes at the Bagnolet competition in 1971, 1972 and 1973;
> –1973–1976: these years saw her fight to introduce contemporary dance as a subject into the University of Paris-III, along with all the events already described. In spite of the convincing results of her earlier endeavours, the scheme to create a course and university diploma in the teaching of contemporary dance failed, confronted not only with a certain degree of hostility, but also with

---

[9] Mireille Arguel, communication to Jacqueline Robinson.

administrative unwieldiness. Nevertheless, Mireille Arguel pursued her research activities in the field; she collaborated in the development of a multidisciplinary course entitled 'Sciences of expression and communication' at Paris-III, which united the arts of movement and music, and continued her technical and pedagogical work at the École Normale Supérieure d'Éducation Physique;

– in more recent years, Mireille Arguel has extended her research and responsibilities; within a course at Paris-III entitled 'Dance and sociology of understanding' she could provide a practical training there once again. She took charge of the Équipe de Recherche et d'Action Culturelle (E.R.A.C. dance) at the Centre Régional de Documentation Pédagogique within the Paris Academy and collaborated with a team from the C.N.R.S. at the Centre D'Études Transdisciplinaires (sociology, anthropology and semiology), taking part in the seminars led by Edgar Morin. She also began work on a Ph. D., and is active in all areas where dance, the quality of the art and its practice, its teaching and the views supporting it, needed to be upheld.

Over and above her numerous articles and communications concerning one aspect or another of this vast subject, Mireille Arguel published *Danse et enseignement. Quel corps?* (Vigot, 1980), and with other authors *Le Corps en jeu* (PUF, 1992).

Alberte Raynaud

French, born in 1938.

As a result of her childhood in Algeria, Alberte Raynaud kept a feeling for matter, light and shapes, and a specific visual and tactile sensitivity. Her unusual path prompts us to trace the various stages that led her to become a sculptor, scene-painter, choreographer and film producer. She states:

> *"I began sculpture when I was thirteen years of age, dance when I was eighteen, filming at thirty, and obtained my doctorate when I was forty-six!"*

She discovered sculpture whilst still in Algeria, and came to France in 1961 where she met Karin Waehner:

> *"this experience revealed to me that dance is a form of sculpture; like sculpture, it too consists of love, voluptuousness, pleasure and joy; it is space, the body in space, like a shape in space; and the rhythm of the shape in the rhythm of the*

body – but the body moves and breathes, it speaks and desires; it is a living miracle".[10]

Although she studied different techniques of dance, she says she feels closest to the Wigman line. She produced sets for several modern dance companies, including those of Karin Waehner, Annick Maucouvert and Teresa Trujillo, and, as stage-manager for Graziella Martinez, she became familiar with lighting techniques. The décor she conceived already established a position/possession/dialogue in relation to space, and gradually she moved towards choreography, thinking in terms of shapes and full and empty spaces. In 1968 she formed her own company, Danse et Sculpture, thus confirming a particular dimension of her conception of choreography, the metamorphosis and manipulation of space. She created several works, including *Noirs et blancs*, that were performed at the Théâtre d'Essai de la Danse in 1968.

She experimented in *Signal* with an electronic sculpture that reacted to the proximity of the dancers, and in 1971 she created *Trilogie*, to music by Maurice Ohana, which involved a semi-circular screen with slide projections and all the technical procedures that this implied, fully integrated into the choreography. The next step in the use of film in dance came in *Amour(s)* which modified both the observer's and the dancer's perception of space. Conceived as a sculpture around which the spectator moves, it reveals the interplay between the multiple presence of the dancer on stage and on the three screens, and creates the sense of *circular space* that was to become one of Alberte Raynaud's constant preoccupations. And so on until she arrived at 'cine-dance', which incorporated the camera into the movement and the choreographic text: the camera-man also dances in intimate dialogue with the dancer.

Anne-Marie Duguet wrote in *Vidéo, la mémoire au poing*:

"Making the camera dance does not mean dancing with the camera, or for, around or in front of it. It means making it dance directly itself. This experience of video-dance is an extremely unusual transitive. 'Making the camera dance' signifies that it aims to prolong the movement of the dancer, embody its suppleness, its breadth and rhythm. It forms an intense presence; far from disturbing the proceedings, the video equipment is in full view and is essential in conveying the body dynamics. The rigid frame of the screen throws the flexibility and fluidity of the shapes into relief. The observer's gaze shifts constantly between the dancer and the image, the electronic equipment and the expression of the group. As a result of the constant movement back and forth a confrontation is created not between the detailed and the general, or between different points of view, but between a subjective approach that seeks to relate the inner space of dance to an external, frontal and fixed position".

---

[10] Alberte Raynaud, 'Le Corps polyphonique' (doctoral thesis, 1984), p. 674.

This particular approach to dance and choreography was to lead Alberte Raynaud to question its logic from a symbolic and psychoanalytical perspective (the mirror, the double, sex, the breaking up of meaning). It is the sum total of this consideration that forms the basis of her doctoral thesis "Le Corps polyphonique", submitted in 1984. *"I choreograph like a sculptor, I make words dance, I sculpt and make images move, whilst the sculpture curves to hold bodies, becomes mobile so as to join with the rhythm of the dancer and finally provide a space for the cinematographic frame."*

Pinok and Matho

(Monique Bertrand and Mathilde Dumont.)

"Here are two pearls who constantly turn into monsters... Two rare and strange human puppets" (*El Dia*, Santa Cruz de Tenerife).

Pinok and Matho have seemed inseparable for so many years that one might almost forget that these two women come from completely different backgrounds. They are not dancers, and yet! Neither are they mimes in the traditional sense of the word. They might be as directly related to clowns as to Shakespearean tragedian actors or actors of Noh movement theatre. They are nevertheless very close to us dancers, all the more since they shared in our struggle.

Pinok and Matho describe their careers in the following way:

"Matho and I were both primary school teachers before embarking on a training in physical education, and choosing to pursue this route (myself in order to go to Paris to study mime, and Matho because she had reached an advanced level). At the age of seventeen, Pinok was already fascinated by Jean-Louis Barrault in 'Les Enfants du Paradis', and by gypsy dance. She was initiated into the world of the theatre and dance by two teachers at teachers' training college. Her experience of theatre and improvisation dates back to her primary school days, however, with a teacher from the Freinet school who had a background in the scout movement. On her admission to the École Normale Supérieure in Paris, she worked with Antonetti and Lombardin at E.P.J.D. for two years and then with Etienne Decroux in her third year. Appointed as a teacher in the provinces, she waited five years for an opportunity to return to Paris where, in 1955, she resumed her studies in mime with Decroux. Her basic training in dance did not begin until 1950 at the École Normale Supérieure with Mireille Fromantel who encouraged her to study modern dance and the current styles of European dance (Wigman-Jooss).

Pinok was appointed as a dance teacher at the École Normale Supérieure in 1958 and continued to work with Karin Waehner and Etienne Decroux. Her collaboration with Mireille Fromantel led her to introduce expressive elements that had rarely been used in dance before, and to become involved in the problem of creation. She worked constantly with the musician Francisco Semprun, whose qualities as an improviser and composer provided an invaluable aid to this type of work".

She met Matho in 1960.

> *"Matho's love of acting and the imaginary has always been such that from an early age she created plays ... for her dolls, her companions at the teachers' training college in Lyons, and the children and young people entrusted to her care as a primary school teacher and as a drama teacher at the C.E.M.E.A. It was therefore quite natural and obvious that she should reconcile her taste for theatre and theatrical writing with her aptitude for sport by working with Pinok in the field of expressive movement and elaborating a form of movement theatre.*
>
> *The first mime pieces were composed in 1962. At the same time Matho continued to perfect her technique with Decroux, and gave her first professional performance at the Kaleidoscope in 1964. Since then, Pinok and Matho have played a part in establishing the unifying concept of "bodily expression" – a term already used by Jacques Copeau but one that they launched into the teaching world well before 1968 – in 1965 to be precise – through their school, the T.E.M.P. (Théâtre-École Mouvement et Pensée). This term subsequently became widely used after 1968 in any kind of context. Until 1977 Pinok and Matho continued to teach in state education as well as in their own school and to develop their careers in mime. Then they abandoned physical education and devoted themselves entirely to performance, touring and their school."*[11]

The dynamism and creative energy of these two women has produced an impressive quantity of works of various genres including performances of mime of course, but also books, films, stage productions and records (with Francisco Semprun and Michel Christodoulides). They performed in the theatre, cabaret, on television and abroad, from Canada to the Congo. The range of students they taught was similarly diverse and encompassed actors, sportsmen and university students. They also produced books, films and videos as aids to their teaching. The titles of their books include *Expression corporelle. Mouvement et pensée, Expression corporelle à l'école, Dynamique de la création. Le Mot et l'expression corporelle* and *Écrits sur pantomime, mime et expression corporelle.*

The following extract is taken from *Dynamique de la création:*

> *"He who creates oscillates permanently between two modes of existence: "inside" his body or "outside" it. Inside his body when it "becomes" his body, animated by gestures of emotion or ideas: an inhabited, pervaded, involved body, a receiver–transmitter body, a deeply touched body, an emotionally moved body. Outside his body when he observes or remembers. Inside his body when he attempts to reproduce sequences he invented earlier by breathing new life into them – the living expression of first improvisations quickly cools down and always seems difficult to recapture; it is surprising how dull a sequence that appeared at first worthwhile, unique and inspired may seem a few days later; outside his body again when he casts a critical eye over what may be preserved and what ought to be changed, making corrections in the mirror.*

---

[11] Pinok and Matho, letter to Jacqueline Robinson (1987).

Plate 37 Pinok and Matho, *Présence d'Hiroshima*, 1969. Photo: Francette Levieux.

> *In this way all creation proceeds towards maturation by means of an oscillation between 'impulsive action' and 'reflexive action' and as a result constitutes an act of liberation. 'Conscious, deliberate, controlled, modulated expression', brought to the precise point at which it has meaning for me at the same time as becoming clear to others".*[12]

Pinok and Matho's particular contribution, their charm, one might say, lies in the fact that they are artists as well as thinkers, humanists, capable of writing works in which they set forth their doctrines, methodological hypotheses and the results of their theatrical and pedagogical research, and of being, in the words of certain critics:

> *"vigilant, supple and uncompromising, these two emissaries of our innermost life draw us unfailingly into their obscure world"* (P. de Rosbo, *Le Quotidien de Paris*); *'Their art lies entirely in the progression from the manifest to the hidden, in this inversion of signs. Extraordinarily rich in their manifold talents, they project on stage the solitary confrontation of the human being with laughter, fear, his fellow beings, with sleep or death. What is left remains in the uneasy and ever changing images of a dream'* (*Politique-Hebdo*); *"Pinok and Matho, their eyes like stone, sharp gestures, bodies anonymous and tough like two fallen angels recreate a celebration that lies on the edge of the abyss in which the sea dances with monsters disguised as cherubs"* (P. Kyria, *Combat*).

Amongst the younger generation of mimes, we should mention the remarkable Claire Heggen and Yves Marc, descended from Decroux via Pinok and Matho; Ella Jarosewicz, of Polish origin, educated at the Pantomime Theatre in Wroclaw with Henryk Tomaszewski, director of the Magenia company and school; and finally Corinne Soum and Steven Wasson, Decroux's last two assistants, and their company L'Ange Fou.

THE EDUCATORS

I have several times in the course of this chronicle pointed out that certain practitioners of dance have appeared more concerned with work of an educational nature than with stage performance. The persons discussed in this chapter have all given priority to this concern and thus feature amongst those supporters of the belief that dance should serve man.

---

[12] Pinok and Matho, *Dynamique de la création*, p. 15.

Denise Coutier and 'Danse Ma Joie' (D.M.J.)

French, born in 1926.

Denise Coutier holds that the development of her personal career is inseparable from the communal work she has carried out through the association D.M.J., the achievements and influence of which have been remarkable in the thirty years since the formation of that initial nucleus is Strasbourg. Her training and varied experiences have served to nourish a whole range of activities, an ideal, in the service of the community:

> *"a form of pedagogy that is an art".*

Denise Coutier wrote:

> *"Why D.M.J.? Out of a love of dance and creation – an artistic activity, freely chosen, without any professional ambitions, non-profit making, and with different motivations for each individual.*
> *– To promote dance and allow everyone to discover and experience the adventure of dance, each according to his potential and level of ability at the time; in towns and small locations. To contribute to the training of teachers. To develop the spirit of research.*
> *Our teaching: technique employed as a means and not as an end in itself. Research involving personal commitment, authenticity and an integrity of expression through dance. The development of group awareness (communication, the acquisition of a common language). The exploration of the body, the attempt to control and master it with a view to increasing its receptivity – Experiencing music: the importance of silence, interaction with other forms of expression.*
> *Dancing is a state; could it become permanent? Perhaps for some people. Knowing how to be through a specific ability. When thought, desire, motivation and concentration reach a certain level of intensity then anything is possible; if the body has been taught to perceive, feel and control, then it will follow. I believe in intuition, premonition, anticipation, but these things can be worked on ... listen to and assert your own motricity, the knowledge that is yours alone.*
> *Assume confidence – Give confidence – Trust".* [13]

Denise Coutier came to dance initially from sports (discus throwing and basket-ball). She trained as a teacher of physical education and sport and dance, eventually opting for dance, which she used in the various fields in which she studied, practised and experimented: psychiatry, maladjusted children, gerontology, music and movement, and "mother and baby", not to mention all her work in schools and the training of amateurs.

Denise Coutier says she owes much to some encounters, her *"mentors in the field of movement"*: Janine Solane, Rosalia Chladek, Fée

---

[13] Letter to Jacqueline Robinson.

Hellès (the latter two were almost like godmothers to D.M.J.), Malkowski, Gerda Alexander, Jean Serry, Jerome Andrews and Karin Waehner, and, in the field of music: César Geoffray, the great choir leader, and Willy Backeroot, together with the many contacts and discoveries she made during her various trips to Scandinavia, Turkey, India and to Burundi in Africa on a mission of cultural co-operation.

Here follows a brief historical account of D.M.J. In 1953, in Strasbourg, Denise Coutier met Marie-Louise Bilger, an infant school teacher who was equally impassioned by dance. They worked together, organizing classes and weekend courses, and formed a group that took part in the choir festival "A Coeur Joie" in 1954; indeed, César Geoffray encouraged them in their projects. They founded D.M.J., the aims of which are adequately expressed in Denise Coutier's statement quoted above. Danse Ma Joie gradually succeeded in reaching a large number of people of all ages and situations, in many diverse places and an ever widening area, an undertaking that required a high degree of local, departmental and regional co-ordination (nuclei of D.M.J. exist not only in Alsace but in the Paris region also).

Denise Coutier wrote further of Danse Ma Joie:

"An unpretentious yet ambitious association in terms of its aspirations, daring to embark on new ventures and take risks. Our five meetings (from 1961 to 1979) took the form of dance festivals: a large number of dancers (200–400) gathered together in a huge space; dancing with one another; various workshops leading to a 'final evaluation performance'. Our weekends of 'choreographic research': monthly meetings in order to provide an opportunity for working together, possibly with a view to giving a performance; the members do not all belong to the same local groups and travel up to 500 km to attend! Our weekends of 'pedagogical research' held three times a month and directed mainly towards pedagogues, school teachers, cultural leaders and teachers of physical education, sport and dance. Performances produced entirely by children with the help of teachers. Our 'Inter-Age research' (5–80 years old!): requiring a large amount of understanding and sharing for the group to arrive at anything like dance! Production of records, cassettes, data files, pedagogical documents and a book entitled Rencontre avec la danse".

Jean Bouffort

French, born in 1931.

Secondary education in the classics; C.A.P. (Certificat d'aptitude Professionnelle) in cookery! Jean Bouffort had been deeply interested in folk dance from his adolescence. From 1952 he worked simultaneously on modern dance with Geneviève Mallarmé and folk dance with Thérèse

Palau, director of the group La Frairie, with whom he rapidly became a soloist and remained for several years. La Frairie frequently performed in school environments and as a result Jean Bouffort developed a taste for stage work and teaching.

From 1963 to 1969 he danced with the Ballets Modernes de Paris (Dupuy) and took part in the creation of several important works from the repertoire, including *Antigone*, *The Miraculous Mandarin* and *Epithalame*. He met Karin Waehner in 1965 and danced in her company, assuming various scenographical responsibilities and producing his first choreographies there, of which *Histoires à deux* (music by Pierre Henry) was one. At the same time, Jean Bouffort pursued his pedagogical activities for youth movements in schools and developed an interest in maladjusted children. Through his association with Georges Dobbelaere, founder of Animation Jeunesse, he became an active member of this organization supported by Philippe Henry, responsible for matters concerning bodily expression and movement on a national level. Jean Bouffort's interest in this type of teaching gradually began to gain the upper hand and he withdrew from stage work as a soloist. His activities in the field of educational enterprise and the training of specialist teachers led him to organize courses in France and abroad. He never completely abandoned the theatre, however, for, within the setting of these youth organizations, Jean Bouffort staged plays in which movement played an important role. Similarly, he became one of the regular stage directors for the choral society A Coeur Joie (choral productions featuring orchestra, choirs, soloists and background choreography).

Educator, man of the theatre, man of fieldwork, a man with roots; there is an attractive logic in the development of Jean Bouffort's career that led him from the roots of folk dance to become a performer, a creator, a teacher, and, in a way, a therapist. In recent years, he has pursued his experiences in the field of expression through the body, voice and theatre, and creativity in general, in a medical context.

Françoise Chantraine

French, born in 1937.

Born into a family in which the arts flourished, Françoise Chantraine was educated in both dance and music from an early age. She studied piano, violin and harmony at the École Normale de Musique in Paris, whilst her studies of dance encompassed classical and rhythmic dance initially, until she found her first true master in Malkowski, who revealed to her '*the spiritual quality of dance*'.

From 1955 to 1958 she studied with Yvonne Berge, and having discovered with her the importance of the *'corrective and centering aspects of movement'*, she began to study physiotherapy.

Between 1955 and 1965 she studied diversely with Janine Solane, Marcelle Albert for folklore, Nora Rubio for Spanish dance, and Françoise and Dominique Dupuy, Laura Sheleen and Jacqueline Robinson for modern dance. It was also in 1955 that she met Maurice Martenot, a great musician and teacher, and pursued a professional training in music education and the plastic arts at his school, subsequently becoming a teacher there. In 1967 she too travelled to New York where she saw the work of Martha Graham, Paul Taylor and Merce Cunningham.

Since 1958 Françoise and her husband Alain Chantraine (trained in psychology and music) have worked together in an enterprising manner. They devised a method that aimed to provide *"an aid to personal development through dance and bodily expression"*, in *"the harmony between the three poles of the human being, the physical, the affective and the intellectual"*. This method is, it must be admitted, by no means revolutionary in itself, for it rests on the principle of unity between the mind and the body, and the awareness of universal rhythms that had been preached for many years by one or another practitioner or philosopher of dance. The Chantraines gave their name to this method, which they disseminated with a sure sense of marketing, and which is directed towards people of all ages, levels of ability and needs; it rests upon the progression of work in *"five stages: rhythm – interiority – technique – creativity – choreography"*, that is, from inner awareness to the liberation and organization of choreographic material.

They were indeed capable of stirring up energies and motivation. The aims of their enterprise were noble and lofty, their manner generous, and Françoise's innate sense of musicality was apparent both in her own dancing and in that of her pupils; nevertheless, in spite of the application of the method, there emanates from their work a rather hybrid, approximate feeling that fails to live up to the observer's expectations. Today Françoise, in collaboration with her husband and their team, teaches and produces both in their school in Neuilly and its branches and in various institutions and at courses and festivals both in France and abroad.

Sylvie Deluz

French, born in 1940.

She received her initial training in dance with Janine Solane, obtaining a diploma with her in 1963. In 1965 she was initiated to the

Graham technique by Anna Mittelholzer and Yuriko, the chief harbingers and conveyors of Martha Graham's teaching, and, in 1969, she studied with Cunningham and Graham herself in New York. Since 1971 she has taught in various Parisian institutions, including the American Centre and the E.S.E.C. More recently, Sylvie Deluz has devoted herself primarily to the teaching of children and adolescents, supporting her work with thorough research in the fields of movement, psychopedagogy and the fundamental principles of the teaching of other artistic disciplines, such as music and painting.

In the period just following this chronicle, Sylvie and her painter husband, Marc Deluz, settled near Montpellier where she directs the group Iseïon together with the centre of the same name where creation, pedagogical experiences uniting dance, music, graphic arts, the natural environment and work on the body, movement and energy all take place.

The 'Science of the Body'

As in the years preceding the war, there were, from the 1950s on, practitioners who were not themselves dancers (gymnasts and/or therapists before the war, mainly therapists today) who had a considerable influence on the approach to techniques of movement and the perception of the body.

These included such practitioners as Mendensieck in the past; today they include:

- the Dane Gerda Alexander and her method known as eutony, which is applicable to teaching in general as much as to therapy or the teaching of the arts;
- Irmgard Bartenieff and her 'Fundamentals' which were inspired by her work with Rudolf von Laban;
- Mosche Feldenkrais and the legacy of Matthias Alexander, Dr Lulu Sweigard and, following on from the work of Mabel Todd, 'ideokinesis' (the thinking body');
- and, closer to home, the internationally renowned Frenchwoman, Françoise Mézières, whose work was developed by a whole network of practitioners. Mézières's theory and practice gained widespread recognition amongst the general public as a result of the 1976 best-seller *Le Corps a ses raisons* by Thérèse Bertherat and Carole Bernstein (English translation *Body Has Its Reasons* (Mandarin, 1990)).

These philosophers of movement differ from their predecessors in that their work is based upon quantifiable medical and clinical data; it incorporates psychotherapeutic and psychoanalytical data also, for today it is only amongst the enthusiasts of Eastern practices that the mode of thought, so dear to their elders, that takes the spiritual, even the cosmic dimension of 'the-being within-the-body' into account, may be found.

THE GRAFT FROM LATIN AMERICA

During the 1930s modern dance had developed most vigorously in Germany, Central Europe and the United States. After the war, another continent began to play an important part and was in fact ahead of Europe (or of France, at any rate): this continent was South America, and in particular Mexico and Argentina.

Modern dance was introduced into Mexico in 1939 by Waldeen, an American independent dancer who had gone there at the invitation of the Bellas Artes of Mexico, and later by Anna Sokolow, one of the greatest choreographers of her generation.

Their initiative was taken up by Ana Merida, Guillermina Bravo and Josefina Lavalle who founded the Ballet Nacional; a number of interesting choreographers emerged from this group. José Limón continued to maintain close links with his native country, of course, and exerted a certain influence there.

In Argentina, too, the American influence was present in the person of Myriam Winslow, and later Pauline Koner, an independent choreographer associated with the Limón company. The most important influence, however, was that of the Europeans who took refuge there, including Dore Hoyer after the war, and briefly Margarete Wallmann, Harald Kreutzberg, the Sakharoffs, Masami Kuni, Kurt Jooss – in other words, the principal descendents of Laban and Wigman. One of the main characters to feature amongst this constellation, due to the quality of her work and the fact that she established herself in Buenos Aires, was Renate Schottelius of German origin and a pupil of Wigman, she had been a member of the Berlin Opera and associated with the Ballets Jooss. Seeking refuge in Buenos Aires, she directed a school and company, and her influence spread throughout the two Americas. It was with her that the majority of those Argentinian dancers who were later to come to France trained. Karin Waehner also studied with her during the years she spent in Buenos Aires. Renate Schottelius appears to have been not only a great dancer and choreographer but a remarkable teacher as well.

Ernst Uthoff and Nadya Franklin, who settled in Chile and Venezuela respectively, also came from the Ballets Jooss.

The National School of Dance in Buenos Aires thus became a privileged place, in which Ana Itelman, another leading dancer, also taught. These Latin American modern dancers thus drew nourishment from three sources: the European source (in the Wigman and Laban/Jooss traditions); the American source (Winslow, Sokolow, Limón); and that very important Hispanic and Indian heritage that without doubt penetrated the very essence and form of their cultural inheritance. This threefold influence explains the particular richness of their skill and audacity.

In actual fact, during the 1950s, there were probably more things going on (and with more significant results) in Buenos Aires than in Paris. Moreover, modern dance seemed to receive greater encouragement from various official institutions there. It was as if the radically different new dance had not had to overcome so many barriers of conservatism there as it had in France. Indeed, almost the same observation was made by two dancers on their arrival in France: Renate Schottelius said

> *"I get the impression that it is in young countries that the development of modern dance is most important, and that interest and recognition are greatest. The Americas (North and South) currently possess a certain know-how and a public full of interest"*,[14] whilst Paulina Ossona maintained that *"Nations with only a recent past, like Argentina, are more aware of the fact that art cannot simply be a restatement of the past, but is above all an indication of the future. And, in these countries, the need to research is most powerful"*.[15]

Why, then, did such a considerable number of Latin American dancers come to France during the 1960s? Sometimes out of political necessity; sometimes, it appears, to discover European sources; and sometimes, of course, by chance! Some of them settled there, became integrated into the French dance world, and created a real graft (yet another, as at other moments in our chronicle). In general, these dancers brought with them technical skill, but above all a more highly developed and penetrating level of thought concerning the very substance of dance and its potential relationships with the other arts than was usual in France. They seem to have injected a breath of excitement through their personal commitment and intellectual and aesthetic freedom and openness.

Arlet Bon

Born in 1935 in Argentina.

Arlet Bon spent her childhood in the pampas, and the memory of its immensity and solitude remained with her throughout her life. She was sure of her vocation from an early age and studied dance at the National School in Buenos Aires with Renate Schottelius, Paulina Ossona,

---

[14] *Danse et rhythmes* (February 1959), p. 29.

[15] *Ibid.* (April 1960).

Pauline Koner, Dore Hoyer and Yuriko Kukushi. On leaving the school, she joined Conjunto Nueva Danza, an experimental group that performed in unusual places and contexts. She also taught history of dance at the conservatoire, and dance to children and the disabled.

In 1963 Arlet Bon visited Paris as a tourist, married and settled there, and became a member of the small band of pioneers of modern dance. Her experience and audacity placed her amongst the avant-garde and she immediately found herself at the forefront of modern dance undertakings. She took part in the Théâtre d'Essai de la Danse, at the Paris Biennale, where in 1965 she presented *Missa Criolla*. She performed at the Sigma in Bordeaux, where in 1971 she presented experiments in collective improvisation entitled *Kamaramix* with a group of musicians and actors; the A.R.C. at the National Museum of Modern Art (in various collaborations with other artists); the Maeght foundation; the underground railway as part of the inaugural ceremony of the R.E.R.* (this production was also staged in the New York bus station); the Pompidou Centre and in the open air. In 1974 she formed Danse Ensemble, a group that consisted of Katy de Kerday, Christian Bugaud, Patricia Passat and herself. Her creative activities and stage work were important not only in France but also abroad. She has never ceased to emphasize the relationships between dance and other artistic disciplines and has collaborated with musicians and plastic artists. A characteristic of her work is the important role she has accorded to chance, experimenting with aleatory methods.

She herself declares:

> *"Ever since the creation performed at the A.R.C. [L' Échelle de Jacob, music by Sikorski], the use of chance has been a constant feature of my work, making each dancer a co-creator. In Le Départ and Viaje II the order of the sequences is aleatory; all the dancers share the same vocabulary of movements, but each one selects their own order in which to perform these movements in time and space; the atmosphere of the open work enriches its form and meaning …".*

This aspect of her work, which was often considered unusual or unprecedented in location as in circumstances (audience participation in *Itinéraire II* or *Voyage III*, for example), together with the use of unexpected scenographical elements, texts and new music, all signalized Arlet Bon as an "experimental choreographer".

She taught regularly in Paris, Oxford and Buenos Aires, and became involved in militant activities promoting dance within the framework of national and international organizations such as the Conseil

---

*Réseau Express Régional.

International de la Danse which is dependent upon U.N.E.S.C.O. and in which she plays a very important part today. More recently, she has become interested in the problems of teaching children and has directed courses and conferences on pedagogical matters on both sides of the Atlantic.

In 1963 Gilberte Cournand wrote of her:

> *"One can but wish that every enthusiast of modern dance could see Arlet Bon dance. She dances with all her soul. The purety of line, the beauty of a body performing with intelligence, and the rhythm and music that radiate from her make everything about her art seem so easy".*[16]

She herself claimed of her work, which was both complex and austere, bare:

> *"This experimental, creative work lies within the spirit of contemporary art and is naturally related to the work of musicians, writers and plastic artists of our time. The use of simple forms, their combinations and the different meanings they engender, together with the use of the aleatory, an essential device that places the dancer, with all his control and sensitivity, in an ever watchful relationship, and the use of space experienced through the body like a partner — thus Dance becomes a language that may be spoken anywhere if it testifies to the presence of the Spirit".*

Sara Pardo

Argentinian, born c. 1930.

She first studied dance in Buenos Aires with Ana Itelman and Renate Schottelius, and subsequently became a member of Schottelius's company, creating her first choreographies there. At an early age she was also appointed as a dance teacher at the conservatoire, which opened wide its doors to modern dance.

In 1958 Sara Pardo was awarded a scholarship to study in Mexico, where she worked with Anna Sokolow and José Limón and joined the Compania Nacional de Danza. She first came to Paris as a dancer with the Peruvian National Ballet, performing within the programme of the Théâtre des Nations. She decided to settle there when, in 1962, she visited the city a second time in order to plan a dance piece at the university of the Théâtre des Nations, in which she brought together various other South American dancers resident in Paris. As a result of this experience, Paris became her home port. She went on tours and, in 1963, collaborated as a choreographer with the Ballets Contemporains de Karin Waehner. She created *Sensemaya* (music by Silvestre Revueltas) for them, in which

---

[16] Gilberte Cournand, in *Art et danse* (December 1963).

Arlet Bon, Aline Roux and Milena Salvini also danced, and produced *Poète à New York* (text by Garcia Lorca, music by Edgar Varèse), which she had created the previous year for the Théâtre des Nations.

She returned to Mexico in 1965 where she created more choreographies. Returning to Europe in 1969, she staged a show for the Maison de la Radio in Paris and the Round House in London. She then found another propitious place in London at the London Contemporary Dance Centre, and worked there in collaboration with Robert Cohan. During all these years Sara Pardo frequently worked with Guillermo Palomares. In the 1970s, following Sara's stay in London, they both went to teach at the recently established Centre du Marais. She then spent a brief period in Chile where the National Ballet engaged her as a dancer and choreographer. Today, Sara Pardo is still resident in Paris and teaches, mainly in Italy and England.

Graziella Martinez

Argentinian, born in 1938.

Graziella Martinez was one of the most curious of all the characters to arrive from Latin America. Alain Nahmias wrote of her:

> *"Graziella Martinez is, even before a choreographer, a poetess, a magician who creates poetry out of a form of dance that is always bare in the extreme, a distant glance or a costume that hardly seems to be a costume at all. We thus experience a miracle".*[17]

And Pierre Lartigue described her as *"a clown, a tit ... this touching acrobat of pure poetry"*. All those who saw her and wrote of her work seem to have been moved by a poetic (surrealist?) quality that was highly personal, even unique, and which, from her very first appearances placed Graziella Martinez outside all accepted trends in dance. Whether innocently or with cunning calculation, this was no doubt how she wished to be perceived. Lise Brunel wrote:

> *"Here (in Giselle Tomorrow), an actress rather than a dancer, she simplifies her dance to extreme in order to stand deliberately outside of ballet".*[18]

From the outset, her career differed from those of her Argentinian colleagues who arrived in Paris at the same time as she. Born in Cordoba, *"a town"*, in her own words, *"at the heart of Argentina, full of tangos and humour"*, she studied classical dance, philosophy and languages and

---

[17] *Pour la danse* (April 1985).

[18] *Les Saisons de la danse* (May 1972).

Plate 38   Graziella Martinez in *Giselle after Tomorrow*. Photo: Noak/le bar Floréal.

became engrossed in numerous different interests. She then went to Buenos Aires, that cosmopolitan capital, which was for her, she claimed, *"the discovery of the world"*. She rarely mixed with the contemporary dance world, however, feeling more at home in that of painters, musicians, writers and theatrical folk, and she showed a certain affinity with Oscar Araiz. It was in Mexico that she acquired the technique she required, and studied assiduously for a year with Xavier Francis and Bodyla Genkel, to whom she has always acknowledged her great debt.

In 1957, feeling physically ready, she began to produce choreographies using props, fabrics and lighting, *"rather like Nikolais, although I had not heard of him at that time!"* Willingly or not an iconoclast, she found herself propelled to the forefront of the avant-garde, and founded the movement Danse Actuelle which gave frequent performances. In 1963 the French government awarded her a scholarship to study music and she came to Paris. There she worked, once again in avant-garde circles, alongside not only dancers but writers, musicians, film producers and graphic artists. She collaborated with Lavelli, Topor, Copi and Savary amongst others. She staged the work of painters and sculptors at the Paris Biennale and gave shows at the National Museum of Modern Art. She danced, challenged received opinions, stirred up passions and went on tour in London, Hamburg, New York and Amsterdam. Her works of that period include *Giselle Today*, *Floating Bird* and *Sainte Geneviève dans le toboggan*.

A studio in Amsterdam was placed at her disposal and she formed a group there known as White Dreams, which was also the title of one of her group pieces. She composed *Giselle Tomorrow* and *Magic Doll*, strange, dreamlike, crazy pieces. Once again she danced in all four corners of the world, alone or with Gaspar Hummel, with a small group, and continues today, ever fascinating and moving to her audience. Her recent works include *Ophélie* (1980), *Graziella par Graziella* (1982), *La Symphonie de la vie* and *A la folie* (1985). Indeed, madness appears like a thread running through all her work: Giselle, Ophelia, archetypes that she turns upside down. *"Graziella Martinez is unique, and represents through her dance her innermost being"*, wrote Bernadette Bonis in *Révolution*. And Hervé Gauville added in *Libération*:

> *"She herself personifies perfection, and is all the more contemporary for the fact that she constantly deals in anachronism"*.

(Working outside recognized boundaries, Graziella Martinez found it increasingly difficult to work and find venues that would welcome her. Following the establishment of democracy in Argentina, she decided to return to her native country at the end of 1988.)

Juan Carlos Bellini

Argentinian, born c. 1925.

He studied dance in Buenos Aires with Renate Schottelius, who subsequently became his partner, and they gave many recitals together. Later he joined José Limón's company and remained with them for several years. Juan Carlos Bellini came to Paris in 1954, where he became associated with almost every modern dance group and established a career principally as a teacher. Rigorous, attentive and warm-hearted in his teaching, he taught the Limón technique at Rose-Marie Paillet's studio and subsequently in Italy and Cannes at Rosella Hightower's school. He now lives in the South of France.

Mara Dajanova

Argentinian.

She studied in Buenos Aires with the Sakharoffs and Matsumi Kuni, in the Wigman tradition. Since 1947 she pursued an itinerant career as a dancer both in Europe and South America and also taught modern dance. It was, therefore, with a solid reputation and wealth of experience already behind her that she arrived in Paris. There she visited the various centres of modern dance and worked alongside Karin Waehner and Jacqueline Robinson. It was at the Atelier de la Danse, moreover, that she began to teach and make her work known. Lise Brunel wrote of her:

> *"Mara Dajanova is an artist endowed with real personality, and intellectual rather than intuitive sensitivity; immense self-control, elaborate compositions and an occasional lack of warmth".*[19]

She later settled in Tel Aviv.

Noémie Lapzeson

Argentinian, born c. 1950.

She received her early training at the National School of Dance with Renate Schottelius and Ana Itelman and was a member of various modern dance groups in Buenos Aires. She then went to New York to study with Martha Graham. She came to France on several occasions, where she was amongst those teachers to introduce the Graham technique to French dancers. Following upon Yuriko, however, she gave a

---

[19] *Danse er rythmes*, 1959.

different, less doctrinaire and more creative perspective on that technique. She also taught in England at the London School of Contemporary Dance. Today she is more active than ever, working in several European countries, including Switzerland and Spain, and performing striking pieces with her group in many different settings. Her work is appreciated for both its moving humanity and striking staging.

Paulina Ossona

Argentinian, born c. 1925.

Paulina Ossona is another of those figures who spent only a brief time in Paris but nevertheless remained there long enough to make an impression on the dance world (and the public; she was an original and powerful dancer/choreographer with a keen intellect and a rich and dynamic personality. Educated at the National Conservatoire of Buenos Aires in the 1940s, she received a training in classical dance initially and subsequently in modern dance with Margarete Wallmann, Myriam Winslow, the Sakharoffs and Matsumi Kuni; she soon became a teacher there, whilst absorbing the traditional Argentinian culture.

She began her career as an independent soloist in 1945, and established her company and school, which produced many well known dancers. She also toured the Americas and Europe, was appointed to positions of increasing importance and sent on missions to a number of different countries. She came to France in 1960, and gave numerous recitals, lectures and interviews; the quality of her stage work and thought on dance testify to her talent. With other artists she worked for television, and has been extremely active as a lecturer and conference organizer. Since 1976 she has published several works, including *Educación por la danza*, *Danza moderna* and *El lenguaje del cuerpo*. She is currently a dance critic and presides over various important professional organizations in Argentina.

Paulina Oca

Argentinian, born c. 1935.

She trained in classical and modern dance at the National School of Music and Theatrical Art (the conservatoire) in Buenos Aires, and studied there with Renate Schottelius amongst others. She came to Paris in 1957 and worked with Karin Waehner (Waehner had herself spent some time in Buenos Aires in 1947 and had worked with Schottelius. It was perfectly natural therefore that she should serve as a point of contact and place of fall in Paris for Argentinian dancers).

Paulina Oca was as much a choreographer as a dancer:

"her work has evolved from impressionism, through cubism, to abstract art, a progression that may be paralleled with her choice of the musicians whose works she danced to: from Maurice Ravel and Claude Debussy to Pierre Schaeffer, and musique concrète".[20]

She performed at the Paris Biennale on several occasions, sharing a programme with Arlet Bon and Graziella Martinez in 1965, and in 1968 she took part in the shows and meetings organized by the A.R.C. at the National Museum of Modern Art.

She also travelled extensively, staged shows and created choreographies in Argentina as well as in France, Italy and Spain. During these years she formed part, if only episodically, of the French dance scene, infusing it with her own brand of rigour and intelligence. She returned to Argentina in 1971 where she pursued a completely independent career.

Diana Obedman

Argentinian.

Educated at the National School of Buenos Aires, she was a pupil of Renate Schottelius and Ana Itelman. Subsequently she became a member of Itelman's company. She continued her studies in the United States before going to the London School of Contemporary Dance, where she pursued an active career as a dancer and choreographer, then continued in Copenhagen and in Paris. In 1968 she joined Sara Pardo's group in Paris and became involved in the activities of the A.R.C. In the same year she obtained the Cologne prize for choreography and finally settled in Denmark.

Gladys Aleman

Venezuelan.

She trained initially in classical dance in Caracas, where she became a teacher at the national school. She subsequently went to Mexico where she studied modern dance and further pursued this path by going to work with Martha Graham in New York. On her return home, she founded the group Danzas Venezuelas and assumed the directorship of the school of dance in Portuguesa. She arrived in Paris in 1967 as a

---

[20] Extract from the introductory text to the A.R.C. in 1968.

delegate of the Venezuelan National Institute of Culture. She performed within various different organizations, such as Sara Pardo's group, and took part in the activities of the A.R.C. In 1970 she was awarded a prize at the Bagnolet competition.

Sonia Sanoja

Venezuelan.

She trained initially in classical dance in Caracas and entered the Theatre of Dance directed by Grishka Holguin in 1953. She then went to Paris to study contemporary dance with Laura Sheleen, Karin Waehner and Winifred Widener. On returning to Caracas in 1961 she and Holguin created the Foundation of Contemporary Dance, which worked in association with the Fine Arts Museum in Caracas.

Sonia Sanoja returned to France on several occasions. In 1965 she took part in the fourth Paris Biennale in a solo programme set to music by contemporary composers Webern, Ginastera and Pierre Henry – a very "physical" type of dance, of which the programme notes may give some idea:

> *"The weight of the earth supports me horizontally. I look around me, my eyes lifted. My feet are uprooted as if walking in the sky. My body raises itself from the ground and begins to grope about: it proceeds, sometimes in a dramatic manner, seeking a vertical position, the full stature of the being, standing, in space".*

She subsequently gave a number of performances in France and Europe and took part in the shows and encounters of the A.R.C. in 1968.

Guillermo Palomares

Mexican.

He trained in classical and modern dance in Mexico and came to France in 1961 where he remained for several years. He became a member of various groups, among which Karin Waehner's company, the Ballets Contemporains. He became associated with the work of Sara Pardo in particular. In 1970 he worked as a dancer, choreographer and teacher in Germany and Eastern European countries. He subsequently divided his time between various venues, including Paris and London. During the 1970s he taught at the Centre du Marais in Paris. Today, he has returned to Mexico, where he teaches.

JAZZ AND AFRICAN DANCE:
ANOTHER TURNING TOWARDS ROOTS

Ingeborg Liptay

Of German origin, born in 1934.

She trained initially in dance with Kurt Jooss in Essen and became a soloist in his company. She came to Paris in 1960 where she studied with Karin Waehner, then in 1963 went to America and worked in New York with Martha Graham, Clive Thompson, Sevilla Fort, Lucas Hoving and Walter Nicks, obtaining a prize for dance at the Clark Centre for the Performing Arts. On her return to Paris in 1966, Ingeborg taught jazz in a particularly lively and creative manner nevertheless built on very firm foundations. She taught at the Schola Cantorum, the C.I.D. and the American Centre, and led courses in the provinces and abroad. She also pursued a career as a dancer/choreographer in collaboration with the musician Morton Potash. Her work was based in part on a certain jazz spirit with its bursting energy and immediacy of impact. Ingeborg says:

> *"the time of dance is nourished by the present".*

In 1972 she settled in Montpellier where she opened her dance school and continued her work with Sylvie Deluz within the framework of the group Iseïon. This work led her beyond dance to a consideration of underlying philosophical and spiritual disciplines. She currently teaches at the Institute of Theatrical Studies at the Paul-Valéry University in Montpellier, and continues today to create dances, solos and group works.

Ingeborg relates her memories of 1960 with a certain sense of humour:

> *"After three years in that "convent" of the Folkswangschule, Parisian life appeared to me rich and sumptuous (even though I didn't have a penny to my name) with the rue Mouffetard and its market, the night life of Les Halles, and the "Chat qui pêche" where my friend Kenny Clark and other jazz musicians played.*
>
> *I can still see Karin; in a parallel first position, full of vigour, with a big smile on her face whenever we discovered something new at workshop, always loyal through good times and bad. The Schola Cantorum, and its directors, Guy Tréal, who seemed like God to me, opening the little garret that was to be my home with his enormous key. I can hear even now Tchemikoff playing his cello at night as I made my way home from the studio across the garden. Do you remember the old Russian caretaker?*
>
> *I eagerly absorbed everything that occurred at the Atelier de la Danse ... Villa-Lobos, Vivaldi, and the scent of Montmartre and those "other worlds" ... the fluid tranquility of your dance.*

The shows at the Récamier in 1963 – a precious memory – that place that felt unreal and opened up imaginary worlds. I danced Miles Sketches and the programme stated: 'she reveals a desire to work 'with' jazz musicians, 'like' jazz musicians, that is, by using choreographies similar to 'arrangements' leaving a certain amount of improvisatory freedom to the performer'. It all seems such a long time ago, but this is what I am still trying to do!".[21]

Christiane de Rougemont

Born in 1942 in Lyons.

She studied at university and began modern dance with Line Trillat in the Lyons descent from Anita Wieskemann and Hélène Carlut. In 1960 Christiane worked with Karin Waehner and Lilian Arlen in Paris, and danced successively in the Ballets Modernes de Paris and the Ballets Contemporains de Karin Waehner. 1964–67 were years of travelling, discoveries and creation for her. She was given a scholarship to study at the Katherine Dunham School in New York and became an assistant there. She appeared in John Huston's *The Bible*. Later she taught in Cologne, at the Katherine Dunham School in Stockholm, and various institutions in Paris. From 1967 to 1970 she devoted most of her time to choreography, before leaving once more for the United States, where she was put in charge of the dance department at the University of Southern Illinois.

Christiane de Rougemont returned to Paris in 1970 where she worked in Lazzini's company and at the Théâtre Français de la Danse, and founded the group Free Dance Song, with which she toured Africa. In 1975 she created a training programme in dance and teaching at the Cité Universitaire of Paris. Free Dance Song performed in France, at the Avignon festival amongst other venues, and abroad. Christiane appeared in several films and television broadcasts.

The chronological boundary of this study prevents me from going further, but I must point out that Christiane de Rougemont has never stopped creating, solos and group pieces, for Free Dance Song, teaching in her centre for research and training in Afro-American dance at the university centre, and directing courses in France and abroad. The path she has followed and the specific focus of her work clearly indicate what lay (and still lies) at the heart of her approach: the search for the primitive roots of dance, not a mythical primitivism, but the very real one of living races and cultures. She wrote me:

---

[21] Letter to Jacqueline Robinson, 1987.

Plate 39 Hideyuki Yano, *Le Fleuve*, 1975, with Christiane de Rougemont and Elsa Wolliaston. Photo: Suzanne Robert, Paris.

"I felt that something was lacking in my training, each time dance did not appear to emanate directly from music, something was lacking in my training. For me, it is the dynamism of the music that gives dance its catalytic dimension, its liberating role, giving balance to the whole being; and I felt that, somewhere in our evolution, we had lost the essence of dance.

My encounter with Katherine Dunham was decisive for me. I realized that through her technique, communication with rhythm could restore to the body and dance a vitality drawn from the very roots of our primitive being, where physical and psychic forces coexist in harmony".

In her discussion of music, it is clear that Christiane is not referring to the practice of our predecessors (Isadora and the rest) who needed 'great' music as an emotional support; but to that functional, physical music, to be found in the percussion and songs of African dance. It is precisely this impression of physical and psychic strength existing together in harmony that emanates from Christiane's dance: beautiful, vigorous, free and subtle. Indeed, one might have said "natural" if this word had not had so many other connotations at previous moments in history! Jeanne Maréschal said of her:

"Particularly sensitive to African cultural themes, her manner confronts the audience with a difficult challenge, for she seeks to make perceptible not images or feelings, but symbolic relationships between the being and primitive forces, the individual and the group, and finally the individual and himself in his intercourse with others".

It is not surprising, therefore, that, seeking in this particular and funda-mental area of dance where the sacred and profane merge and links with the community are particularly strong, Christiane should have developed an interest in therapy. For in no other field of investigation is the indis-solubility of body and mind more apparent; indeed, since 1973 she has led workshops in psychiatric hospitals.

Christiane de Rougemont writes most pertinently for her students:

"Modern dance in France suddenly seems to be experiencing rapid growth, schools and young companies are multiplying, as is the number of amateurs on courses of various types. And the best thing about this all too belated movement is that it appears full of a new vitality; this, coupled with the fact that several of the major trends in modern dance have already witnessed such a degree of expansion, offering the creators of today a wide range of experiences, and the results of these: openings or impasses. There is also what was learnt from a long and testing process of liberation in relation to the many fetters and taboos that several generations of dancers have had to confront within our society. Young creators thus find themselves benefiting from a considerable achievement and of ground that has already been prepared and is still to be used.

Are we going to bury modern dance, as with the forms of dance that preceded it, in rationalism and abstract technicality even before it has had a chance to exist? We strongly risk doing so if we do not assimilate technique into our personal seeking. There is no such thing as dance without technique, and modern dance is in the process of defining its own, building upon analysis and organization of new concepts such as dynamism, weight, space, energy and impetus, concepts that had not until this time been seen as the motives behind movement but simply as the consequences of it; thus a vocabulary emerges that speaks of the quality of a movement in the same breath as of its form, and of its perception in the same breath as of its mechanical procedure. Anatomical consciousness, physical rather than cerebral, evolves simultaneously from a knowledge of the placing of the body and the evidence of feelings and experiences. The language of modern dance is the language of the body itself; the mere consciousness of movement is a form of expression that affects us all for it is perceived by other bodies that are capable of identifying with the same experience".

EPILOGUE

This chronicler would not like the curtain to fall abruptly at the end of her story. The story goes on, the actors do not leave the stage, even though the chronicler makes her exit.

And as the chronicler moves backwards, as it were, off stage, she can still see what is happening ...

The chronicler that I have chosen to be plays a dual role: to be now in the wings, and yet to foretell what we all know is going to happen.

Apart from wishing to remind the reader who the next actors and what the next events were to be, however, I am almost surprised to note how rapidly contemporary dance has evolved since 1970 on two levels: first on that of conception and second on that of practice.

Far be it from me to wish to say that all goes well in the best of worlds. Has dance really won the place it deserves in the life of society? Are dancers normally acknowledged? More significantly, is the choreographer acknowledged as a creator? No, not really, not in all cases. He is too often considered as an 'arranger of steps' and, at worst, simply as a coach.

It was a real battle to obtain recognition for the choreographer as a creator by the S.A.C.E.M.* or by the S.A.C.D.† Could a choreographer claim royalties, rights, acknowledgement? Even today, as far as certain legal matters are concerned, the choreographer is considered on a par with stage producer or ballet-masters. (The latter professions work from someone else's text, whereas the choreographer writes, invents, his own text.) There lies in this a total misunderstanding of the choreographer's work. I admit that the problem lies outside the scope of this book, but it is nevertheless extremely important and can be listed amongst the concerns of this adventure, this chronicle.

Furthermore, I do not wish to put forward any judgement of the kind "it was better before" concerning the practices of today compared with those of yesterday. There is, to be sure, a huge difference between what constituted modern dance even in the 1970s (much more so earlier) and what it is today. What can be seen today would have been quite

---

*Société des auteurs, compositeurs et éditeurs de musique.
†Société des auteurs et compositeurs dramatiques.

inconceivable as much for the dancer as for the public of the past. Could the dancer of 1930, for instance, have imagined, let alone foreseen the manner in which the body would be used, the physical and chore-ographic behaviour? Would he have found then, within himself, the mode of gesture, the way of moving, acting, speaking and showing the body that is current today? It is a question, I feel, of more than a matter of convention or mores; I would suggest that it might be a mutation.

The same applies to the discourse surrounding dance and the motivations of the creators. New concepts, be they of a philosophical, aesthetic, scientific or even a political nature, have penetrated every field, including that of contemporary dance which seems to have become a favourite sphere for intellectual speculation. Discourse about dance takes its references from elsewhere, including graphic arts, music, literature and cinema. It is at the same time sharp, subtle, open and extremely complex indeed even complacent. This widening of the field and degree of complexity would have bewildered the dancer of the past who, naïve and earnest, and so completely involved in fighting for something more simple, fundamental and direct, would not have foreseen that much.

The level of much of the current thinking and writing about dance may not be easily accessible to the 'ordinary dancer'. Nevertheless he can-not escape the varied consequences of this thinking which has spread with the times. It may yet be necessary to promote a mode of thinking about dance that would link a relative illiteracy to an excessive intellectualism.

Taking things to extremes, we may wonder what there is in *common*, between those out of date forms of dance that were so new, and current forms? Beyond the fashion factor which always plays a more or less visible part, could it be that notion to which I referred at the beginning of this book, the notion of *virginity*? The desire, the need, the potentiality to explore ever further? (At the risk of getting lost or having to return to the centre.) And to build, be it only a house of cards, upon an individual or a collective dream. This evolution, like all other forms of evolution, is visible only from a distance. We have surreptitiously moved from one way of conceiving and making dance to another.

I feel it is important to point out that for a long time, there has been in the mind of both the public and the critics a confusion between so-called contemporary and what is referred to in France as neo-classical dance. It should be remembered that neo-classical dance, born, in fact, out of the works of Serge Lifar, still depended to varying degrees upon the vocabu-lary of classical dance. (Distortions added to this particular mode of movement do not make it contemporary.) Movement here is not yet freed from actual staging, nor from literary pretexts, and does not yet speak ac-cording to its specificity. (Dare I say that I hope my reader can distinguish a form of dance that is *new* (virgin) from one that is based on a conventional movement language, on clichés). According to this view, we may designate as neo-classics, Roland Petit and Janine Charrat, Joseph Lazzini, Joseph Rusillo, Françoise Adret and, of course, the great Maurice Béjart.

Whatever label he might wear, it should not be forgotten that Béjart has initiated a vast public. He offered another image of dance, set in a captivating theatrical framework, performed by wonderful dancers and promoted by the mass media, which was a revelation to thousands of people who in turn became open to unfamiliar forms of dance. Classified as modern by the classics, and still today by the greater part of the non-specialized public for whom 'Béjart' means 'contemporary dance', and as classical by the moderns, Béjart is, in fact, a creator with a hybrid style, and this is in a way puzzling, as though he had chosen not to take that final step out of academicism.

I will go no further than to list those new developments that occurred in the landscape of French modern dance in the 1970s, developments which were, in spite of an apparent break, simply the living sequel of all that happened in the preceding decade, based on the work of earlier practitioners.

There were breaks, progressive or sudden, towards a personal language on the part of a number of dancers and choreographers trained and working within the classical or neo-classical tradition. The most noteworthy of these were probably Brigitte Lefèvre and Jacques Garnier, who in a way became the heralds of the new French dance. They left the Opéra having experimented creatively within Michel Descombey's Ballet Studio, then with the Groupe des Sept and the Jeunes Chorégraphes de l'Opéra. They founded the Théâtre du Silence in 1974, which established its home in La Rochelle, and achieved international renown. Both dancers explored on American ground, and collaboration with Merce Cunningham in 1976 made their 'conversion' to contemporary dance obvious. In 1973 the programme of their show at the Palace Theatre in Paris bore the following lines:

> "Theatre of Silence: that is significant. Theatre means a happening, drama or comedy: dance as entertainment, dance as decoration, dance as candy will be excluded. Dance is a language and does not want to speak any more without significance".

Later, in his book *Histoire de la danse en Occident*, Paul Bourcier wrote of what Garnier and Lefèvre had undertaken:

Plate 40   Christine Gérard and Alejandro Witzman-Anaya in *Algorythme*, choreography by Jacqueline Robinson, 1970. Photo: Yves van Veerbeke, Paris.

"We have here a denial of anecdote, even of logical discourse, and a desire for spareness which call for respect, but which demand a lot from choreographers as well as from their public".

Félix Blaska took a similar path after working with the Ballet Théâtre Contemporain and having studied in America, and gradually moved away from a neo-classical style. In 1968 Joseph Rusillo arrived in France and in 1970 founded the Compagnie Béranger-Rusillo with Anne Béranger (who had danced with Nikolais), and in 1973 the Ballet Théâtre Joseph Rusillo. In 1976 he was appointed to teach modern dance at the Opéra. (As a choreographer, however, he was rather neo-classically minded.)

It was at this time that some of the characters who were to play a leading part came onto the stage: first, the Americans Carolyn Carlson and Susan Buirge, two remarkable women who introduced Alwin Nikolais's view of dance, strict and subtle, to France.

And, in a very different vein, the Japanese Hideyuki Yano and African Elsa Wolliaston.

As creators and teachers, these characters were to draw a whole generation of French dancers in their wake. The appointment of Carolyn Carlson at the Paris Opéra in 1973, and the founding of the Groupe de Recherche Chorégraphique de l'Opéra de Paris (G.R.C.O.P.) in 1974, where several other creators such as Wilfride Piollet and Jean Guizerix revealed their talents, promoted by the media, made this as yet unfamiliar type of dance more accessible to the public at large.

It is true that in this period there could be noted in France a very strong American influence, mostly that of Cunningham and Nikolais, together with that of José Limón, especially through the much appreciated choreographic and pedagogical work of Peter Goss. This took place simultaneously with the new awareness of contemporary dance on the part of many young practitioners and a large section of the public, which may account for the current (misguided) notion that, prior to 1970, France was from that point of view a desert.

This American influence was due not only to those who came to work, permanently or temporarily, in France, but also to those numerous young choreographers stemming from the French school who went to further their studies in the United States and became known in the 1970s. Several of these attracted attention at the Bagnolet competition, which was a true springboard towards recognition, including Catherine Atlani, Dominique Bagouet, Christine Gérard, Jean-Claude Gallota, Michel Hallet-Eghayan, Serge Keuten, Maguy Marin, Jacques Patarozzi, Jean Pomarès, Jean-Claude Ramseyer, Delphine Rybinski, Brigitte Réal, Anne-Marie Reynaud, Quentin Roullier and Karine Saporta. And those who came from abroad, such as Gigi Caciuleanu, Peter Goss, Myriam

Berns, Jane Honor and Alejandro Witzman-Anaya amongst others, must also be added to this list of promising artists. All that happening before the unfurling of today's new wave, who are winning public acclaim and making for the international repute of French contemporary dance.

Furthermore, this period witnessed on an international level a much greater circulation of ideas, people and works, as well as an inter-penetration of cultures – Indian, Japanese and African – from a choreo-graphic point of view.

Several projects of a more institutional nature were undertaken:

- the setting up of French contemporary dance companies in the provinces;
- the founding of festivals where dance held an important position: 'Action-Danse' at the Théâtre des Deux Portes in Paris, directed by Lise Brunel, the Val-de-Marne festival by Michel Caserta, the Avignon, Aix-en-Provence and Châteauvallon festivals, and the Montpellier festival devoted entirely to dance;
- the founding of the Centre National de Danse Contemporaine (a very high-level professional training centre directed for a while by Alwin Nikolais);
- the founding of the Maison de la Danse and the Biennale Interna-tionale de Danse in Lyons, both directed by Guy Darmet;
- the somewhat uncoordinated activities of federal, associative and trades union groups;
- the (rather modest) presence of dance at the ministry of culture, and the slight increase in government subsidies.

Alongside this new string of official initiatives, all the work carried out in private settings, be it creation, teaching or promoting, by practitioners, some of whom we met in preceding chapters, should not be underrated. It was great work carried out with small means, which made the actual soil upon which French dance may grow, infused with vital energy.

Throughout the whole of this chronicle, I have used an agricultural metaphor, from ground breaking to flowering. I would like to remain there, to note bad weather and good, droughts and frosts, to appreciate the plentiful flowering, to observe how harvesting and vintage are going on, to taste the fruit, to delight in the diversity of flavours, and above all to feel life flowing through this earth tilled by so many men and women who have lived through the adventure of French modern dance, who have been the Pioneers of Modern Dance in France.

I recall these lines by Bertholt Brecht:

"Each thing belongs to him who makes it better:
The child to loving hearts, so that he may grow well;
The cart to the good driver
So that it should not fall by the way;
The valley belongs to him who feeds it
So that the loveliest fruit should spring from the earth".

APPENDICES

THE SPECIALIZED PRESS AND WRITERS ABOUT DANCE

It seems to me that the specialized dance press reflects in a very true manner the tastes, fashions and tendencies of a community at a given time.

The dance community in France grew enormously during this half century with which we are concerned, a community made up of professionals and a wide public that had not only grown in size but changed in nature. From 1920 to 1940 dance was still very much the concern of an 'elite', of a cultured proportion of the public, whatever the current aesthetic opinions might be. (We must not forget that 'ballroom dancing' was a widely practised leisure activity and even had its own specialized press.) Those who were in charge of the dance items in the daily, weekly or monthly periodicals were often specialists in the field of music or of theatre. There were very few specialists in dance, Fernand Divoire and André Lévinson being exceptions.

It was in the 1950s that an increasing number of dance magazines appeared in response to the need for all kinds of information demanded by professionals belonging to different age groups and by an ever growing public. Many people found themselves moved to write for this good cause: journalists, critics, often belonging to the worlds of theatre or music, teachers and gossip columnists.

I have listed a dozen or so reviews amongst those which came out since 1948. (I do not mention those quasi private ones, aimed at a small specific audience and of an essentially didactic character, even though they might be most interesting, as was Jean Serry's *Danse et enseignement*.)

These reviews existed diversely for many or only a few years, the chief reason for their disappearance being generally financial.

These specialized magazines should not lead us to overlook the important part played by the daily press. Little by little, columns devoted to dance, with a regular critic, were introduced, and initiated a wider public than that already informed one that read the specialized reviews. Whether this initiation was well carried out is another story!

Amongst these critics there were, of course, ones of a more conservative nature, such as Olivier Merlin and Claude Baignères, who did not cast an appreciative eye upon modern dance. Nevertheless, we should not forget the positive roles played by, amongst others, Dinah Maggie in *Combat* and later in the *Quotidien de Paris*, Lise Brunel in *Le*

Matin and *Lettres françaises*, Marcelle Michel who took over from Claude Sarraute in *Le Monde,* and Gilberte Cournand, to be found in many pages.

This list, which I admit is clearly incomplete, aims to provide specific information, but is unfortunately limited. It was, for instance, impossible to obtain information upon some matters that would have been of interest, such as the respective number of editions printed and circulated. Nearly all the reviews were centred mainly on classical dance, and promoted the Opéra and the large international companies; however, gradually modern dance took its place and was written about in a more respectful manner. In a more or less similar way, all these reviews published after the war included pages of critiques, advertisements for performances, articles about this person or that, a few about historical subjects, advice on legal, technical, medical matters, some leading articles – hardly any difference, apart from a matter of style, from what we can read today!

Before the War

La Danse
Founded in 1921 by Jacques Hébertot. This review added to the efforts of Hébertot to promote 'new dance' by his regular performance initiatives: *Les Vendredis de la Danse.* The review was sponsored by Rolf de Maré, director of the Ballets Suédois and the Archives Internationales de la Danse.

La Tribune de la Danse
Founded in 1923 by Jean Dorcy. Intended as a bulletin of information for dance critics.

Revue Internationale de Musique et de Danse
Founded in 1926. The dance section was run by Carol-Bérard whose wife was librarian at the Paris Opéra.

Arts et Mouvement
Founded by Pierre Conté. A didactic bulletin devoted to his theories about dance and his notation system.

Archives Internationales de la Danse
Founded in 1932 by Rolf de Maré. Regular publication until 1937. (I have referred to this review in the chapter devoted to the A.I.D.)
... not to mention the numerous magazines of a cultural nature such as *Comoedia, Conferencia, Musica, La Revue Musicale, L'Illustration.* etc.

After the War

Art et Danse
Founded in 1944 by E. Mourier in Rouen, as a bulletin for ballroom dancing teachers. The chief editor was Matias Desève. In 1954 the review opened up to other forms of dance. In 1959 it was edited in Paris by Ginette Chabetay and Jean Dorcy. Amongst the regular contributors were Jacques Baril, Gilberte Cournand, Jean Dorcy, Jean Laurent, Marie André-Lévinson, Maurice Louis, Jacqueline Robinson, François de Santerre, André Schaikevitch.
Format I: 21 × 27; format II: 28 × 38.
Last issue: no. 162, October 1975.

Revue de la Danse
Founded in 1948, incorporating *Terpsichore 48*, the bulletin of the association Les Amis de la Danse. Directors: Jacques Lebar, Baron-Renouard. Editors: Madame Jacno-Stéphane and Yves Bonnat. Chief contributors: Jean-André Balthus, Baird Hastings, Serge Lifar, Irène Lidova, Pierre Michaut, Jean Silvant, Françoise Reiss.
Format: 28 × 38.

Danse
Founded in 1948; cyclostyled. Editors: Edmond Linval, Dinah Maggie, Ferdinando Reyna, Pierre Tugal.
Format: 21 × 27 (a very modest publication ...) .

Les Cahiers de la Danse
First run of publications: founded in 1956 by Edmond Linval; cyclostyled. Texts by Pierre Conté, Lycette Darsonval, Guy-Georges Duret, Nil Hahoutoff, Maurice Louis, Ferdinando Reyna.

Second run of publications: March 1957 later added as subtitle: *Revue internationale de recherches, d'esthétique, de critique et d'information*. Director: Edmond Linval. Chief editor: Guy-Georges Duret. Chief contributors: André Boll, Youra Bousquet, Paul Bourcier, Jean Coquelle, Maurice Tassart, Ferdinando Reyna.
Format : 21 × 27; paperback as from 1958.
Last issue: no. 9, September 1958.

Toute la Danse
Founded in 1952 by Guy-Georges Duret. Director in December 1952: J. Cusset-Valdes. Chief contributors: Germaine Laurent, Irène Lidova,

Pierre Michaut, Maurice Pourchet, Françoise Reiss, Guillot de Rode, Jean Silvant, Maurice Tassart, Pierre Tugal, Jean Coquelle.
Format: 16 × 24.
Enlarged in 1953; returned to previous format in 1954. Chief editor: Jean Silvant.
Contributors: Jacques Baril, André Boll, Jean Coquelle, Marie André-Lévinson, Ferdinando Reyna, Pierre Thiriot.
In 1955 turns into *Toute la danse et la musique*, directed by Jean Monfisse, later by Albert Combe.
Last issue: no. 108, August 1962.

La Danse
Founded in 1954 by Guy-Georges Duret. As from 1955, press medium of the Club International de la Danse. Director: Jean Mayeur. Chief editors, successively: Helène Martinelli, Charles Imbert, Raymond Lyon. Chief contributors: Marie Brillant, Antoine Goléa, Charles Imbert, Norah Lidart, Pierre Michaut, Michèle Nadal, Maurice Louis, Michel Petit, Georges Reymond, Françoise Reiss, Jean Rollot, Maurice Tassart.
Format: 16 × 24.
As from no. 35, October 1957 becomes:

Danse et Rythmes
Chief editor: José Atienza. For a while, it was edited in French and in Spanish. Chief contributors: Marie-Jean Béraud-Villars, Lise Brunel, Martine Cadieu, Atty Chadinoff, Luc Christophe, Trudi Goth, Delfor Peralta, Jacqueline Robinson, D. Saint-Pierre. (This eclectic review was very favorable to modern dance.)
Format: 16 × 24.
Last issue: no. 63, July 1960.

Les Saisons de la Danse
Founded in 1968 by André-Philippe Hersin and Jean-Claude Diénis. Chief contributors: Jacques Baril, Monique Babsky, Paul Bourcier, Lise Brunel, Marie-Françoise Christout, Irène Lidova, Lucile Rossel, André Schaikewitch.
Format: 28 × 28.

Chaussons et Petits Rats
Founded in 1970 by Elyane Richaud, teacher of classical dance in Montpellier. This was at first a liaison bulletin between schools. It grew and became:

Pour la Danse
Based in Marseilles, then in Paris. Director: Annie Bozzini. Chief contributors: Bernadette Bonis, Antoine Livio, Odon-Jérôme Lemaître, Marcelle Michel, Geneviève Vincent ... and in 1989, some of the avant-garde dance writers: Daniel Dobbels, Hervé Gauville, Alain-Paul Lequeux, Bernard Rémy, Chantal Aubry, Patrick Bossatti, Laurence Louppe ...
(This review ceased to be published in 1990.)

Danse Perspective
Founded in 1975. Directors: Philippe Braunschweig and T.V. Suppan. Chief editor: Antoine Livio. Chief contributors: Ghislaine Juramie, Pierre Julien, O.J. Lemaître, Claude Langel, Marcelle Michel.
Format: 21 × 29 as from no. 11.
Last issue: no. 20, 1977.

Danse No. I
Founded in 1977 by Thierry Mathis (from Maurice Béjart's school 'Mudra'. Irregular publication. Chief collaborators: Serge Keuten, Bernard Lefort, Brian de Martinon.
Format: 21 × 29.

Empreintes-Écrits Sur la Danse
Founded in 1977. Irregular publication. Chief editors: Patrick Bensard, Daniel Dobbels, Hervé Gauville, Bernard Rémy ...
Format: 21 × 29.
Last issue: no. 6, 1983.
(This was a remarkable review, presenting the deepest approaches to dance, and of a high literary quality.)

Danse
Founded in 1979 by Richard Flahaut, Jean-Pierre Lavolé, and from no. 7, by René Joly. Chief editor: Laurence Lavolé. Chief contributors: Guy Darmet, Anne Duvernoy, Didier Laurent, Jeanne Mareschal, Sonia Millian, François de Santerre, René Sirvin.
Format: 21 × 29.
Last issue: no. 10, February 1980.

Danser-Voir et Vivre la Danse
Founded in 1983. Chief editor: Jean-Claude Diénis. Chief contributors: Bernadette Bonis, Dominique Frétard, Agnès Izrine, Patrick Jaquin, Antoine Livio, Alain Nahmias, Dominique Passet, Geneviève Prudhommeau ...

And so, today, in 1989, there are three major publications devoted to dance on the French market: *Les Saisons de la danse, Pour la danse, Danser* (in chronological order). They each have their own tone, as it were; diversely more 'high-brow', more technical, more fashionable, but most of the ancients feuds are over and modern dance is fully accepted, although there are still cliques and factions, as there will doubtless always be!

I wish to thank the late Monique Babsky, documentalist and archivist passionately devoted to dance, who helped so many researchers, and helped me check this data concerning the specialized press.

A FEW AUTHORS WHO WROTE ABOUT DANCE

I also want to mention and praise those who devoted part of their talent to celebrating and furthering dance. I have included in the following short list only those (French) writers who fought for modern dance, or whose opinions brought about new approaches, and I have not included the great classics such as Paul Valéry's *L'Âme et la danse* or Noverre's *Letters* ...

Léandre Vaillat
French (1876–1952)
Literary studies. Became a journalist in 1904, subsequently an art critic. He fought, at his own costs, for Matisse and Picasso. For twenty-five years he was in charge of a column on problems of urbanization in the periodical *Temps*. He published books on such diverse subjects as Rabindranath Tagore, Morocco, painting, regionalism and Paris. From 1939 on, Léandre Vaillat was almost exclusively interested in classical dance. He was critic for *Carrefour*, and published several books on dance: *Histoire de la danse* (Plon, 1942); *La Taglioni* (Albin Michel, 1942); *Ballets de l'Opéra de Paris* (Cie française des arts graphiques, 1943 and 1947); *Olga Spessivtseva* (ditto, 1945); *Réflexions sur la danse* (Éditions de l'Artisan, 1947); *La Danse à l'Opéra de Paris* (Amiot-Dumont, 1949); *L'Invitation à la danse* (Albin Michel, 1953-a re-edition of *Réflexions*).

A writer with an elegant style, which unfortunately modern dance was not able to turn to its advantage.

Émile Vuillermoz
French (1878–1952)
A musician, composer and writer. In 1910 he founded the Société Musicale Indépendante which was to champion young composers. He wrote librettos for ballets, books on music and musicians and articles.

Endowed with a subtle and original mind, he was for almost half a century one of the leading French critics of dance and music. Amongst the works he published were: *Musique d'aujourd'hui* (Crès); *Clotilde et Alexandre Sakharoff* (Éditions Centrales Lausanne, 1933); *Histoire de la musique* (Fayard, 1973); *Claude Debussy* (Kister).

Maurice Brillant
French (1881–1953)
He studied history and philology and was a specialist in ancient Greek civilization. Both poet and scholar, he was interested in all the arts and especially theatre and dance. He was, as Françoise Reiss describes him in *Sur la pointe des pieds*, "*a devoted and strict servant of classical dance*". After the war, Maurice Brillant wrote many articles for several periodicals and reviews mainly for *Arts*. He wrote several important articles on the Ballets Russes for the *Revue Musicale* in 1929, and *La Technique de Pomiès* in *Pomiès* (Tisné, 1939). In 1953 he published *Problèmes de la danse* (Colin) which is in fact a history of dance.

Fernand Divoire
French (1883–1950)
He is the ancestor of the (public) supporters of modern dance! Fernand Divoire was above all a poet; his major work in this field is *Itinéraires*. He wrote essays about occultism and philosophy. He was also a journalist, writing articles and critiques for several periodicals including *La Revue Musicale*, *Art et Médecine* and *La Semaine à Paris*, the latter being read by a very wide public. Furthermore, he was for twenty-five years editor in chief of the important daily paper *L'Intransigeant*.

Enthusiastic about dance, captivated by Isadora Duncan, he made her, as it were, the gauge of his emotions and judgements.

He was a friend of many of those artists who had something to express. He was curious, strict, given to occasional prejudices, but generous and impassioned. Fernand Divoire made a real effort to understand dance and dancers, not just from the point of view of technique, but from that of the many motivations. Contrary to the clique of defenders of tradition, such as Lévinson, Brillant, Boll, etc., he furthered the development of modern dance in France. I have referred several times to two important works, which left their mark at the time: *Découvertes sur la danse* (1924) and *Pour la danse* (1935). He also wrote *La Danseuse de Diane*, illustrated by Dunoyer de Segonzac, and *Isadora Duncan, fille de Prométhée*, illustrated by José Clara.

(I had the opportunity to meet Fernand Divoire on several occasions at the studio of Mila Cirul, whose work he admired and for whom he had written ballet scenarios. I remember the venerable poet, his sharp glances and sometimes caustic speech, full of youthful enthusiasm.)

André Lévinson
Of Russian origin (1887–1933)
He settled in Paris in 1918 and soon became the first specialist. As early as 1922, he wrote articles for *Comoedia*, at that time a very important review devoted to the arts. He published several important books including *La Danse au théâtre* (1924), *La Danse d'aujourd'hui* (1929), *Les Visages de la danse* (1933) and works about Taglioni, Lifar and La Argentina.

He was most erudite, had a very sectarian attitude and defended tradition to the point of condemning Fokine's reforms, which indicates how hostile he was towards the new dance! Much of what he writes, however, is so apposite as to be stimulating.

Pierre Tugal
Of Russian origin (?–1964)
I referred to Pierre Tugal quite extensively in the chapter devoted to the Archives Internationales de la Danse, which he directed. He wrote prolifically and published many knowledgeable articles. He also published *Petite histoire de l'art et des artistes – la danse et les danseurs* (Nathan, 1950).

Valentin Parnac
Of Russian origin.
He was a music, theatre and dance critic in Russia, Germany and, from 1927, in Paris, in particular for *La Revue Musicale*. He also wrote about music hall, Jewish dance, Spanish dance, dervishes, the Ballets Russes and notation. His *Histoire de la danse* was published in 1932 (Éditions Reider). He did not accept Isadora's work, but I would like to quote the last paragraph of this book, which seems to be prophetic:

> *Those gentlemen who run music halls are certainly not aware of the fact that through the revues and turns they stage, to the sound of fox-trots and charlestons, can be discerned many things, greater, more moving than those which lie within the boundaries of the imagination. A mind avid for music is making no mistake when, in the midst of sumptuous triteness, he has a sudden direct feeling of pending disaster. Wars and revolutions have been foretold by dance songs. Vulgarity can hide aspirations filled with pathos. Without particular emphasis, in a light and elegant style, a musical fragment can reveal the condensed soul of our time. What music, what dances, or what silences are telling us of approaching upheavals?*

Ferdinando Reyna
Of Italian origin (?–1969)
Literary studies and activities. Historian of Italian dance, a specialist in classical dance, but not hostile to modern dance. As a critic, he wrote for several French periodicals, and held several posts connected with dance, such as chairman of the Ballet Club de Paris. He published *Des Origines du ballet* (Tallone, 1955), *Histoire du ballet* (Somogy, 1964), *Dictionnaire des ballets* (Larousse, 1967).

Françoise Stanciu-Reiss
French, born in 1915.
Dance critic since 1949, Françoise Reiss is a specialist on the Ballet Russes and on Nijinsky. She has written for many periodicals, reviews and encyclopedias. She has published several works of literary criticism, including *Pour une critique vivante* (Nizet, 1981). *Sur la pointe des pieds* is a survey of what took place in dance in Paris from 1951–53, but her most remarkable work is that concerning Nijinsky *Nijinsky ou la grâce* (1957; re-edited by Éditions d'Aujourd'hui, 1980). Still very active, she founded the International Association of Friends of Nijinsky in 1989.

Germaine Prudhommeau
French, born in 1923.
This enthusiastic historian obtained her Ph.D. with *La Technique de la danse grecque antique*. She was appointed research director at the Centre National de Recherche Scientifique (C.N.R.S.) in 1948, and initiated the first courses in history of dance and of general culture at the Paris Opéra School. She is currently professor of dance history at Paris University-I and lectures the world over.

Germaine Prudhommeau has published *Grammaire de la danse classique* (Hachette, 1969; translated, various works into Spanish and English); *Histoire de la danse – des origines à la fin du Moyen-Age* (Amphora, 1986), and *De la Renaissance à la Révolution* (Amphora).

Jacques Baril
French (1924–1984)
Jacques Baril, open to all forms of art, especially sculpture, and thereby to movement, discovered dance through the work of Janine Charrat, whose *gestures filled with will and power* seemed akin to his own style. He wrote his first articles on dance in 1953 for *Toute la Danse*. From 1956 he taught dance history and sociology at the École Supérieure d'Études

Chorégraphiques, and in 1968 became one of the founders and editors of *Les Saisons de la Danse*.

He published *Dictionnaire de danse* (Le Seuil, 1964), *Janine Charrat – la tentation de l'impossible* (Michel Brient, 1964) and *La Danse moderne – d'Isadora Duncan à Twyla Tharp* (Vigot, 1977).

Marie-Françoise Christout

Whilst pursuing university studies in arts, archeology and aesthetics, Marie-Françoise Christout took lessons, just for pleasure, in classical and modern dance. She wrote two theses concerned with dance. From 1951 she wrote didactic articles for *Dance Magazine* (U.S.A.), *Dance and Dancers* (G.B) and for the rising French specialized press. She was appointed secretary for the Institut Chorégraphique of Serge Lifar.

She is an authority on matters of performing arts and dance history, holds important positions in diverse institutions, writes and teaches. She has published amongst other works *Le Merveilleux et le Théâtre du Silence* (Mouton, 1965), *Le Ballet de cour de Louis XIV. 1643–1672* (Picard, 1967), *Maurice Béjart* (Chiron, 1987), *Le Ballet de cour au XVIIe siècle* (Minkoff, 1987), *Le Ballet Occidental* (Desjonquières, 1995) … and has contributed texts for many specialized books, encyclopedias, etc.

Jean Silvant

He was born in Lyons, intended to be a painter and grew interested in dance through Hélène Carlut and Françoise Michaut (Dupuy). He became one of the most eager supporters of modern dance and through his writings helped many young choreographers in the 50s and 60s who were working for the acceptance and understanding of the new dance. Much may be owed to him and his early death prevented him from seeing the flowering of what he sowed.

Paul Bourcier

Being in charge of the department of cultural information at the France-Presse Agency, Paul Bourcier gradually became very interested in dance. In 1962 he wrote articles and became dance critic for the review *Nouvelles littéraires*, being well acquainted with all the trends in France and abroad. In 1973 he was appointed teacher of the history of movement at Paris University-VII. He has published *Histoire de la danse en Occident* (Le Seuil, 1978), *Danser devant les dieux* (Chiron, 1989).

Lise Brunel

She pursued at the same time university studies and training in different types of dance. She furthered her knowledge of contemporary techniques with Ludolf Schild, Karin Waehner and Jean Serry. Since 1958 she has been called to write, as dance critic, in several periodicals.

She collaborated with Françoise and Dominique Dupuy in the organization of the dance programmes of A.R.C at the Museum of Modern Art. After this closed in 1974, she founded 'Action/danse' uniting some twenty modern dance companies, with the object of giving a coherent structure and organization to the profession. She was put in charge of several radio and television programmes on dance.

Lise Brunel has published *Nouvelle danse française* (Albin Michel, 1980), *Trisha Brown* (Bougé, 1987), *Danse, l'expérience de La Rochelle* (Rumeur des Ages, 1982) and has contributed to several collective works and encyclopedias.

Gilberte Cournand and La Danse

A rallying point, a treasure-trove for teachers, dancers and scholars, Gilberte Cournand is an important person in the world of French dance. Her understanding of the problems with which dancers are faced led her in 1951, to found La Danse, a gallery as well as a book-shop. She is an historian, lecturer, writer and dance critic, and has produced a collection of gramophone records to accompany classes in classical and contemporary dance. She married a well known doctor, studied music, dance and singing. Highly attracted by art, she commissioned sculptures, portraits and drawings connected with dance from talented artists. An expert collector, she put on exhibitions of works by Louis Legrand, Charpentier-Mio, Benois, Bakst, Berard, Charcoune, Carlotti and Doboujinsky amongst others. She also launched the books of Serge Lido and Irène Lidova.

Gilberte Cournand has used all her knowledge and abilities to render homage to artists such as Serge Lifar, Anna Pavlova, Lycette Darsonval and Yvette Chauviré. Never will be forgotten those private views of paintings, photographs and books in springtime at her gallery at the charming Place Dauphine which became an extension of her 'salon'. For truly she held a permanent 'salon', always filled with people wishing to listen, contemplate, meet, discuss and learn, like the centre of a network she had woven at a high level.

Alas, Gilberte Cournand closed her shop and gallery, La Danse, in April 1989.

PERIOD PIECES: A FEW HOWLERS

Without wishing to point an accusing finger at any particular person, it seemed amusing to me to quote a few 'period' opinions about this poor style of dance (free, populist, expressionist, modern, contemporary ...), just to indicate how long it takes, beyond any special individual temperaments and approaches, for a new idea to be understood and eventually accepted. I shall, therefore, quote a few paragraphs, simply giving the year of their publication except for the first example, which has now become history, and the author of which, from the hereafter, will bear me no malice ...

With the Populist Dancers by Jean Dorcy
(from *Toute la Danse*, Sept–Oct 1955)

> *In Paris, the general staff of the retarded floor-bound creatures worry and thrash about. Their concern? Certainly not the state of the lower limbs of their followers but the search for a name to replace 'German Expressionism' no longer approved of today.*
>
> *The Americans, of the same church, describe the Swedish gym set to music and the various bodily collapses – the subject of current research – as Modern Dance.*
>
> *Over here, 'Modern Dance' is first and foremost ballroom dancing. Confusion would certainly arise if the same word were used to describe two sorts of dance. 'German Expressionism' is well and truly finished and there is no question of replacing it by one of the words in use in the muscle business: Rhythmic, Harmonic, Body Melody, Expressive Dance, or yet some Feminine Gymnastics. This is where we stand.*
>
> *What does 'German Expressionism' represent? For some, including myself, a speaking actor's method. But if it is to be classified in the universe of dance, one can only refer to it as 'low dance',* [Reference is to "basse danse" that type of gliding dance of the fifteenth century, in opposition to 'danse, haute' which implied leaving the ground in leaps, hops etc. J.R.] *Low dance: that which is unable to make full use of space, which lacks vigour, and the beating of whose wings is similar to the heavy, lumbering flight of the bat. Our puffing maenads place the problem elsewhere, limiting it to 'expression through movement'. This states or at least implies that the abstract writing of an accomplished classical dancer is inexpressive. A matter of understanding obviously, and of taste as well. I will accept that Yvette Chauviré as Istar, Vyroubova as the Swan (the Lifar-Chopin version), and Adabache as Salome can leave one cold. But I must ask for reciprocity. That it should be accepted that the crawling about of Madame Graham's girls and boys, wiping the stage with the best-covered parts of their anatomy, only gets one reaction out of me: the sweepers will have rather less to do tomorrow.*
>
> *Low Dance!*
>
> *It can be understood that Folklore is not competing.*
>
> *Popular Dance? This term covers all kinds of dance, popular and*
practised to the point where it becomes part of a tradition.

The People's Dance! Such a term implies a biased attitude, referring to the revels of a certain social class.

Populist Dance! Here we are very close. I think this term goes beyond a squabble. Populist dance would in any case deserve more universal application than 'German Expressionism'. Populist dance would be that which immediately pleases the majority. The faithful, those who want to learn a dance in five lessons, would innocently think that simple images may be learnt easily. The consumers, for their part, would find comfort in a direct gesticulation not based on a system of gymnastics. Goodbye to problems of transposition!

To flee from myths, to copy life, to say nuts to any morphology, what more does one want to be able to breathe freely?

After all, 'German Expressionism' was all of that, with, in addition – and this made the Latin's skin crawl – a love of the unpleasant, an inhuman desire to include this in gestures.

Briefly, if I joined in the discussion, I would not have the curiosity to go further than Populist Dance.

I know fairly well the Parisian practitioners of Populist Dance. One of them, Raymonde Lombardin, has, according to my view of the populism of the dance, signed the masterpiece of 'The Third Man' type. The theme: the cheap suburban pimp. Here Raymonde Lombardin makes use of gesticulations from which has been banished all idea of bodily architecture: the dancer reads a newspaper on stage, walks about hands in pockets, tired-looking clothes and the inevitable characteristictics. Here we have in dance sequences 'Prosper' as popularised by Maurice Chevalier. Raymonde Lombardin's piece resorts to ready-made stuff. An artist looks for the unseen, rare and telling image. 'The Third Man' is such a well known, banal image. If populism in visual images calls for signs of daily routine, Raymonde Lombardin could not do otherwise.

Raymonde Lombardin possesses the secret of movement. It is to be regretted that such gifts do not serve more dancing solos.

With Anne Gardon, the problem becomes more complicated. This maenad is an unusual character. When the frenzy takes her, she bucks and pranks, tearing through the backcloth. Creations such as her 'Danses Gnossiennes' (Satie) confuse us. We could and perhaps should not classify them as populist dance where everything is thought out, for we have there a succession of signs with no relationship to any particular verism. What a poet the wild Anne Gardon is here!

There is something else with this artist: a real concert dancer. In days when a dance is composed on Wednesday to be performed on Thursday, Anne Gardon imagines, composes, recomposes, decants – as the nice Sakharoffs used to do – and offers us some striking moments.

Now here is Olga Stens. She makes us realize how illusory is any absolute classification. I believe this dancer has read everything, as I know she has studied all types of dance. She remains faithful to her dear Mila Cirul. But must I say

*nothing of her daily work over many years with the greatest classical masters –
Zvereff, Egorova, Anna Stephann, Peretti? It is not one but several masterpieces
which this artist has in her repertoire. I would mention, in order of my preference,
'L'Indifférent' 'Images de la Russie ancienne, the revolutionary 'Rencontre' (a
hundred per cent acting). Never anything common in Olga Sten's solos. Quite the
contrary. The catch is that the artistic intent is so obvious in what she signs, which
robs us of a full appreciation of her pieces. Although she plays in many styles,
Olga Stens must be classified with the populists. A point to consider, neither
Raymonde Lombardin, nor Anne Gardon, nor Olga Stens are Latins.*

*Now we have to realize that this type of dance is in constant develop-
ment. Borrowings from the classical school are countless in number. Obviously
the nuns of the low dance claim that the classical school has absorbed their
contribution. We shall come back to that.*

*We must conclude, however, by saying that we await from low dance
performers who can be set on a parallel with the goddesses of high dance.*

Jean Dorcy

One can easily imagine the reaction of the "nuns" to this article. They got
together and drafted an answer which was published in January 1956, in
this same review, of course. Jean Silvant, the chief editor wrote: *Following
the article by Jean Dorcy entitled 'Chez les danseurs populistes', which appeared
in the September–October issue of the review, we have received the following reply
from Raymonde Lombardin, Anne Gardon, Suzanne Rémon, Jacqueline Robinson,
Claude Stéphane, Karin Waehner, Geneviève Mallarmé, and Messrs Paul d'Arnot
and Jean Serry, which we are happy to include in our correspondence column, open
to all and making no aesthetic distinctions,* to introduce the following:

*For anyone who knows, prizes and admires Mr Jean Dorcy, it was
painful to read the article which he published in 'Toute la danse' of September
1955. It seems difficult to understand how this man, usually courteous,
cultivated, elegant even in the very simplest of words when he speaks in public
could suddenly drop all these characteristics to attack modern dance in writing.*

*Is it courteous to describe women using expressions such as 'retarded
floor-bound creatures', or 'puffing maenads'? Is it courteous to affirm that
dancers 'wipe the stage with the best-covered parts of their anatomy'? We can
also note that, after describing modern dancers twice as maenads, he then calls
them 'low dance nuns' ... Are we to understand that as an involuntary
expression of Mr Jean Dorcy's desire to see nuns become maenads, or vice versa?*

*So much for courtesy. For the rest, let us say that Monsieur Jean Dorcy
is simply badly informed. He suggests replacing 'Modern dance' by the expression
'Populist dance'. He backs up this proposal with statements that are odd, to say
the least: modern dance in France means 'Ballroom dancing' which is almost true.*

But when we know that 'Modern dance' means 'Modern dance' in England, Germany, Canada, the United States and the whole of Latin America, one may wonder whether French terminology might not benefit from adopting the same interpretation. Besides, to be exact, we should note, that 'ballroom dancing' is called 'ballroom dancing' in French. Within this 'ballroom dancing' there exists a 'modern' category, as in all dancing and that is all. The waltz has always been called ballroom dancing and not a modern dance.

So far as the 'populist' label is concerned, we are sorry to have to tell Jean Dorcy that it has existed for a long time. It is used to describe a literary school which has the self-imposed task of bringing the people to life in literature. It has been brilliantly successful in this task. It would seem appropriate to render to Caesar what is Caesar's and to leave to the founders of 'populism' the ownership of the term 'Populist' which they forged.

Monsieur Jean Dorcy is once again ill-informed when he states that a group of modern dancers are 'worrying and thrashing about'. Its concern? In no way the condition of the legs of the flock, nor the search for a term to replace that of 'German Expressionism'.

The information gleaned by Monsieur Jean Dorcy is incomplete and we believe that it would have been preferable for him to obtain his information at source rather than make fatuous remarks without background knowledge: it is true a group of modern dancers has been meeting regularly throughout the year, but it is false that they meet to find a title. Not only were the modern dancers concerned with their legs at these meetings, but they made them work too, as their main aim was to exchange the results of their work. These meetings took place in working clothes; tights in other words. The modern dancers, during these work sessions, also had their arms, bodies, lungs and breath working. Monsieur Jean Dorcy seems to think that only legs count. We choose to believe that this is a typographical error.

That is not all: the modern dancers also met to work on elements of choreographies, to compare different ways of giving life to space and of building a choreographic architecture. Because, still something else which Monsieur Jean Dorcy was not told, modern dancers have concerns of this type.

A lack of information once again as regards the significance of the words 'expression through movement'. We greatly admire muscular achievements and, within the compass of our feeble means and puffing breath, we subject ourselves to a daily training of several hours. But we believe that the condition for expression is not muscular achievement. Expression is something far more subtle.

'A matter of comprehension' says Monsieur Jean Dorcy. We can only repeat after him 'a matter of comprehension'. If Monsieur Jean Dorcy fails to understand Martha Graham, it is a pity ... for him.

Monsieur Jean Dorcy also makes a mistake when he says that the dance he labels 'popular' will be that which will naturally seduce the greatest number.

The truth, in fact, is quite the reverse: it is classical dancing which seduces the majority, whilst the modern dancers are constantly fighting for their existence.

Monsieur Jean Dorcy is mistaken one again on the ethnic origin of those modern dancers whom he says are not 'Latins'. Amongst the 'retarded floor-bound creatures' (a Latin floor), we would mention Françoise and Dominique Dupuy, Paul d'Arnot and Raymonde Lombardin, Geneviève Mallarmé, Suzanne Rémon, etc.

Finally, Monsieur Jean Dorcy casts doubt on the fact that classical dancers may have absorbed a part of modern dance's contribution. He has doubtless not seen the admirable Modern Ballets of Maurice Béjart, entitled 'Voyage au coeur d'un enfant' and, 'Symphonie pour un homme seul'. He perhaps has not understood the humour with which Maurice Béjart, in the 'Belle au boa' has satirized, the thirty-two 'fouettés' and the arduous 'portés'.

It seems to us that these various adjustments are necessary to allow Monsieur Jean Dorcy to review his rash statements more closely. We hope he will read them in an indulgent frame of mind and earnestly hope to find him soon as we have admired him.

(So far as I am concerned, as one of the signatories of this letter at the time, I find it very timorous today – our irony too wrapped up. But perhaps it was better to meet rudeness with courtesy. Were there other arguments for our defence, with which to win others to our cause?)

Referring to Lisa and Isadora Duncan

... She can be attractive, and could have been a dancer. But she was a pupil of Duncan. And nothing of what (at the time) made Isadora's renown can be learnt or taught. As to her elementary doctrine, her doubtful musicality, her lack of technique they could in no way provide a pedagogical grounding. It is pitiful to see a Lisa Duncan, naturally graceful and blest with a tiny choreographic flame, struggle against the consequences of an illusory education, and attempt to fill in the gaps of a childhood wasted for a then fashionable game – no more so today ... (1929)

Concerning Mary Wigman

... German opinion was almost unanimous in praising 'Der Feuer' a liturgical, funereal, triomphal action. We have found this secular ceremony unbearably tedious, filled with intellectual conceit, perverted in its humanity by the overflow of sentiment. Truly is it a megalomanic art, bombastic and wanting ... (1929)

Referring to German Dance

... most of the dance pieces where an ever stilted imagination is at work, belong to the area of mime. They imply a painful tension of the whole being. The

dancer's eyes stare, his fingers splayed; his body twisted by terror, he drags himself along the ground, stamps furiously, and falls, exhausted.

The classical dancer defies gravity and spurns the sense of weight. The modern German dances with all his mass and weight. The ballet dancer seeks grace; a pupil of Madame Wigman seeks to impress by the breaking up of bodily harmony, in a would-be eloquent distortion. Our ballerinas move and exude a feminine charm, a subtle sexual attraction, distilled and sublimated through the dance. The feminity of a 'rhythmic' dancer is well-nigh abolished. Manlike and resolute, with a wide pelvis and robust legs, she goes to it all of a piece ... (1929)

Referring to Anne Gardon
... Why does she offer us certain terrifying visions when she is beautiful and refined, elegant? Why look for what is horrible, when one can put across mischievousness or poetic charm? ... (1948)

Referring to Isadora Duncan
... this impassioned missionary, wielding a poor and woolly philosophy, was a great artist and even had a stroke of genius. But she was not a dancer. To the balletomanes and orthodox dancers her principles are simply heresies ... (1953)

Referring to Expressionism in Germany
... more akin to mime than to dance, lacking in means, technique, vocabulary, its great apostles were the rough theoretician Rudolf von Laban and his emancipated disciple, later his opponent, Madame Mary Wigman. It would seem that a deliberate search for ugliness (a somewhat romantic view), takes the place we give to harmony and beauty. In this case, we hover on the one hand, between overdone pathos, unbridled paroxysms, and on the other, grotesque, wry, even macabre distortion. Never any lightness (always the heavy tramping of the earthbound artist), never a smile nor any grace ... (1953)

Sundry
... the German Terpsichore sticks like glue to her adepts' ankles ... the tortuous dead-ends of so-called free dance ... (1956–57)

Referring to Metaphysics
... Why must those who use modern techniques display a perverse liking for metaphysical themes? Nothing could be more tedious in a ballet. Miss W.'s 'Quo Vadis' succeeds in being pompously boring. Why does Miss P. want to offer us 'Inner faces' to music by Bartók? Is that the purpose of dance? If the attitudes of the human body, the rhythms and figures that can be built with dancers are to suggest any transcendence, it were better not to underline it, but let it pervade

our mind as an added effect. Preferable are the innocent capers composed by Miss C. ... (1959)

Concerning Happy Themes

... It would appear that in our time there is a tendency to move away from happy and poetic themes; the subjects are increasingly morbid, or refer to philosophy. Modern choreographers have no more imagination to create ballets that are lively and healthy ... (1963)

Referring to Free Danse

... the price of an ideal, that is, complete freedom, both spiritual and physical, in the practice of an art that only the most unrelenting of disciplines may bring to life, an art that must go beyond technique to be an art at all; and that going beyond, is that not the very condition of the initial acquisition of technique? The price of freedom is the impossibility of creating a school, of building a tradition, or putting down rules. Laban, father of 'modern' dance, gives the impression of having created a school, of having had disciples who furthered his work. The most important of these are Mary Wigman, Martha Graham, Kurt Jooss. But there too, the diversity of techniques and styles was immediate. An overall view of the aspects of free dance may be drawn by calling to mind the solitary personality of Harald Kreutzberg, a total artist in the line of these great silent mimes of yesteryear, a particularly clear symbol of the greatness of free dance and of its limits; its greatness lying in the personality of he who makes and embodies it; its limits being the impossibility of forming disciples and having followers who pursue the work ... (1967)

Concerning Modern Dance

... 'modern dance', which we see reappearing from time to time as a youthful and revolutionary novelty, is a very limited form of creation and seems to have been invented for those dancers who, ignorant of dance, hide their shortcomings beneath aesthetic dogmas that are fortunately hazy. Around 1920, 'modern' ballet reached us from Germany. It has returned after a detour to America, those German dancers who fled from Hitlerism having had imitators in the United States. To sum up, the 'modern' ballet, when it is not actually pantomime, falls into the worst of negative clichés: dancers are barefoot (because classical dancers have shoes), wear leotards (because classical dancers wear tunics and tutus), feet turned in (because classicism demands turn-out), arms akimbo or stiffly held behind the back (because classicism seeks beauty of gesture), fighting or crawling in the dust (because clas sicism means elevation), and finally, superimposed bodies and more or less realistic simulations of what gentlemen and ladies do more comfortably in bed. All that is dreadfully childish ... (1969).

BIBLIOGRAPHY

This list comprises those works of interest that have come to my knowledge and are to be divided into two categories:

– Those published in France or in French during the period 1920–1970 (or later …) covering various aspects of dance: specifically French and more general.
– Those works published in other countries, indispensable "classics" or concerning events, persons, trends to which I refer in this book.

A short list, to be sure, and, moreover, a subjective choice …

In France

Allard, Odette, *Malkowsky, le danseur philosophe* (Editions Poliphile, 1984).

Arguel, Mireille, *Dance et enseignement – quel corps?* (Vigot, 1980). *Le corps en jeu* (PUF, 1992).

Arout, Gabriel, *La Danse contemporaine* (Nathan, 1955).

Les Ballets Suédois (joint authorship) (Editions du Trianon, 1931).

Baril, Jacques, *La Danse moderne de I. Duncan à T. Tharp* (Vigot, 1977).

Barrault, Jean Louis, *Souvenirs pour demain* (Le Seuil, 1972). *Comme je le pense* (Gallimard, 1975).

Béjart, Maurice, *L'Autre chant de la danse* (Flammarion, 1974).

Berge, Yvonne, *Vivre son corps* (Le Seuil, 1975). *Danse la vie* (Le Souffle d'Or, 1994).

Bernard, Michel, *Le Corps* (Editions Universitaires, 1972). *L'Expressivité du corps* (Chiron, 1976).

Bertherat, Thérèse, *Le Corps a ses raisons* (Le Seuil, 1976).

Bourcier, Paul, *Histoire de la danse en Occident* (Le Seuil, 1978). *Danser devant les dieux* (Chiron, 1989).

Brosse, Jacques, *Cinq méditations sur le corps* (Stock, 1967).

Brunel, Lise, *La Nouvelle danse française* (Albin Michel, 1980).

Challet-Haas, Jacqueline, *La Danse – les principes de son enseignement aux enfants* (Amphora, 1983).

Christout, Marie Françoise, *Histoire du Ballet* (PUF, 1966). *Le Ballet de Cour de Louis XIV* (Picard, 1967). *Maurice Béjart* (Seghers, 1972). *Le Ballet Occidental* (Desjonquères, 1995).

Copeau, Jacques, *Les Registres du Vieux-Colombier* (Gallimard, 1974).

Calais-Germain, Blandine, *Anatomie par le mouvement* (Association Médiane, 1984).

Dalcroze, Émile Jaques; *Souvenirs, notes et critiques* (Akinger, Neuchatel, 1942). *Le Rythme, la musique et l'éducation* (Foetisch, Lausanne, 1965). *La Musique et nous* (Slatkine, Genève, 1945).

Danilo, Albert and Stévenin, Philippe, *Le Corps dans la vie quotidienne* (EPI, 1974).

Dictionnaire du ballet moderne (Hazan, 1957).

Divoire, Fernand, *Découvertes sur la danse* (Grès, 1924). *Pour la danse* (Saxe, 1935).

Dobbels, Daniel, *Empreintes* (magazine 1977–84).

Dropsy, Jacques, *Vivre dans son corps* (EPI, 1973).

Dullin, Charles, *Souvenirs et notes de travail* (Mieuthier, 1946).

Durand, Gilbert, *Les Structures anthropologiques de l'imaginaire* (Dunod, 1969).

Ellipses (joint authorship) (Danse à Lille, 1992).

Eyquem, Marie-Thérèse, *Irène Popard ou la danse du feu* (Editions du temps, 1959).

Feldenkrais, Moshe, *L'Expression corporelle* (Chiron, 1965).

Fous de danse (joint authorship) (Autrement, 1983).

Garaudy, Roger, *Danser sa vie* (Le Seuil, 1963).

Guy, Jean Michel, *Les Publics de la danse* (Documentation Française, 1991).

Jousse, Marcel, *L'Anthropologie du geste* (Resma, 1969).

Jouvet, Louis, *Créativité de l'acteur* (Librairie Théâtrale, 1952).

La Danse art du XXe siècle? (joint authorship) (Editions Payot, Lausanne, 1990).

La Danse, naissance d'un mouvement de pensée (joint authorship) (A. Colin, 1989).

Lapierre, A. and Aucouturier, B., *La Symbolique du mouvement* (EPI, 1984).

Le Boulch, Henri, *Vers une science du mouvement humain* (ESF, 1971).

Legendre, Pierre, *La Passion d'être un autre* (Le Seuil, 1978).

Lévinson, André, *La Danse au théâtre* (Paris, 1924). *La Danse d'aujourd'hui* (1929, Actes Sud, 1994).

Lidova, Irène, *Ma vie avec la danse* (Editions Plume, 1992).

Lifar, Serge, *Le Manifeste du chorégraphe* (Hachette, 1935). *Les Mémoires d'Icare* (Hachette).

Lobet, Marcel, *Le Ballet français d'aujourd'hui* (Librairie Théâtrale, 1958).

Loux, Françoise, *Le Corps dans la société traditionnelle* (Berger Levrault, 1979).

Martinet, Susanne, *La Musique du corps* (Chiron, 1990).

Michaut, Pierre, *Le Ballet contemporain* (Ides and Calendes, 1952).

Niclas, Lorinna (*et al.*) *La Danse dans le monde* (Armand Colin, 1991).

Parnac, Valentin, *Histoire de la Danse* (Reider Paris, 1932).

Pinok and Matho, *La Dynamique de la création* (Vrin, 1976). *Expression corporelle, mouvement et pensée* (Vrin, 1979).

Porte, Alain, *François Delsarte* (Editions IPMC, 1992).

Prudhommeau, Germaine, *La Danse grecque antique* (CNRS, 1965). *Histoire de la danse* (Amphora, 1986).

Pujade-Renaud, Claude, *Expression corporelle, langage du silence* (ESF, 1975). *Danse et narcissisme en éducation* (ESF, 1976).

Reiss, Françoise, *Sur la pointe des pieds* (Adam, 1952; Lieutier, 1953). *Nijinsky ou la grâce* (Editions d'aujourd'hui, 1980).

Reyna, Ferdinando, *Histoire du ballet* (Aimery Somogy, 1981).

Robinson, Jacqueline, *L'Enfant et la danse* (Chiron, 1975). *Éléments du langage chorégraphique* (Vigot, 1981). *Introduction au langage musical* (Chiron, 1989). *Danse chemin d'éducation* (self-published, 1993). *Une certaine idée de la danse* (Chiron, 1997).

Rouquet, Odile, *Les Techniques d'analyse du mouvement* (Fed. Fse de Danse, 1985).

Schott-Billmann, France, *Le Primitivisme en Danse* (Chiron, 1989).

Serry, Jean, *Par le mouvement* (Pro Musica, Freiburg, 1973).

Sheleen, Laura, *Théâtre pour devenir autre* (EPI, 1983).

Solane, Janine, *Pour une danse plus humaine* (Vautrain, 1950).

Soupault, Philippe, *Terpsichore* (1928, Actes Sud, 1986).

Tugal, Pierre, *Initiation à la danse* (Grenier, 1947) *La Danse et les danseurs* (Nathan, 1950).

Vaillat, Léandre, *Histoire de la Danse* (Plon, 1942). *Réflexions sur la danse* (Editions de l'artisan, 1947). *L'Invitation à la danse* (Albin Michel, 1953).

Vuillermoz, Émile, *Clotilde et Alexandre Sakharoff* (Editions Centrales, Lausanne, 1933).

Waehner, Karin, *Outillage chorégraphique* (Vigot, 1993).

Elsewhere

Anderson, Jack, *Ballet and Modern Dance* (Dance Horizons, NY, 1986).

Armitage, Merle, *Dance Memoranda* (Duell Sloan, NY, 1949).

Aube, Hermann and Marianne, *Der künstlerische Tanz unserer Zeit* (Königstein, Leipzig, 1930).

Bach, Rudolf, *Das Mary Wigman Werk* (Reissner, Dresden, 1933).

Blom and Chaplin, *The Intimate Act of Choreography* (Univ. Pittsburgh, 1982).

Rosalia Chladek Tanzerin, Choregraphin, Pädagogin (joint authorship) (Öster-reichischer Bundesverlag, 1965).

Cohen, Selma-Jeanne, *The Modern Dance – Seven Statements of Belief* (Wes-leyan Univ. Press, 1966). *Doris Humphrey – An Artist First* (Wesleyan Univ. Press, 1972). *Dance as a Theatre Art* (Harper, NY, 1974). *Next Week, Swan Lake* (Wesleyan Univ. Press, 1982).

Coton, A.V., *The New Ballet, Kurt Jooss and his Work* (Dobson, London, 1946).

de Mille, Agnes, *Dance to the Piper* (Hamish Hamilton, London, 1951). *The Book of the Dance* (Artists and Writers Press, NY, 1963). *Martha* (Hutchinson, London, 1992).

Denby, Edward, *Looking at the Dance* (Horizon Press, NY, 1968).

Delius, Rudolf von, *Mary Wigman* (Reissner, Dresden, 1925).

Duncan, Irma, *The Technique of Isadora Duncan* (Kamin, NY, 1937).

Duncan, Isadora, *The Art of the Dance* (Theatre Art Books, NY, 1970).

Elsworth-Todd, Mabel, *The Thinking Body* (Dance Horizons, NY, 1937).

Forti, Simone, *Handbook on Motion* (New York Univ. Press, 1974).

Fraleigh, Sandra-Horton, *Dance and the Lived Body* (Univ. Pittsburgh Press, 1987).

Gleister, Martin, *Tanz für Alle* (Hesse and Becker, Leipzig, 1928).

Graham, Martha, *Notebooks* (Harcourt Brace, NY, 1973). *Blood Memory* (Doubleday, NY, 1991).

H'Doubler, Margaret, *Dance: a Creative Art Experience* (Crofts, NY, 1940).

Hawkins, Alma, *Creating through Dance* (Prentice Hall, N. Jersey, 1966). *Modern Dance in Higher Education* (Columbia Univ. 1955).

Hodgson, John and Valerie Preston-Dunlop, *Rudolf Laban – An Introduc-tion to his Work and Influence* (Northcote House, Plymouth, 1990).

Horst, Louis and Russell, Caroll, *Preclassic Dance Forms* (Kamin, NY, 1953) *Modern Dance Forms* (Dance Horizons, NY, 1961).

Humphrey, Doris, *The Art of Making Dances* (Grove Press, NY, 1959) (translated by Jacqueline Robinson as *Construire la danse* (Coutaz, 1990)).

Hurok, Sol, *Impresario* (Macdonald and Evans, London, 1947).

Laban, Rudolf von, *Ein Leben für den Tanz* (Reissner, Dresden, 1935) (translated by Lisa Ullmann as *A Life for Dance* (Macdonald and Evans, London, 1975). *Choreutics* (Macdonald and Evans, 1966). *The Mastery of Movement* (Macdonald and Evans, London, 1966). *A Vision of Dynamic Space* (trans. Lisa Ullmann) (Falmer Press, London, 1984).

Lloyd, Margaret, *The Borzoi Book of Modern Dance* (Dance Horizons, NY, 1949).

Louis, Murray, *Inside Dance* (St Martin's Press, NY, 1980).

Martin, John, *The Modern Dance* (Dance Horizons, NY, 1933). (translated by Jacqueline Robinson as *La Danse moderne* (Actes Sud, 1991). *Introduction to the Dance* (Norton, NY, 1939). *The Dance* (Tudor, NY, 1946).

Morison-Brown, Jean, *The Vision of Modern Dance* (joint authorship) (Dance Books, London, 1980).

Muller, Hedwige and F.M. Peter, *Mary Wigman* (Quadriga Verlag, Berlin, 1986). *Dore Hoyer, Tänzerin* (Edition Hentrich, Köln, 1992).

Nagrin, Daniel, *Dance, the Specific Image* (Pittsburg Univ. Press, 1993).

Ossona, Paulina, *Educación por la danza* (Buenos Aires, 1976). *El lenguaje del cuerpo danza moderna.*

Peter, Frank Manuel, *Valeska Gert* (Fröhlich and Kaufmann, Köln, 1985).

Pirchan, Emil, *Harald Kreutzberg* (Frick Verlag, Wien, 1950).

Preston-Dunlop, Valerie *A Handbook for Modern Educational Dance* (Macdonald and Evans, London, 1963) (second edition: *A Handbook for Dance in Education* (1980). *Practical kinetography* (Macdonald and Evans, London, 1969). *Dancing and Dance Theory* (Laban Centenary Publication, 1979).

Russell, Jean, *Modern Dance in Education* (Macdonald and Evans, London, 1958).

St-Denis, Ruth, *My Unfinished Life* (Harper, NY, 1939).

Schliche, Susana, *Tanz Theatre, Tradition und Freiheit* (Rowalt Taschenbuch Verlag, 1987).

Seigel, Marcia, *The Shapes of Change* (Univ. of California Press, 1979). *Days on Earth – the Dance of Doris Humphrey* (Yale Univ. Press, 1982). *The Tail of the Dragon – New Dance* (Duke Univ. Press, 1991).

Selden, Elizabeth, *Elements of the Free Dance* (Barnes, NY, 1930). *The Dancer's Quest* (Univ. of California Press, 1935).

Shawn, Ted, *Dance We Must* (Haskell House, NY, 1940). *Every Little Movement* (Dance Horizons, NY, 1954).

Sorell, Walter, *The Dance Has Many Faces* (Columbia Univ. Press, 1966). *Hanya Holm* (Wesleyan Univ. Press, 1969). *The Mary Wigman Book* (Wesleyan Univ. Press, 1975) (in German: *Mary Wigman – Ein Vermächtnis* (Noetzel Verlag, Wilhelmshaven, 1986). *Dance in its Time* (Columbia Univ. Press, 1986). *Looking Back in Wonder* (Columbia Univ. Press, 1986).

Stanislawski, Constantin, *An Actor Prepares* (Theatre Arts Books, NY, 1936). *My Life in Art* (Geoffrey Bles, London, 1924).

Terry, Walter, *The Dance in America* (Harper, NY, 1956). *Miss Ruth* (Dodd Mead, NY, 1969).

Stebbins, Genevieve, *The Delsarte System of Expression* (Dance Horizons, NY, 1978).

Taylor, Paul, *Private Domain* (North Point Press, SF, 1985).

Wigman, Mary, *Deutsche Tanzkunst* (Reissner, Dresden, 1935). *Die Sprache des Tanzes* (Battenberg Verlag, Stuttgart, 1963) (translated by Walter Sorell as *The Language of Dance* (Wesleyan Univ. Press, 1966) (translated by Jacqueline Robinson as *Le Langage de la danse* (Chiron, 1986).

Winearls, Jane, *Modern Dance – the Jooss-Leeder Method* (A. and C. Black, London, 1958).

Zivier, Georg, *Mary Wigman, Harmonie und Ekstase* (Wasmuth, Berlin, 1956).

Other books by Jacqueline Robinson

ON DANCE:

L'enfant et la danse (auto-edited, 1975, 1988, 1993)

El niño y la danza – translated by Sara Lopez Santos & Carlos Murias Vila. (Ediciones Octaedra Barcelona 1992)

Éléments du langage chorégraphique (Editions Vigot, 1981, 1988, 1992, 1997)

L'aventure de la danse moderne en France (Bougé, 1990)

Introduction au langage musical (Editions Chiron, 1991)

Danse chemin d'éducation (auto-edited, 1993)

L'Atelier de la Danse 1955–1995 – Souvenirs (auto-edited, 1995)

Une certaine idée de la danse (Editions Chiron, 1997)

TRANSLATIONS (into french)

Le langage de la danse – Mary Wigman (Die Sprache des Tanzes)

Construire la danse – Doris Humphrey (The Art of making Dances)

La danse moderne – John Martin (Modern Dance)

POETRY

Epiphanies
Visitations
Ce chant dans mon œcur
Chemins critiques

INDEX

Abiléa, Arie   166
Abraham, Pierre   68
Abramovitch, Ruth   144
Adabache, Olga   201
Adret, Françoise   201
A.F.R.E.C. (see Maggie)
Ailey, Alvin   319
Akesson, Birgit   115
Albert, Blondine   244
Albert, Marcelle   382
Albertieri, Luigi   234
Aleman, Gladys   **393**
Alexander, Gerda   380, 383
Alexander, Matthias   383
Alexandre-Debray, Janine   344
Algaroff, Youli   125, 223
Algo, Julian   124
Allard, Edith   231, **269**, 273, 283
Allegra, Claudine   205, **349**
Allen, Maud   234
Alvarez, Isaac   351
American Students and Artists
   Centre, Paris   321, 327, 383
Andrews, Jerome   84, 125, 143,
   198, 201, 204, 225, **233**, 259, 266,
   269, 279, 283, 286, 296, 305, 320,
   345, 347, 366, 380
Anik, Djemil   44, **93**, 124, 366
Animation, Jeunesse   322
Annenkov, Georges   299
Antonetti, Charles   189, 213, **217**,
   303, 375
Antony, Mary   251, 348
Araiz, Oscar   390
Archives Internationales de la
   Danse (A.I.D.)   49, 63, 77, 88,

114, **118**, 135, 143, 155, 205, 242,
   281, 291
Argentina   42, 44, 115
Argentinita   42
Arguel, Mireille   331, 335, **371**
Arlen, Liliane   **167**, 396
d'Arnot, Paul   201, 214, 231, **267**,
   281, 422
Art, Recherche, Confrontation
   (A.R.C.)   227, 271, 318, **345**,
   355, 386, 393
Ashido, Sakae   42
Atelier de la Danse, L'   97, 240,
   253, 285, 296, 321, 354, 369,
   391, 395
Athanassiou, Nikos   246
Athanasoff, Cyril   201
Atienza, José   329
Atlani, Catherine   405
Aveline, Albert   23
Azagury, Odile   361

Babilée, Jean   167, 342
Babillot, Claire   279
Babillot, Marie-France   155, 159,
   200, **278**
Babsky, Monique   412, 414
Backeroot, Willem   380
Baddeley, Diana   369
Bagouet, Dominique   359, 405
Baignères, Claude   409
Baker, Josephine   49, 115
Balachova, Alexandra   369
Bales, William   251
Balieff, Nikita   42
Ballet de l'Ile de France   66, 287

Ballet National de Danses
    Françaises 323
Ballet Studio de l'Opéra 319,
    342, 403
Ballet Théatre Contemporain
    319, **341**
Ballets Contemporains de Karin
    Waehner 264, 273, 320, 358,
    372, 387, 394, 396
Ballets Modernes de Paris
    (Dupuy) 149, 218, **220**, 252,
    261, 267, 270, 288, 320, 347, 364,
    381, 396
Ballets Russes (Diaghilev) 3, 23,
    47, 72, 181
Ballets Russes de Monte
    Carlo 23, 181, 269
Ballets Suédois 23, **47**, 118
Balthus, Jean-André 411
Bara, Charlotte **78**, 115
Bari, Tania 231
Baril, Jacques 75, 343, 411, **417**
Barrault, Jean-Louis 104, 127,
    162, 189, 197, 201, 216, 291, 303,
    343, 375
Bartenieff, Irmgard 383
Basil, Colonel de 24
Bastin, Christine 296
Bataille, Nicolas 299
Baty, Gaston 68, 78, 88,
    104, 199
Bauhaus 41, 139
Bausch, Pina 7, 359
Bayle, Christine 365
Béchade, Jean-Jacques 231
Beckett, Samuel 130
Bederkhan, Leila 97, 124
Bedou, Anne 231
Béjart, Maurice 201, 285, 342,
    403, 424
Bellini, Juan Carlos 266, 391
Bellugue, Paul 115, 123

Benesch, Rudolf 370
Benois, Alexandre 201
Bentley, Alise 239
Béranger, Anne 405
Beraud-Villars, M. J. 412
Bereska, Dussia 36, **61**, 113,
    124, 135, 204
Berge, Yvonne 13, 53, 113, 167,
    191, 198, 284, 289, **291**, 295, 382
Berlant, Alexandre 125
Bernhardt, Sarah 72
Berns, Myriam 405
Bernstein, Carol 383
Bertherat, Thérèse 383
Bertrand, Monique (see Pinok and
    Matho)
Bessy, Claude 201
Biennale de Paris 320, 386, 394
Bilger, Marie-Louise 380
Bing, Suzanne 44
Birkmeyer, Anton 168
Birmelet, Mme 223
Blaise, Michel and Michèle 323
Blancpain, Suzanne 275
Blanc-Raillard, Denise 69,
    159, **277**
Blaska, Félix 344
Blaue Reiter 41, 72
Bleu, Annette 213
Blin, Roger 127, 137, 161,
    189, 218, 223
Blondé, Gabriel 299
Blum, René 24
Bode, Rudolf 30
Bodenweiser, Gertrud 121, 168
Boll, André 411
Bon, Arlet 227, 320, 345, **385**,
    388, 393
Bonis, Bernadette 390, 413
Börlin, Jean **47**, 118, 123
Botbol, André 344
Bouffort, Jean 212, 231, 323, **380**

Bougai, Marguerite   106, 113, 143, **160**, 189, 212, 223, 266
Bouland-Vinay, Yvette   201
Bourdelle, Antoine   87
Bourcier, Paul   205, 342, 403, 411, **418**
Bourgoin, Mytho   137, 189, 242
Bousquet, Guy   246
Bousquet, Youra   411
Bouxvilliers, Jérôme   33, 157
Boyer, Guillemette   209
Bozzini, Annie   413
Brady, Erina   241
Bravo, Guillermina   384
Braunschweig, Philippe   413
Breton, André   299
Briansky, Oleg   299
Brieux, Yves   66, 211
Brillant, Marie   205, 412
Brillant, Maurice   **415**
Brodier, Jean-Pierre   246
Brown, Doryta   113, 124, **144**, 222
Brunel, Lise   135, 227, 259, 356, 388, 406, **418**
Bugaud, Christine   386
Buhne Studio, Zurich   299
Buirge, Susan   246, 277, 322, 367, 405
Butler, John   342, 358

Caciuleanu, Gigi   404
Cadieu, Martine   412
Calais, Blandine   296
Cantarelles   295
Caquille, Simone   85
Carlut, Hélène   113, 129, 147, **148**, 223, 322, 396
Carol-Bérard   410
Casarès, Maria   301
Caspari, Marguerite   351
Cébron, Jean   352

Cendrars, Blaise   22, 48
Chabetay, Ginette   202, 411
Chadinoff, Atty   219, 246, 321, 352, 369
Challet-Haas, Jacqueline   204, 246, 266, **369**
Champagne, Anita   64
Chantraine, Françoise   79, **381**
Charrat, Janine   7, 66, 88, 125, 167, 201, 320, 403, 418
Châteauvallon, Festival de   273, **344**, 360
Chauchet, Nicole   129
Chaumont, Jacqueline   44, **64**, 113, 124, 287, 325
Chaurand, Jaque   205, 324, 346
Chauviré, Yvette   201, 269
Chevalier, Maurice   67, 236
Childs, Lucinda   358
Child, Ludolf (see Schild)
Chipiloff, Nadia   136
Chladek, Rosalia   105, 115, 123, 144, 145, 148, 168, 223, 274, 289, 292, 379
Christout, Marie-Françoise   412, 418
Christiaens, Jean   266
Christodoulides, Michel   246, 376
Centre International de la Danse (C.I.D.)   271, 321, 327, 356, 395
Centre International de Documentation pour la Danse (C.I.D.D.)   126
Conseil International de la Danse, U.N.E.S.C.O. (C.I.D.D.)   126, 386
Cirul, Mila   60, 113, 124, 125, **140**, 143, 201, 211, 242, 266, 270, 281, 415
Clair, René   48, 330
Claudel, Paul   48, 104

Clustine, Ivan   23
Cocteau, Jean   48, 127, 225
Cohan, Robert   388
Collantes, Nathalie   346
Comité Français de la
   Danse   126
Compagnons de la
   Danse, Les   237, 259, 283
Concours de Bagnolet   324, 333,
   346, 372, 394, 405
Contamin, Lili   148
Constant, Anne-Marie   331
Constant, Marius   142
Conté, Pierre   5, 121, 361, 370, 411
Conty, Jean-Marie   137, 189, 218,
   242, 304
Copeau, Jacques   44, 87, **185**, 192,
   199, 284, 301, 304
Coquelle, Jean   412
Cothenet, Suzy   149
Cournand, Gilberte   254, 387,
   410, **419**
Cousin, Gabriel   155, 352
Courtiade, Odette   31, 124
Courville, Xavier de   350
Coutier, Denise   166, **379**
Cramer, Ivo   122, 129, 270
Cremona, Kilina   359
Crevier, Eliane   231
Cruixart, Modest   232
Cullberg, Birgit   44, 122, 129,
   319
Cunningham, Merce   137, 225,
   251, 259, 319, 327, 345, 355, 358,
   382, 403
Cuny, Alain   167

Dabert, Roger   87, 94
Dajanova, Mara   246, **391**
Dalcroze, Émile Jaques-   9, 30,
   32, 35, 44, 106, 145, 148, 151,
   168, 223, 277, 337

Damour, Michèle   95
Daniel-Lesur   245
Danse et Culture   44,
   153, 199, 205, 210, 233, 261, 276,
   283, 347, 355
Darmet, Guy   406
Darsonval, Lycette   167, 411, 419
Dasté, Catherine   352
Dasté, Jean   189, 284, 295,
   304, 362, 364
Davesne, Alain   201
Davis, John   358
Dazy, Marcelle   64
Debatte, Anne-Marie   155, 159,
   191, 195, 284, **295**, 322
Decaillot, Claude   205, **352**
Decroux, Etienne   128, 161, 192,
   199, 212, 223, 258, **300**, 305,
   367, 375
Decroux, Maximilien   303
Delattre, Bernard   231
Delaunay, Sonia   22, 64
Delieuvin, Marie-France   231
Delsarte, François   54, 60,
   140, 167
Delsarte, Maximilien   167
Delsarte, Ria   167
Delsout, Mireille   321
Deluz, Sylvie   159, **382**, 395
Demange, Paul   48
Demeny, Georges   30, 84
Derp, Clotilde von   69
Descombey, Michel   205, 319,
   342, 403
Desève, Matias   411
Deshauteurs, René   352, 367
Devi, Rita   225
Devos, Raymond   303
Diaghilev, Serge de   23, 128,
   342
Didion, Marie-Louise   125
Diénis, Jean-Claude   412

Divoire, Fernand   26, 27, 31, 48, 55, 57, 67, 78, 81, 82, 85, 109, 135, 147, 156, 209, 409, **415**

Doat, Jean   186, 209

Dobbelaere, Georges   323

Dobbels, Daniel   245, 413

Dolin, Anton   269

Dolto, Boris   292

Dorcy, Jean (see Danse et Culture)   194, **199**, 205, 214, 233, 318, 354, 420

Douai, Jacques   218, 296, 323

Dougnac, Paul   128, 213

Dravet, Agnès   231

Drayson, Phyllis   **293**, 348

Drengwicz, Régine   **274**, 361

Dropsy, Jacques   253

Druckman, Jacob   266

Dudan, Jean   345

Dudde, Borghild   249

Dufilho, Jacques   218

Dufour, Denis   232

Dullin, Charles   68, 104, 128, 185, 189, 199, 217, 222, 305

Dumont, Mathilde (see Pinok and Matho)

Duncan, Elisabeth   **53**, 55, 61, 113, 143, 168, 291

Duncan (girls)   27, 53

Duncan, Irma   **54**, 61, 156

Duncan, Isadora   **26**, 31, 40, 45, 50, 72, 79, 84, 87, 140, 166, 169

Duncan, Lisa   **55**, 68, 113, 123, 143, 275, 305

Duncan, Raymond   **50**, 88, 291

Dunham, Katherine   327, 396

Dupuy, Françoise and Dominique   13, 122, 153, 162, 198, 204, **220**, 233, 237, 242, 261, 271, 279, 286, 296, 320, 344, 347, 351, 381, 418, 424

Dupuy, Dominique   126, 145

Duquesnoy, Richard   319

Duret, Guy-Georges   411

Duvernoy, Anne   413

Duvivier, Julien   104

Dynalix, Paulette   125

École Normale Supérieure d'Éducation Physique (E.N.S.E.P.)   85, 159, 261, 294, **335**, 355, 372

École Supérieure d'Études Chorégraphiques (E.S.E.C.)   205, 266, 322, 369, 383

Éducation par le Jeu Dramatique (E.P.J.D.)   130, 137, **189**, 218, 242, 286, 299, 323, 375

Egger, Muggi   237

Eglevsky, André   125

Egorova, Loubov   24, 88, 115, 121, 267, 286

Egri, Susanna   225

Ellis, Lucile   231

Epinoy, Katherine Henry d'   225, 231, 246, 253, **270**, 288, 327

Erdman, Jean   251

d'Erlanger de Rosen, Thomas   125, 205, 322

Escudero, Vicente   49, 95, 115

Essenine, Sergei   26

Etchessary, Isabelle de   **78**

Etorki   225

Eyquem, Marie-Thérèse   85, 336

Fabri, Patricia   244, 372

Fajon, Madeleine   249

Farber, Viola   319

Faure, Hélène   136

Fédération Française de Danse, d'Art Chorégraphique et d'Expression Corporelle (F.F.D.A.C.E.C.)   250, 276, 325, 349, 353

Feïlane, Dora   167, 345, **354**

Feldenkrais, Mosche   383

Fenonjois, René   201

Festival International de
    Danse de Paris   319

Fielden, D.   346

Fibisch, Felix and Judite   126

Finkel, Heinz   63, 113, 124, **133**,
    183, 212, 218, 219, 295

Foatelli, Josette and Renée
    125, **165**

Fokine, Michel   24, 48

Forster, Elle   366

Fort, Sevilla   395

Fortin, Edée   129

Fosca, Igor   345

Frag, Pierre   299

Frairie, La   218, 323, 380

Franchini, Frédérique   **286**

Francis, Xavier   390

Franck, Paul   67

Franklin, Nadia   384

Free Dance Song   396

Frémiot, Marcel   354

Fromantel, Mireille   **294**,
    336, 371

Fryer, June   50, 125

Fuchs, Elisabeth   84

Fuller, Loie   **36**, 44, 77

Gallé, Émile   36

Gallois, Anne-Marie   231, 244

Gallotta, Jean-Claude   155, 405

Ganeau, François   231

Garby, Annie   337

Gardon, Anne   113, 153, 201,
    204, **208**, 421, 425

Garnier, Jacques   319, 403

Garsky, Brigitte   246

Gaudelette, André   82

Gauville, Hervé   390, 413

Gérard, Christine   7, 231, 248, 405

Gémier, Firmin   64, 87, 343

Genkel, Bodyla   390

Geoffray, César   148, 223, 380

Georghiu, Marie-Christine   333

Georgi, Yvonne   111

Gert, Valeska   44

Gide, André   104

Gielgud, Maina   201

Gilbert, Saul   237, 259

Glegolski, André   355

Golea, Anne   237

Golovine, Serge   225

Goron, Pierre   126, 287

Goss, Peter   405

Graham, Martha   2, 7, 132, 143,
    204, 234, 251, 266, 271, 279, 327,
    330, 332, 345, 348, 355, 367, 382,
    393, 395, 420

Grantseva, Tatiana   350, 354

Gropius, Walter   41

Groupe de Recherche en
    Expression Corporelle
    (G.R.E.C.)   335

Greco, José   125

Gregory, Tony   **164**

Gsovski, Tariana   364

Gsovski, Victor   168

Guédy, Antoinette   64, 287

Guédy, Pierre   64

Guilcher, Jean-Marie   364

Guillot de Rhode, François   412

Guitry, Sacha   66

Guizerix, Jean   169, 319,
    365, 406

Gurdjieff   146

Guyon, Eliane   303

Haeger, Bengt   130, 344

Hahoutoff, Nil   411

Hallet-Eghayan, Michel   405

Halphen, Doris   113, **151**

Hastings, Baird   125, 411

Hébert, Georges   30
Hébertot, Jacques   44, 114, 410
Heggen, Claire   378
Hellès, Fée   **166**, 291, 354, 380
Hellerau-Laxenburg   33, 105,
   124, 146, **151**, 223, 358
Henry, Philippe   249, 323, 381
Herba, Hélène   237
Herrera, Nana de   124
Hersin, André-Philippe   205, 412
Holm, Hanya   33, 108, 111, 236,
   329
Holzer, Suzon   159, **358**
Honegger, Arthur   24, 82
Honor, Jane   406
Horst, Louis   234, 251, 263, 348
Hoving, Lucas   321, 358, 359
Howell, Mary   53
Hoyer, Dore   329, 344, 384
Hightower, Rosella   125, 350,
   360
Hinkson, Mary   321, 354
Hubert, Denise   331
Hummel, Gaspar   390
Humphrey, Doris   66, 234,
   251, 326
Husset, Michèle   237, 288
Hutchinson, Ann   63
Hutton, Loïs   **76**
Hyon, Brigitte   231

Illic, Mme   223
Imbert, Charles   412
d'Indy, Vincent   81
Ione, Geneviève   44, 66
Institut Pédagogique d'Art
   Chorégraphique (I.P.A.C.)   347
Ionesco, Eugène   130
Inyoka, Nyota   44, **90**, 115,
   125
Itelman, Ana   384, 393
Izrine, Agnès   413

Jacquelin, Claudie   364
Jacquemont, Maurice   223
Jacque-Mortane, Simone   85
Jacques (Frères)   303
Jacquin, Patrick   413
Jaër, Muriel   320, **366**
Janko   106
Janoli, Noëlle   237, 266, **348**
Jarosewicz, Ella   378
Jarrell, Jean   273
Jodjana, Raden Mas   42, **95**, 115,
   137, 246, 366
Joie, Norman de   231
Jolivet, André   104, 231
Joly, Andrée   85, 124, 350
Jones, Betty   321, 352, 367
Jooss, Kurt   10, 24, 36, 66, 123,
   214, 234, 267, 304, 344, 352, 355,
   361, 372, 384, 395
Jouvet, Louis   104
Julien, Pierre   413
Juramie, Ghislaine   413

Kalfon, Jean-Pierre   155
Kalfouni, Dominique   169
Kamadjojo, Indra   125
Kandinsky, Wassily   41, 76,
   106, 139
Karmitz, Fernanda and
   Renée   237
Kaufmann, Hedy   266
Kaufman, Susan   205
Kempel, Helga   276
Kerday, Katy de   386
Keuten, Serge   405, 413
Kintzel, Renée Odic   13, **81**, 113,
   124, 143
Kiss, Nora   281, 361
Klee, Paul   41
Klein, Nita   273
Kniaseff, Boris   121, 219, 281
Knust, Alfred   361, 369

Kochno, Boris 115, 201
Komatis, Henri 344
Kokoshka, Oscar 41
Komori, Toshi 97
Koner, Pauline 386
Korène, Vera 211
Kousnetzoff, Maria 125
Kressel, Trudi 274
Kreutzberg, Harald 10, 44, 111,
    115, 133, 144, 148, 208, 267,
    274, 329, 384
Ksetchinskaya, Mathilde 24
Kuni, Matsumi 384, 391
Kratina, Valéria 145
Kummer, Marie **66**, 113, 123

Laban, Rudolf von 10, 13, **35**,
    106, 124, 140, 167, 204, 209, 256,
    266, 303, 337, 383
Laban Centre, London 36
Laban Institute, New York 36
Labis, Attilio 201
Lamballe, Lucienne 87, 200
Lamy, Emilienne 349
Lancelot, Francine 169, 231,
    246, 283, **363**
Landowski, Marcel 211, 325
Lang, Maurice 246
Lang, Nadine 354
Langel, Claude 413
Langlère, Marie-Odile 249
Lartigue, Alain 249
Lartigue, Pierre 388
Lapzeson, Noémie **391**
Laskine, Lily 291
Laurent, Jean 411
Lavalle, Josefina 384
Lavelli, Jorge 390
Lavolé, Laurence 413
Lazzini, Joseph 205, 320, 342, 403
Lecoq, Jacques **304**, 351
Lecouvreur, Anne 249

Ledain, Nicole 333
Leeder, Sigurd (see also
    Jooss) 36, 184
Lefébure, Yvonne 241
Lefèvre, Brigitte 319, 403
Le Flem, Paul 49
Lefort, Bernard 413
Léger, Fernand 22, 48
Legros, Annie 353
Lemaître, Odon-Jérôme 413
Lemarchand, Isabelle 249
Lenthéric, Christine 349
Lequeux, Alain-Paul 413
Le Rolland, Anne 249
Lerondeau, Michèle (see Blaise)
Lescaut, Poumi 273, **360**
Levant, Jacquèline 137, 153, 190,
    204, **218**, 223, 231, 242, 252, 259,
    270, 286, 323
Lévinson, André 45, 64, 110,
    201, 409, 416
Lévinson, Marie 411
Levitzky, Bella 352
Lidart, Nora 412
Lido, Serge 419
Lidova, Irène 411, 419
Lifar, Serge 7, 23, 85, 115, 152,
    181, 269, 281, 299, 411
Limón, José 195, 251, 264, 266,
    321, 327, 330, 332, 349, 355, 367,
    384, 405
Liptay, Ingeborg 372, **395**
Linval, Edmond 125, 140,
    205, 411
Livio, Antoine 413
Lobov, Youra 223
Lombardin, Raymonde 87, 135,
    183, 189, 204, **212**, 267,
    375, 421
London School of Contemporary
    Dance 361, 367, 388, 393
Louppe, Laurence 413

Luigi   271, 372
Ludin, Fritz   321, 372
Lundin, Birgit   244
Luz, Lutys de   321
Lytton, Madeleine   61, **305**

MacDonald, Brian   342
MacGehee, Helen   137, 321
MacKaye, Steele   54
MacMurray, Lynn   273
Madden, Dorothy   321, 358
Madika   122, 363
Maeterlinck, Maurice   87
Maggie, Dinah   193, **203**, 252,
   266, 306, 409
Mail, Léone   122
Maison de la Danse   353, 406
Malavika, Kumari   93, 344, 364
Malkowski, François   13, 44, 66,
   79, 113, 294, 348, 363, 371, 380
Malherbe, Henri   49
Malraux, André   104
Mallarmé, Geneviève   142, 201,
   204, **211**, 288, 347, 422
Marc, Yves   378
Marceau, Marcel   128, 192, **305**
Marcus, Julia   113, 124, 133,
   143, 164, 236
Maré, Rolf de   47, 118, 200, 410
Mareschal, Jeanne   413
Marin, Maguy   405
Martenot, Maurice   129, 161, 190,
   211, 382
Martin, Claude   189, 218
Martin, Etienne   231
Martin, John   111, 342
Martinez, Graziella   320, 345,
   355, 374, **388**, 393
Martinon, Brian de   413
Mathis, Thierry   413
Mattox, Matt   327
Massine, Léonide   24, 234, 361

Maucouvert, Annick   205, 320,
   331, 345, **355**, 374
Mauriac, François   104
Menassol, Danièle   237
Mendel, Deryk   225, 232,
   273, 345
Menessier, Marianne   349
Mensendieck, Bess   30, 123, 383
Menslova, Ludmilla   136
Merida, Ana   384
Merlin, Olivier   409
Mertz, Max   53
Méry, Mimose   285
Messiaen, Olivier   104, 225
Meyerhold, Vsewolod   140
Mézières, Françoise   383
Michaud, Françoise   125, 133,
   149, **223**, 267
Michaut, Pierre   201, 411
Michel, Marcelle   205, 245, 413
Midière, Alberte   293
Mignoton, Solange   237,
   259, 266
Milhaud, Darius   48, 104
Miloss, Aurel   361
Millian, Sonia   142, 231, 413
Min, Tanaka   358
Minot, Anne   349
Mirova, Isabelle   232, **350**
Mistinguett   236
Mitchell, Linda   333
Mittelholzer, Anna   285, 321,
   345, 383
Mille, Agnes de   95, 115, 329
Montessori, Maria   289, 293
Montherlant, Henri de   104
Mordkin, Michel   60, 140
Montalvo, José Jaen   231
Morandière, Françoise
   de la   231, 273, **348**
Morf, Yvonne   358
Morris, Margaret   76

Motta, Gilberto   205, 246, 270, **273**, 355
Mouloudji   127
Mourousy, Paul   300
Muray, Philippe   11

Nadal, Michèle   231, **361**, 364, 412
Nahmias, Alain   388
Nagrin, Daniel   227, 345
Nicks, Walter   285, 321, 327, 352, 395
Nikolais, Alwin   139, 239, 319, 344, 390, 405
Nijinska, Bronislava   23
Nijinsky, Waslaw   23, 24, 281, 417
Nolde, Emil   41, 106
Nordmann, Anne   231
Nureyev, Rudolf   365

d'O, Marc   288
Obedman, Diana   **393**
O'Brady   223
Oca, Paulina   227, 320, 345, **392**
Ogier, Bulle   288
Opéra de Paris   23, 115, 319, 342, 365
Ortus, Pedro   125
Ossona, Paulina   385, **392**
Ostrowski, Alice   274

Padani, Paula   274
Pagava, Ethery   125
Page, Ruth   234
Pagneux, Monica and Jean   253
Paillet, Rose-Marie   159, 205, 253, **275**, 391
Painlevé, Jean   362
Palau, Thérèse   218, 323, 380
Palucca, Gret   111
Paquet, Gérard   344

Pardo, Sara   274, 345, 367, **387**, 393
Parmeggiani, Bernard   232, 364
Parnac, Valentin   415
Passat, Patricia   386
Patarozzi, Jacques   405
Paul-Boncour, Dominique   237
Pavlova, Anna   23, 49, 94, 123, 419
Pearce, Barbara   345
Peerbohm, Hilde   13, 113, 191, 284, **288**, 291, 295
Peralta, Delfor   329, 412
Perinetti, André   344
Perrotet, Suzanne   143
Peters Renate   237
Petit, Michel   412
Petit, Roland   7, 66, 181, 330, 342, 403
Petroff, Paul   298
Picabia, Francis   48
Picasso, Pablo   22, 164
Piesen, Ferdinand   246
Piguet, Geneviève   153, 159, 240, **284**, 345
Pilates, Joseph   236
Pilobolus   341
Pinok and Matho   273, 303, 337, 344, 367, **375**
Piollet, Wilfride   319, 365, 405
Pitoëff, Georges   104, 199
Philippe, Pierre   232
Pledge, Miss   295
Poiret, Paul   22, 91
Pomarès, Jean   346, 405
Pomiès, Georges   7, 57, **67**, 88, 123, 211, 415
Pomiès, Hélène   69
Pontan, Maïan   113, **151**
Pontois, Noella   169, 201
Pook, Renate   **359**
Popard, Irène   5, 31, **84**, 277, 337, 352

Potash, Morton   395
Preobrajenska, Olga   24, 87, 223, 234, 369
Pourchet, Maurice   164, 201, 209
Prudhommeau, Germaine 413, 417
Pujade-Renaud, Claude   335, **367**
Poudru, Florence   146
Pyros, Odile   55, 204, **306**

Radio City Music Hall   234, 269
Rachell, Jérôme   238, 348
Raffinot, François   365
Rakoczi, Basil   246
Ramseyer, Jean-Claude   405
Ranay, Jeanne   125
Rao, Shanta   124
Rasch, Albertina   44, 115
Ravel, Maurice   24
Raynaud, Alberte   205, **373**
Réal, Brigitte   231, 405
Redgis, Yvonne   **77**, 124
Reine, Bella   143, 201, 246, **298**
Reinhardt, Max   54
Reiss, Françoise   411, **417**
Réjane   87
Rémon, Suzanne   153, 201, 208, **219**, 422
Rencontres Internationales de Danse Contemporaine (R.I.D.C) 227, 250, 271, 322, 351, 365
Rétoré, Guy   271
Reymond, Georges   125, 412
Reyna, Ferdinando   126, 204, 411, 417
Reynaert, Christine   79
Rezvani, Nahide and Mejid   97, 115, 124
Ribes, Roger   231, 237, 271, 283, **287**, 345, 351
Richaud, Elyane   412
Ricaux, Gustave   23, 152

Rijbek, Hans   124
Risler, Jean   64
Robbins, Jerome   266
Robert, Marie-Béatrice   249
Robin, Jean   319
Robinson, Elisabeth   246
Robinson, Jacqueline   125, 190, 201, 204, 220, 227, 237, **240**, 271, 273, 275, 277, 285, 296, 299, 321, 347, 354, 382, 391, 411, 422
Rochereau, Jean   231
Roehmalaiselan   97, 246
Roelens, Mathilde   128
Rogge, Lula   359
Rollot, Jean   412
Ronsay, Jeanne   44, **87**, 95, 126
Ross, Bertram   321
Rossel, Lucile   412
Rothschild, Bethsabée de   125
Rouché, Jacques   23
Roudanez, Louise   91
Rougemont, Christiane de   169, 205, 364, **396**
Rouiller, Quentin   405
Roussel, Albert   82
Roussel, Stéphanie   248
Roux, Aline   205, 320, 335, 346, **354**, 372, 388
Rubinstein, Ida   24
Rubio, Nora   200, 382
Rusillo, Joseph   344, 405
Rybinski, Delphine   231, 233, 249, 405

Saint-Denis, Ruth   25, 42, 72, 234
Saint-Hubert, Titane   159, **280**
Saint-Thibault, Françoise   205, 212, 231, 244, 253, **346**
Sakharoff, Alexander and Clotilde   13, 44, **69**, 78, 115, 123, 206, 279, 321, 329, 347, 358, 384, 415

Salvado, Jacinto   147
Salvini, Milena   388
Samson, Joseph   284
Sanasardo, Paul   342
Sanders, Dirk   201, 342
Sanoja, Sonia   320, 345, **394**
Santerre, François de   411
Saporta, Karine   405
Sarabhai, Mrinalini   125
Sarraute, Claude   410
Satie, Erik   48, 87
Sauguet, Henri   24
Sauvage, Nadia   125
Savary, Jérôme   390
Schade, Monika (see Pagneux)
Schaikewitch, André   126, 411
Scène Française, La   66, 355
Schiele, Egon   41
Schild, Ludolf   113, **135**, 143,
   218, 259
Schlemmer, Oscar   41, 122
Schmidt-Schäfer, Norbert   231
Schmitt, Florent   82, 146
Schmucki, Norbert   205
Schola, Cantorum   274, 321, 341,
   351, 395
Schoop, Trudi   115, 121
Schottelius, Renate   258, 384,
   385, 391, 393
Schwartz, Jean   232
Seatelli, Lucienne   64
Seigneuret, Michèle   231
Semprun, Francisco   232, 244,
   246, 259, 273, 358, 375
Sérac, Yvonne   **78**
Séréville, Jacqueline   231
Serre, Jean-Claude   335
Serreau, Jean-Marie   217, 303
Serry, Jean   105, **152**, 183, 193,
   197, 199, 208, 222, 251, 259,
   270, 279, 281, 286, 293, 380,
   406, 422

Serry, Viviane   155, 231, 365
Shankar, Uday   88, **94**, 115
Shapiro, Lilian   266, 270, 283
Shawn, Ted   25, 234, 299
Sheleen, Laura   183, 204, 231, 237,
   246, **250**, 263, 271, 277, 320, 327,
   347, 354, 367, 369, 382, 394
Sie, Edo and Liong   246
Silvant, Jean   149, 411, 412, 418
Simkie   95, 125
Simon, René   286
Sirvin, René   413
Skibine, George   125, 205
Skouratoff, Vladimir   320
Snell, Gertrude   63
Société des Auteurs et
   Compositeurs Dramatiques
   (S.A.C.D.)   401
Société des Auteurs,
   Compositeurs et Éditeurs
   de Musique (S.A.C.E.M.)   401
Sokolow, Anna   266, 384, 387
Solane, Janine   13, 33, 60, 105,
   155, 193, 275, 278, 284, 286, 294,
   350, 354, 367, 379, 382
Sombert, Claire   201
Sonnier, Pierre   129
Sorell, Walter   109
Sosa, Richarth   356
Soum, Corinne   303, 378
Spear, Gayle   231
Srimati, Usha   126
Staats, Léo   23, 93, 156, 234
Stanislawski, Constantin   298
Steiner, Rudolf   30
Stens, Olga   125, 142, 153, 183,
   201, 231, 269, 279, **280**, 287, 421
Stephan, Anna   199, 422
Stéphane, Claude   201, **219**, 286,
   422
Stravinsky, Igor   24
Susana and José (Udaeta)   125

Swan, Paul **77**
Swann, Patti 299
Syndicat National des Auteurs et
    Compositeurs (S.N.A.C.) 227,
    250, 325

Talbot, Danièle 231
Tallchief, Maria 125
Tansman, Alexandre 126
Tassart, Maurice 411, 412
Taylor, Paul 319, 327, 344, 382
Tels-Rabanek, Ellen **60**, 113, 124
    140, 156, 168
Teresina 115
Terpis, Max 111
Théâtre de l'Atelier 68, 364
Théâtre des Champs-Elysées 49,
    68, 72, 78, 109
Théâtre d'Essai de la Danse **203**,
    261, 273, 276, 287, 320, 347, 352,
    355, 368
Théâtre Français de la
    Danse 319, **343**, 396
Théâtre National de la Danse et
    de l'Image **344**
Théâtre des Nations **343**
Théâtre du Silence 319, 344, 403
Thiriot, Pierre 87, 412
Thompson, Clive 395
Tikanova, Nina 286
Todd, Mabel 383
Tomaszewski, Henryk 378
Topaz, Muriel **266**
Topor, Roland 390
Torrès, Emilia and Filémon 125
Traguth, Fred 347
Travail et Culture (T.E.C.) 130,
    153, 200, 208, 213, 217
Trillat, Ennemond 147
Trillat, Line 147, 396
Tugal, Pierre 122, 125, 193, 211,
    223

Tugdual, Georges 231
Tzara, Tristan 106

Ullmann, Lisa 36
Umemoto, Rikukei 97, 115
U.N.E.S.C.O. 126, 343
Uthoff, Ernst 384

Vaillat, Léandre 414
Valentin, Lola 220
Van de Rohe, Mies 41
Vanel, Hélène **76**
Van Tu, Nguyen 128
Van Veen, Marie-Louise **63**, 64,
    113, 123
Vaudoyer, Jean-Louis 23
Veltchek, Vaslav 156
Vendredis de la Danse 44, 87
Verdy, Violette 201
Vieux-Colombier 44, 82, 87, 114,
    199, 208, 237, 284, 301
Villard, Pierre du 205
Vincent, Geneviève 413
Vladimiroff, Serge 298
Vronska, Alice 211
Vyroubova, Nina 201

Waehner, Karin 153, 183, 201,
    204, 231, 237, 244, **257**, 266, 273,
    274, 276, 283, 286, 294, 319, 320,
    345, 348, 350, 355
Wallmann, Margarete 111, 143,
    234, 384, 392
Wanger, Nadia 143
Warnot, André 223
Wasson, Steve 303, 378
Watteau, Georgette 155, 208
Weidt, Jean 13, 113, 122, **127**,
    143, 170, 183, 223, 295
Widener, Winifred 327, 394
Wiener, Jean 67

Wiesenthal, Grete and Else   168
Wieskeman, Anita   113, **146**, 148,
   183, 396
Winslow, Myriam   384, 392
Wigman, Mary   10, 13, 33, 36, 40,
   42, **106**, 113, 140, 143, 144, 148,
   167, 170, 204, 208, 233, 234, 241,
   253, 267, 274, 276, 283, 358, 364,
   371, 374, 384, 424
Wittop, Freddy   165
Witzman-Anaya,
   Alexandre   249, 406
Wolliaston, Elsa   405

Yami, Vanah   97
Yano, Hideyuki   359, 405
Yuriko   271, 274, 321, 351, 354,
   386, 391

Zambelli, Carlotta   23
Zimmermann, Daniel   368
Zullig, Hans   208, 214, 267
Zvereff, Nicolas   201, 212, 223,
   269, 281, 422

Other titles in the Choreography and Dance Studies series

Volume 10
First We Take Manhattan
Four American Women and the New York School of Dance Criticism
Diana Theodores

Volume 11
You call me Louis not Mr Horst
Dorothy Madden

Volume 12
Dancing Female
Lives and Issues of Women in Contemporary Dance
Sharon E. Friedler and Susan B. Glazer

Volume 13
Modern Dance in France
An Adventure 1920–1970
Jacqueline Robinson. Translated by Catherine Dale

Volume 14
Anna Sokolow
The Rebellious Spirit
Larry Warren

Volume 15
What's So Funny?
Sketches from My Life
Lotte Goslar